Celebrating our Norwegian-Minnesotan Heritage
A Sesquicentennial Celebration of Minnesota's Norwegian Pioneers

Compiled by
The Norwegian Statehood Pioneer Project

Celebrating Our Norwegian-Minnesotan Heritage:
A Sesquicentennial Celebration of Minnesota's Norwegian Pioneers

Published by
The Norwegian Statehood Pioneer Project
6938 State Highway 200 NW
Laporte, Minnesota 56461
Anne Sladky, Editor
info@mn-nspp.org

Library of Congress Control Number: 2008942841

ISBN No. 978-0-615-25348-0

© February 2009 Norwegian Statehood Pioneer Project
All rights reserved
Second Printing

Applications, photos, biographies, and supporting documents submitted to the project will be housed at the Norwegian-American Genealogical Center and Naeseth Library in Madison, Wisconsin.

This book is available for purchase on-line at
http://www.cafepress.com/nspp/

This book is dedicated to all of the Norwegians who made Minnesota their home and the descendants who have kept their stories alive for over 150 years. We hope this book helps to insure that our Norwegian pioneer ancestors will be remembered with respect and great affection for at least 150 more!

Thanks to the following organizations that participated in the Norwegian Statehood Pioneer Project

Hadeland Lag
Hallinglag
Landingslaget
Nordfjordlaget
Nord Hedmark & Hedemarken Lag
Opdalslaget
Ringerike Drammen Districts Lag
Romerikslaget
Telelaget
Toten Lag
Trønderlag
Norwegian-American Genealogical Center & Naeseth Library

And to all the individuals who donated their time, efforts, stories, and enthusiasm to this special Sesquicentennial project

Minnesota Counties

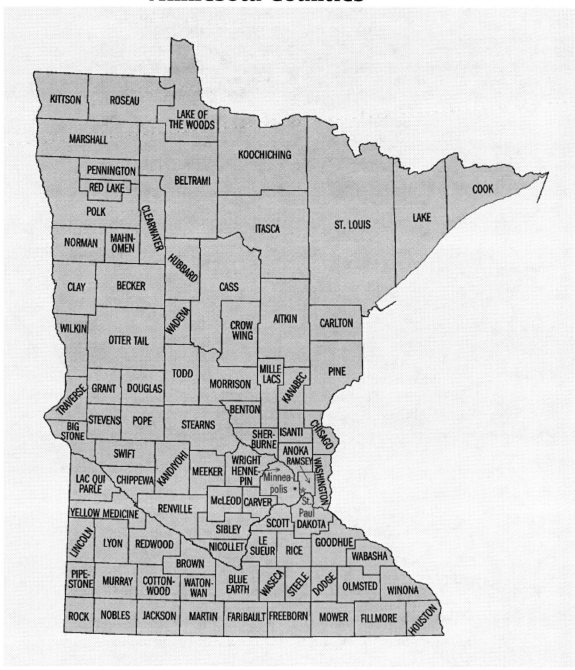

Map found on Wikipedia.com

Foreword
By Verlyn Anderson, Ph. D.

Verlyn Anderson was a member of the faculty of Concordia College, Moorhead, for 36 years. He served as director of the college library and as a professor of history and Scandinavian studies. Dr. Anderson has lectured and written extensively about Norwegian-American history in both the United States and in Norway and has given generously of his time and talents to promote knowledge and appreciation of Norwegian culture, language, and history. His ancestors, all Norwegians, settled in western Minnesota in the second half of the nineteenth century. For a lifetime of tireless work in the Norwegian-American community, by order of His Majesty King Harald V, Dr. Anderson received the St. Olav Medal on June 25, 2008.

More Norwegian immigrants settled in Minnesota than in any other state in the United States. There are several reasons why so many Norwegians chose Minnesota. At about the same time as the line of settlement reached Minnesota, the number of Norwegian immigrants arriving in America was increasing rapidly every year. The vast majority of the Norwegian immigrants lived in rural Norway and wanted to continue their rural way of life in the New World. In Norway tillable land was not only scarce, but virtually not acquirable to the younger sons of farm owners. Millions of acres of government owned fertile farmland were available in Minnesota for $1.25 an acre. The opportunity to own land in America became even more enticing when the *Homestead Act* was signed by President Abraham Lincoln on May 20, 1862. That law provided that any adult citizen, or intended citizen, could claim 160 acres of surveyed government land for a filing fee of $14. A homesteader was required to "improve" his/ her homestead by building a dwelling, "breaking up" and cultivating the land, and living on the property for at least 5 months each year. After 5 years, the original filers could receive full legal ownership to the land upon "proving-up," that is, submitting evidence that they had fulfilled the requirements of the law. After the Civil War ended in 1865, the number of Norwegians immigrating to America surged dramatically. To the land-starved Norwegians the opportunity to acquire 160 acres or about 640 Norwegian *mål* of farm land of their own was nearly unbelievable! By 1900 Norwegian Americans in Minnesota were farming four times as much land as was tilled in all of Norway that year! Of all the immigrant groups who came to America, the Norwegians acquired more land than immigrants and their descendants from any other nation.

The Norway from which they came —

The Norway from which our ancestors emigrated during the Nineteenth Century was very different from the prosperous social democracy that it is today. After living under Danish and Swedish domination for more than five centuries, Norway finally achieved full political independence in 1905. With the discovery of the rich oil reserves in the North Sea in 1969, Norway, like *Askeladen* of the country's well-known folk tales, is no longer the impoverished member of the Scandinavian nations, but today is probably the wealthiest nation in Europe.

In 1800 there were almost 900,000 people in Norway and the population was increasing rapidly. By the end of that century, Norway's population reached 2.2 million even though hundreds of thousands of her citizens had immigrated to the United States and Canada. Historians point to many reasons for this rapid rise in population. Living conditions improved markedly. The potato, which had been introduced in the 1780's, together with the increased consumption of herring, allowed Norwegians to replace the monotonous and less nutritious barley porridge that had been the daily fare of the common people with a much healthier diet. Vaccination for smallpox became mandatory shortly after 1800. This dramatically lowered the death rates, especially among children. With the end of the Napoleonic Wars in 1814, Europe experienced a century of peace that also stimulated population growth. Not only did that mean that fewer people died as a direct result of a war, but also that soldiers returning to Norway after the fighting were not carrying foreign bacteria and diseases that had often resulted in epidemics and widespread death in earlier centuries.

Compared to other, more prosperous European countries, Norway had very little industry in the 19th Century, and it could not begin to absorb this large increase of people seeking a livelihood. The majority of the population was rural, living on small farms. Less than three percent of the land could be cultivated which offered little opportunity for the expansion of agricultural endeavors. The ancient *odel law,* the primogenitor law that was in force throughout the land, decreed that the oldest son would inherit the land, leaving the younger siblings landless with limited chances to improve their economic lot. Employment opportunities in other occupations in Norway were few. As a result a new class of citizens was created, - the *husmenn* or cotters, basically landless rural workers who lived on small plots of land and paid for that privilege by working for a contracted number of days for the farmer who owned the land on which their cottage stood. Wages were low in Norway in the 19th century and continued to sink even lower as the population grew, creating an oversupply of potential workers.

In addition, improvements in education, communications and transportation helped the Norwegians to become more aware of what was happening in the rest of the world. "America letters" received from friends and relatives who had immigrated to the United States were often passed from farm to farm and some were even published in local newspapers. These often glowing reports encouraged Norwegian relatives and friends to join them in America. From these letters, many caught the "America Fever" and sold their earthly belongings to finance their journeys to a new future. Politically, America seemed like the land of opportunity and freedom to the Norwegian immigrants. Almost everything that Norway lacked was apparently readily available in America! Living conditions in Norway were probably not any more difficult than they had been for centuries, but the awareness of the possibilities of America caused especially young people seeking a better economic future to become steadily more dissatisfied with their lot in life. As Einar Haugen, well-known linguist and immigration historian, has written, "They emigrated because they had learned to be dissatisfied, and because a changing world had provided them with a hope of escape from their dissatisfaction." (Haugen, Einar, *The Norwegian Language in America*, Indiana University Press, 1969, p.22.)

The Norwegian emigrants' routes to The New World –

The first group of Norwegian emigrants left Stavanger on the sloop "Restauration" on July 5, 1825 and arrived in New York City some three months later, on October 9th. No ships left Norway with America-bound emigrants for another eleven years. From 1836 to 1842 only two or three emigrant ships left annually for New York from Stavanger, Bergen or Drammen. The rate of Norwegian emigration to America rose dramatically during the decade of the 1840s from only seven sailings in both 1846 and 1847 to16 in 1848 and 29 sailings in 1849. The vast majority of these were bound for New York. This trend began to change in 1850 when some Norwegian emigrant vessels began sailing to Quebec, Canada instead of to New York. The revoking of the British Navigation Act in 1849 allowed the shipping companies to carry a larger number of passengers on their ships to Quebec than they could to New York and it was considerably easier for the ship owners to get lucrative cargoes to haul back to Europe from Canada than from New York. Therefore, if the ship owner could carry more passengers and have freight to take back to Europe, he could generate more income and thus lower the price of each trans-Atlantic passage. The result was that after 1855 no Norwegian immigrant ships docked in New York; all headed for Quebec. It was also probably less expensive for the immigrants to get passage to their Midwest destinations from Quebec than from New York City.

Sailing ships dominated the trans-Atlantic emigrant traffic until later in the 1860s. In 1853, the first combination steam and sailing ships began to transport Norwegian immigrants to Hull, England. From there the emigrants took the train across England to Liverpool where they boarded a British steamship bound for the New World. That route via Hull became the dominant trek for the majority of the Norwegian emigrants in the early 1870s. During the period from 1865 to 1874, some sailing ships continued to operate directly from Norway to the United States and Canada, but each year there were fewer of them. Finally, in 1874, the last two sailing ships, the *Brødrene* and the *Pontecorvo* left Norway on voyages that took 44 and 53 days respectively. The emigrant route via Hull-Liverpool-New York on steamships usually took only 14-16 days. The website www.norwayheritage.com is a rich resource of information about Norwegian emigrant and passenger ships, 1825-1925. I highly recommend this website for individual research about the emigrant ships on which your Norwegian ancestors traveled to the United States and Canada.

After the Norwegian immigrants arrived in New York or Quebec, they still had a long distance to travel before they would reach their destinations in the Midwest. There were two basic routes for them to continue their long journeys. Those who arrived in New York before 1850 usually traveled by water, north on the Hudson River from New York City to Albany and then continued westward on the Erie Canal which took them slowly to Buffalo, New York on Lake Ontario. From there they could take a river boat to Detroit, Michigan. The majority of the immigrants most likely continued north on Lake Huron sailing above Michigan, and then continued south on Lake Michigan to Milwaukee or Chicago. Once the railroad between Detroit and Chicago was completed in 1852, that leg of the journey was most often completed by train. The Norwegians who emigrated after 1850 arrived at Quebec and from there traveled on the St. Lawrence River to Lake Erie, then through the Welland Canal to Lake Ontario and continued on the same route as the immigrants who traveled from Norway via New York. From Milwaukee or Chicago, the early immigrants continued on to their Midwest destinations with ox or horse drawn wagons, that is, if they could afford to buy them when they got off the river boat. There are numerous accounts of immigrants having to walk to their final destinations.

The railroad reached Detroit, Michigan in 1848 and Chicago in 1852. The railroad from Chicago to Galena, Illinois was completed in 1853. From Galena it was only a few miles to Dubuque where the immigrants could board a riverboat on the Mississippi River and continue north into Minnesota Territory. However, some Norwegian immigrants left the river boats at Lansing, Iowa and then traveled overland west to the Decorah, Iowa area or north into Minnesota. By the time Minnesota joined the union in 1858, the railroad had reached La Crosse, Wisconsin. It was from there that news of Minnesota's acceptance into the Union traveled by steamboat up the Mississippi River to Winona, Wabasha, Red Wing and finally to St. Paul, the capital of the new state. The railroad from Chicago to Minneapolis-St. Paul was delayed by the Civil War and was not completed until 1867. The Duluth, Minnesota to Fargo, North Dakota railroad line was completed in 1870. The following year, the railroad from Minneapolis reached Fargo, North Dakota. For decades, the rails dominated transportation, not only for arriving immigrants, but also for the products that were produced and the farm equipment and other supplies and goods that the Minnesota citizens needed.

Norwegians reach Minnesota

The first destination in the United States for newly arriving Norwegian immigrants was usually the home of a friend or relative who had already established himself, or to the settlement area from which they had received an "America letter." Norwegians, like immigrants from other countries, tended to settle in communities where there were people who spoke their language. However, the Norwegians were often even more selective. Not only did they want to settle among other Norwegians, but they preferred to settle with fellow Norwegians from their own valley or district in Norway who spoke the same Norwegian dialect. There are many Norwegian dialects in Norway.

During the immigration period, Norwegians from the western fjord districts would have had some difficulty in understanding the dialects of eastern or southern Norway. It was more comfortable to join people from one's own area than to feel like an outsider in another Norwegian community. As a result, there are a large number of Norwegian settlements in the Midwest that attracted concentrations of immigrants from particular areas of Norway. For the diminishing number of Americans who spoke Norwegian as their first language in childhood, it is still possible in 2009 to detect where in Norway their ancestors had lived before coming to America. Norwegians have told me countless times that my ancestors must have emigrated from eastern Norway and have often indicated that I speak with a Hadeland dialect, - more than 130 years after my ancestors arrived in America - from Hadeland!

The Norwegian immigrants arrived in the Fox River Valley of Illinois in 1834. As more Norwegians arrived, they soon began moving north into Wisconsin. Einar Haugen, in his history entitled *The Norwegians in America, 1825-1975*, (published by the Royal Ministry of Foreign Affairs, Oslo, 1975, p. 11-12) summarizes well the Norwegian settlements that were established in Wisconsin before 1850:

> By 1838 the Norwegians had moved into Wisconsin to found the "Jefferson Prairie" settlement in Rock County, followed by nearby Luther Valley in 1839. "Muskego" in Racine and Waukesha counties and "Koshkonong" in Dane County, both of them dating back to 1840, were famous in pioneer history. Madison is surrounded by a wreath of Norwegian settlements to the southeast, southwest, and north, going back to the early 1840's…. In western Wisconsin there is an almost solid strip of Norwegians in the coulee country along the Mississippi River from Crawford to Barron counties, including the cities of La Crosse and Eau Claire. There are large concentrations here known as "Coon Prairie" and "Coon Valley" around Westby and Viroqua in Vernon County, founded as early as 1848."

Prior to Wisconsin becoming a state on May 29, 1848, Minnesota was a part of the Wisconsin Territory. After long debates, on March 3, 1949, Congress finally passed the act creating the Minnesota Territory that included all of the future state of Minnesota and the land west to the Missouri River in the future Dakotas. By 1850, individual Norwegians began to cross the Mississippi River into Minnesota, settling first in western Houston and eastern Fillmore counties. The terrain of that area was particularly attractive to Norwegians because the deep valleys and rugged ridges reminded them of their native land. Spring Grove in Houston County is recognized as the first Norwegian settlement in Minnesota. Many of the early Norwegian settlers had spent some time in Rock, Racine and Dane counties in Wisconsin before moving to Minnesota. In turn, Spring Grove and Lanesboro in neighboring Fillmore County later became the first settlement destination for many Norwegian immigrants, especially those moving into western Minnesota. "Newcomers" often lived in established communities for several years, earning enough money to purchase their own "stake" before they moved further west where government land was available. During those first several years, the emigrants also learned some English and became acquainted with the farming practices in their newly adopted land. This pattern of residing in an established Norwegian community for several years, and learning some basics of American culture, was one that many Norwegian immigrants followed.

In 1852, Goodhue County was opened for settlement. By 1854, the land had been surveyed and immigrant caravans began to move in, one after another. The majority of these early settlers were Norwegians from the Koshkonong settlement, Dane County, Wisconsin who had arrived a few years earlier and now were ready to purchase farm lands of their own in the newly opened area. To the west of Red Wing there were thousands of acres of fertile farm country which were soon purchased by Norwegians. Goodhue County became a major Norwegian settlement area, with St. Olaf College in Northfield at its center.

Norwegians also continued moving west from Fillmore County into Mower, Freeborn and Faribault Counties. From there they spread into the counties bordering the upper Minnesota River Valley and then on into the Park Region area northwest of Alexandria. By 1870 they were settling in Otter Tail and Clay Counties in western Minnesota.

The majority of the 19th century Norwegian immigrants became farmers in America. However, after 1880 there were an increasing number of Norwegians who settled in Minneapolis and in smaller cities in other Norwegian areas. These included Red Wing, Northfield, Alexandria, Fergus Falls and smaller villages in dominant Norwegian settlement areas. During that period, a larger percentage of the immigrants were single young men and women who preferred to find employment in urban environments instead of on the farms.

According to the Census of 1860, there were 7,738 foreign-born Norwegians living in Minnesota. By the Census of 1880, that number had grown to 69,255! (Qualey, Carlton C. and Jon A. Gjerde. "The Norwegians," in *They Chose Minnesota: A Survey of The State's Ethnic Groups*, edited by June Drenning Holmquist, Minnesota Historical Society Press, 1981, p. 224). More people in Minnesota in 2009 claim Norwegian heritage than they do in any other state in the Union.

Pioneer life was difficult, especially for those first immigrant farmers whose days were filled with hard work and seemingly endless toil. Eugene Boe, in his essay "Pioneers to Eternity" has written eloquently about his grandparents who settled in west central Minnesota in the mid 19th century -

> "The wonder is not that so many of these first settlers
> succumbed, but that so many survived. A partial
> catalogue of the trials that beset them would show such

entries as grasshopper plagues, blizzards, long Arctic winters, stupefyingly hot summers, prairie fires, cyclones, tornadoes, hail storms, torrential rains that turned the grain to rot, poor seed and ignorance of good farming practices, oxen running wild, horses and cattle driven insane by mosquitoes, nerve-shattering winds, droughts, crop failures, money panics, stem rust in the spring wheat, killing strikes by pneumonia and influenza and tuberculosis and black diphtheria and typhoid fever, death by freezing, back-breaking labor without end, and the aching loneliness." Boe, Eugene, "Pioneers to Eternity" in *The Immigrant Experience: The Anguish of Becoming American,* Penguin Books, 1972, p. 59.

Congratulations to editor, Anne Sladky and all the various lag members who have assisted her in producing this unique contribution to the celebration of Minnesota's 150 years of Statehood! I highly encourage you to read it from cover-to-cover. It is my hope that this volume will encourage you to research, record and retell the immigration and settlement saga of your Norwegian ancestors. It is certainly worth the effort. Future generations of your family will be thankful for what you record.

Verlyn Anderson, Ph.D.
Moorhead, Minnesota
January 2009

Table of Contents

Dedication	iii
Map of Minnesota	iv
Foreword	v
Table of Contents	xii
Contributors, Photo Credits	xiv
Preface	xv

Stories of the 1850's

Crossing the Atlantic	2
Traveling by Covered Wagon	5
A Letter to Territorial Governor Ramsey	7
Settling Highland Prairie	9
A Poem by Ivar Vaeting	13
Houston's Stone Church	14
From Gol, Hallingdal to Wilmington Township, Houston County	15
Journey to Spring Grove	18
The Beginning of the Norwegian Settlement at Spring Grove	26
History of Bear Creek	31
Settling in Fox Lake	40
Pioneer Life in Dodge County	49
Historic Buildings in the Rock Dell Area	54
Statehood Pioneers and a Minnesota Governor	56
A Letter Home	58
Ole Torgerson, Road Builder	61
Urland's Most Difficult Citizen	66
Land Immigrants in Minnesota before 1858	69
Norwegian-Minnesotan Pioneers from Sigdal, Eggedal & Krødsherad	71

Biographies of Statehood Pioneers ... 74

Minnesota's Norwegian Century Pioneers

Century Pioneer Roster	176
An American Adventure	182
War Comes to Norway Grove	185
Christian Ahlness Leaves Norway	193
Pastor Brandt's Travels in Minnesota in 1869	199
To the Northwestern Frontier!	203
Turn of the Century Pioneers	214

Norwegian Fishermen on Lake Superior 216

Norwegian-Minnesotan Sesquicentennial Celebration
Schedule of Events 219
"They're All Bound for Minnesota" 222
On the Importance of Religion 228
Prayer of Remembrance 229
Photos: Norwegian Marketplace 230
Photos: Afternoon Program 231
Photos: Reception & Banquet... 233
Attendees 234

Minnesota's St. Olav Medal Winners 235

About the Participating Organizations
Hadeland Lag 240
Hallinglag 242
Landingslaget 243
Nordfjordlaget 245
Nord Hedmark & Hedemarken Lag... 247
Opdalslaget 248
Ringerike Drammen Districts Lag 250
Romerikslaget 252
Telelaget 253
Toten Lag 255
Trønderlag 257
Norwegian-American Genealogical Center & Naeseth Library 259

Acknowledgements 261

Reading List 262

Index of Names 264

Original Articles Written, Contributed, or Translated by

George H. Anderson, Dr. Verlyn Anderson, Gary Bakko, Joel Botten, Jr., Pastor Nils Brandt, Scott Brunner, Ole Ellingson translated by Stanley Uggen & contributed by Janice Johnson, Gene Estenson, Ingeborg Grønsten contributed by Nora Boyum, Stan Guberud & Chad Olson, James Joseph Hefte, Ole Jorgens & Lars G. Hanson with additions from O. M. Norlie, Alice Kirn, Dr. Odd Lovoll, Charlotte Stangeland Morsch, Percival Narveson contributed by Chad Muller, Martin Olson, Audrey Overland & Lorna Anderson, Iver Rommegen, Anne Esterby Romo, Arvid Sandaker contributed by Carol Olson, Jim Skree, Guri Sandersdtr Slettemoen, Levi Thortvedt, Ivar Vaeting translated by Dordi Round, Pastor Per Inge Vik, and Deana Williams.

Participating organization profiles provided by Joel Botten Jr., Helen Buche, Robert Fossum, Blaine Hedberg, Sandra Hendrickson, Evelith Kuecker, Elaine Nordlie, Anne Sladky, and Narv Somdahl.

Photo Credits

Cover graphics: Selected photos of Statehood & Century Pioneers submitted by their descendants; collage by Anne Sladky

Photos of the Statehood Pioneers were supplied by their descendants, unless otherwise noted.

Photos in other sections of the book were supplied by the contributors or the editor, unless otherwise noted.

Page	Description	Credit
Page 230	"Photos from the Marketplace"	Gerald Ziesemer, Fergus Falls
Page 231-232	"Photos from the Afternoon Program"	Sandra Hendrickson, Lakeville; Jim Skree, Caledonia; Georgia Rosendahl, Spring Grove
Page 233	"Photos from the Reception & Banquet"	Jim Skree, Caledonia
Page 238	Conrad Morck's St. Olav Diploma	Diane Langill, South Pasadena, CA

Preface

Baby-boomers (of which I am one) are perhaps the last generation with a strong personal connection to a Norwegian-American culture that was an integral part of everyday life, almost a part of the air we breathed. In the decades after World War II, strong ethnocentric neighborhoods and communities became more diverse and a more compartmentalized interest in ethnic heritage replaced a sense of "being Norwegian." Norwegian heritage is now one among many that vie for the attention of Americans whose family trees have roots not only in Norway, but in many other parts of Europe - and Africa, Asia, and the rest of the Americas as well.

We who never questioned the importance of our Norwegian ancestry are today faced with an unexpected responsibility. Successive generations can choose which parts of their ethnic quilt to embrace and celebrate. We must explain the value of Norwegian heritage and demonstrate its relevance to our children and grandchildren. For Americans of Norse descent who were brought up in a culture where reticence and humility were valued more than marketing skills, that's a tall order!

It therefore seemed not only appropriate but incumbent upon us to celebrate our Norwegian-Minnesotan ancestors as part of Minnesota's Sesquicentennial. The Norwegian Statehood Pioneer Project was organized to provide a visible acknowledgement of the role played by Norwegian pioneers in the development of the state. NSPP offered descendants the opportunity to purchase a plaque for the earliest Norwegian pathfinders; Norwegian Statehood Pioneers lived in Minnesota when it became the 32nd state on May 11, 1858. Much of Minnesota wasn't open for settlement until long after 1858, and it was soon obvious that the project could not ignore the brave pioneers who came later and spread that special Norwegian perspective from the border with the Dakotas to Lake Superior. The Century Pioneer Certificate was developed to offer recognition for all the Norwegians who lived in Minnesota by 1908. NSPP also sponsored a day long Sesquicentennial Celebration in October, 2008.

This book is the product of all of those Sesquicentennial activities. Although it tells only a handful of stories and profiles just a few of the Statehood Pioneers, it paints a picture of what life was like for the first Norwegians who cleared the land and laid the cornerstones of life in Minnesota today. All of Minnesota's pioneers shared the same joys and trevails, but the Norwegian sense of family and commitment to community set them apart, and allowed their influence to exceed their numbers.

My hope is that you will enjoy reading this Sesquicentennial volume as much as I have enjoyed the privilege of being its editor. This book wouldn't have been possible without the organizations that joined the project, publicized its efforts, accepted applications, and gathered information. The enthusiasm of those who applied for pioneer recognition and contributed content for this book was contagious, and the wonderful stories they had to tell made my job a real labor of love.

A great effort has been made to carefully transcribe all the names and dates, and to present the biographical information provided by pioneer descendants in a consistent and equitable way. I have no doubt a few mistakes will be found in the final product despite our best efforts, and my sincere apologies if your pioneer's story is so afflicted.

Applicants were required to provide documentation proving an ancestor's presence in Minnesota at the time of statehood, and designation as a Minnesota Statehood Pioneer was granted only after an independent review and verification. The content of life stories submitted with applications was accepted without further scrutiny. Biographies were edited to standardize presentation, add additional facts found in supporting documents, accommodate information from multiple descendants, and/or to focus attention on the pioneer rather than ancestors or succeeding generations. Some biographies were shortened to conform to the 500-word guideline.

The dates and places listed for Century Pioneers were verified against documents submitted with the application or the project's research in other sources. Although we worked hard to determine the earliest date of residence, the reality is that immigrants often did not appear in church or civil records for some period of time after their arrival. If you believe your ancestor arrived in an area earlier than the date listed you may well be right, but at least for this compilation, we just couldn't prove it!

All of the materials collected and created by NSPP will find a permanent home at the Norwegian-American Genealogical Center and Naeseth Library in Madison, Wisconsin. Many of the applications included family trees, photos, and other information that did not find its way into this book. Thanks to NAGC-NL, all of the information submitted will be available to genealogy researchers in the years to come.

I hope that seeing a Statehood Pioneer plaque on the wall, a Century Pioneer certificate in a scrapbook, or reading the stories in this book will catch the imagination of the descendants of all the Norwegians who made Minnesota their home, and instill a sense of pride because *Norwegian* pioneers played an important role in building this state, beginning in Territorial times. The work of the Norwegian Statehood Pioneer Project will have been a success if our efforts encourage interest in and conversations about what we all know – that it is an honor and a privilege to be a descendant of Norwegian-Minnesotans!

Anne Sladky
Editor

Section One
STORIES OF THE 1850's

We of Norse blood, but American birth, if we are true to the best that is in us, cannot fail to have an interest in the trials and the achievements of the pioneer fathers. We must recognize the true heroism of the men and women who braved the hardships and suffered the privations of frontier life.

Norwegian Immigration to the United States, p. 17
George Tobias Flom ©1909

Crossing the Atlantic in the 1850's

Reprinted by permission from "Williams-Nelson Family History" pages 27-29, self-published by Deana Williams in 1992

The three-masted barks that brought the early immigrants from Norway were powered only by the wind. It was still the era of sailing ships. These ships were usually only about 120 feet long. Although some ships had one or two "guest cabins" available, the primary purpose of ocean-going vessels at this time was moving cargo. The idea of a ship dedicated solely to transporting passengers was still a decade or two away

To accommodate immigrants, the cargo hold of the ship was modified and held a row of wide (holding 3-4 people) bunks stacked two or sometimes three high against each wall of the hold. Larger ships might also have a row of bunks down the middle. The ceiling heights varied from slightly less than six feet to as much as eight feet. Access to the remodeled cargo hold (renamed the "between deck") was usually down long ladders that extended up to the deck through the cargo hatches.

The journey was estimated to take ten weeks, but unfavorable winds or stormy seas could extend the voyage to three months or longer. A one way ticket typically cost from $20-$30 dollars. The ship provided straw mattresses (an ideal home for lice and fleas) on the wooden bunks. Passengers were expected to bring their own bed clothes, cooking utensils, and food. Water and wood (for cook stoves) was included in the price of passage, although there were often reports of water shortages when winds and storms extended the crossings.

Every traveler was responsible for bringing enough food for the 10 week voyage, – a typical list might include loaves of bread, a large cheese round, butter keg, coffee or tea, a sack of flour, and a hefty chunk of salted sausage, salt pork, and perhaps a smoked sheep shoulder. Some captains allowed a stove in the between deck; most, because of the fear of fire, insisted that all cooking be done in a galley on deck. Since each family cooked for itself, there were often long lines waiting to use the cooking facilities; some families simply gave up on cooking and ate all of their meals cold.

Each passenger was allowed one trunk. The charge for excess baggage was dear and few could afford it. Trunks were usually made specifically for the voyage. Along with the owner's name, many included the year of immigration, and some were beautifully decorated with rosemalling. The trunks contained the food and utensils required on the trip along with the most necessary and most important of his or her possessions. Everything else had to be given away, sold, or thrown out. The child's rocker that Great-great Grandma Nelson is said to have brought with her from Norway would have been packed in her immigrant trunk. We can only imagine what she chose to leave behind, and how valuable this treasure from her childhood must have been for Guro to have given it so much precious space in her trunk!

On some ships, provisions and trunks were kept in a cargo hold beneath the between deck. The cargo hold was often tightly packed, with the immigrant trunks stacked on top of regular cargo. It was sometimes very difficult for the passengers to get to their provisions and possessions, and only a handful of them might be able to descend to the cargo hold at one time. On some ships, trunks were kept on the between deck. That made access much easier, but could create serious problems in stormy weather. Passengers often reported that the trunks, which were not always tied down, were tossed around in the dark of the between deck, seriously injuring passengers who had the misfortune of being in the path of sliding or flying trunks!

Ventilation was usually a serious problem. Most passengers spent as much time as possible on the decks of the ship. Because a between deck was just a cargo hold filled with bunks, on most ships the only openings through which fresh air could pass were the cargo hatch and a small number of vents. Bathroom facilities were often just a pail in a corner that was to be brought up on deck each morning and dumped over the side. During bad weather, the hatch and vents were closed to prevent the between deck from filling with water. Although lamps were usually allowed during calm seas, they were forbidden during storms. Imagine being in almost total darkness, with the "Johnny can" sloshing all over and people vomiting from seasickness. The stench could be almost unbearable.

Water was brought onboard for drinking, but many ships depended on rainwater collection for water for washing both passengers and crew and their clothing. When a water shortage developed, personal hygiene was the first thing to suffer. This only added to the odor problems suffered by the passengers.

Most captains required that passengers organize cleaning parties so that, at least once a week, the entire between deck was scraped and cleaned. The most effective room deodorizer for the space was an often daily visit from one or two crewmen who brought red hot pokers down from the deck and dipped them in tar. The smoke and steam from the tar covered the most offensive odors.

The voyage was considered extremely dangerous. The possibility of a ship sinking was always there, although it did not happen often. Many people did not survive the crossing because of disease and accidents. The tight quarters were the perfect breeding ground for diseases such as cholera, dysentery, and measles, and the accumulating filth from extended periods of bad weather, coupled with the weakness brought on by bouts of seasickness, often proved a death sentence. Children and the elderly were often the first to be lost. Ships of that era did not have a staff doctor or an infirmary on board. Most often the passengers had to look to each other to fashion home remedies and provide care for the ill. There was no way to isolate the sick from the healthy, so disease spread easily.

Those who died were very quickly buried at sea. Services were held on deck, by a clergyman among the passengers if one was onboard or the ship's captain. Bodies were wrapped in canvas or, if wood was available, placed in simple boxes built by the ship's carpenter. After a few words and a prayer, the body was sent over the side into the ocean. There are many reports that such burials often attracted sharks that would then continue to circle the boat waiting for their next meal to hit the water. When there were a large number of deaths and burials, the sound of the sharks' feeding frenzies as passengers and crew held the somber funeral ceremonies created nightmares that would haunt parents, children, siblings, and spouses of the departed for a lifetime.

Certainly few could have imagined what was in store for them as the ships set sail from the Norwegian ports, and few wanted to speak about it when the ordeal was over. Conditions improved on the steamships that replaced the sailing ships, but for the Norwegian immigrants of the 1840's and 1850's, the cost of seeking a better life in America was paid in more than dollars.

Traveling by Prairie Wagon
Submitted by George H. Anderson

Most of our Norwegian ancestors made their way from the ports where the immigrant ships docked in New York and Quebec to Chicago and Milwaukee on public transportation – at first by boat on the Great Lakes, and later on the trains that ran from New York or Detroit. Many who stepped off the boats and trains walked to their destinations or arranged for a friend or relative to meet them. For families with the means to do so, the purchase of a prairie wagon and a sturdy set of horses or oxen was often their first business transaction in the U. S. After spending time in the established settlements of Illinois, Wisconsin, and later, Minnesota, Norwegian families set out to pre-empt or homestead government lands on the frontiers. Once again, the prairie wagon served as the combination RV and moving van of its day.

Prairie wagons typically measured 8-12 feet long, although with the tongue and yoke included their total span was closer to 24 feet. The wagon bed was 4 feet wide, with walls that were 2-3 feet in height. Sometimes tar was used to make the wagon bed water tight for crossing streams. The cover was often homespun cotton or linen doubled over and soaked in linseed oil to make it waterproof. The cover was supported by 4-6 bent wood bows. The total height of the wagon with its cover in place was usually about 10 feet.

Wheels were made of wood, typically with iron wrapped around the outside to make them more durable. Front wheels were slightly smaller than the back wheels, which improved the wagon's turning radius and made it easier to maneuver.

Most of us imagine horses pulling these "prairie schooners" (so called because they reminded the pioneers of ships on a sea of prairie grass), but actually most of our Norwegian ancestors used a team of 2 or 4 oxen – they were usually less expensive and required less feed on the trail.

The driver's seat served as the cover of a storage box in which were kept staples like flour, sugar, and dried meats. Often the seat/top of this box could be removed and used as a table. A hole was drilled in each corner, so that legs could be put into place.

The wagon had to be packed to allow easy access to everyday things like cooking utensils and travel clothing. Other goods being moved were packed securely and placed so that they did not have to be disturbed during the journey. Flat trunks were usually arranged so that they could be used as a bed at night. Sometimes a couple slept in the wagon and children beneath it; often the women slept in the wagon and the men and boys bedded down "under the stars" and took turns keeping watch.

The outside of the wagon had a number of hooks that could be used to secure wash tubs and other larger items. A "jockey box" was usually attached to the outside of the wagon, and it carried tools and the spare parts needed to make repairs to the wagon along the way. In addition, a water barrel, butter churn, lanterns, a shovel and ax, or a small feed trough might also be attached to the outside of the wagon.

Wagons typically had a set of springs at the front of the wagon that made riding on the driver's seat tolerable, but even on relatively even ground, riding inside the wagon was a bumpy and uncomfortable experience.

Once the pioneers arrived at their destination, the schooners continued to provide a home until land was cleared and a cabin built. The bows and cover would then be removed and the prairie schooner continued to serve the family as a farm wagon.

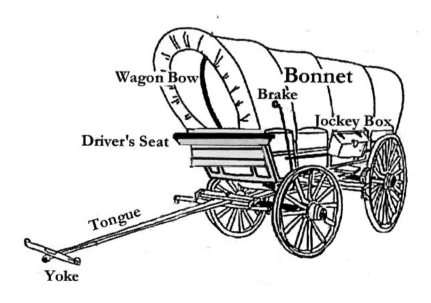

A Letter to Territorial Governor Ramsey
by Audrey Overland and Lorna Anderson

Original letter in Ramsey Papers, Minnesota Historical Society, reprinted from "Overland Family History – Volume I" pages 51-53, published in 1986 by River Falls (WI) Journal Commercial Printing Department

Reverend C. L. Clausen was a young Dane who had hoped to become a missionary to Africa. Instead, he was convinced to come to America to teach religion to the sons of the pioneers. He began his service in Muskego in 1843. He was ordained later that year. Pastor Clausen went on to minister in Koshkonong and Rock Prairie.

While pastor at Rock Prairie and previously at Muskego, Clausen was brought into direct contact with the problems of immigration. Hundreds of Norwegian immigrants came to the Wisconsin settlements annually, and the pastor was forced to take measures to aid these people in earning temporary subsistence and to find land. The increasing number of immigrants coming, many people taking advantage of the language barrier to swindle the newcomers by overcharging for land, and the gradual exhaustion of the good government land, made the problem of the care of new immigrants a very serious one. Clausen was deeply concerned by this state of affairs and personally set out to find new areas where the Norwegians might obtain good farming land from the government. His attention was naturally drawn to Minnesota. This new area had just become a territory and steps were being taken to acquire the land from the Indians.

Clausen wrote to Governor Ramsey in January, 1850, inquiring about the opportunities offered in the Minnesota Territory for immigrants:

```
                                   Luther Valley, January 22d, 1850

His Excellency, Alexander Ramsey, Governor:

Sir! I feel assured in my mind that you will pardon the liberty I hereby
use in addressing you, as a stranger to you, and asking for some
information from you, when I tell you my motives and situation. I am now
and has (sic) been for nearly seven years, a minister amongst the
Norwegians in this state and the Northern Illinois, and having in that
time acquired some knowledge of the American language, institutions, and
other matters, my advice has often of late been asked by the large bodies
of Emigrants from Scandinavia, especially from Norway, who annually come
into this country, as also from those in the old country who propose to
emigrate, concerning matters here of importance for them to know, and
especially about where the best locations for settlements on public land
are to be had. A large number of Emigrants who came in last season, are
now staying over the winter around here in the settlement, purposing to
look out in the spring for public lands to settle upon, but as they are
alike unacquainted with the country and the language here, it is to be
feared that many of them may be misled to their serious disadvantage, if
```

left entirely to themselves or, which is often worse, to the guidance of interested speculators.

They have appealed to me for advice and assistance, but the time is past, when I from my personal acquaintance with the government lands - of which there are none here now in this section of country - could be able to advise them where to go. But Minnesota has often during the last year been noticed in the papers in such a way, as to make me believe that some parts of that country in the vicinity of Lake Pepin and St. Croix River and Lake, would be most preferable for my hardy and enterprising countrymen, both as to climate, soil, and the principal natural advantages. This belief has been strengthened by conversation with persons who has (sic) been through that country, and give it a high character, but before advising my country-people to go there, I still wish to have more information about it myself, and from sources that I could rely on, and no better way to get information about that country occurred to me, than by addressing Your Excellency, who both from your residence in that country, and from your official situation, that commands so numerous sources of information, probably is more able than any other person to give me the desired information. If you would therefore deign to give me a description of the country adjoining the lakes and River aforementioned: the climate, soil, timber, water, etc.; or refer me to some sure and reliable source to get the information about it. You would thereby greatly benefit and oblige myself and my country-people. Those Norwegians, in whose behalf I now principally write, are generally poor, but sober, hardy and industrious farmers and mechanics; but I have received letters from Norway and Denmark informing me that several men with considerable capital, wish to go over here, if I can lead them to places where they can invest their capital profitably, in improving water powers, erecting mills and other machineries, and building towns, etc; and I should therefore be very much gratified, if Your Excellency would please let me know how far those objects might be gained in your section of country, and perhaps point out to me the most favorable places.

If your Excellency's answer is so, as to encourage an emigration up there, I am determined to go there myself, and will in all probability have a considerable Norwegian settlement on the banks of one of the lakes or water courses next Fall. Hoping your Excellency will consider this letter favorably and favor me with an early answer, I remain most respectfully, Your obedient servant.

C. L. Clausen

Please direct your letter to:
   Rev. C. L. Clausen
   Immansville Post Office
   Rock County, Wisconsin

Settling Highland Prairie

Compiled by Lorna Anderson from material in "Overland Family History with Roots in Telemark Norway" by Audrey Overland and Lorna Anderson, published in 1987

This is written as a tribute to two sets of great grandparents who explored and chose land to settle in 1853 in the southeastern part of Minnesota Territory and the pioneers who accompanied them. Ole Overland and Halvor Erickson emigrated from Telemark, Norway, in 1849 and 1850, and came to a Wisconsin settlement started by relatives in 1843 bordering Jefferson and Walworth Counties, near Palmyra. A church was organized in this area called Skoponong. Johannes and Tone Overland and the rest of the children came to America in 1851. Halvor married their daughter Kari after they moved to Minnesota.

The second pastor to serve in this parish was a young Dane, Pastor Clausen. As early as 1844, Knud Langeland traveled through Dane County, Wisconsin, and said all the best land had been taken and there was hardly room for newcomers. Knud and Pastor Clausen visited Jefferson and Rock Counties in 1849 visiting farms. In *Nordmændene i Amerika* Knud reports that "Almost all the cultivable land was taken up and everywhere well-built farms were to be seen which indicated industry and well-being among the farmers."

In January of 1850, Pastor C. L. Clausen wrote to the Territorial Governor of Minnesota, Alexandria Ramsey, telling him that many Norwegians had asked for advice in obtaining government land. Minnesota had been advertised in the papers and other acquaintances had been there making him believe that it would be a good place to settle.

Ramsey's reply must have been favorable, for in the summer of 1850, Clausen and others made the trip up the Mississippi to St. Paul and St. Cloud, southeastern Minnesota, and part of Wisconsin. On this trip Clausen saw a good deal of Minnesota which was still Indian land.

In 1853 the company of the Johannes Olsen Overland family, Ole Overland family, Halvor Erickson, and a couple of Rue families left the Skoponong Settlement and traveled west. Their wagons were pulled by oxen. The wheels of the wagons were made of solid sections of oak logs. The men drove the animals while some walked and others rode in the wagon. The trip of 200 miles to Iowa took about three weeks. The route took them through Madison, which was a little village at that time. Those who had room enough slept under the wagon covers, the others slept on the bare ground under the wagons.

The Wisconsin River had to be crossed on a small ferryboat. The propelling power was furnished by a horse placed on a tread-power, which worked the paddle wheels. Only one wagon and a team at a time could be taken aboard. The herd of loose cattle had to swim over the river. The ferry boat at Prairie de Chien was larger and propelled by a four mule tread-power. The Mississippi River was wide and much time was taken to get everything across.

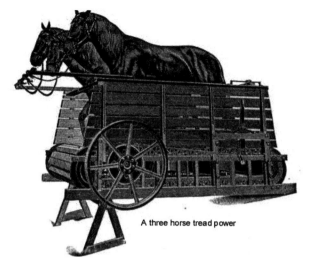
A three horse tread power

The pioneers set out northwesterly, coming to the Washington Prairie settlement in Winnesheik County, Iowa. Here they found land and proceeded to build a dugout ¾ mile northeast of Calmar, Iowa, where they stayed for the winter. As the available land had been taken in this area, Ole Overland and Halvor Erickson set out to explore the region in Minnesota about which they had heard reports from others. This was done in spite of rumors that it was too cold a place to raise corn and other crops. There were also reports of danger from unfriendly Indians. The explorers came to Highland Prairie and were impressed with its possibilities, but there was no available water supply. They continued northward to the Root River. In this valley, west of what became known as Rushford, they found two Norwegian settlers, Halvor Goodrich and Ole Tuff. These men came that same year directly from Norway by way of McGregor and Decorah, Iowa, and had taken claims on the south side of the river.

Ole and Halvor were favorably impressed with this area, but after some deliberation, decided to explore the possibilities of the Highland Prairie area. They returned by a more westerly route. As they were preparing to camp for the night on the northwestern edge of Section 15, they discovered a little spring of water trickling out of a hillside. Having found a source of water supply, they returned to Calmar for the winter. They planned to return in the spring of 1854 to stake their claims. On their return, they could report in glowing terms of having found an ideal place to settle – Highland Prairie in Minnesota Territory.

In March of 1854, Johannes Overland, his three sons, Ole, Knut and Steinar; future son-in-law Halvor Erickson; nephew Hans Franson Rue; and Hans' cousin, Harold Olson Rue set off with oxen and wagons to stake their claims in Section 15 and 16. They built the first dwelling on the prairie, a sod-thatched log cabin measuring 14 feet wide and 18 feet long. This home was built for the Johannes Overland family. Hans Franson claimed the distinction of having felled the first tree on Highland Prairie as they joined together in the task of providing material for the shelter.

They completed the structure in April and returned to Iowa to get the rest of the families. They returned May 18, 1854, and sent word to the families in Wisconsin that they had good land available for settlement

Highland Prairie or "*Vaslans Prairien*" (Waterless Prairie), as it was called in the early years of the settlement, was indeed an attractive site for settlers. The land was all open, with wooded areas on the hillsides and in the valleys. Repeated prairie fires had destroyed upland trees and underbrush, so the problem of clearing the land was simple. Lush prairie grass abounded, which made the breaking of the sod for fields a strenuous but not impossible task. The wooded slopes and valleys were a ready source of logs for buildings, and for fuel for cooking and heating the homes. The little spring in section 15 was enlarged into a reservoir by digging out a large hole in the clay soil around and below its source. This became the source of drinking and cooking water for the settlement. The rest of their water needs were supplied by catching the abundant rain water in stock ponds and cisterns. Wooden barrels were later used to store rain water for household use. The Overland farm had water rights for the land on which the spring was located.

In June of 1854, a very large company came trekking the long distance from the southern corner of Wisconsin with their cattle and household goods. Thus the Waterless Prairie was all at once heavily populated. About 60-100 of these people lived the first summer and fall in their wagons which were gathered in the grove by the spring. The place became very lively with so many cattle, pigs and chickens.

In spite of the reports that had been made concerning the unsuitable climate of Minnesota for raising crops, the settlers here found that their plantings thrived. Having succeeded in breaking their plots, the settlers' field crops yielded abundantly. It is said that the first field plowed was just north of the present Highland Prairie church parsonage, and was broken with a borrowed plow from settlers in the Root River Valley.

The plantings in 1854 were potatoes, beans, wheat, oats, and corn. All of these yielded a very satisfactory harvest. The corn not only ripened, but proved an irresistible attraction to the numerous blackbirds and crows. The meat supply was adequate thanks to the abundance of game, especially deer and prairie chicken. As was usual with early Norwegian settlers, those coming to Highland Prairie brought some livestock with them. These animals were a source of milk and meat, in addition to serving as foundation stock for the large herds of animals that came to be such an important factor in the successful settlement.

Winona was the main market. Farmers hauled their wheat, oats and pork there and would return with necessities such as flour, flannel and linsey material. The trips would take two days, requiring a night in a Winona hotel, with the oxen and horses in a livery barn. Sometimes the trip would be made to LaCrosse, Wisconsin, and the evening would be spent in the hotel located about a mile below Hokah.

Clothing usually consisted of flannel undershirt and drawers, linsey shirt, vest coat, homemade woolen pantaloons that were lined, muskrat cap, woolen mittens faced with deerskin, woolen socks, and cowhide boots.

There were quite a number of Indians the first years. They would often come and beg for something to eat. They asked for pork, butter, flour and soap. During storms they would, without asking, walk into a home and simply stay until inclined to leave. The pioneers tolerated this odd behavior because they needed to be seen as the Indians' friends in order to establish their homes without creating problems.

As the years went by, there were many who paused to rest at Highland Prairie on the long and tiresome journey by foot and ox cart to other Norwegian settlements farther west and in northern Minnesota, South Dakota and North Dakota. It was estimated that from 60 to 100 immigrant wagons per year stopped or passed through the Highland Prairie Settlement.

Torkel Oftelie wrote in the *Telesoga*: "I came up on Highland Prairie which is known throughout the entire Northwest because many have been here of those that moved westward in the old days. This high ground is situated between deep valleys of the Root River. The Root River runs through a large valley on the north side and on the south side is the South Fork. Highland Prairie takes all of Norway Township and small parts of others. Arms of this highland reach out between side valleys on all sides like spreading arms of an ink blot. Some of these have names: Olav Ridge in the east, Øien Ridge in the north and Busil-Rova in the west. The land here is not really flat. It has hills, draws and groupings of trees."

Torkel tells about the village of Bratsberg: "There are two stores, a creamery, a blacksmith shop and several farms around so it looks for the most part like a town. It is two Telemarkings who are storekeepers here, Olav Overland and Sveinung Byholt."

"The farms are quite close and the church stands in the middle of the circle surrounded by a fine oak woods and in with it is the Pastor's farm. The first church was built in the 1860's and the one that now stands in the 1890's. The ministry belongs to the Synod and comprises this church plus Elstad and Oak Ridge. Old Christian Magelson has been pastor over 40 years. His son Nils Magelson is now assistant Pastor."

A Poem by Ivar Vaeting

When sagawriter Torkel Oftelie came for a visit in 1913, Ivar Vaeting composed a poem about the Telemark settlement in Houston County. The original (written in Norwegian dialect), a literal translation, and a poetic translation composed by Dordi Round were published in "Telemark to America-Volume II" by Telelaget of America. The poetic translation appears here with Telelaget's permission.

It was in the 1850's
They came to Houston's vales,
From Telemark's old homesteads,
With all their chests and bales.

Here they found hills and valleys,
With woods, and brooks, and streams,
Resembling their old homeland,
They chose the best, it seems.

They built their simple cabins
Of woods with foreign names,
And it was cause for boasting
When they saw their first hearth flames.

No church was here for worship,
Not a single town or street.
The boys learned independence,
And to stand on their own two feet.

They thought about their choir,
Which had sung in days of yore:
"O let us have a church now,
We cannot worship Thor."

They built the church they wanted,
Hard labor they did not shirk;
It isn't boasting when we say
Its an impressive piece of work.

The Yankees, their first neighbors,
Complained about their speech;
They couldn't grasp the Telemaal --
And were too dumb to teach.

But the Telers didn't like "Yankee,"
Which sounded whiny and shrill,
So they kept on speaking Telemaal
And we hope they always will.

We honor our old people,
Admire their courage and drive,
And when they sleep beneath the sod,
We must keep their faith alive.

Houston's Stone Church

The church mentioned in Ivar Vaeting's poem is the Norwegian Evangelical Lutheran Church that straddles the Houston-Sheldon Township line in Houston County. It is commonly known as the Stone Church. This venerable old congregation, along with Highland Prairie Church, in nearby Fillmore County, are the two oldest Norwegian Lutheran congregations in Minnesota.

The Stone Church has been designated as an historic site. The marker at the church is inscribed as follows:

With a Bible in one hand and an axe and a gun in the other, Norwegian emigrants settled in the area in 1853. Realizing their dependence on the Lord and his guidance, with the help of a traveling minister of the Gospel, Rev. V. Koren, a Lutheran congregation was established in this community in 1855. Construction of this beautiful church was started in 1863, the rock quarried from the adjacent hills. The work was stopped during the Civil War, but the church was completed in 1866 at a cost of $4,385. It was dedicated to the glory of God in the same year. Desirous of maintaining complete harmony, this church is located in Houston and Sheldon townships, the township line running up the center aisle of the church. May the Blessings the Lord has poured out on this community never be forgotten.

From Gol, Hallingdal to Wilmington Township, Houston County
Compiled from information submitted by James Joseph Hefte

"*Gofa*" (Grandpa) Ole Olson Hefte was born in Reinli, Valdres, in 1796. He volunteered to fight the invading Swedes in 1814, and was still listed as a soldier when he married Ingrid Kinneberg in March of 1819. In 1820, they took title to the Hefte farm in Gol, Hallingdal. It was a small plot, with no road, and despite adding more land over the years, Ole and his family had to work very hard to make their meager living. In 1853, *Gofa* Ole sold the Hefte farm to Ola Nilson Brekke. *Gofa* Ole, his wife Ingrid and their children "*Storre*" (Big) Ole and his wife Inger, Lame Ole, Nils, and Bergit joined others from Gol seeking new and better lives in America.

Their preparation for this long and wearisome voyage to America had to be carefully planned, for the cost of the tickets depended on the amount of luggage. They made large wooden chests in which to pack their clothing and a few cherished treasures. These huge white pine chests were iron bound to withstand abuse. They had high round lids and were equipped with large homemade locks and a huge key, five or six inches long. The chests were painted a rust color with the name and birthday of the owner painted across the front and top in fancy script, together with some rosemaled designs.

Besides clothing, these chests contained enough food for the trip across the ocean of sixteen weeks. Women would stand by the fire and bake flatbread for several days. Other foods included butter, several kinds of meal, dried meat, herring and salt. Dozens of rounds of lefse were made to be used up first, as lefse did not keep as long as flatbread. The family Bible was the most cherished possession and was carefully packed. It served as a great source of strength and comfort during the passage and in the family's first years in Minnesota.

During the early days of their voyage, many of the passengers were homesick and sea sick. For those who weren't sick, there were various forms of entertainment enjoyed on top deck, such as violin and accordion music, *Springdans, Hallingkast*, and wrestling. Whenever possible, the passengers would fish. Sunday worship was conducted on board with the Captain as minister. He also had charge of funerals, of which there were quite a few. Cholera took many lives.

Gofa Ole's wife Ingrid became violently ill and died on the sail boat. She was buried at sea. What a mournful event! *Gofa* was left alone to face a rigorous life in the new land. He was then about fifty-eight years old.

After arriving in New York, the company traveled by rail to Chicago, then to the Norwegian settlement at Fox River, Illinois. In the same year they went by riverboat to Brownsville, Minnesota. From Brownsville they set out westward for about thirty miles, stopping in what would become Wilmington Township in Houston County. Before these stout-hearted pioneers had traveled more than a few miles in this new area, they found a hilly and wooded country to their liking.

Ready access to water was the most important asset a farm could have. *Gofa* Ole's son, *Storre* Ole scouted the land and one morning discovered a pond which was about halfway between the site of what would become the Hefte farm and the village of Caledonia, Minnesota. He walked on through the day, however, hopeful of finding an even better location. This he failed to do, so at dusk he returned to the pond, determined to claim that land. When he arrived at his goal, he found much to his dismay that three covered wagons had already squatted there. Eventually he discovered and squatted on the ground which would become the Hefte Homestead.

Much of the land in southeastern Minnesota wasn't available for legal claim until 1857. Before selling the land for $1.25 an acre, the government had to complete an official survey. The early settlers staked out their homesteads and began building their farms long before they could become legal owners. As it was for many new arrivals, the forced delay in registering a claim offered a great advantage. The money obtained by selling the Hefte farm in Gol paid the family's passage from Norway, but other travel and living expenses left *Gofa* Ole and his oldest son *Storre* Ole without the money to buy land, or even the simplest tools to develop it. A Mr. Sprague, however, furnished a grub hoe and an ax on credit, and with these *Storre* Ole set to work.

The first shelter was a cellar dug in the hillside. The second building was made of logs with a dirt covered roof. There was no furniture, not even beds, but willing hands and a determination to make a better home soon changed things for the better. *Gofa* Ole had been a carpenter in Norway, and his well-honed skills were of great assistance to his family and the larger community.

In 1856, *Storre* Ole lost his wife Inger during the birth of their daughter, Guri. He hired Sigri Engen as a housekeeper and soon realized that this tiny woman, who weighed just 90 pounds, was the wife and helpmate he was looking for. They rode the same horse to the home of the justice of the peace in Portland Prairie, a distance of about five miles, for their marriage ceremony. Although the service was conducted in English and they could not yet speak the language, they understood and were very happy to have been united in matrimony.

Storre Ole expanded his holdings, 40 acres at a time. The story of how he acquired the fifth and final 40 acres of his homestead is a good one. Neighbor Kari Stenehjem warned Ole that he had better buy the 40 acres he wanted because there was someone else interested in purchasing it. Ole took the information seriously and scraped together fifty dollars. At two o'clock in the morning, he started the twenty-five mile walk to Brownsville where the US Land Office was located. He arrived late in the afternoon and completed the purchase. The next day, when Ole was walking home, he met his competitor on the road, bound for Brownsville to purchase the property Ole had bought just hours before!

Gofa Ole lived with his son and family until his death in 1881. He was able to see that the decision to come to America, although it cost him his beloved wife, had been a good one. His sons and daughters had found land and built a much better life for themselves and their descendants in Minnesota.

Journey to Spring Grove

Excerpts from the Gubberud family history written and researched by Stan Guberud and Chad Olson

The Gubberud family traces itself to about 1826 and the marriage of Kjersti Gudbrandsdtr Haugsrudeige and Anders Øestensen Haugsrudeige. In 1844, they purchased the north Gubberud farm in Bagn, Valders, Norway, so their last name changed to "Gubberud". Anders and Kjersti (Haugsrudeige) Gubberud had 5 children: Gulbrand, Øesten, Olia, Gunhild and Martin. Anders was also in the business of floating stray logs down the river. He would purchase these from the lumber company and sell them for a profit.

In Norway, the development of a smallpox vaccination allowed more babies to survive infancy and childhood. Potatoes, introduced in the late 1700's, provided better nutrition. These two factors caused the population to increase. Tillable land for farming did not, so the chances of buying land or improving one's situation were small. The people lived under a strict social system where, among other things, they were expected to show public signs of respect to members of the upper class, a very humbling experience. Only the upper classes were allowed to vote. In the mid 1800's the country had a series of crop failures causing food shortages and hard times. Even with all the dangers of the ocean crossing, by comparison America looked like the Promised Land.

When a family made the decision to cross the ocean in hopes of a better life, it meant leaving behind friends, family members, and possessions. It was a pretty big gamble with no guarantees. Emigrants faced a long and dangerous journey, sickness, and death. The motivating factors had to have been the stories of abundant tracts of fertile land in America which could be purchased for $1.25 to $5.00 an acre.

To make this journey there was lots of work that had to be done beforehand. Before being allowed to leave Norway they had to be free of debt, and the price of their one way ticket from Norway to Quebec was about $25. With the decision made and passage paid for, they had to pack up their immigrant chests, and decide what was being taken and what was being left behind. Unwanted possessions were sold off, as extra freight was very expensive. When the time came to depart, passengers would assemble near the port and wait, and there were usually delays. When this happened the wait wasn't just for a few hours, but weeks at a time.

The first ships used to freight passengers were originally built for cargo. This meant that the passengers were placed in the cargo hold, rebuilt to carry passengers. The passengers were lodged "between decks," often just called steerage. The origin of the term steerage comes from steers (cattle), and indicates that the emigrants traveled under the same conditions, and on the same decks as were used for transporting cattle (often with very little cleaning in between).

These ships of course were wooden sailships. The most commonly used for transporting immigrants was called a barkentine. Other types were brigs and schooners.

A barkentine was 3-masted: square rigged on the foremast, and both fore- and aft-rigging on the main and mizenmasts. Barks were used for coastal shipping because of their ability to go into the wind with the fore-aft sails, and to catch long wind currents with the square sails.

After arriving in Quebec and being examined by a doctor, passengers transferred to a succession of large river steamers, canal steamers, and trains. These transported them to Montreal, down through the Great Lakes, and on to Detroit, or Milwaukee if their final destination was further west.

The Skiftuns, Gubberuds and Lunde would make the crossing on 5 different ships, probably leaving from Stavanger and/or Christiania (Oslo).

In 1850, Ole Gudmundson Skiftun and his wife Sissela and their four daughters, Anne, Anna, Sissel, and Malene came to America. Ole sold half of his farm in Hjelemenland and signed the other half over to his son Gudmund, the oldest of the Skiftun children. Gudmund chose to stay behind in Norway with his much older wife.

At the quarantine station on Gross Isle, Quebec, the Skiftuns mingled with hundreds of other immigrant passengers before continuing their journey. They received a clean bill of health to travel on to Montreal, but were probably exposed to cholera there. This was the 1850 Cholera Epidemic, sometimes referred to simply as the cholera season because the epidemic returned summer after summer, killing year after year. Cholera is a nasty disease spread by contaminated food or water, with major outbreaks occurring in late summer. Large unclean cities and hot summer temperatures also made a ripe environment. Cholera thrived in densely populated areas and among travelers who spread the germs wherever they went. The disease was an infection of the intestinal tract that caused dehydration and flu-like symptoms, and in 1850 it killed 50% or more of the people infected.

The Skiftuns made it as far as the state of Michigan (probably Detroit) before things took a very bad turn. They were struck by this deadly scourge. Ole died and was either buried at sea or along Lake Michigan. Most of the family was likely infected with cholera by this time; regardless, they had no choice but to continue on. The remaining family members traveled as far as Milwaukee, a thriving port city of 20,000 people. Here, mother Sissela perished from the same sickness. She was taken away by the authorities and buried, and the children never knew at what place.

Surely the girls would have liked to have given their parents a proper burial, funeral, or, a chance to lay some flowers on their graves to say their good-byes. As for Sissela Skiftun, she was likely taken to a pauper's cemetery, or "potter's field." Over the years there were a number of these located in or around Milwaukee where county officials buried the dead of families who couldn't afford a proper burial, including not only immigrants but also the homeless, insane, or individuals separated from family members. Consider this: In 1991, 5,000 graves from a 19th century pauper's cemetery were discovered in Milwaukee under a parking lot and nearby county buildings. The bodies were exhumed and examined by archaeologists. They discovered many coffins contained two bodies, most of them unidentified, usually with no personal effects. Some had missing or severed legs. The researchers learned that a decision had been made to purchase coffins less than 4 feet long, so amputations were required at time of burial for the corpses to fit in the coffins. There would be no peaceful rest for these forgotten souls. Over the years these graves were dug up, moved, built on, desecrated, or the remains were boxed up and placed in some archeologist's storeroom.

Anne, Anna, Sissel and Malene found themselves alone in a strange city, unable to speak English. They were in a terrible fix with no idea what they should do next. The four orphan girls, of whom the oldest was 27 and the youngest only 12, sadly continued their way west. They luckily got a ride with Eric Skavland, of Numedal, Norway, to Jefferson Prairie, Wisconsin, which is near what is now Beloit, Wisconsin. They stayed with friends and made their home there for some years. Malene's sister Sissel died in Jefferson Prairie, and Anne was married to Anders Peterson (Haugen). Anna married Nels Olsen Blexerud and moved to Spring Grove, Minnesota Territory. Malene later named two of her daughters Anna, one of them being Anna (Rustad), and this no doubt reflects her deep feelings for the older sisters who saw her through the loss of her parents and her teen-age years.

Gulbrand Anderson Gubberud was born on December 14, 1827, and came to America in 1852. Since he was the oldest son at age 25, he was chosen to be the first to make the trip. Gulbrand was to see for himself the opportunities this new country had to offer, and then send for the remaining family members.

Gulbrand's voyage must have been uneventful. Traveling alone he was sure to have made the trip more efficiently, going straight to Dane County, Wisconsin. He worked there for a time and then moved on to La Crosse, Wisconsin, where he worked on farms and in lumber camps, earning money to help pay for Øesten's voyage. His brother Øesten joined him in Wisconsin in February of 1853, possibly with his Aunt Sigrid and Uncle Amund Lunde (Sigrid was a sister to Anders).

Once in Wisconsin, brothers Øesten and Gulbrand teamed up cutting timbers in the pinery during the winter and working in saw mills during the summer. They saved up enough money to send for the remaining family members.

Their parents Anders and Kjersti and siblings Olia (age 19), Gunhild (16), and Martin (13), came over in 1854. They landed in Quebec on July 30 after being tossed about the ocean for 81 days. The Bark *Urania* piloted by Captain Thesen, sailed in 1854 and possibly was the ship on which they traveled. The *Urania* left Stavanger, Norway, on May 6 and landed in Quebec on July 24. This ship had been built in 1847, at Jordfallen in Larvik, Norway.

This Norwegian immigrant described the last part of his 1854 journey like this: "We left Quebec at five in the afternoon. There were some eight hundred people on this boat, but it would have been permitted to carry fourteen hundred. There were Norwegians, Swedes, Irish, and German, black Negroes and brown Indians. This is the most beautiful city we have seen and has the largest church, and many other large churches besides. At Montreal our baggage was hauled by horses and wagons up to a canal where we boarded a steamer again. We passed through a canal having twenty locks. We passed many stopping places and arrived in Kingston at eight o'clock in the evening of the ninth. Here we boarded a much larger boat, which left at once to cross Lake Ontario. We passed many ports and arrived at Hamilton. At this place our baggage was weighed and we took a train for Detroit. The train left Hamilton at twelve during the night and arrived at Detroit at ten the following morning. At Detroit we crossed the river by steamboat. We left, again by train at one in the afternoon and arrived at Chicago at nine in the evening. We remained there till morning, when our baggage was transferred to the pier. We went by steamboat to Milwaukee, leaving at nine in the morning of the thirteenth. We arrived in Milwaukee at four in the afternoon of the same day."

Anders, Kjersti and their children started the final leg of the journey to Spring Grove. At Blue Mounds (near Madison, Wisconsin) Anders hired a man to haul their belongings to Minnesota. They had to walk behind the wagon over the trail-less terrain by day, and sleep on the bare ground at night. Madison to Spring Grove is about 150 miles as the crow flies, much longer walking. At some point they stopped and asked for directions to Norwegian Ridge (Spring Grove, Minnesota). They were informed that there was no certain trail, but that Norwegian Ridge lay to the northwest. So, off they went again, following these instructions, keeping in line with the tallest trees through the forest (which served as a compass). After many days of traveling they reached what would become the city of Decorah, Iowa, but which at that time consisted of two small huts. The family then traveled north, likely on the ancient Indian Highway also called the Winona-Fort Atkinson trail. The trail ran north from Fort Atkinson, Iowa, through Decorah, Spring Grove and Houston village. This trail was first laid out by the ancient mound builders and later used by the Mdewakantons, Chippewa, and Fox-Sauk tribes. It was worn deep and wide by much travel and the dragging of teepee poles.

The travelers finally arrived at Amund and Sigrid Lunde's hut in Spring Grove, which had just been prepared for the winter. After a short stay here, in the late fall, they went on to live at Gulbrand's farm. With this adventure over the Gubberud clan was again together in one spot, home at last. For a dwelling, Anders dug a cave in a hillside and this served as their home for some time. This dugout apparently is still there.

Gulbrand's dwelling was slightly better, a small log-cabin built by the two boys. Later, Anders homesteaded 80 acres next to Gulbrand, which later became part of the Gubberud farm. Olia was soon courted by John O. Bakken, and they were wed in October of 1855.

The township of Spring Grove is one of the most densely settled Norwegian-American colonies in the United States. The Spring Grove settlement or, as it was previously called, "Norwegian Ridge," has retained the language and customs of Norway longer than most of the other Norwegian settlements. The Norwegian language is today sometimes heard on the streets of Spring Grove. There is only one church in the township, a Norwegian Lutheran congregation.

This settlement was also one of the important distribution points for Norwegians in the American northwest, and there are hundreds of Norwegian-Americans in western Minnesota and the Dakotas whose ancestors stopped for a time in Spring Grove Township before going further west.

Although this tract in the southeastern corner of Minnesota was acquired from the Indians in 1850, it was not legally open to settlers until the Act of Congress of August 4, 1854. The act extended the right of pre-emption to public lands in Minnesota Territory. Surveys were begun in this area in 1853, but the first block of land was not offered for sale until 1855.

Before 1855, thousands of people crossed the Mississippi River into Minnesota Territory and a considerable number of settlers took land in Spring Grove Township. More Norwegians arrived in the summer of 1853 and in 1854, and by the close of the latter year the sections of land in the eastern part of the township, surrounding the later village site, were almost all taken. Western Wilmington Township, east of Spring Grove, was likewise being settled by large numbers of Norwegians. When one of these pioneers found a piece of government land to his satisfaction, he would put up a sign with his name upon it at each corner of his claim.

A few Americans also took up land in these townships. The Norwegian settlers naturally preferred to establish themselves as near as possible to people who spoke their own language and who were of the Lutheran faith. In such a community, a Yankee was almost an alien, but the barriers didn't remain long, for the Norwegians quickly learned to speak English and some of the Yankees found it both desirable and enjoyable to learn enough of the Norwegian language to transact business.

Once the government survey was complete, the lands in the Spring Grove area could be purchased at the land office at Brownsville, Minnesota, thirty-five miles to the east on the Mississippi River. The town also served as one of the first markets for settlers in southeastern corner of Minnesota Territory.

In the early part of 1854, when Gulbrand came to Wilmington Township near Spring Grove to establish his home and homestead, all the land that contained open water, such as springs or creeks, had already been taken. Timber land and good water were the main objects in view when the settlers decided where to establish their homes so, naturally, all of the nice fertile prairie land was left by the former settlers.

Gulbrand had courage enough to establish his home and homestead on prairie tracts that had no open springs. The spot he chose had previously been marked and then abandoned by Amund Lunde and other land seekers. Strange, or maybe strategy – Amund was an in-law and had this property previously claimed. Gulbrand obtained 160 acres of wild land in section 4, Wilmington Township for $1.25 an acre. Øesten bought the adjoining section which was later known as the Halvorson farm.

In 1856, Malene, then 17, came to Spring Grove to visit her sister, Anna Blexerud. Gulbrand met this beautiful young girl, and after a short but proper courtship they were married August 1, 1856, in LaCrosse, Wisconsin. There was no church in Spring Grove at this time, and the pastor only came through occasionally, so they made the journey to LaCrosse. This trip took them down the territorial road to Brownsville and across the Mississippi River on a ferry. Along this route near Caledonia they may have had to rest at a curious edifice known as the "Seven by Nine", a very small hotel owned by a Yank named Joseph Ober. Mr. Ober spoke with a drawl, was nicknamed 'Powerful Weak,' and could have passed for Rip Van Winkle.

Gulbrand and Malene didn't waste much time starting a family, with their first child Christine born in 1857, followed by Inger Olava in 1859. Of course they suffered in the years to come; nobody but those who have had the actual experience can picture the struggles and hardships these pioneers suffered when they settled on land that had neither timber nor water. Gulbrand had learned to eke out a scanty living from the rocky earth during his days in Norway, so hard back-breaking work was nothing new.

Water used in the Gubberud household had to be carried from a spring located about a half mile away, or further by some accounts. This was done in two pails suspended from a water harness laid across the carrier's shoulders. At times, Indians who crossed their trails would see the women carrying the water and would take the pails away from them and drink the water, as they were usually thirsty from a long march. Other times, the Indians approached their dwelling, but they didn't harm anyone. They normally just pointed to each other and said, "Me good Indian." Malene was usually ready to offer them chickens that pecked their food from the ground in the yard. When this happened an Indian would pick up a pebble, aim at the chicken's head, and the bird would drop long enough to be caught by their fleet-footed and shrewd ways. These Indians were probably from the local Winnebago tribe or possibly Sioux that were traveling on the Winona-Fort Atkinson trail.

Marrying Malene was the greatest investment Gulbrand made. He got a wonderful helpmate, one who stuck by him through thick and thin. Not only did she bring up their children whom she mothered and cared for like only a mother could, but she helped her husband in his farm operations, and took her place in the fields with the rest of the men. Even in the later years when Gulbrand was bent with old age and couldn't do physical work anymore, Malene took charge and managed the everyday farm operations.

Cattle had to be driven many miles into the valley for water, and it is said that at times during the hot weather, when the cattle were brought back to their home they were just as thirsty as when they left. When they finally acquired oxen, life became slightly easier because they then were able to dig up large holes that collected the flowing water after a rain storm and could save it for awhile in their man-made ponds. In the later years they gathered rain water in cisterns from the roofs for the household requirements.

On such a place there gradually grew up a number of small buildings, some of these being a horse stable, cow barn, hog house, chicken coop, wagon shed, corncrib, granary, hay shed (usually merely a roof supported by four posts), smokehouse for meats, privy, and the living house, which was the first erected. All of these were built and arranged somewhat like farm places in Norway. The living houses were small. The so-called "cellars" had only one room, while the log cabins might have two rooms and a low dark attic to which one ascended by means of a ladder. Within the house everything was simple.

The pioneers could not purchase furniture as you can now. At first there was little or nothing with which to make any purchases, and in the nearest market towns there were no dealers in these articles. They had to get along with homemade furniture. The Norwegian red-painted chest served as a table, stools and benches were shaped with axes, and oak trunks served as chairs. Other pieces of furniture, such as beds and shelves, were of the same construction. The mattress on the bed was filled with hay or straw, and the sheepskin brought from Norway served as bed covering. In many of the Norwegian homes, fireplaces were built for heating the cabin and preparing food, but after a time stoves replaced them. For illumination they made candles such as they had learned to make back in Norway, and, if there were not enough candles, they placed lard in a small cup with a bit of linen as a wick.

The food was all prepared in Norwegian style, and Norwegian dishes and manners prevailed for many years. The evening meal was usually corn-meal mush, either hot or cold, served with sweet or sour milk. Pork was a staple food item, the lowly hog played an important role in both the household food supply and in the farmer's income. When a cow had been procured and bred, steers could be raised to serve as driving oxen.

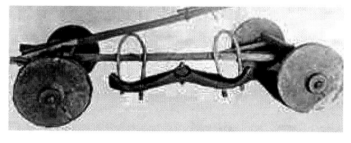

Finally, when the *kubberulle* (a crude wooden cart with solid wheels) had been constructed, the farmer could get along very well. Many pioneers have said that the first time they drove their own oxen hitched to a *kubberulle*, they actually felt independent, if not rich.

The nearest markets were MacGregor, Iowa, fifty miles to the southeastward; Brownsville, Minnesota, thirty-five miles directly eastward on the Mississippi River; and Winona, Minnesota, fifty miles to the northeast, also on the Mississippi River. A trip to any one of these points by oxen and wagon took between one and two weeks. Consequently, one or two trips a year were all that the pioneer attempted. In the early years the pioneer had little to sell by way of exchange for articles such as salt, spices, shoes, and cloth. The principal trips from home were to the nearest gristmill to have the wheat or corn ground. At first the nearest mill was at Decorah, Iowa, about thirty-five miles southwest of Spring Grove Township.

Gulbrand was the type of person that found it hard to say no when somebody came to him for help. He of course had his faults like all of us, but he also had many good points. If any of his friends or neighbors wished to bring their relatives or families over from Norway, they would ask Gulbrand if he would guarantee their passage from

Norway to Spring Grove, and Gulbrand was always willing to help his countrymen immigrate to America. Many people worked for him to pay off these debts, but many a time those with families had to receive cash to buy the necessities of life, so the debt remained unpaid. Sometimes these people would move away and the debts were forgotten. Gulbrand lost several hundred dollars by helping people in this way, and most of them could have paid him back if they had really wanted to. The 1860 census shows many people living with Gulbrand and Malene: farm hands, probably immigrants working for Gulbrand along with their children, plus Anders, Kjersti, and Martin.

    Gulbrand Gubberud, the person whom people looked to for a helping hand, the pillar of the family, a generous man, died March, 18th 1898, from gangrene. By this time he and Malene had increased their farm holdings to about 562 acres. Through hard back-breaking work, dedication and ambition, his gamble paid off. Coming from Southern Norway and meager hard scrabble beginnings, in America he became a successful landowner and farmer. He was also responsible for creating a huge family. Gulbrand is buried in the old pioneer cemetery in Spring Grove, along with Anders, Kjersti, his brother Øesten, and his daughters Thina, and Anna.

The Beginning of the Norwegian Settlement at Spring Grove
By Percival Narveson

Reprinted by permission from "Percival Narveson's Historical Sketches" published in 2002 by Stonegrimson Press, Spring Grove MN. Chad Muller, editor

While early histories of Houston County tell of James Smith, an Englishman, as being the first to stake out a claim and to start a business in Spring Grove, no mention is made of the Norwegian settlement started in that area in 1852. There are probably many who are not acquainted with the fact that the Norwegian settlement at Spring Grove was one of the first and largest Norwegian settlements to be started in the territory of Minnesota, and of the events that led to the starting of this large settlement.

When Torger Johannesen Tendeland, in 1852, staked out his claim in what later became Section 15, Spring Grove Township, he little realized that it was the start of a Norwegian settlement that a decade later would extend from the Iowa state line and north to the Root River, and would embrace much of Wilmington township, all of Black Hammer and Spring Grove and the eastern tier of townships in Fillmore county.

Although Norwegian emigration into Iowa territory did not assume large numbers until in 1849, a small group of Scandinavians had as early as 1840 crossed the Mississippi from Illinois and formed the nucleus of a Norwegian colony along Sugar Creek, west of Keokuk, in Lee County. The settlement had increased to about thirty families but, as the settlement was located in an area where Quakers and Mormons were very active, the colony never prospered since it appears that settlers of other faiths had difficulty in securing title to their claims, and the Norwegians gradually moved out of the area. The abandonment of the Sugar Creek colony seems to have had little or no effect on the later emigrations of Norwegians into Iowa territory.

The first Norwegians to make their appearance in northeastern Iowa were Ole Halverson Valle and Ole Tollefsrud Kittilsland, who in 1843 ventured across the Mississippi and secured employment at the Indian Agency at Fort Atkinson. This fort had been built in the southwestern part of Winneshiek County in 1840, to protect the white men from the Indians, and to protect the Winnebago, who were occupying this area from the marauding of other tribes.

At the time Valle and Kittilsland were employed at the fort an attempt was being made by the government to instruct the Indians in the white man's way of farming, and the two Norwegians worked at this along the Iowa River bottoms near the site of Decorah. In 1846, Valle quit his position at the fort and he was replaced by his cousin, Soren Olsen Sorem. He secured a job in the culinary department at the fort. A year later he secured a job as an assistant cook at the fort for another cousin, Ingeborg Nielson. Soren and Ingeborg later became man and wife. When the Winnebago tribe in 1846 was moved out of this area and into Todd County, Minnesota in 1848, Mr. and Mrs. Sorem accompanied the cavalcade and so became the first Norwegians to enter Minnesota.

After Norwegian emigrations into northeastern Iowa in 1849 began in large numbers, the starting of new settlements followed in rapid succession. By 1850 Norwegian settlements had sprung up in various parts of Winneshiek, Allamakee, and Clayton Counties. All these Iowa settlements later became a haven for settlers when scouting around for land in Fillmore and Houston counties.

The first Norwegian to make his appearance in the southeastern Minnesota was Even Ellertson Dahl, who in 1851 staked out a claim north of Hesper, in what later became Newburg township. Although this was a beautiful prairie country it seems to have attracted Norwegian settlers more so than the rugged country found farther north in the county. One reason may have been the lack of springs; and the sheltered valleys in the northern part of the county were more like what they were accustomed to back in Norway. Whatever the reason, Even Ellertsen in 1856 sold out and moved to the hamlet of Bratsberg in Holt Township.

When settlers in 1852 began prospecting for land north of the Iowa line, there were several accessible routes into Houston and Fillmore Counties. One was an ancient Indian trail that extended from the mouth of the Yellow River across Allamakee County and over to the Root River. The other was the Winona-Fort Atkinson Trail, commonly referred to as the Government Trail. This trail came up from Iowa, and north through Spring Grove Township, and on into the Root River Valley. After Houston County was created in 1854, a territorial road was laid out west from Brownsville, across Houston County, and over to Newburg in Fillmore County. This then became the route followed by emigrants that were ferried across the Mississippi River at La Crosse and Brownsville.

While not known with certainty, it is believed that Torger Tendeland, the first Norwegian to make his way into the Spring Grove area, may have come by way of one of the settlements in Allamakee County. Tendeland was born in Stavanger, Norway in 1818. In 1849 the family immigrated to America and settled first at Beloit, Wisconsin. In 1852, the family crossed the Mississippi at McGregor, Iowa and traveled by a covered wagon drawn by oxen until they reached one of the Norwegian settlements in Alamakee County. Here he left his family and belongings and continued by foot northward until he reached what later became Spring Grove Township, where he staked out a claim to his liking.

When the first comers began scouting for the land in the Spring Grove area they were plagued by a number of land speculators — that is, scoundrels who claimed priority to the land. After Torger Tendeland had staked out his claim, he was accosted by Arthur Bow, the most notorious of these scoundrels. He claimed priority to the finest land in the area, and is known to have intimidated many land seekers so that they moved on to other communities. Bow was an arrogant, insolent Yankee, a man of large build, who was always armed with a pistol — so there were few, if any, who cared to argue with him. Tendeland then went back to his family in Iowa, but after finding out that Bow did not have priority to the land, he came back to Spring Grove later on that summer and established himself on his claim.

By the time Tendeland came back to Spring Grove, a party of four—Haakon Narveson, Knud Knudson Kieland, Fingal Aslesen Flaten, and Truls Haga—had arrived and established themselves in Section 10, north of Tendeland's claim. They had been tricked into paying a scoundrel named John Vale, for what Vale termed his preemption rights. Soon after, Peter Johnson Lommen, his brother John Lommen, and Knud Bergo established themselves in Section 3; and in that same fall came Ole and Tollef Amundsen Berg, Knud Olsen Wold, and Ole Ulen.

The years of 1853 and 1854 saw the arrival of a large number of Norwegians who were destined to be long-time residents of the Spring Grove community, some of whom were to play an important role in the civic, political and religious history of the township: Ole Steneroden, George and Levor Temandsen Quarve, Knud and Ole Sagedalen, Knud and Teman Gilbertson, Hans and Gulbrand Nielsen Myrah, Anders Kroshus, Jens Elemoen and his son Thore Jensen Elemoen, later a well-known pioneer doctor in Houston County; Nels Tweito, Hans Bakke, Even Hoime, Hans and Elling Ellingsen, Gunder Traaen, Lars Reiersen Halstenrud, Elling Kieland, Embrick Knudsen Opheim, Ole Stensrud, Embrick Benson Enderud, Truls Paulsen, Hans Rosendahl and his son Paul Rosendahl; and there were many others whose exact years of arrival is not recorded.

By the end of 1854, most of the land in the township, except what had fallen into the hands of land speculators, and small parcels along the valleys, had been occupied. Later emigrants had to purchase their land at inflated prices from speculators. After the Money Panic of 1857, some were lucky enough to purchase land from speculators who were trying to get rid of their holdings at any price.

Although the village of Spring Grove was located in an area settled almost exclusively by Scandinavians, the actual founder of the village and its first business men were all of other nationalities. As we have stated, the village had its start in 1852 when an Englishman named James Smith staked out a claim, built a cabin and opened a store in the eastern half of Section 11. In 1854, he platted his claim, secured a post office for the community, and from the many springs in the area he gave it the name Spring Grove. In 1858 he sold out his holdings to Robert McCormick, who continued to operate the store and to accommodate travelers. This is probably the Stage House referred to in early township records.

About 1855 an Englishman named William Fleming moved into the Spring Grove settlement and purchased the forty of land on which the main business section of the village is now located. Here he built a large log cabin which he fitted out as a tavern and a community hall. This place became known as the Pumpkin Tavern. This appears to have been the main social gathering place in town until Fleming's death in the late 1850s. In 1857 another Englishman named William Hinkley arrived in Spring Grove and built a frame building along the side of the territorial road in the western part of Section 11, where he opened a hotel and a tavern. After buying out McCormick's stock of goods he began operating a general store in the same building.

Hinkley appears to have been at heart a speculator and probably never intended to make Spring Grove a permanent home, for by the early 1860s we find him operating a store and tavern, and engaged in selling land and town-site lots in Riceford. Among the attempt by non-Norwegians to establish a business in an all Norwegian community can be mentioned a saloon started by James Demeron of Caledonia.

Another short-lived business venture was the mercantile firm of Tart and Smith. This was started by J. C. Tart and T. C. Smith of Dorchester, but after a couple of years they also closed their doors. Whether the Spring Grove community did not appear to have a future, or that Englishmen found it difficult to carry on a business in an all Norwegian community, is not known, but by 1866 the only businessmen left in Spring Grove were Norwegians.

The year of 1859 saw the arrival of Mons Fladager, the first Scandinavian businessman in Spring Grove. In that year Mr. Fladager, who is regarded as the father of Spring Grove business, opened a general store. This was the beginning of the Fladager family's connection with the mercantile industry in Spring Grove, a connection that was to last until 1967, when Maurice Fladager sold out to Robert Hillman.

The next Scandinavian to establish a business in Spring Grove was Nels Hendrickson Stoen, who in 1864 opened a general store. For almost forty years Mr. Hendrickson was one of the town's leading merchants. He was connected with the mercantile business in Spring Grove until his death in 1912. In 1865, he was joined by his cousin Nels Onsgard. For about fifty years, Mr. Onsgard was one of the town's leading citizens. After a short while he dissolved his partnership with Nels Hendrickson and went into the implement business.

After continuing in the implement business until about 1879, he next went into partnership with Haaken Kieland in a general store. It was while in this partnership with Kieland that he began banking in a small way. About 1890, he organized the Onsgard Bank. In 1907, this was organized into the Onsgard State Bank, an institution of which he was president until his death in 1915.

During the 1870s and the 1880s many Scandinavian businessmen and professional men established themselves in Spring Grove: Asle Halvorson; Ole Iverson; Sven Ellestad, printer-merchant and jeweler; hardware and implement dealer Charles Hoegh; merchant and restaurant man Bruun (Brown) Anderson; merchant and banker Ole B. Tone; druggist and merchant, Elling Reierson; veterinarian, druggist and hotel keeper, Mathias Schmidt Nilsen; druggist and farmer, Ingvald Muller; jeweler and clock maker, Ole Hasledalen; photographer and undertaker, Christian Engell; grocer, Truls Paulsen and Steiner Reierson; physician, Dr. Thore Jensen; hotel keeper and merchant, Teman Gilbertson; and grain and stock buyer, Ole Roppe. Most of these well-known business men were in business until well after the turn of the century.

It is now one-hundred and nineteen years ago since the Norwegians began staking out claims and establishing their homes in the Spring Grove area, and while many changes have taken place during these many years, we still find that many of the old homesteads are in the hands of the descendents of those that obtained the land from the government. The Scandinavians have always cherished their Norse heritage, and as most of the pioneers were Norwegians they naturally tried to preserve this heritage and the language that was handed down from their ancestors.

History of Bear Creek

On the 4ᵗʰ of July, 1914, community members of Norwegian birth and descent met at the home of Syver Hovda to celebrate the sixtieth anniversary of the arrival of the first Norwegian settlers in the townships of Frankford (Township 103, Range 14), Racine (Township 104, Range 14), and Grand Meadow (Township 104, Range 15) in Mower County, Minnesota. By a unanimous vote of the assembled people, Lars G. Hanson and Ole Jorgens were asked to write a history of the early life in the settlement. This article is based on, and its content is largely made up of unedited excerpts from, the wonderful history they produced over 90 years ago. Additional information was drawn from "Norsk Lutherske Prester i Amerika" published in 1915 by O. M. Norlie.

The beginning of the Bear Creek community can be credited to Ole O Finhart. He had read of the land along the upper water courses of the Root River in Minnesota Territory and was seized with a desire to "go west." A number of others were inspired by his enthusiasm and a colony was organized.

The first party of colonists were nearly all native Norwegians — except for a few young children — and all born in the church parishes, Aurdal south and Aurdal north, in the judicial district name Valdris, and at that time, Christiana stift (state), at this it is called Hamars stift — it is a part of the old Christiana stift.

All these first colonists or settlers left Norway as emigrants for America during the years between 1840 and 1853. All came across the Atlantic Ocean in sailing vessels and nearly all of them temporarily made their homes in Wisconsin, in Dane County. These first Bear Creek colonists started out on the journey for Minnesota from Dane County, Wisconsin, and the real starting point was Spring Dale. It may be asked, what route did these emigrants follow through Wisconsin into Minnesota? It is stated by Syver Hovda at this date that so far as he remembers they passed through Blue Mound and Dodgeville and crossed the Mississippi River at Prairie du Chien. They and their teams and cattle were taken over the Mississippi River on a ferry drawn across by horses in a treading power. They landed in McGregor, Iowa and proceeded in a northwesterly direction passing Postville and Frankville, and next Decorah. Leaving Decorah they traveled almost in a due northerly direction through Winnesheik County into Minnesota Territory and entering Minnesota in Fillmore County, they followed the most passable trail thru this county till they reached Spring Valley and here they were on the border of their point of destination.

This body of first settlers, thirty-six in number, arrived in township 103, Range 14 — this township was in organization given the name Frankford — on the first of July, 1854. From Wisconsin and to the point of first camping ground, the colonists moved in two separate bodies, all in tented wagons drawn by oxen and bringing with them household goods and a few carpenters and blacksmith tools.

Nearly all single persons and families brought one or more milking cows, some sheep and hens and small pigs in boxes attached to the wagon boxes. The two moving caravans arrived in Frankford Township on the same day and constructed their camp on Section 9, in town 103, Range 14.

From this point or camping ground the colonists, individual or the head of families, started out in search of lands for his future home. All the land within the townships now called Racine, Grand Meadow and Frankford was government land except a few quarter sections claimed by land speculators under soldier warrants. In Frankford, including the new arrivals, so far as known, there were only fifty white persons stopping or camping on this date.

In a few days, all persons entitled to preempt public land had each selected his prospective homestead. However, Ole Simonsen was by common consent allowed to make his home on the southeast quarter of section five in Township one hundred and three in range fourteen. For the sake of getting a temporary dwelling shanty ready, as quickly as possible, four men, heads of families, joined hands in building a log house twenty-two feet by sixteen and twelve feet high. The roof was thatched with pieces of bark and over the bark was square pieces of sod carefully laid.

In this house the four allied families lived the first winter. In this house on November 2, 1854, the first child of the colonists — a girl — was born to the parents Nils Syversen Moen and his wife, Elen. The next summer, 1855, the three families who had over the winter lived together, with Ole Simonson, moved on their own claims and during the next winter the first English school was held in this said family dwelling house, one Mrs. Henry Moore, was the teacher.

This early settlement being largely along a small stream of water which they named Bear Creek due to the following incident: Ole Olson Severud was an ingenious man, a gunsmith. Soon after his arrival he shot a bear with the gun made by himself. The bear was shot somewhere in the woods along the creek between the old Sever Temanson farm and the farm now owned by the Anderson Brothers. The people of the settlement adopted the name "Bear Creek Settlement" and it has always been recognized by this name by other Norwegian settlements in Minnesota and this was legally established in the organization of the Lutheran Church Association by the adoption of the name "Bear Creek Norwegian Lutheran" as the incorporated name of the congregation.

Early in the spring of 1855, Ole Finhart decided to get married and wanted to get married by a Lutheran preacher. He with his betrothed, Kari Hovda, started for St. Ansgar, Iowa, to find Pastor Clausen, and with him went Nils Syversen Moen and his wife. Mr. and Mrs. Syversen wanted their first child baptized. The party started across the unsettled prairies in a wagon drawn by a yoke of oxen. The first night the party camped on the prairie. The second day they reached Cedar River near St. Ansgar. At this point Ole and Nils left the women in the wagon and walked over to the parsonage, there to find out that Pastor Clausen was absent from his home in some distant place in Iowa or Minnesota. The parties in their wagon returned and reached their homes. Ole Finhart didn't want to put off his marriage any longer and in his wagon drawn by his oxen he went a long distance into Fillmore County, and there discovered a lawfully qualified Justice of the Peace, by whom Ole and Kari were made lawful husband and wife.

We will mention in connection with Ole Finhart's marriage history that he and his wife were the first couple married in the Bear Creek Settlement and perhaps the first in Mower County. Finhart came to America in the year 1848, had acquired a fair common school education in Norway and during his residence in Wisconsin he attended an American English school. With these qualifications he was the natural leader in the settlement and a staunch supporter of the Lutheran Church. In the War of the Rebellion, he served in the First Minnesota Battery and in 1872 was a member of the House of Legislature of Minnesota.

By memory it will be stated that on Sunday, the 22nd of June 1856, the first regular Lutheran Church service was held in the settlement by Rev. C. L. Clausen, and on this same day the church was organized. The service and organization meeting was held in the house of Ole Simonson Jobraaten. During the delivery of the sermon the pastor stood under the spreading branches of a young burr oak tree on the farm of Sever Temanson, somewhat apart from the others of its kind. This tree is still standing like a Silent Sentinel, guarding the Hallowed Memories of the Past. At this first church service, six children were baptized. Names as follows: Gunhild, daughter of Nils and Elen Syversen, born Nov. 2, 1854, and Marit, born March 6, 1856; Ole, son of Ole and Kari Finhart, born April 10, 1856; Joseph, son of Chresten and Anne Tuf, born ? ; Anne, daughter of Hans and Ragnhild Andersen (Gamlemoen), and Engebret, son of Amund and Marit Johnson Lindelien. When it was organized, the congregation had forty members. The first church council included Gullik A. Dalen, Ole Simonson Jorbraaten, Ole A. Finhart Sr, Hans Gamlemoen, Arne Bohn, and Ole Jorgens. The church building was not erected until 1869-1870.

The date of the organization of school district No. 28 is not known to the writer, but part of the deed given for the school house ground is in the writer's possession, and bears date the 17th day of January, 1859, and signed by Ole and Liv Simonsen and certified to by Walther S. Booth, Justice of the Peace. The land contained one half acre and situated in the SE$^{1/4}$, Section 4, Town 103, Range 14. On this ground the school house was built — the writer thinks during 1857 -- while Minnesota was yet a territory. The house was built by voluntary work. The men of the settlement each bought a certain number of logs, squared and hewed and then fitted them into the building. The house from foundation with walls, roof and furniture included was all completed by free and voluntary contribution. The settlers built the house for school and temporary church meetings and for many years it was so used. The next winter the first English school was held in this family dwelling and Mrs. Henry Moore was the teacher.

After the log school house was built the settlement had visits now and then, irregularly, from one pastor, Jensen, preacher in charge of Highland, Fillmore County, Minnesota, and one Rev. Fredriksen, a peculiar character who traveled from settlement to settlement clad and wrapped in sheepskin, and by his peculiar appearance he was generally known as the sheepskin (Skinfeld) preacher.

About 10 rods east of the school house and little to the south of a due east line, a grave yard privilege was granted or donated to the Church A a due east line, a grave yard privilege was granted or donated to the Church Association by Ole Simonsen, and the first person buried in this cemetery was Anders Torhaug who died from overexertion trying to drive a pair of young steers. The second person buried here was Erland Bruflat, father of Gulik Erlandsen Bruflat. The family adopted the name Dalen at the time becoming citizen of the United States. In 1864, Ole Simonsen died and was buried in this graveyard. In the year 1870 the Bear Creek Church was built, and around it was formed a new and beautiful place of burial. In 1928 a number of families, desiring to perpetuate the memory of the first pioneers of the community, erected on the site of the old cemetery a beautiful monument bearing the following inscription: To the Memory of The First Norwegian Lutheran Pioneers of Bear Creek, 41 Buried 1856-1870

We will return to a few remarks about the hard struggles of the first years in the settlement. Nearly all the colonists were without money sufficient to insure them against great suffering during the first years before they could raise grain for bread and this condition was general among all settlers of all nationalities in the territory. Our Norwegian settlers were all young and strong people and able and willing to work, but could find little or no employment for pay.

It must be understood that the first great necessity for all the settlers or homesteaders was to build shelters to live in and some kind of hovels for their domestic animals. It was also necessary to get as many acres of ground broken the first summer as possible so as to enable them to grow something for food the next year. The settlers brought their steers together and put 4, 5 or 6 pairs together as a breaking team. In this way each and all got a patch of an acre or few acres broken. Many of the settlers were so poor that they didn't own a yoke of steers, but those who had oxen broke a patch for them.

Nearly all the men settlers travelled far and near in search of work the first winter, but seldom found a chance to work for any kind of money compensation. It is well known to the writers that strong and young men considered it a great luck to find a chance to cut and split rails and cut cord wood a whole day for 25 to 50 cents, and some of them had to walk 6 miles in the morning to the work and of course that same distance back to their homes in the evening.

During the first winter there was a general scarcity of flour or meal for bread. One woman told the writer that as far as she knew, there was not so much wheat for flour in the settlement that a loaf of bread could be baked. In this flour famine Ole Finhart undertook to drive to Decorah, Iowa with his yoke of oxen to buy flour, but there was not one pound to be gotten. All he could get was a sack of corn meal, and this sack was divided among the destitute families.

The settlers of mixed nationalities among and about the Norwegian colonists were mostly all as poor in money wealth as the Norwegians. None hired men or women for money wages. Kari Hovda, later Mrs. Ole Finhart told often that she worked several months for an American family in the new village Frankford without any compensation except her board — said she was glad to get her board. After a couple of years girls as kitchen servants were paid from 50 cents to one dollar and fifty cents a week and it may be added that these servant girls were used or rather abused by their employers as slaves or beasts of burden. A hired girl was janitor, water carrier, clothes washer, floor scrubber, house cleaner, nurse and in some houses she had to calcimine rooms with lime mixture. Her hours of work were not limited to a certain number of hours but in most cases she had to get out of bed at four o'clock in the morning and work till late in the night, often till 12 in the night. Her bedroom was never heated. In some homes she had to sleep in a rustic bedstead in the garret where snow often drifted in and covered her bed cover. It was an exception to the rule if a Norwegian hired girl was allowed to mix with the Yankee family in the sitting room except when she had to come in to work. She was not permitted to serve the family at the table. She was only allowed into the door of the dining room with the food she had cooked or prepared. There she was met by the lady of the house or some other appointed or privileged lady waiter who took the food from her hands and served it. These conditions lasted for more than ten years. The Norwegian girls and her parents had to submit to these hardships and indignities on account of poverty, but it was often expressed by parents of the poor girls, "If we were not so penniless and hard up, we would rather have our daughters feed pigs and milk cows than to be degraded servants of the Yankees."

The second winter in the Bear Creek settlement, 1855 and 1856 nearly all the men population went down the Mississippi River toward Rock Island, Illinois, and into the woods to cut cord wood. They all found work and got fair pay. It was a lucky venture.

They worked till late in the spring and returned to Bear Creek with their hard earned savings. This relieved the money stringency for all the families in connection with the wood choppers and most of these and others with them repeated the enterprise the next winter.

At this time the Bear Creek settlers began to have some farm products to sell. Wheat grew abundantly on their few acres of breakings. The herd had increased in cows, oxen and sheep. The food shortage had at this time disappeared.

The great question now was a marketing place for what farm products they could sell. There were no railroads in Minnesota at this time and the nearest steamboat station was Winona on the Mississippi River, and the distance from Bear Creek to Winona was about 60 miles. Roads to Winona there were none, and no bridges, so to get there with a yoke of oxen before a primitive lumber wagon with a load of wheat on was a perilous and slow undertaking. If rain had softened the ground, it often took the ox teamster two weeks to reach Winona and back home. During the winter season a journey of this kind was impossible. It could only be done during the bare ground season.

The price of a bushel of wheat at this time was about 50 cents and the pay was generally in merchandise at the stores owned by the wheat buyer. The nominal price of the wheat was not governed by a continental or world's market, but by the speculative notion of the grain buyer, and the price of the goods in the stores on which the farmer had his order was just as arbitrary in the opposite direction as on the wheat. The goods were always of job lot qualities such as could not be sold in the market in eastern towns and cities. As an example to illustrate this, the writer will state his own experience. In the summer of 1861, I bought a pair of heavy, low, split leather shoes, and paid two dollars for them in wheat at 50 cents a bushel. In other words, I gave four bushels of wheat for my shoes.

In the villages about the Bear Creek settlement, small stores were started, but their trade was mostly a bartering business. The farmer's wife or daughter carried butter and eggs to these stores. Eggs were sold for from 5 to 8 cents a dozen and butter from 8 to 10 cents a pound. The pay for butter and eggs was always in goods in the store. The farmer's wife or daughter accepted for her burden of products, coffee, tea, sugar, needles, calico, thread, etc. The price on products sold by the farmer and the goods received in payment was not regulated by a competitive market, but by the more or less avaricious disposition of the shopkeeper. He fixed the price on the butter and eggs, and likewise the price on his merchandise. The new settler had no choice. He had to do the bartering unconditionally or carry his butter and eggs home.

During the first ten years at the Bear Creek colony the people lived on their own production. The only thing for the table bought was coffee; sugar was looked upon as a luxury. From cane raised on the farms they made their own molasses. Several enterprising persons on different sections of the towns built molasses mills where the cane was pressed and the liquid boiled into molasses.

For clothing nearly everything was made at home. The sheep furnished the stuff which was carded and spun and woven into clothes in the little cottage houses of the settlers. Nearly every family owned a home made loom and this occupied a corner on the floor of the main living room. Entering those primitive homes you were generally met by the metric strokes of the batten in the strong hand of the operator, the mother of the family or one of her daughters. In another corner of the house was the spinning wheel busily turning out woolen yarn or linen thread from flax hemp raised on the farm. Some of the children were busy carding wool for the spinning wheel.

In the same little house and on the same floor with the weaver and spinner was the lord of the home chopping and shaving a yoke and bows for his oxen on an oaken wooden block brought into the room as a necessary utensil in making the heavy equipment for the oxen to work in.

The description given of the industries carried on in the early log house is not yet complete. There was often a woman or man tailor near the table making clothes out of the home manufactured cloth, and often a cobbler was a momentous necessity and he had to have a corner of the house.

On Sundays this house of week day activities was frequently changed into a room for social gatherings or a school room for religious instructions of the settlement children; and sometimes it had to be used instead of a church for worship. These houses were all small in room space. The largest of them was not more than sixteen feet wide by eighteen or twenty feet long, and still the first years, in many of them, two families were sheltered. These settlers applied the old Norwegian saying: "Where there is heart room there is house room."

The settlement in social relation was very much like a large family and many instances could be written of one family or several aiding where temporary wants were known, and to the honor of the colony it can be said that little or no friction disturbed the general fraternal feeling in connection with the selection of claims, etc. In the few cases where greed made ripples, it was not of such serious nature that it led to any lasting feud among any of the families.

This colony was a competent collection of skilled mechanics as well as farmers. Many of them were carpenters; several blacksmiths, one an artistic turner, a couple wagon makers; three shoemakers and tanners; several stone masons and plasterers, and every man could hew and fit a log into the wall of a log house.

During many of the first years the Bear Creek colonists took no part in town or county politics, from sheer modesty, fearing they were not competent in language or knowledge of American Governmental methods, they never advanced a suggestion in town or county organization. A few Yankees as they called their English speaking neighbors were allowed free actions to name the towns and to organize the county, and the results show even today that those assumptive first officials were incompetent and careless. The county commissioners of Mower County allowed the Olmsted County commissioners to take one whole tier of sections from Mower County and annexed them to Olmsted County without a protest. To Mower County this blunder is a permanent loss.

The first township official in Frankford Township was Ole Finhart. He was elected township supervisor. Some years after Finhart's election, Ole Jorgens was elected Justice of the Peace. Mr. Bostwick, who by Jorgens' election had to give up the office made the remark, it was a disgrace to Frankford Township to elect an ignorant boy foreigner for a Justice office. He said he had never heard of any such thing before in all his life, and he was at that time an old man. J. H. J. Weeks was about the same time elected constable. The Norwegian settlers began by this time to attend town caucuses and town elections.

The Earliest Bear Creek Settlers

Following are the names of the first arrivals in Bear Creek:
- Ole Olsen Finhart from Vang, Aurdal South. Ole Simonson Jobraaten and wife, Liv, and children, Simon, Beret and Syver, from Begnedalen, Aurdal South.
- Ole Olsen Hovda and wife Kari, born on the Gaard Boen and children, Ole, Kari, Syver, Hermand, Arne, Engebret and Guri, all born Reinli, Aurdal South.
- Amund Lindelien and wife, Marit, born Vang, Aurdal South, and a child, Beret, born in Wisconsin.
- Anders A. Lybeck and wife, Signe, and child, Kari, born Vang, Aurdal South.
- Ole Olsen Sjurud, born Etendalen, Aurdal South and wife, Magdalena, born Reinli, and children, Trond and Anne, born in Wisconsin.
- Hans Andersen, born Gamlemoen, Begnedalen and wife, Ragnhild, born Berg, Etnedalen, Aurdal South.
- Nils Syversen (Moen), born Vang, Aurdal and wife, Elen, born in Lands parish.
- Amund Johnson (Klastolen) and wife, Anne, born Etnedalen, Aurdal South.
- Ole Julsen, and a young woman engaged for marriage but dissolved — her name is not known to the writer.
- Knud Nilsen (Haugerstuen), Aurdal North.
- Syver Olsen Skalshaugen and brother, Erland, both born Vang, Aurdal South.

Other families and individuals also came this same early spring and summer, namely, Ole Froland, (Florand) born in Telemarken, Norway, and his wife, Martha, and child Ragnhild, born Oxnaberg, Voss, Norway, and Jonas Nelsen Berg, born Etnedalen, Aurdal South, two daughters, Ragnhild and Kirstin, and his wife, Marit Halvorsdtr Milevandet, Vang, Aurdal South.

In the spring of 1855, the following Norwegians came to Bear Creek: Halvor Olsen Klastolen and wife, Johanna, and with them a sister of Halvor Klastolen, name Kjersti; all of these were born in Etnedalen, Aurdal South, and Christen Tuff, born West Slidre, Valdres, and his wife, Anna, born Lier, Norway; and Nils Nelsen Haugerstuen, born Aurdal North and his wife Anne, — her birthplace is unknown. Aslak Knudsen Aamot also came in the spring of 1855.

In 1856 came Halvor Johannesen Vig (Week) and wife Jorand born Haugerstuen, and children, Johannes, Siri, Ragnhild and Kari, all born Aurdal north. Together with the Week family came Ole Lunde, Nils Lunde, Peder Huset, Gulbrand Renna, and Anders Torhaug, all from Aurdal north. All the persons as arrivals in 1856 came to the Bear Creek settlement on Sunday, the 22nd of June of said year.

In the fall of 1856 came to Bear Creek, John Amundsen Lindelien, born Hedalen, Aurdal South, and wife, Beret Knudsdaughter born Vang, Aurdal South, and with them were the following named children: Thora, Ole, Gulik, and Gunhild. We will note here that Thora Lindelien became the wife of Aslak Knudsen Aamodt, and Gunhild the wife of Dr. O. W. Anderson of Rochester, Minnesota. She was generally known by the name Julia Johnson and married by this name. John Amundsen Lindelien moved to Bear Creek from Springdale, Wis.

During this year 1856, came Anna Oxnaberg, born Voss, Norway and her son Torgeir. She became the wife of Syver Olsen Skalshaugen. She was a sister of Martha, Mrs. Ole Florand.

In 1857 came Helge Johnson and wife Barbra, from Wisconsin. Helge was born Aurdal North on farm named Odegaarden.

After Minnesota became a state, many more settlers arrived both from Wisconsin and directly from Norway.

To learn more about the history of the Bear Creek Congregation, visit http://www.bearcreeklutheran.org/

Settling in Fox Lake

Based on the story written by Ole Ellingson and translated by Stanley Uggen. From "Fox Lake Norwegian Community: Its People, Its Church" pages 11-17, contributed by Janice (Uggen) Johnson, editor

Four families who were in company together from Milwaukee to Jefferson Prairie, Wisconsin, became the seed and the root for the small Fox Lake, Minnesota, congregation, of which I here at least will give a little description. They were Erik A. Uggen, his wife and two daughters; bachelor Ole. O. Juvrud; bachelor Ole Hanson Korsdalen; and my father Elling O. Strand, wife and three children, of which I was the eldest, and was then twelve years old. These here named families and persons were all from Norderhov Parish in Norway and were true neighbors in the old country.

Erik Uggen's wife became sick soon after we came to Jefferson Prairie, and died three weeks later. He traveled then, immediately after the funeral, about fifty miles farther west and bought 160 acres of land where there was broken about 12 acres, and built a little log house about 16 feet square.

We others stopped there at Jefferson Prairie and got work with the farmers through haying and harvest. My mother took in sewing and ironing from farmers wives and earned with that more than enough provisions to support our whole family, so that now we thought that we certainly had come to the Land of Canaan.

After about three months, it was agreed we should move to where Erik Uggen had bought land. My father then took land on shares to get a home, and farmed it two years. Erik Uggen was married again the first winter to a widow, Mrs. Ingebord Iverson from Sogn in Norway and moved to her home.

Ole H. Korsdalen was also married the first winter to Kristi, the eldest daughter of Erik Uggen. And since Korsdalen was a wheelwright from Norway, he began immediately to seek work in that, and got employment with a wheelwright in Darlington and worked there two years.

Ole O. Juvrud also had a desire to learn the wheelwright trade, and went in with a wagonmaker in Wiota and worked there with him for two years. And now it was that Juvrud and Hanson got together, built a shop, and began a business with their own hands and worked together for two years, until they moved to Minnesota

And now it was in '53 when I got a sister, so that now we were six in the family.

A day's pay at that time was rather low, and difficult when work should be paid with money. There was almost no money then among the people, but one would work for cattle or food. So it was much easier to come to an agreement with a man about daily pay.

Father worked for the most the last two years we were in Wisconsin on the first railroad which was built west from Chicago to Dubuque, Iowa. But the lack of money developed so the company broke up at last, so that Father as well as many others lost not so little with that.

Our desire and decision was to travel west, either to Iowa or Minnesota, where there was Government land to find, and get us a home which we could call our own. This should be accomplished as soon as we got the necessities to travel with, as oxen, wagon and some cattle.

When the time came, the place chosen was Rice County, Minnesota. So it was the 8th of June, 1855, when my Father, Elling O. Strand with his family, Ole Hanson Korsdalen and Ole Olson Juvrud who during the winter was married to Martha Iverson, left for the Wild West and immediately were out of the civilized boundary. At that time one could scarcely call the place which we went out from civilized. We took with us so much of the most necessary provisions which we could easily haul, and experienced later that this was a wise plan. We were ferried over the Mississippi at Prairie du Chien, traveled over the northeast corner of Iowa, and came into Minnesota near Decorah, which at that time had not much more than the name to show.

The trip went without special incidents which can be worth mentioning. On such a trip through an almost uninhabited country and in many places almost no road and no bridges one must expect and be prepared to meet hardship and unpleasantness. After about four weeks travel we came at last to the township of Wheeling, Minnesota, to an acquaintance by the name of Peder Thompson.

This Thompson with many others moved there the year before, so there already was a not so little settlement of Norwegians there already. We searched in all directions after unoccupied land and found enough of both fine and good prairie, but there was not more of that to get because it was already taken by those who had come there before us. And woods and good hay land was the foremost we looked for, because without woods one could not then build a house, and neither raise cattle without hay.

Raising wheat here in the west, at this time, even in Wisconsin, was very little made use of. The prices were then so low and almost no market just then on this side of Milwaukee and Chicago because the Milwaukee and St. Paul railroad was not opened on this side of the Mississippi River before about twelve years later.

There it was told to us that some miles west from there on the west side of the Cannon River the big woods began, but we could not meet anyone who had been in these big woods or knew anything about what kind of land there was in the big woods. And so Ole Juvrud and my father decided to make a discovery expedition and left early one morning in the direction which they were told there were woods to find. When they had gone six or seven miles in a southwesterly direction they met both the river and the woods, but the river lay between them and the woods, and they did not how they should come over the river. But they then walked a ways along with it and found at last a place where the water was so low that they could wade over when the stretched their necks so far as possible and walked on their toes. When they came over they were as jack rabbits and went to the woods as fast as they could, and had not gone far before they were convinced that now they had found enough woods, but yet there were two things they lacked, namely hay fields and cultivated land.

They then went the whole first day in different directions without meeting people or just such land which they wished, because they had not yet seen water since they walked over the Cannon River, and water was already now which they yearned most after. Because they had tramped almost the whole warm day without water, since It bad not rained for a long time. In that direction they happened to go there was no creek or water to find. Towards evening they sought more after water than anything else, but still found nothing.

At last it became so late and dark that they could not see to go farther. Now they made a fire and they sat in the smoke of it to keep the mosquitoes away as much as possible. But they could not eat because first they must get water. Here they sat now, and coughed from the smoke and were weary. The mosquitoes were severe the whole night and they waited with longing for the coming morning. And as soon as it became light enough so that they could see to walk, they continued their travel and looked for water, and several hours went by without their finding what they sought.

At last they became so weakened from thirst that they didn't like to strain any longer, but they laid down in the shade and were on the lookout. Father discovered a place a ways away where they saw it was lighter, and where the woods were not so thick. He was eager to discover what they could be and said to Juvrud that he had a desire to go a little father ahead to see; he must not leave the place before Father came back. He went then away in the direction where he had made this discovery and the farther he went the lighter it became, and after a little while he discovered in great joy and surprise a big water or lake. He ran more than he walked till he came there, and there he found good clear water, and he had possibly the most best tasting drink of water which he had ever had in his life.

He now filled his hat with water and burned back to Juvrud with it, and he agreed that it tasted good. They now felt already very refreshed, and both went down to the lake and made a fire, cooked coffee, ate and drank, rested a while so that at least they felt that everything was good again. Now again, eagerness awakened in them to discover the new home which they had traveled so far to find.

They went now along the lake a ways in a westerly direction and came right away to a big creek which emptied into the lake, and here in this creek they found a great number of both big and small fish, of many different kinds, aid cleaned some of them, which they fried on the coals and ate supper that evening.

They followed this creek a little ways uphill and came directly to a big, smooth bottom as the creek divided in about two equal parts, and where blue grass reached clear up under the arms.

On the south side of this bottom there was thick and hay woods of almost all kinds, and on the north side there was a big area of good and fertile cropland when it was cleared and broken.

And after they had viewed the land and the benefits as were expected, then at last they agreed to settle down here and make this place their future home.

There they made their marks in different places to show that the land was taken.

But there was not enough time to fool around and to dig out every place. But in the greatest hurry they traveled back the next day so as soon as possible to move their families, select everything, and take possession of the land, which also happened.

Therefore about four days later, namely the 11th of July 1855, they were there once more again with their families and all that they owned. We selected our camping place on a little hill in the vicinity of the before mentioned big creek, where we later built a little cabin of hay and rails where we camped the whole summer till far out in the fall, and for this hill we call the cabin Bakken, even today.

And here in this creek in the deep pool there was a great number of big fish of almost all kinds the whole summer which appeared to be there at our disposal any time we needed them. I remember well what Mother often used to say to me in the morning when she saw that I was idle. "You must take the fishing spear, Ole, and go down to the creek and catch a couple big fish. We must have fish for dinner." As ordered, so done, for it did not take a long time to carry out her order.

From now on we became quite busy for the whole summer, yes, till far out in the winter. Because for the first must we now cut and get hay together for the cattle, next a house for ourselves, together with a barn for the cattle, and not that alone, but we must also try to get some fields broken so that we would have a little to seed the next spring. And that we got carried out, more or less, as we wished.

But yet the worst was not over, for we had winter ahead, and it already began to come to us now and then.

The provisions which we brought with us were now for the most used up. Shoes and other things which we must get to endure the winter cold, and these things which we needed did not come closer than Hastings, which then was about fifty miles away, when we should figure all the things we should do when we came there. But the greatest worry of it was that we feared that we would come to lack money when we should come to buy and pay for the provisions. Credit was impossible, nor was a loan anything to think about, for we all had too little capital in relation to what we needed. One thought we had nevertheless, and that was that we did not need to starve to death, for fish and game we could catch what we needed to support life. But it was this also, that the flour which we had brought with us was now soon used up; no potatoes, nothing of any kind of garden stuff. Milk began to shrink and in a short time nothing.

When I so often here used the expression "we", so I mean us, all three families, for after all we went about almost as one family. For we share with each other both sorrow and happiness.

I will also report here about the same time as we moved in here, then also came two American families in here and settled a mile north from us, and their names were Jones and Sargent, but they were not acquainted with us, as we did not have a great association with them the first winter.

It was then one day about in the middle of October that Father and I left for Hastings to buy the most needed things for winter supplies for our family. (Juvrud and

Ole Hanson went together a little later.) Flour or bread stuff we considered to be the most necessary, and bought as much there of that we had need.

Moreover we bought a little of the most necessary which we could not very well manage without, including a grindstone. Since one shall grub so one must also have a grindstone. We came home from this our trip the fifth day after much difficulty and trouble which is unavoidable on such a trip through a virgin forest and wild prairie.

Here I will also report that Oline, daughter of Mr. and Mrs. Ole Juvrud, was born here in a hay shed *(other sources indicate Oline was born in their covered wagon)*. She was their oldest child and also she was the first white child born in the town of Forest, Rice County, Minnesota.

The Uggen farmstead. It was said that the house was built on the same spot where Oline Juvrud was born in 1855. Oline lived in the house until her death in 1889.

Now we have done about all that stood in our power to do before winter came; the food supplies we had, at least enough to last till spring. We had already moved into a house sixteen feet square, and although after old Norwegian style without ceiling, sod roof; and split basswood logs for the first floor, it was nevertheless warm so that nobody, neither big or little, suffered for any need in it.

Stable and shed for the cattle were now also more or less ready, as now we were not so far from a snowstorm if it should come. It was rather not long for we got a deep snow before Christmas and a continual cold with many big snowfalls went on almost the whole winter, so that by the first of March we had about three feet deep. We had no thaw or mild weather the whole winter before the 25th of March when we got a thaw which lasted several days, and then the snow shrunk considerably. We had it busy the whole winter with different things, for at first we must split enough rails to build a fence around the land we intended to seed and plow the coming spring.

Also there got to be quite a market for shingles here in Faribault this winter, for all who had decided to build here the coming summer must have shingles, and then they could split and scrape the shingles here in the woods around Faribault cheaper than they could transport them from the pinery to here. So there were here many in and about Faribault who made a great number of shingles and sold them for a good price. We were of those who made use of this opportunity. We also sold not so little hay through the winter to different ones who had come to Faribault with a team to earn money with hauling of different things. So that through the course of the winter we had earned not so little money, so that now so far as money was concerned we could manage well, but the thing which we needed the most was not to be disheartened.

And here I will give a description of the settler's conditions and living here through March and April of 1856.

We had done not so little preparation to cook and make maple sugar and syrup, and from the sweet stuff we made quite a bit. But what did this give us when the bread was finished? We had, as before said, an abundance of fowl and fish for our use, but so the reader must remember that this here was merely simply high in water. For we didn't have fat or butter to fly or brown it in, and we ate one time cooked fish and meat, and the next time cooked meat and fish.

It was then in the first of April when we were, so to say, completely bare of all kinds of flour stuff, and so Father said that I should go to Faribault and see if I could get flour, for he who had the store there had several teams on the road between St. Paul and here to carry merchandise here when the road was so that they could go ahead. This here was in the worst condition and almost impassable. But I left and waded in the snow and water, in many places to the knees, and came at last to the Cannon River and found it so big that it was impossible to get over without a boat. Here traveled a group of five or six men who had come before me and who would go to the store to get a little food supplies. Fortunately for us who was there but an Indian with a little canoe which was just big enough to carry a man by his side and was hired to row these men over the river. He got ten cents from each to row them over and this went by turns, so that I was standing there a long time before my turn came. Nevertheless I came over at last. But when I came here to the store I found what I already expected, namely that all remaining supplies were gone and sold. No matter what I have said, what Mr. Mills (the storekeeper) as yet has not sold is about 25 pounds of crackers in that barrel. He pointed to an apparently empty barrel away in a corner of the store. "Yes, those, you must let me get them," I said. "I cannot let you have them all," he said, "because there are many small children who cannot live well without a little bread, but you shall get 5 pounds of them" he said. 1 got then 5 pounds of these crackers, paid 25 cents per pound for them and went on my way home. And when I came to the river again there stood a group who waited for the Indian to bring them over the river again. And while we stood and waited for the ferryman I told a man, Mr. Dutton, who lived about a mile north from town what kind of luck I had to get to buy flour in town. He said that perhaps he had a little more flour than he needed until he could get more, and that if I would follow him home he would try to spare me a few pounds.

Because he was a man who was not pinched for money, and had made a big purchase of provisions in the fall so that he was well supplied, I went home then with the man and took out a $2.50 gold piece which I gave him, also with a bag which I had brought with and asked him to ladle the flour in the bag which he could give up for the gold piece. He then took a ladle and began to look and smell of it. He ladled a little more, and then he said "Now, I believe you are not able to carry more because you have a long way home." "If you consider what I can carry" I said, "you can safely ladle the bag full because I am stubborn to carry when it comes to a test, but you may ladle in the bag so much as you think you can give for the money, and I am satisfied?' He ladled in there some and asked if I was satisfied, and considering the circumstances I was more or less satisfied and thanked him for his volunteering to sell me the flour. And before I left this man he showed me some corn which he had raised from seed the summer before and was planted so late that it froze before it was ripe and was somewhat damp. He said that if we could make some use of that to live on we could come down and get some of it. It still stood in the shocks and was not shelled.

I went home again the same rough and wet way as I came down with my cracker package and flour bag on my neck, quite hungry and tired, but arrived happy that we had gotten a little for pancakes again, because I almost did not have flour enough to bake bread. The flour was not weighed but we assumed that it was about twenty-five pounds.

We went down again several days later and bought some of the corn which the man had, took it home and shelled it, dried it well in the baking oven and ground it two times in an old fashioned coffee mill which we had so that it became quite fine and firm. From this meal we baked corn cake which we thought tasted quite good, then we did not have anything which was better when we mixed this with a bit of maple syrup. In this way we had not so little of it, just the same. Now the last of April we also got milk which also helped to improve the corn cake not so little. And now as time sped forward it was good that we were able to have corn cake till the first of May. For we traveled again to Hastings and bought what we needed the coming summer, because we had earned enough money through the winter to buy that which we probably needed through the summer. From now on we shall not complain any more on the dry food or lack of daily bread.

In the summer of '56 there was here not so little emigration and many families of different nationalities came in here and settled in different directions around us. Among these were two Norwegian families who came in here in our circle. These were Andrew Fredrickson, wife and two children, and Christian Hanson and wife (they were newly married). So that now we were already five Norwegian families. They took land in the vicinity of us and others and became as if adopted into our family.

It was also this year that my brother Theodore was born the 27th of October. As said before, although in poor circumstances we were more or less well provided for in the secular, but in the religious we lacked everything. Here were already two children who were not baptized. My oldest sister was now old enough to be confirmed but school and minister was lacking. But time passed and we followed into the fall of 1857. Then we got information that Pastor Larson would make a mission trip through Goodhue County and visit the Norwegian settlements, among them Valley Grove, Rice County, and that was the nearest place where we could meet with him. So most of the families here in Fox Lake went there at the determined time and were administered both baptism and communion by an ordained Lutheran minister which they appreciated very much.

Father met with Pastor Larson and learned he had already organized a confirmation class there in the area. In this class my oldest sister Martha was admitted. She with the others got lessons in different places, but met the pastor every day where he heard their lessons and taught them the necessary things.

When the lessons were done, the Pastor gladly followed you out and pointed for you the direction where the house was, perhaps one, two or several miles away. Then you took the direction and often over the wild prairie without a road and at last you usually found what you sought. But on the way you would perhaps find one or several creeks without bridges and must often take a long detour to come over it, and at this time you were also liable to meet or come together with one or several Indians at any time or place, which was not considered by far the safest company, especially for a young girl.

After 25th of March we had several days of mild weather so that the snow went down considerably. We had been busy the whole winter with different things. For the first, we must split enough rails to fence in the land where we cultivated so that we could seed and plant the coming spring.

There were then not so few came into Faribault that fall and winter who intended to build the next spring and summer, and the material which should be used for this must be brought from either Hastings or St. Paul. And so there was a real market for shingles because they could be made cheaper around Faribault than one could bring them from Hastings. And so we made many thousand shingles that winter and sold them for five dollars a thousand, cash. Besides we had cut many more tons of hay than what we needed for our own use, and that we brought to Faribault and got a good price and cash money for it.

In the spring and summer of '56, most of the good land was taken, but the most by speculators who by a kind of self-fulfilling law claimed that they could hold the land until it came to the market and then preempted it; it is that they paid $1.25 per acre. Then they abandoned the land and let it lie uncultivated for no one's benefit for years until it had risen double and more in value. Then the poor people who were sincere and would get themselves a home must pay these speculators a high price for the land which some would never be able to pay, but would have to leave the land again after they had struggled for years to make themselves a home from it.

It was now a longer time which we had not had or heard some kind of preaching in the Norwegian language. But then came there a lay preacher from Christiana, Dakota County. His name was Olson. He had a congregation in Waseca County which he visited as a minister at certain times, and on these trips to Waseca he also stopped here with us and held prayer meetings, until he made arrangements with Pastor Muus so that he came and visited us as minister when he had opportunity for it.

The ten Norwegian pioneer families that came together to organize the Fox Lake congregation were:

        Elling O. Strand   Ole Ellingson
        Ole Hanson   Halvor Meland
        Ole Juvrud   Thosten Thompson
        Andreas Fredrikson Gunlek Olson
        Christian Hanson   K. A. Knudson ✤

The relationships among founding families in the early pioneer communities were often many and complicated, and this is certainly true in Fox Lake. Ole Ellingson was the son of Elling Strand. Halvor Meland and K. A. Knudson married daughters of Elling Strand. A daughter of Ole Ellingson married Ole Juvrud's son, Thomas.

Erik A. Uggen was Fingar Uggen's brother. His daughter Kristi married Ole Hanson and Erik Uggen's second wife was Ingeborg Iverson, mother of Ole Juvrud's wife Martha.

Ole Hanson's son Anton married Ole Juvrud's daughter Anna. Hanson's daughter Karen became the second wife of Engebret Oppegaard who married Serena Juvrud, Ole Juvrud's youngest daughter. Ole's son Hans Hanson married Elsie, sister of Andrew Uggen.

Andrew Uggen married Ole Juvrud's daughter Oline. Kolbjorn Haugen's son Christian married Inger Juvrud, another of Ole Juvrud's daughters. Gunlek Olson married Axel Iverson's daughter, Synneva.

These connections were reinforced and expanded in the next generations of Fox Lake, and reflect the familial patterns of many Norwegian settlements. They help explain the blending of community and family that allowed mid-19th century Norwegian dialects and traditions to flourish in Minnesota until after World War II.

Pioneer Life in Dodge County

Excerpts from the Grønsten family history written in Norwegian by Ingeborg Grønsten Aaby and translated by Nora Boyum.

My father, Hans Johnson Grønsten, was born on the farm Grønsten in Holla, Telemark, Norway, the 26th of May, and baptized the 30th of May 1819 in the Holden Church. He was married on September 8, 1842, to Karen Kjerstine Eich who was born on the 19th and baptized the 29th of September 1816, also in the Holden Church. They lived at Grønsten and he was successful as a spinning wheel maker. Born to them were John in 1842, and Anne Marie three years later, with a twin sister that died.

In 1846 they migrated to America. A great deal of preparation was needed for such a long journey, and for getting started in the new country. They took what they could of food and clothing which was packed in large wooden chests. The chests were hand made with hand wrought hinges, handles, and locks, beautifully painted in scroll and flower designs and bright colors. These contained all their belongings: household linens, bedding, clothing, food, such as dried foods of various kinds and flat bread, tools, and what was most precious, the Bible and devotional books.

They started the 17th of May and had a very stormy passage to Havre, France. When they arrived they were badly disappointed to find that the ship they were to have taken had already departed so there was nothing to do but stay in Havre for six weeks to wait for the next ship. These ships were sailing vessels and they had to rely on the winds to take them across the ocean which generally took around six to eight weeks. They had a long and stormy voyage to New York; from there they were taken in canal boats (horse drawn) to Buffalo, New York, and then another ship to Milwaukee, Wisconsin. With the unexpected delay and with helping fellow travelers who were less fortunate, their money and provisions were sadly depleted and they were forced to leave their baggage and proceed on foot, carrying each a child a distance of seventy miles to Whitewater, Wisconsin, where my mother's uncle, Anders Johnson Shipnes lived.

There was want and sickness the first year. At one time when the whole family was stricken with some disease, little Anne Marie died and kind neighbors came and buried her for them. Father built a five-room frame house and dug a 100-foot well on his 40 acrew farm, and lived there ten years.

Their land contained a small lake and some bluffs and was not well suited for farming so in the spring of 1856, he sold his place for $500 and along with some neighbors moved with covered wagon which had *kubberulle* (wooden wheels) and oxen to Minnesota, and settled on 80 acres of school land in Canisteo Township, Dodge County, thus going through all the hardships of pioneering a second time. (This farm is the one now occupied by Wallace Beaver). They had to go to Decorah to buy flour and when they finally had wheat to sell they had to take it by wagon and oxen team to Winona to be ground which would take at least three days.

(Most important to the new settlers was good spring water and good timber to build their houses and furnish fuel. Most of this territory was heavily wooded then.) They lived in their covered wagon most of the summer as the first thing to do was to clear some land and put in some crop, after which father cut logs and built a small log house. This was covered with a turf roof at first but during the winter father made oak shingles which made a good roof. The first year's wheat crop was a failure and as they had not much money to buy flour they got along with cornmeal but they had plenty of meat and vegetables. They lived in this small log house for five years, and here I (Ingeborg Georgine Grønsten Aaby) was born July 19, 1858.

One of the interesting stories mother used to tell was about a neighbor lady, Ingeborg Dahl. Ole and Ingeborg Dahl lived as close neighbors, (they probably came in their company from Wisconsin) and their cattle ran together with ours. At first the cattle stayed near the wagon but as they became accustomed to the surroundings they began to wander farther away and had to be fetched for evening. One day when Ingeborg Dahl came for her cows they had wandered way past the high hill which is about three-fourths mile away but she went after them. She had gotten the whole herd together when she was suddenly startled to see a large band of Indians come riding on their ponies over the hill. There were 35 or 40 of them. She let out a frightened yell and started running and in haste grabbed the tail of the bell-cow which started for home with great speed with Ingeborg hanging on while the others scattered in all directions.

The Indians must have thought it was funny - she could hear them laughing and talking loudly amongst themselves. They good-naturedly gathered the cattle and brought them home. They stopped about 10 or 12 rods from where our log house stood. Here they set up their tents and stayed until the next spring. They were friendly however, and came quite often to beg for a little bread which mother always gave them. They looked quite formidable as they jumped off their ponies with knives and tomahawks in their belts and carrying guns but when father had to be away for several days at a time, mother even thought it was good to have them near. Father made friends with them, helped them repair their guns, and make snowshoes which they needed for that winter which was later called by the Indians as the winter of the big snows. They never stole anything from father but some of the neighbors were not so lucky and would catch them stealing most anything. There were two other camps, one large one by Sjur Saettre, and the other near Anders Mohn. In the spring of 1858 all the Indian camps broke up and left and the deer seemed to disappear with them.

There were other settlers - many came in 1855, some as early as 54. Some came directly from Norway; many came from earlier settlements in Koshkonong and Bonnet Prairie and others in Wisconsin. My father came in 1856. Others to come that year were John Tverberg who built a large log house and Ole Hellekson Flata who gave of his land for Flata schoolhouse. These settlers were from many different parts of Norway and due to the different dialects there were even some neighbors that had difficulty understanding each other.

Salem and Rock Dell Townships in Olmsted County and the southeast part of Dodge County were predominantly Norwegian Lutheran. Visits from pastors from earlier settlements in Wisconsin and Iowa were welcome. Some of these were Clausen, Preus, Brandt, St. Munch, Jensen, and Muus. St. Olaf's Norwegian Evangelical Lutheran Congregation was organized, also some land purchased and a cemetery dedicated in 1856, which is now the East St. Olaf ALC.

In the first years, young people walked as far as from Hayfield to study for confirmation. In the many years before the churches were built services were held outdoors in summer, probably under some wide spread oak tree and in winter in people's houses and later there were schoolhouses. Most frequently used were the roomy log house of John Tverberg, the first large frame house built by Aslak Aaby in 1861, and homes of Tollef Golberg (Olmsted County) and Hans Grønsten Johnson, my father.

In the spring of 1858, word came that H. A. Preus would conduct services at the Sjur Saettre place the next day and there would be baptism, confirmation, communion and marriage ceremonies for those that desired. Before they had a resident pastor there were three or four such meetings a year. My brother John was then 15 years old and my parents would like very much for him to be confirmed but father had gone to Decorah to get flour and my brother did not have suitable clothing. They had bought cloth as there wasn't such a thing as ready-to-wear in these days.

Mother wasn't generally at a loss what to do. She made all the clothing, for father as well as the rest of us so she got busy making a confirmation suit for John. Evening came and with it a storm with thunder, lightening, and heavy rain. The roof started to leak badly and mother had to put the children in the bed and was lucky to have an umbrella to put over them to help keep them dry, then she moved the table to a dry spot and worked all night sewing by hand and by candle light and when morning came it was all finished.

Then she didn't know what to do about money as there was none in the house but she decided to go to a neighbor, Aslak Aaby, who had just moved into the settlement. He was pleased to loan her a $5 gold piece for John to give the pastor. She hurried home again to get ready and they walked the three miles or more to the Saettre place. John had no other religious instruction then what he had learned with help of parents by reading the Bible and memorizing long passages from both Old and New Testaments but passed easily the catechism and was confirmed that day among others. Along with preaching and the confirmations, there were also baptisms, communion and marriage ceremonies performed that day.

One other such meeting was held in the same place that summer where I was baptized together with John Aaby (son of Aslak) and many others. At age 17 John went to school two months at Salem Corner, at 18 went a winter to Engen where they had a remarkably good teacher that year. At 19 he received a teacher's certificate and taught for several years in different districts. At age 23 he became Justice of Peace in Canisteo (1866) and was town clerk until he moved away (1882). John Johnson and Anders Aaby (son of Aslak) organized Mutual Fire Insurance Co. in Dodge County.

Having celebrated church festivals in both East and West St. Olaf (1931) memories go back to childhood days. Then the commonplace was oxen team hitched to wagons, log houses, small fields surrounded by zigzag rail fences. It is wonderful to remember the coziness of these log houses and how close we were to father, mother, sister, and brother as we grew up together. Often it was used for church services, having been scrubbed and tidied the day before, the table laid with white linen, and as people sat tightly packed together, it was truly a 'God's House Built of Living Stones'. The pastor came, probably a two-day journey.

Sunday services were often held at the John Tverberg home as they lived in the west part of the congregation and had a large log house. I remember very well once we were there in winter when my sister Anne Marie was confirmed. We drove with oxen and sleigh and it got quite late getting home again.

Another time was summer - the house was packed with people, with others crowding open windows and doorways. A flock of us children were sitting on the lawn and there was some old ladies out there also. A young man came riding up the lane and as he came close enough for us to hear, shouted "Lincoln is dead! President Lincoln has been shot!" and rode on. One of the ladies clapped her hands together and said, "God be praised that Lincoln is dead. Then there will probably be an end to this terrible war." This seemed to me such an awful thing to say - really sacrilegious I thought.

Little by little more land was cleared and crops were better and they prospered beyond their expectations. After five years father built a bigger and better log house, and added more government land until he had nine forties. Land was bought at that time for $1.25 an acre. The land office was at Mantorville. However money was not plentiful and some who had to borrow had to pay 25 to 40% interest. Father also acquired three oxen teams and John became an expert at driving them.

During the first years the wheat was harvested with scythe and cradle. With this they cut the grain and left it in neat rows which then would have to be gathered into bundles and tied, then set up in shocks. This was slow and tedious work as the fields got larger. Father seeded grain by hand. We children would often walk a space ahead at the edge of the last row so he could see how he should throw the grain and get it even.

One day I walked in the seeding all forenoon and we seeded quite a few acres. When we had eaten our dinner and came out to the field again it was entirely covered with the small blue wild pigeons which were so common in those days. They moved with rolling, turning, tumbling movements and glimmered, twinkled and sparkled in the sunlight - a beautiful wonderful sight to behold, but as we drew near - swish! Vips! It was as though an enormous blanket were lifted which as it rose, shaded the sun and made a noise like the sound of far away thunder. When we came to where they had been, there was hardly a kernal of wheat left, so we had to sow the field all over again and the boys followed up with a rake to rake the grain into the soil. These blue pigeons came in large flocks in springtime for several years. Later they were not seen anymore, whether civilization drove them away or what I do not know. I have to tell a few are occasionally seen at the inland lakes in the north. These seemed to be harmless except for the seed grain they ate which that day amounted to several sacks full.

My father, Hans Johnson Grønsten, had only a few months of schooling but had read a great deal, especially history, both ancient and modern. It seemed he knew times and dates and the wherefore of all European wars. He predicted World War I and said that when Germany was ready there would be the greatest war that the world had ever seen and hoped he would not be living then.

He also knew church history and his favorite reading was Martin Luther's writings. He considered him very wonderful, loved Luther's hymns and sang them enough so we children learned them too. He sang well, had a very good voice and liked to sing national songs and all kinds of Norwegian songs; he almost always sang while at work.

Father was handy with all kinds of tools, was a spinning wheel maker by trade and did well at that while in Norway. Here he did the necessary blacksmithing for himself and others, also carpenter work. The panel doors he made in 1862 are still doing good service although the house is now rebuilt and modern. He also built the pews in the East St. Olaf Church which were very nice. He was an active member of the church and especially interested in schools and our education. He might maybe have done better at something else than farming although he farmed well but was too easily taken in by agents who were so numerous in the country in those days.

Politically he was staunch Republican until after President Grant's administration. He admired Grant as a soldier and commander but not as a statesman. He said it was in those years after the war that the monopolies and trusts got such a foothold in the country which one can readily believe when we consider that to borrow money then one had to pay from 25 to 40% interest. So in later years he was as staunch a Democrat as he had been a Republican.

With large families growing up, many looked about for more land. In 1881 father went to Dakota Territory to take a homestead and a year later he sold his land here and moved out together with sons John, Jens and Nils, who all took land out there. Jens lived there for some years and then moved to Colorado, due to a bad asthmatic condition of his son Henry. Jens retained the name Grønsten while the other brothers went by the name Johnson. Father built a house and barn and farmed it there. He married again and had two more children: Inga Kinstad Groves and Johnny Johnson. His wife died when the children were little. Inga was adopted by the Kinstad family in Wallace. Father stayed with us some of the time in 1906 and 1907. Norman accompanied him to Brother Jens in Colorado and he died there in 1909.

Historic Buildings from the Rock Dell Area
By Scott Brunner

Tverberg Cabin

John Peterson Tverberg was born March 10, 1811, in Tinn, Telemark, Norway. He was married on January 17, 1840, to Gro Sondresdatter of Tinn. In 1842 this couple and their young daughter came to America. They first lived in Dane County, Wisconsin, where more children were born. In the late 1850s the family moved to Vernon Township in Dodge County. They lived in a large log home which was built about 1856. John P. Tverberg died May 31, 1895. The Tverberg couple is buried in the West St. Olaf Church Cemetery in Dodge County, Minnesota.

The St. Olaf Norwegian Lutheran Church was organized June 12, 1856, under a big oak tree south of the present East St. Olaf Church. It would be a number of years before actual structures were built (East and West St. Olaf churches). Because of its size, the Tverberg log house was used most frequently for church services. Rev. Lauritz Steen, the first resident pastor, stated that he had held 101 services in this house. Before schools were built, the home was also used to conduct school. The John P. Tverberg home was moved from its original site in Vernon Township, to just south of the East St. Olaf Church. Now it sits preserved in the oak grove where the St. Olaf congregation was originally formed.

Erikson Stabbur

Hans Erikson was born June 12, 1824, in Norway. He immigrated to America, and settled in Salem Township, Olmsted County, Minnesota Territory, in the mid-1850s. He married Kristi Iversdatter and they had nine children. Hans died February 28, 1885; he is buried at the East St. Olaf Cemetery in Rock Dell, Minnesota. From his farm an early Norwegian-style stabbur building has been preserved. It is now located on the Vesterheim Museum grounds in Decorah, Iowa.

The plaque in front of the building reads:
"Hans Erikson built this storehouse near Rock Dell in Olmsted County, sometime after 1860. It served as storage for food and was set on posts or pillars to deter pests. The Norwegian term for a storehouse like this is stabbur. A building of this type was seldom found on a Norwegian immigrant farm. However, the stabbur style of storehouse was common on more substantial Norwegian farms and in fact announced one's status."

Statehood Pioneers and a Minnesota Governor
By Gary Bakko

Ole and Margit Bakko Family - 1893

In 1853, Knut Knudson Finseth and Margit Olsdtr Finseth and their six children emigrated from the Hemsedal area of Hallingdal, Norway. Sons Knut, Herbrand, Ole, and daughter, Margit, were already in their twenties.

Their two youngest children were Anders, 17, and Anne, 11. The family went first to Rock Prairie, Wisconsin, an active Norwegian settlement at the time. In 1854, Margit married Ole Jorgen Bakko, also from the Hemsedal area of Hallingdal. In 1852, at the age of 20, Ole Bakko had immigrated to America, and taken up residence for a time in Green Bay, Wisconsin.

On May 5, 1855, Finseth brothers, Herbrand, Anders and Knut, along with their brother-in-law, Ole Bakko, left Rock Prairie, Wisconsin, and came to the farm of Halvor Odegaard, by way of Cannon Falls and Cannon City. Odegaard had settled in Richland Township, Rice County, Minnesota, in 1854. These were the first of about 700 Hallings who came and settled in and around the western sections of Goodhue County and eastern Rice County. Each of the four brothers pre-empted lands in that part of Goodhue County's pristine prairie area lay in Holden Township. The Finseth elders, Ole and Anne, along with daughter Margit and her infant son arrived later.

The Bakko's 160-acre farm proved to be ideal land and was endowed with a gushing spring, near where the couple's 12x14 log home was built. One year later a village was platted 1 ½ mile south of the Bakko farm near the south bank of the Zumbro River, which today is the City of Kenyon. But in 1855 members of the Sioux and Dakota tribes continued to traverse the yet game-abundant areas along the Zumbro River for their sustenance.

George, the first of eleven children born to Ole and Margit Bakko, was the one who as an infant was left alone while his mother went to the spring for water. An Indian woman who had wandered by took advantage of the unguarded moment and hurried away with baby George. Perhaps she was a grieving mother whose child had recently died. But whatever the motive, she ran off with the child in her arms toward a timbered area that led down toward the Zumbro River. Upon hearing her baby's cry and watching him being carried off, Margit let out a scream that only a mother would make if confronted with such an unthinkable situation. Immediately a race to recover her baby son ensued. The impediment of carrying a child on the run created a disadvantage, especially when being pursued by the child's mother. The gap between the two racing women closed significantly as they entered a grove of timber and soon baby George was placed on the ground. The Indian woman, probably expecting to pay with her life for running off with another's child, drew a knife in self defense and began backing away, all the while facing the infant's mother. As Margit picked up her son, a momentary glance between the two women assured the kidnapper that the child's mother was only interested in returning to the safety of her home, not committing some act of retribution.

Ole and Margit never lived far from Finseth family members, as all had either settled or married a settler in the same general area. A number of Knut and Margit Finseth's grandchildren went into business for themselves in the nearby village of Kenyon.

Knut Finseth married Bergit Odegaard, a daughter of the farmer he first met when he, his brothers and Ole Bakko stopped at the Halvor Odegaard farm on June 3, 1855. In 1868, he was elected to serve in the Minnesota House of Representatives.

Anders Finseth was elected a county commissioner for Goodhue County, and Minnesota state senator, 1875 – 1879 and 1887 – 1891. He was appointed state dairy and food commissioner in 1891 and served as a presidential elector for Rutherford B. Hayes in 1876.

The youngest member of the Finseth family, Anne, married Halvor Quie, a neighboring farmer from Rice County. Quie was a Civil War veteran who served with the Minnesota Sharpshooter Volunteers, 2nd Company from December 20, 1861, to January 8, 1863. He participated in 11 battles and was wounded at Antietam. They had seven children. One child, Albert, married Nettie Jacobson, to whom was born a son, Albert. Albert Quie went on to serve in the Minnesota Senate from 1954 – 1958, U. S. House of Representatives from 1958 – 1979 and then as the 35th governor of Minnesota.

A Letter Home

Guri Swenson (center front) with children Paul, Swen Jr., Ole and Sander (back) Lars and Kristi (front). Photo taken about 1890

The following letter was written by Guri Sandersdtr Slettemoen, (Mrs. Swen Swenson Sr) to her mother, Gunnar Tollefsdtr Slettemoen at Hol, Norway. Swen and Guri emigrated from Norway in 1857 with six sons and one daughter. They were destined for the Norseland Settlement, Nicollet County. Minnesota. One son, Tolleiv, age six months, died en route and was buried at sea. Swen and Guri pre-empted land in what became Section 15, New Sweden Township, Nicollet County. Sadly, this letter was written and received after the death of Guri's mother in Norway on May 8, 1859.

Unforgettable Mother and Siblings.

    Finally the time has come that we happily can take pen in hand to let you know how we are doing here in the far West. And it is such a long time gone since we were separated. And we have always been thinking about how you are in our old home. When we almost 2 years ago wrote a letter to our old Father, Svend Rodningen who was asked to greet you from us. But we have not received any reply. We do not know if the letter has reached the owner, and that is the reason it has been such a long delay before writing to you. It is a great pleasure and enjoyment to hear from our relatives and friends. That is the only thing we can enjoy together this side of the grave.
    We have all been in good health to this day and are, all things considered, well. On October 20 in the year 1858 I brought into the world a baby girl who was stillborn. I had

no birth pains to mention and I thank the Almighty who knows what is best for us. We should tell you that we have taken Government land which consists of 160 acres of prairie and also forest and this land is located about 5 English miles from Lars S. Rodningen and 12 English miles from the town of St. Peter. And our neighbors are Ole Lofthus and our son Svend, and also a bachelor from Torpe annex. We took over our land last May. And last summer we built a cabin with a loft and a cow barn for our animals. And our animals consist of 3 cows, a span of driving oxen, 2 pairs of 2-year old oxen, 3 - 1year old oxen, a heifer, 2 pigs and 2 sheep. Last fall we slaughtered 6 pigs.

We can also tell you how much land we have cleared for grain on our farm which consists of 13 acres. Of these 13 acres we planted 5 acres with maize, roots (rutabaga) and potatoes and of that seeding we harvested 60 bushels of maize, 70 bushels of rutabaga and 70 bushels potatoes. We can also tell you that last year we had 7 acres at Lars S. Rodningen where we had one half, he the other half. And the harvest was 30 bushels wheat, 60 bushels barley, and 15 bushels oats on our part. To give you more details I will return to our land. I have fenced in 40 acres which I partly use for grain, partly for haying. And I regard my land as having a good location for water, grain field and haying, and an excellent building site. I think it is 70 acres with good grain fields. I also think I can feed a herd of 40 and have enough pastures. I almost forgot to tell that we have bought 10 acres forestland which is about 3.5 English mile from my home, which cost 85 dollars and shall be paid next winter. And this should be sufficient for me.

I suppose I should tell you my true opinion of our departure which many of you perhaps might be interested in. I truthfully do not regret my move to here and particularly when I think about the many heavy burdens I got rid of. Then I feel happy about it, for example the move to the saeters, the animals starving in winters and our fear for the hay-buying and for things we need in life. All this I now, with God's help, think I got rid of, but do not think that we thereby are rid of all worries. When one comes here it is a great difference, particularly for women. But it all depends how one was situated in Norway. A man's burdens are made easier because here one does not have to do hay-driving in the wintertime and cut leaves and twigs for extra fodder and manure-driving which one had to do in Norway. When one has fenced one's land then all his work is to get firewood and take care of the animals by bringing them the hay like we did for the sheep in Norway. Except when the weather is too cold, then the hay must be brought in to them, and then it is common that one brings in so much that the animals can lay down on the hay, because here one does not have to be so stingy with the hay, because it is plenty of hayfields, where one can cut 12-18 skipund a day (16 pounds to a skipund), and that is fast!

Let me tell a bit about times here. We had a very good year, but there is not much money to have, but we hope that will change. The labor wage is not high. A good worker can get 50 cents a day in wintertime, but there is not much work to get in the winter. During summers it is 75 cents to 1 dollar a day, and for a girl 4 to 6 dollars a month, and there is plenty of work for them. I can now tell about the food prices, for 1 bushel wheat

70 cents, for 1 bushel maize 35 cents, for 1 bushel potatoes 25 cents, for 1 bushel barley 40 cents, for one barrel wheat-flour 5 dollars, for 1 pound butter from 10 to 15 cents, for 1 pound pork 4 to 4 1/2 cents. As for the
animals they cost; for a span of driving oxen, 60 to 75 dollars; for a team of good workhorses, 200 to 300 dollars; for a cow, 20 to 25 dollars. For one year-old heifers, 5 to 6 dollars, and equipment and tools are very expensive here. A wagon costs 50 to 100 dollars, a plow 12 to 15 dollars, a breaking plow 15 to 24 dollars, and a cooking stove 15 to 35 dollars. And we have bought a cooking stove which cost 36 dollars, and with that one we can cook, fry pork, bake bread and make coffee, all at the same time.

I have to end my letter and my reports with the dearest wish that these lines will arrive at its destination and find you all well and healthy. I must also ask you to write to us soon, as soon as you have read this letter, as I have not heard anything from my people since my departure. You can therefore imagine how much I yearn to hear from you about everything.

Also remind those at Rodningen to write to us as we think it is peculiar that we have not heard from them while it is so long ago when we wrote to them. As there is no more paper left I have to end my letter. And then, for the last time I have to say farewell to you, my dear Mother, as it is so uncertain that we with pens, can speak to each other anymore, but if that is the way it will be, then let us do what we can to meet each other again on the other side of the grave, where there are no more separations and where there will be no more sorrow for us. As there is no more space left I can not mention all the names, but all our siblings, relatives and friends are given our heartfelt greetings, and greet all at Rodningen, at Fosgaard and at Kvamen. But above all, my most heartfelt greetings to you, dear Mother, who is always in my thoughts and closest to my heart. Do not forget to write and do not delay, but write as soon as possible. And greetings to Paul and Kari Nerol from Syver K. Foss.

Rodning, February 4, 1860

Svend Svensen
and Guri Sandersdtr.

Goodbye! Live Well!

Original letter published in Folk og fortid i Hol Book II; pages 768 – 771, by Lars Reinton and Sigurd S. Reinton.
Few translated excerpts of letter in Land of Their Choice – The Immigrants Write Home; pages 423 – 425, by Theodore C. Blegen, 1955.

Ole Torgerson, Road Builder

Ole's mother carefully saved each letter from her oldest son. In 1968, Martin Olson's father translated the letters. Martin built this story from excerpts from letters written in 1855-1856.

Ole left his parents' home in Rock Prairie, Wisconsin in 1855 for his father's brother's home in Houston County, Minnesota Territory. He faithfully wrote his mother Siri every 3-5 weeks for the next 8 years. He moved to the West Coast in the early 1870's, and the Wisconsin family doesn't know what happened to him after that. Ole may have continued to keep the family informed, but after Siri died no one kept his correspondence. This story is told with actual translated excerpts from his earliest letters:

I have made it fine to Uncle Torger's house, and there is plenty of work for me to do here. I have told him not to pay me directly so that I am not tempted to waste my money. I want to find myself some good land and set to farming a year from this spring. Uncle Torger thinks I am being too ambitious and should set my sights for my own farm toward 1858. By then his oldest son will be 12 and more able to take on work around the farm, so I think he may be looking after his own interests in telling me such a thing. I did not tell him as much, as he may know more than I do on that account.

These Yankees are worse than the ones we've had to deal with at home. You can't trust a word they have to say. I am lucky that I can speak good English, as most have yet to learn it. I was to the mill here last week, run by an awful sneaky fellow. He was charging way too much to those who couldn't speak English, and not just Norwegians. So I took on their defense and made sure they paid no more than was necessary for their grinding. The owner did not seem too pleased with me, as if his dislike of my ways would shame me into being an easy victim of his games, but I did not allow him to get the better of me or those around me. I can guess that as soon as I left with my wagon, he went back to his usual ways.

Whether it is in a store or a mill, or even at government meetings where road and bridges are decided upon, these Yankees act like they are the kings of the world and we are their servants and should accept what they decide and be grateful for anything that by coincidence is helpful to our community. We are large in number but have not yet organized ourselves as well as we should, language being just one barrier, but that will change. Sooner or later the Yankees will maybe get a lesson on how they are not so smart or so much better than the immigrants that buy at their establishments and secure them a good living.

I am enjoying the extra work of milking cows for our Scottish neighbors. They are a jolly bunch, with much talking and joking to see the sun up each morning. I heard from them about an opportunity it may be hard to turn down, although I don't think it will make Uncle Torger too happy, so I would be much pleased to hear your advice. It seems that the territory is building a road through the wilderness, paying the workers a dollar a day. This would put me much closer to my goals, but the work runs from early spring until late in the fall, and I must agree to work the whole time, and that would leave Uncle Torger short during the whole crop season. The benefit to this, so they say, is that we can have first pick of the land along the roadway as we go along, and such a chance is hard to ignore. I am so grateful for Torger's generosity and being as a part of his family that it is hard for me to think of bringing it up to him. I also have to consider my own future, and this may be the chance to better myself. So I will await your good advice on my decision.

We were surprised when we recognized cousin Bendik walking up the road toward the farm. Your letter to Uncle Torger, saying that he had come to find some employment, and the letter to me in which you so kindly saw the wisdom of being part of the road workers, was all I needed to bring up the subject with Uncle Torger. He agreed that it seemed to be a good opportunity for me. I asked him to give me only $10 of the money I have earned so that I can go up to St. Paul and find out all about it. He says that I am welcome to return if the situation is not to my liking. The Scotsmen next door said the same, and in fact one of the sons, a husky fellow we call Briedy, will come with me on this adventure. His father gave us his fine tree saw so that we could promote ourselves as a good pair of sawyers. We will leave our homes as soon as we can see the sun on Tuesday morning.

Ole and Briedy went to St. Paul, where they found the right office and signed a contract to work from April to November on a new territorial road. They were to receive their meals, a place to sleep, and a dollar a day working as treefellers cutting through the wilderness to connect Chaska with St. Paul.

This is a very interesting experience that I find hard to describe. There are many nationalities working on this road, as well as many Yankees, who are usually the boss of course. The Germans are very hard workers, as are the Irish. But the Irish, I must tell you, are not to be insulted in any way. They carry around clubs and, when they take offense, have no reserve in swinging them at the person who they think has insulted them. Even the bosses tread softly around them. Briedy has made friends with other Scotsmen on the crews, and since I have not found any other Norwegians here, I am associated with the Scotch among the workers, which is sure to give Poppa a good laugh. These Scots at least are not associated with the Pope and all of that malarkey, although they are not good members of the Lutheran church. Still, we can read our Bibles together on Sunday morning without much argument. The food is not so good, but it is hot and fills our stomachs. We sleep under the stars most nights, with the blanket we were given as part of the bargain to keep us warm. Mosquitos cause a great bother to most, but for some reason they leave me well enough alone, although the buzzing by itself is not very pleasant. A few of the little varmints do see me as a good lunch, which they pay for with their lives.

There is an engineer from St. Paul that has laid out the road, but sometimes the way he has set out the road does not match too well with the ground. There are two man crews who go in front of us and mark the trees to be cut, and sometimes there are arguments when the engineer takes a look and sees that the road is not going exactly where he wanted it. To go through a swamp or over a high hill when with just a little change it will be easier makes no sense, but I guess he thinks with all his education he is better than the practical workers who see things as they are, and not just as he has put it on the map. It is a good laugh to watch from a distance when the engineer tries to take these fellows to task, with all the arm waving and pointing that goes on. We are making good progress, I think, and the main road boss has said that he is quite happy with the work we do.

Some of the men have had problems to get their pay each week, and there is quite some grumbling. Breidy and I have not had much problem in that regard. Some of the Yankees encourage everyone to play cards and gambling games with their pay, and then are angry to have no money as soon as the next morning, often with a black eye to boot. I keep to the other side of the camp from that kind of goings-on, with my eye firmly fixed on having enough money to build my farm. Some of these men would rather give you a poke in the eye than to talk sensibly about a disagreement, so it seems best to keep to ourselves and not get caught up in a melee of any kind.

It has been raining here the last many days, and so we deal with mud up to our ankles in some places, putting everyone in a very bad mood. The horses that pull the logs are having a mighty hard time because of the mud, and the mosquitos swarm around them so even the poor animals are miserable.

We were given the 4th of July off, and I was surprised to find that I was paid for not working that day. This tells me how important the day is to the Yankees. Briedy and I set off on Tuesday night to take a look at some of the land ahead. We have got to an area that offers some promise of productive farms. It is possible to see where the spring floods come along, as no trees grow there. The usual farm here is 160 acres. I will need to guess that size when I stake out a claim, as I am told the survey of this area will not be completed for as much as two more years.

We spent a pleasant evening with a Swedish family just recently arrived, and slept in their barn. They have staked their claim far from the road, I believe, but he was pleased to show us a good field of corn and one of wheat, which he is sure is just the start of his good luck. There is a good area where a creek runs and it is my hope that the road will be close by this acreage and I can lay claim to some of it. On Wednesday as we were about to turn back to the camp, we found a good hill with a spring flowing halfway up the side on which to put the house and buildings, and bottom land that should be rich and fertile for growing crops. This is some miles from where we are now working, so I will anticipate making this my home, should we pass close to it. Briedy thinks the same, and I would not mind so much to have him as a neighbor again. We both must work until November, so I am not sure how to protect this land from others, but there is some time to consider this, I believe.

I am fine, Momma, but there was very nearly a real bad accident this week. There is a big turn over of workers, I guess signing a contract doesn't mean much to some men. For reasons good and bad, they decide to quit in the middle and then are angry when they don't get paid as much as they think they should. If they break their contract, I don't see as how they should get paid at all. The ones that come in new to take their places don't always know so much of what to do and how things work.

Briedy and I have been taking the bigger trees to cut down, we have a good rhythm and know how to make them come down as they should. One of the new tree fellers was working on smaller trees around us and one of them came down right on Briedy. This young Yankee fool didn't call out, but just watched it coming down. At the last minute I saw and gave warning, but even as he stepped away, it knocked Briedy down and did his shoulder some damage. There is a good man with some medical experience from the Mexican War, he came up within the hour, Briedy laying on the ground in pain the whole time, with many of the men coming around and offering what help they could but I said to leave it for someone who knows better.

They took him back to the camp on a wagon and got him wrapped up. He has been told he should not work the rest of this season to be sure the shoulder sets right. This is a disappointment to him, losing so much money. The road boss come up though and said he would be paid $25 for his trouble and said that the two of us were worth every cent of our wages. Briedy had himself quite a headache for a day or two and his shoulder has hurt him quite a bit, but this evening when I got back to camp he was feeling much better. They tell him he can travel out of here in just a day or two more.

I am now working with a German, he is a Catholic and doesn't speak much English, but we can get a good rhythm and he is a good worker. His partner went back to St. Paul last week, and he was glad to get off the digging crew. It isn't like working with Briedy, but at least this man is not a fool!

Well, don't you suppose that Briedy's accident has worked well to our advantage? The day he was about to get a wagon ride back to St. Paul, he says to me that maybe he could come back and hold both of our claims until I can get done and join him. We will get to that nice hill with the spring in two weeks at the most, so he thinks he will go to St. Paul and contact his younger brother to join him and then come back to our claim. I wrote a note to Uncle Torger to give him my pay. We must spend about $150 for a good pair of oxen, $50 for a wagon, $100 or more for tools and necessities to build the house and prepare for the winter. Between us two we can do this, and a Frenchman who came down from Pembina country and has a warm cabin close to the river says we can get enough pelts over winter to pay to put in our first crop. In the spring I can build my own house and maybe a barn, all the while saving so when the land is surveyed I can pay for it.

Momma, you should not worry so much that I might forget my good Norwegian roots, or stop honoring our Lutheran faith. Briedy and I have become good friends despite our differences, and have good respect for each other. He and his family are not the sort of rascals to not make their word their bond. There are plenty of them to be found on the road crews, but he is a good man from a good family. That is how it should be in America, where we can trust people that we would not even know back home in Norway. There is plenty of room here for more claims, but know that in spring many will be coming.

    My contract is complete, dear Momma, and I can now return to my new home for the winter. I will buy some sugar and salt and other such things to bring to the cabin Briedy and his brother have built to see us through to spring. It would be good if you and Poppa, brothers and cousins could all come out to this new country. I think it will be a good life here!

Urland's Most Difficult Citizen
By Ann (Esterby) Romo

Odd and Randi Otterness and their family are in front of their house in Leon Township, Goodhue County. From left to right they are: Lawrence, father - Odd Otterness, Ellen, Ingeborg, mother - Randi Otterness, Ben, Lars, Eddie, and Jensine.

Odd Larsen Otterness was born in Aurland, Sognefjord, Norway. He was baptized and confirmed in the Vangen Church in Aurland.

In 1857, Odd and his parents, Lars Oddsen and Marta, his brother, Lars, and sister Marta came to America and settled in Leon Township, Goodhue County, Minnesota Territory. They joined one of Odd's brothers who had come two years previously. Odd lived there with his parents for seven years until he bought his own property.

His obituary stated that Odd's first desire was to familiarize himself with American ideas and methods, and to acquire some knowledge of the English language. To achieve this goal, Odd attended the common schools and mingled with English speaking neighbors. His second desire was to become a farmer and own his own home. Seven years after coming to America, Odd bought the 160 acre farm (80 acres in section 28 and 80 adjacent acres in section 33) where he lived out his life.

In 1866, he married Randi Olsdatter Berekvam. Odd (E.L.) and Randi and his parents belonged to Holden Norwegian Lutheran congregation, which was started in 1855. Then in 1872, he was one the three signers of the Articles of Incorporation for

Urland Lutheran Church, located seven miles north of Holden. Odd was also on the building committee for the church that was erected that year. The family maintained their memberships in the Urland congregation for the rest of their lives.

Dr. Lloyd Hustvedt, professor at St. Olaf College wrote about the Urland Lutheran Church and members in the book *Crossings*, published by NAHA:

> Odd Otternes was born in Aurland in 1840 and emigrated in 1857, and from that time on he worked tirelessly at becoming Urland's most difficult citizen. Few have harbored a more lofty disdain for public opinion than he. Had the poet John Donne known him, Donne would not have written the words 'No man is an island.' Odd was intelligent and at times quite right about things. This only compounded the problem. The dynamics of this man's presence defy measurement. When a proposal to install a pipe organ first came up in 1887, he reminded the assembly that the church needed painting. When the proposal came up to paint the church, he argued that this could wait until next year. Once the church was painted, the matter of an organ resurfaced. Odd then reminded the congregation that on top of the initial cost of an organ, they would have to hire an organist, and organists did not come cheap. After twenty-one years, Urland got its pipe organ in 1908. It was Odd who came up with the apportionment plan, but later railed against it for its many injustices.
>
> He had an uncanny nose for sniffing out disciplinary cases and could be the single holdout on a motion to forgive. This created a problem for Pastor J. N. Kildahl, who believed that congregational forgiveness was worthless if not unanimous. Kildahl once denied Odd future speaking rights until he recanted. As early as 1888, Odd argued that there would be no sense to the parochial school system unless they went over to the English language. 'It will come,' said Kildahl, 'but not just yet.' Odd had a grandson, William that took after him in this respect because William loved to discuss and argue with anyone.

Odd was a staunch Democrat. In the township he held the offices of assessor, treasurer, supervisor at various times and was also member of the school board.

From childhood and during all his life, up to the last three years, he was a robust healthy man. Then he suddenly took sick, perhaps a stroke of paralysis, from which he never fully recovered. His strong nature seemed to prevail to such an extent that he recovered somewhat, and it was only the last two days preceding his death that he was wholly confined to his bed.

Odd and Randi had eleven children: Anne, Lars, Ellen, Benjamin, Lawrence, Ingeborg and Eddie all lived to adulthood. Four other children died as infants.

My grandfather, Benjamin Otterness inherited 40 acres in section 28 from his parents. He bought his brother, Lars' 40 acres and another sibling's 40 acres in section 33.

My parents, Andy and Edith Esterby bought the farm from her parents, Bennie and Randi. I remember as a child going next door to the house that Grandpa Odd (E. L.) Otterness built for his family in section 33. Grandpa's sister, Ingeborg had inherited that 40 acres. Ingeborg's daughter Randi and her husband, Joseph Nelson, lived in the old house. There was a back stairway going upstairs from the kitchen. Next to the front parlor was a beautiful stairway. Randi and Joe's nine grandchildren would come to visit and several were close to my age so I liked to play with them. There were many bedrooms upstairs. The old house was taken down and replaced in the 1970's.

About 1989, the farm passed out of the family when it was sold to the Larry Olsons, neighbors from across the fields.

Land Immigrants in Minnesota before May 1858
By Carol Olson

This article contains a <u>partial</u> list of Land immigrants to Minnesota before 1858. The names were extracted from Boka om Land IV, written by Arvid Sandaker and published in Norway in 1973. The book deals with various aspects of immigration from Land, the last section of the book containing biographies of many of the immigrants. As part of his research Mr. Sandaker interviewed members of Landingslag to gather information about their ancestors. If you were not a member at that time it could be that your ancestor's name does not appear on this list.

There are additional lists of Land immigrants which appeared in a series of annual publications of the Lands Museum, Landingen. *If your ancestor's name doesn't appear in the list below, it could be it is included there.*

1843: Søren Olsen Sørum (1823-1091) was the first Nordman to live in St. Paul, Minnesota. He was son of Ole Sørensen and Kari Madsdtr Ruud. His wife was Ingeborg Nilsen (b. 1827) and she came from Numedal. (p. 149-150)

1844: Andreas Nilsen Erstad, b. 1815 and his wife Oline Karine Olsdtr Jørondlien Gaarder, b. 1826 came first to Illinois, then came to Zumbrota, Minnesota in 1854 with their son Nils who was born in Illinois. They are buried at Lands Lutheran Church there. (p. 151)

1846: Erik Johansen Nerhaugen, Frøslidieie, b. 1824, went first to Rock Prairie, Wisconsin. He was married to Marie Syversdtr in 1860. Brothers Andreas and Christian P. Lunde moved in 1854 to Goodhue County, Minnesota. Ingeborg Olsdtr Ommelstadsæteren, wife of Christian, came to the US in 1849. (p. 155-156)

1848: Christoffer Hovelsen Tollefsrud, b. 1831, married Ingeborg Haugen (from Nordre Land) in 1856 and they came to Minneola twp in Goodhue County, Minnesota. After Ingeborg's death in 1871, Christoffer married Stenetta Larsdtr Sæteren. His brother Hans Hovelsen Tollefsrud, b. 1834, moved to Zumbrota, Minnesota but date of the move was not given. Johannes Tollefsrud, b. 1836, lived along the Des Moines River in Jackson County, Minnesota. Date of entry into Minnesota is not certain and need to be verified. Sister Christine Lovise married Syver Dahl and they lived in Zumbrota. (pp. 158-159)

1848: Andrew Johnson (Andreas Nerhaugen) was born in Land, lived first in Wisconsin and moved to Zumbrota in 1855. (p. 160)

1848: Andreas Olsen Sørum, b. 1826, immigrated to Goodhue County, Minnesota in 1854 and he was brother to Søren Olsen Sørum. (p. 160)

1849: Johannes Olsen Ommelstadsæteren, b. 1822, lived from 1855 in Minnesota and was a member of Lands Lutheran Church, Zumbrota, Minnesota in 1867. (p. 165)
His sister Ingeborg Olsdtr Ommelstadsæteren, (1825-1919), married Mathias Pedersen Ringdahl from Fåberg (d. 1884) and lived in Zumbrota from 1855 on. One of their sons was Peder M. Ringdahl (1861-1922), a Democratic candidate for governor in 1912. (p. 165)

1851: Kristen Johansen Rud (Rood) (b. 1802 in Aurland) and his wife Olava Olsdtr (b. 1806 in Land) left Land with their children Agnete, b. 1836, Ole, b. 1844; Kristian (1848-1918) and Oline

(1848-1937). Their other children also immigrated to the United States in 1850: Johan, b. 1829 and Mari, b. 1831. Johan was a farmer in Albert Lea, MM but date was not given as to when he moved there. (p. 171)

1852: Ole P. Anderson moved to Granite Falls, Minnesota after the Civil War—not known where he was at first. (p. 172)

1853: Lars Hansen, b. 1827 at Røsteengen, and his wife Kari Nilsdtr Gaardersæteren lived first in Rock Prairie, WI, moved to Zumbrota and finally to Montevideo, Minnesota. (p. 175)

1853: Ole Paulson b. 1825 and his wife Helene Hansdtr b. 1835 in Lyshaugen in Østsinni moved to Spring Grove, Minnesota in 1856. (p. 175-176)

1853: Haldor Olsen Ommelsæteren b. 1833 came first to Red Wing, Minnesota. He ended up in California. (p. 178)

1853: Christian Olsen Skogstad b. 1831 came to Zumbrota. (p. 178)

1853: Widower Johan Hansen Lybeck b. 1831 and four children came to Zumbrota. He married Guro Strand and he served as Goodhue County Clerk 1874-1886. (p. 179)

1853: The daughter-in-law of Johan Hansen Lybeck and wife of his son Hans Johansen) claimed link to Peder Aadnes by way of the daughter of the latter. (p. 179)

1853: Berthe Hansdtr Aasen (1826-1914) ended up in Linden, Minnesota and married John R. Johnson. (p. 180)

1854: Erik Gudbrandsen Kapperud b. 1830 came first to Eau Claire, WI and then in 1859 to Norway Lake, Minnesota. *(not qualified as a Minnesota Statehood Pioneer)* (p. 183)

1857: Kristoffer Hansen Engen b. 1832 and brother Hans came first to Allmakee County, IA, then to Norway Lake, Minnesota in 1859. *(not qualified as a Minnesota Statehood Pioneer)* (p. 188)

1857: Olave Sophie Pedersdtr was married to John Hoovel (Tollefsrud) and they were residents of Jackson County, Minnesota from 1858 on. (p. 190)

Norwegian-Minnesotan Pioneers from Sigdal, Eggedal, & Krødsherad in Buskerud County, Norway
By Scott Brunner

Sigdalslag is an association of Norwegian-Americans with roots in Sigdal, Eggedal and Krødsherad, Norway. Established in Fergus Falls in 1911, the purpose was to help preserve the heritage from those areas of Norway. But long before the Sigdalslag formation, Norwegian immigrants from this region of Norway became pioneers in Minnesota. As early as 1852 our first immigrants settled at Spring Grove, Minnesota. In the ensuing years more and more settlers arrived, following the general path of Norwegian immigration throughout Minnesota: first in the southeast corner, then spreading across southern Minnesota. In later years after statehood, settlements continued northwesterly up to the Red River Valley.

A sampling of our immigrant families who pioneered Minnesota is as follows:

Spring Grove, Houston County
1852: Haaken Narveson, Knud Knudsen Kieland, Fingal Aslesen Flaten, Truls Haga
1854: Elling Knutsen Kieland, Engebret Gundersen Benson Enderud, Ole Olsen Gulbrandsgutten, Lars Reiersen Halstenrud
1855: Even Olsen Haugen's wife Goro, Ole Christiansen Stensrud, Anders Christiansen Stensrud, John Steingrimsen Bergrud, Elling Erlandsen Snedkerpladsen, Hans Erlandsen Snedkerpladsen
1857: Elling Pedersen Engar

Black Hammer, Houston County
1854: Elling Bjertnes

Highland Prairie, Fillmore County
1857: Bjørn Gunderson

Manchester, Freeborn County
1856: Anders Libæk, Thor Anderson, Halvor Peterson Slette, Ole Kittelson, Ole Peterson Slette, Anders Evenson

Glenville, Freeborn County
1857: Torsten Eriksen Hagen, Lars Torkelsen

Emmons, Freeborn County
1857: Erik Erikson Braaten, Steingrim N. Jellum, Helge Gundersen Emmons

(Helge anglicized his farm name Ommen to Emmons, and the town of Emmons, Minnesota, is named for this family).

Wanamingo, Goodhue County
1854: Torsten A. Aabye

Rock Dell, Olmsted County
1854: Tron Christensen Sæthre, Guttorm Olson Fraagot, Beret Olsdtr Fraagot, Anne Olsdtr Fraagot
1855: Anders J. Rud, Jon Gundersen Eidal
1856: Christopher Kittilsen Vasslia
1857: Christian C. Bergan, Even Gulliksen Neggen

Now in our 10th decade, the Sigdalslag is still in business and has a membership range of 250-300 family units. A big part of the Sigdalslag's mission these days is in genealogy – helping people to find their roots in Norway. To this end, the Sigdalslag genealogist maintains a substantial library that includes books and microfilmed church records. These books are a wonderful resource for these seeking to learn about the life of their immigrant forefathers.

The Sigdalslag publishes a newsletter, *Sigdalslag Saga*, three times a year, and holds annual meetings, usually in July. Membership in Sigdalslag is available for any person who was born in Eggedal, Krødsherad, or Sigdal, Norway; any person having ancestry from these areas of Norway; spouses or family members of such a person; or anyone who has a specific interest in the activities of Sigdalslag. We encourage everyone to share the history of our Norwegian immigrants to Minnesota. Our website and personal contacts can be found at: www.sigdalslag.org

Section Two
Minnesota's Norwegian Statehood Pioneers

They lived in Minnesota when it became a state on May 11, 1858, and helped pave the way for the tens of thousands of their countrymen who built new lives in Minnesota and points west in the decades to come.

All applications were reviewed by the genealogists of participating organizations to assure Norwegian Statehood Pioneer status. Photos and biographies were submitted by these pathfinders' proud descendants.

Aaby, Aslak Anderson

Aslak Anderson Aaby and his family moved to Minnesota Territory in early 1858. Previously Aslak had lived in Wisconsin for 13 years. The Aabys settled and farmed in Section 1, Vernon Township, Dodge County.

Aslak Anderson Aaby was born November 26, 1826, in Kviteseid, Telemark, Norway, to Anders Jonsen Aaby and his wife, Ingeborg Johannesdatter Kleivstaul. Aslak's parents were very poor and, once confirmed, he was obligated to go out and find work. Kviteseid church records list the Aaby family leaving May 9, 1845. They came to America aboard the ship *Industrie*, which sailed out of Porsgrunn under Captain Böye Adzlew. The ship arrived in New York on August 12, 1845. They first lived at the Koshkonong settlement in Wisconsin.

Aslak married Aaste Nilsdatter Grovum on August 20, 1848, in Beloit, Wisconsin (the marriage is recorded in the Koshkonong Church records). Aaste was born August 9, 1823, in Nissedal, Telemark, Norway. Her parents were Nils Olavson Grovum and Jøran Aanesdatter Omland. Aaste came to America in 1843.

The following was written by their granddaughter, Aaste Jensen:

> "Aslak Aaby was a sedate and very industrious man and had a great knack for building. He acquired quite a considerable tract of land. It was said that while he had no schooling he could figure material for buildings very accurately without paper and pencil. His main interest during his life was to build on his several farms. He built five complete sets of farm buildings and never moved out of Vernon Township. He was a very persistent worker in matters pertaining to the church; he was one of the charter members of the West St. Olaf Church. Even though Aslak was a farmer and raised cattle he never learned to milk cows. Aaste, his wife, was a woman of all work. Though she never helped in the fields, she was expected to attend to the chores. To her befell the duty of milking the cows and caring for the family. She was strong and healthy, always the first one up in the morning and last to bed. She was of a very quiet and even temperament, very seldom volunteered advice but when asked, her opinions were considered sound. Aaste's health, in spite of her strong physique, did not last. She had to retire from active work early at the age of sixty. As long as I can remember she always had hired help. Besides raising their own children they often took in other children to care for, for periods of time."

In 1861 Aslak built a large frame house which was regularly used for early services of the St. Olaf Lutheran Congregation. He was elected to the building committee for the West St. Olaf Church. He continued to purchase more land and at one point held deeds to 15 forties, some of the land located in Northern Minnesota.

Aslak and Aaste were parents to nine children: Anders, Jøran, Nils, Ingeborg, John, Jul, Aane, Aslak, and Severin. Aaste Nilsdatter died August 5, 1903, and

Aslak Anderson Aaby died January 15, 1905, both in Vernon Township, Dodge County. Both are buried in the West St. Olaf Lutheran Church Cemetery.

Aaker, Knud Saavesen
Knud Saavesen Aaker was born on the Moen farm in Brunkeberg Annex, Kviteseid, Telemark, on January 27, 1797. His parents were Saave Knudsen and Aslaug Halvorsdtr. Knud married Mari Larsdtr Haegtvedt on December 5, 1818, in Norway. Her parents were Lars Knutsen and Asborg Halvorsdtr.
Knud and Mari moved with their children to Holden Township, Goodhue County, Minnesota Territory in 1857.
Mari died on July 20, 1869, and Knud died February 17, 1873. Both of them are buried in Holden Lutheran Church Cemetery.

Aaker, Lars Knudson
Lars K. Aaker was born on the Aaker *gård* (farm) in Lårdal Parish, Telemark, on September 19, 1825. He moved to Holden Township, Goodhue County, Minnesota Territory in 1857.

Anderson, Andrew
Lewis Anderson came to America in the early 1840's. He and his wife Anne settled in Dane County where their children Susan, Andrew, Nels, Ole, and Lewis were born. They relocated to Wanamingo Township, Goodhue County, Minnesota Territory in 1855, where their sons John and Cornelius were born.
Andrew was 8 years old when the family moved to Minnesota. He grew up on his father's farm in Wanamingo County. He married Amelia Olson and they had one child, Caroline, before her death in 1877. He remarried quickly, and Andrew and second wife Olina had a number of other children.
Andrew was a partner in the Martinson & Anderson hardware store in Red Wing. He was a successful businessman and a respected member of the community.

Anderson, Elling
Elling Anderson was born February 22, 1832, in Sogndal, Sogn og Fjordane, Norway, to Anders Ellingson Kvaale and his wife, Synneva Ellingsdatter Ruggeseter. In 1848 Elling came to America with his father, stepmother, and half-siblings. The family farmed in Dunkirk Township of Dane County, Wisconsin. Their original home has been preserved. Built in 1848, the Kvaale log home has been restored to its 1865 appearance, but moved to a new location. It is now featured as the Norwegian homestead at Old World Wisconsin in Eagle, Wisconsin.
Elling married Gunhild Andersdatter Aaby on October 21, 1856, in Stoughton, Wisconsin. Gunhild was born October 9, 1837, in Kviteseid, Telemark, Norway, to

parents Anders Jonsen Aaby and wife Ingeborg Johannesdatter Kleivstaul. Elling and Gunhild were the parents of eight children: Anders, John, Edwin, Susan, Isabelle, Albert, Albert, and Gunarius.

The Andersons moved to Mantorville, Dodge County, Minnesota Territory, in early 1858. Elling spent 55 years as a dealer in retail shoes and boots. *The History of Winona, Olmsted, and Dodge Counties – 1884* reports that Elling learned the shoemaker trade in Janesville, Wisconsin, and in 1855 opened his first shop in Stoughton, Wisconsin. Elling built a store and shop on Main Street in Mantorville, where he remained until October 1873. The family then moved to Kasson, where Elling ran a shoe store in partnership with his brother until 1908.

Elling was recorder for Kasson Village in 1874. The family became charter members of St. John's Lutheran Church of Kasson in 1876. Elling moved to Dodge Center, and in 1909 opened a shoe repair shop. After suffering a stroke, he moved to his son's home in Hayfield, Minnesota, where he lived for the last year and a half of his life.

Gunhild died May 27, 1877, from childbirth complications in Mantorville, Minnesota. Elling died June 15, 1911, in Hayfield, Minnesota. Both of them were laid to rest in West St. Olaf Lutheran Church Cemetery in Dodge County, Minnesota.

Andersen, Gulbrand

Gulbrand Andersen was born in 1796 in Nittedal, Norway. He was the son of Anders Larsen Moe and Ingebor Olsdtr. He married Dorthe Amundsdtr Bleikedammen on December 10, 1823. She was born in 1804 in Gjerdum, Norway. On March 30, 1853, Gulbrand and his family left Akerhus for America, landing at the port of Detroit. They made their way to Carrolton Township (Township 103) in Fillmore County where they established their farm.

Their daughter Kierstine was born February 22, 1825. She did not emigrate with the family. Gulbrand and Dorthe's other five children immigrated with them to America.

Karoline Henrikke was born March 2, 1828. She married Gulbrand (Gilbert) Olson in Minnesota and died January 18, 1910 in Albert Lea, Minnesota.

Ole Gulbrandson was born June 16, 1832. He married Martha Olson on July 19, 1861 and died in Fillmore County on November 13, 1909.

Martha was born January 9, 1837. She married Jon Ellingson in 1865. He died in 1882 in La Moure County, Dakota Territory. A second marriage to Jon Nelson is recorded that same year. Martha married for a third and final time in 1883 to Johan Nilsen Hårsaker (Horsager). Martha died June 30, 1904. Johan apparently returned to Norway, where he died on August 31, 1932 in Sør Trøndelag.

Anders "Andrew" Gulbrandson was born October 23, 1841. He married Karen Marie Danielson Stubberud in Fillmore County. He left her and moved to Ransom

County, Dakota Territory. On October 3, 1881, he married Anna G. Fetten in Otter Tail County, Minnesota. Their three children, Emelie Dorothea, Gustav Oscar, and Henry Alfred, took the surname "Anderson." Sadly, Andrew spent his last years at the Jamestown State Hospital in Jamestown, North Dakota. After he was hospitalized, Anna and the children returned to Otter Tail and Wilkin Counties in Minnesota. "A. Gulbranson" died February 12, 1926, and was buried in the Jamestown State Hospital Cemetery.

Fredericka was born June 3, 1845. She married Jens Christian Dunham on November 25, 1867. Fredericka died on January 24, 1930 in Maddock, North Dakota.

Applen, Ola Tostensen and Ambjor Olsdtr Forlie

Ola (Ole) Tostensen Appelen, son of Thorstein Olsen Appelen and Inger Olsdtr, was born September 20, 1820, in Tinn, Telemark, Norway. He was baptized November 18, 1820, and confirmed November 26, 1837, in Norway. On February 4, 1847, he married Ambjor Olsdtr Forlie, daughter of Ole Hoejesen and Gunhild Johnsdtr Forlie. Ambjor was born January 18, 1827, baptized March 21, 1827, and confirmed October 16, 1842, in Tinn. Two children were born to them in Norway: Inger, born June 16, 1846; and Ole O., born April 1, 1850.

Ola and Ambjor then decided to leave for America. He left behind his parents and nine brothers and sisters. They received their release from their church in Norway on April 30, 1851, and arrived in New York on the ship *Centurion* on August 21, 1851.

They first located in Muskego, Racine County, Wisconsin, and in 1852 they moved to Locust Lane, Howard County, Iowa, where they stayed for two years. In 1857, they settled in Bristol Grove, Bristol Township, Fillmore County, Minnesota Territory. Their farm was located in Section 12.

Nine children were added to the family in America: Nellie (1852), Tosten (1853), Susan (1857), Emma (1858), Henry (1861), Maggie (1862), Knut and Johnny (1868), and Otto (1870). Ola died in 1879 and Amjor died in 1915.

Applen, Tosten and Esther Felland

Tosten Applen was born November 7, 1853, to Ole and Ambjorg Applen on their farm in Howard County, Iowa. He moved with his parents to Fillmore County in 1857. He grew to manhood on the home farm and attended school in District 131.

He married Esther Felland on March 8, 1879. She was born in Minnesota Territory in 1857 to Torger Tollefsen and Ingeborg Felland. The house was built in 1878 and remodeled in 1907. The 240 acre farm specialized in breeding Short Horn cattle.

Tosten and Esther had 11 children: Oline (1880); Theodore (1882); Ingman (1884); Albert (1885); Arnold, (1888); Carl (1890); Mabel (1892); Ole (1894); Christina (1896); Fremont (1899); and Tudor (1903).

Tosten died February 9, 1920. Esther outlived her husband by over 25 years, passing away on September 1, 1945.

Aslakson, Peter S.

Peter S. Aslakson was born June 3, 1852, in Vinje, Telemark. He emigrated with his parents, and they claimed land in Minneola Township, Goodhue County, in 1858.

Bakke, Hallstein Torson and Kari Nilsdtr Viljugrein

Hallstein Thorsen Bakke was born in Gol, Hallingdal, Norway in 1829. In 1852 he married Kari Nilsdtr Viljugrein. On May 10, 1853, they left Hemsedal in the Hallingdal Valley and sailed to America from Bergen on the brig *Hans Holmboe*, arriving in New York on June 29th. Their infant son Ola was with them.

The family settled first in Rock Prairie (Luther Valley), Wisconsin. In 1856, they moved to Kenyon, Goodhue County, Minnesota Territory.

Their first home in Goodhue County was a log cabin. In the 1870's it was replaced by a large red brick house with a wrap-around porch that still stands today. Hallstein was a successful farmer; the Bakke farm would grow to 500 acres.

The Bakkes were charter members and one of many families who helped build the Gol Lutheran Church in Kenyon.

Hallstein and Kari had nine children. Ola, who traveled with them from Norway, died at the age of 12. Three daughters – Mary, Lena, and Greta – married and farmed near Lake Park in Becker County, Minnesota. Nils became a Kenyon merchant. Peter and Ole became doctors. Thor moved to North Dakota, and Gunhild remained in Kenyon.

Hallstein passed away in 1899 and Kari died in 1906.

Kari Nilsdtr Bakke

Berekvam, Botolv Botolvsen

Botolv Botolvsen Berekvam, son of Botolv Johannesen Berkvam and Ingeborg Torsteinsdtr Melhus, was born November 26, 1825, in Flam, Aurland *kommune* (township), Sogn og Fordance, Norway.

He immigrated to America in 1852, at the age of 27, and joined his brothers, Jens and Torstein, in the Koshkonong Settlement in Dane County, Wisconsin. All of Botolv's brothers emigrated in the years from 1845 to 1852. In 1854, Botolv and four brothers, Johannes the Elder, Johannes the Younger, Ole and Iver migrated to Black Hammer and the surrounding townships in Houston County, Minnesota Territory. Jens and Torstein remained in Wisconsin. By 1860, all of Botolv's siblings had arrived in America. Variations in the spelling of the family name included Bottolson, Bottelsen, Berkvam, Bergkvam, Bergman, and Berekvam; the most common spelling of the family name is Berquam.

Botolv was a farmer and purchased land in 1855 from the US Government for $1.25 an acre. He married Brita Amundsdtr on January 27, 1860, in his residence in Caledonia Township, Houston County. Brita was the daughter of Amund Erickson Vickesland/Holum and Anna Torsdtr Holum. She was born in Flam, Aurland *kommune*, Sogn og Fordance, Norway on May 22, 1842. Brita and Botolv had been neighbors both in Norway and in America. Of all those who came to Black Hammer and its surrounding townships from Aurland *kommune*, the Berekvam family was the largest.

In 1863, Botolv's mother Ingeborg died in Norway. Two years later, eighty-five year old Botolv Johannessen Berkvam joined his seven sons and three daughters in America. He lived with Botolv and his family on their farm in Caledonia Township until his death on May 3, 1869. He was buried May 7, 1869, in Black Hammer.

Brita and Botolv had eight children: Botoh Andrew (1860-1864); Ingeborg (b. 1863), Anna (1865-1921), Andrew Botoh (1868-1952), Karen (1870-1943), Amund (1873-1967), Martha (1875-1916), Bertha (b. 1878) and Johan (1881-1886).

Botolv died October 13, 1897, at his home in Caledonia. Funeral services were held at the Norwegian Evangelical Lutheran Church of Norwegian Ridge in Spring Grove, Minnesota. Reverend S. S. Reque officiated. Botolv had been a charter member of the congregation. He was one of the last to be buried in the old Norwegian Ridge Cemetery.

Bergetongen, Knute and Beret
In 1857 Knute and Beret Bergetongen and their two year old son, Ole, left Sigdal, Norway and boarded a ship bound for America. After seven weeks on the fierce Atlantic Ocean, they finally landed safely in New York City. Several members of the group joined a wagon train that was destined for Rochester, Minnesota

Territory. As they traveled west, Beret wrote letters back to her sister at Sigdal, Norway. Her sister Ragna saved the letters, and also gathered interesting letters from other people that she knew who were traveling in that same wagon train. Many years later she mailed the letters to a nephew in Appleton, Minnesota.

After many weeks of traveling, the wagon train finally arrived at Rochester on the 14th day of August in the year 1857. The wagon train disbursed at this point and each family went its separate way.

The Bergetongen family went west 13 miles and settled on a farm five miles south of Kasson. Beret gave birth to a baby boy five days after they arrived in Minnesota. The family drove the eighteen miles to Rochester and helped observe the statehood of Minnesota on May 11, 1858. While they lived at Kasson, the Civil War took place. They attended church services in a large log cabin building that later became the congregations of East Saint Olaf Lutheran and West Saint Olaf Lutheran churches. The log cabin still stands in the cemetery of one of these churches.

Three years before the churches were built, the Bergetongens moved to Atwater in Kandiyohi County. In 1873, Knute donated land for Bethlehem Lutheran Cemetery, a small two acre cemetery at the very east edge of what is now Atwater. Maude and Beauty, their faithful old team of horses, died during the winter of 1876 and are buried at the edge of the little cemetery, as this was the location of their farm yard at that time. Since the town of Atwater was expanding, Knute and Beret sold their farm to the Atwater Town Site in the spring of 1876.

Their last move was to Lac Qui Parle County, locating in Hantho Township. They were very much involved with the founding of The Minnesota Valley Lutheran Church. Knute died in 1897 and Beret died in 1915. They rest from their labors in the shade of this church they helped found and loved so dearly.

Knute and Beret were the parents of eight children. Their oldest daughter Elsa Marie was born in 1861.

All the members of the family have been gone for many years, but the churches they helped start in three different locations in Minnesota are still doing the wonderful task of spreading the Word of God. Blessed be the memory of these brave pioneers who helped settle early Minnesota! By learning about the past, we can appreciate what future generations have to offer this great country of ours.

Blixerud, Ole Lewison

Among the first immigrants who came from Ringerike to America were Knut O. Blixerud and his father, Ole Lewison. The family had its origins in Eggedal in Buskerud County, Norway. They had lived in Eggedal in their earlier years before moving to the Blixerud farm or *gaard* in Soknedalen. The family adopted the surname Blixerud or Blexrud from the name of the farm they had rented for many years before leaving Norway.

"In the spring of 1850, Knut, Ole's son, married Maria Mokastad. Shortly after their marriage, Knut's mother passed away. Following her death, Knut, his father Ole, and brothers and sister immigrated to Jefferson Prairie, Wisconsin, where they lived for three years before moving to Houston County, Minnesota Territory. In 1853, they settled about a mile northeast of Spring Grove on government land."

(from *The Immigration History Book of Ringerike*, 1919) Ole was 60 years old when they arrived in the USA. The 1860 census finds him, at the reported age of 70, living with his son on the Spring Grove farm. Knut's son, Hans Johann (John) was one year old at the time of the census. (Hans Johann is pictured on the far right in the back row in this 1920 church bulletin photo.) Active in the life and mission of Immanuel Lutheran Congregation were many members of the Ole L. Blixerud family. Today there are many descendants of Ole of Eggedal, Norway, scattered all over the USA.

Hans' great-grandson Christopher was the son of John H. and grandson of Henry S. Blexrud. In 2005, John and Christopher traveled to Norway and found the Blixerud *gaard* where Chris' great-great-great-grandfather, Ole Lewison, had farmed prior to coming to America. What a blessing that was!

Bøen, Ole Østensen

Ole Østensen Bøen (Ole Estensen) was born January 28, 1827, in Tinn, Telemark, Norway and his wife Astrid Jonsdtr Bøen was born April 11, 1831. They left Tinn for America in 1851, accompanied by their baby daughter Aase, Astrid's father Jon Gunleiksen Bøen, and her brother Gunleik Jonsen Bøen.

They arrived in America on October 10, 1851. Daughter Aase did not survive to reach her first birthday. Ole worked on the railroad and a son, Jon Olsen Bøen (John Estensen) was born in a railroad shanty near Galena Illinois, on February 18, 1853.

The family followed Ole's brother Torstein Østensen Bøen to Norseland in Nicollet County near St. Peter,

Minnesota. Ole and Astrid settled on what was called Norwegian Grove in Granby Township, Nicollet County.

Ole swore his support for the Constitution of the United States and the Territory of Minnesota on June 9, 1855. At the land office of Red Wing he obtained the land in Nicollet County on September 12, 1856, for $168.45. Ole and his brother Torstein were charter members of Norseland Lutheran Church at Norseland in 1858. The family survived the Sioux Uprising of 1862. The war came to their doorstep; there were deaths at Norwegian Grove, and Ole and Torstein served in the Scandinavian Guard of Nicollet County.

A son, Østen Olsen Bøen (Austin Estensen) was born in Minnesota Territory on July 24, 1856. Other children of Ole and Astrid were Nils, born August 13, 1858; Louis, born December 5, 1860; Augusta, born March 2, 1863; and Louise, born August 22, 1865. Astrid died on August 6, 1867, shortly after giving birth to a daughter and namesake Astrid, on July 25, 1867.

Ole died at Norseland on May 21, 1886.

Børtnes, Astri Herbrandsdtr

Astri Herbrandsdtr Børtnes (1792-1878) came from Nes in Buskerud, Hallingdal, Norway. Astri's son, Jens Guttormsen (born 1825) emigrated in 1846 on the ship *Columbo*, however no additional information about Jens has been found. In 1848 Astri's daughter, Gunhild Guttormsdtr, immigrated to Wisconsin on the ship *Drafna*. Gunhild married Knud Knudsen in 1851.

In 1857, Astri along with her second husband, Tosten Larsen Ursdalen Nøbben (1795-1877), and their two daughters, Gunhild Tostensdtr (Evans) and Ingeborg Tostensdtr (Gunvalson), joined the Knudson family in Amherst Township, Fillmore County, Minnesota Territory. An obituary reports that Astri and her family made the last leg of the trip on foot walking all the way from McGregor, Iowa to Amherst.

The 1857 census for Amherst Township (T-102-N & R-9-W), Fillmore County, records three generations - Astri, her daughter Gunhild and husband Knud Sævre, and their son, Mikkel - all living in the same household. The families are buried in local Lutheran cemeteries: Henrytown, Elstad, and Highland.

Brokken, Tallack W. and Aase Tarjesdatter

Tallack Brokken was born in Valle, Satterdalen, Norway, on February 3, 1828. He was confirmed in 1842. Aase Tarjesdtr was born July 20, 1828. She and Tallack were married two weeks before leaving for America on April 24, 1853. They landed in New York on August 10th.

Tallack and Aase lived at Watertown, Wisconsin, for a year before moving to Harmony Township, Fillmore County, Minnesota Territory, in the summer of

1854. They traveled in a prairie schooner drawn by oxen, and took up 120 acres in sections 21 and 22.

Tallack built a log house, and worked hard. The log house was replaced with a fine frame home, and his land holdings grew to include thousands of acres. From nothing, he became one of the wealthiest men in Fillmore County. Tallack was a leader in the community, held many public offices, and served in the state legislature in the 1876 session. Tallack helped organize Greenfield Lutheran Congregation and was one of the founders of the Harmony State Bank, where he was a stockholder and served as a director and vice president until his death on November 17, 1910.

Tallack and Aase had ten children: Their three oldest children died in infancy. Tilda, Isabelle, John, Julia, Thaddeus, Amy, and Ole survived to adulthood.

Aase died September 5, 1894. In 1895 Tallack married a widow, Mrs. Guro Bakken, and they moved to the village of Harmony where they spent the rest of their days. Guro died in 1912.

Tilda married George Wralstad and moved to Wahpeton, North Dakota. The rest of the Brokken children remained in the Fillmore county area. Isabelle and Julia married brothers – Isabelle married Aanond Harstad and Julia, his brother Samuel. John married Julia Erickson Solseth. Thaddeus married Anna Olson. Amy married Edward Haugrud, and Ole married Oline Olson.

Bronson, Ole Herbrandsen Sire and Ingebor Jorgensdtr

Ole Herbrandsen Sire Bronson was born to Herbrand Olsen Skuleslatta and Ragnild Tomasdtr Trettrudhaugen on March 4, 1822, at Aal, Norway. He came to America on the ship *Drafna* in 1849.

Ole first settled at Luther Valley, Wisconsin. There on May 7, 1853, he married Ingebor Jorgensdtr Bakkene. She had come to America a year earlier with her 4-year old daughter, Barbro.

Church and census records indicate that Ole and Ingebor were in Iowa when they had their first child, Herbrand, on February 3, 1854. They moved to

Seated: Mother Ingebor, daughter Ingebor, Herbrand, Carl, Ragnild, and father Ole. Standing: Ole, Jorgen and Knu'

Minnesota Territory and settled on land in Wheeling Township, Rice County, near the town of Nerstrand before their second child, Jorgen, was born. He arrived on April 14, 1855, and was baptized on July 1 at Holden Church. Ole and Ingebor had six more children, all born in Rice County: Knute, born September 2, 1856; Ragnild, December 16, 1857; Karine, April 30, 1859; Ole, May 19, 1862; Carl, March 19, 1865; and Ingebor, born September 9, 1866.

Ole and Ingebor spent the rest of their days on their Wheeling Township farm. He died December 2, 1902, and Ingeborg died May 5, 1879. They are buried in Valley Grove Church Cemetery in Rice County.

Brynsaas, Gudbrand Pedersen and Anne Maria Pedersdtr

Gudbrand Pedersen Brynsaas was born April 17, 1816, on the Dvergsten farm in Hadeland, Norway. He was the son of Peder Carstensen and Mari Gudbrandsdtr. He married Anne Marie Pedersdtr on December 29, 1840. She was the daughter of Peder Ellingsen and Marthe Isaksdtr.

In April of 1854 they immigrated to America from the port of Christiania on the ship *Christina* with their children Peter, Martha, and Johanna (Hanna). Their son Martin was born during the voyage. After 12 weeks at sea, they landed in Quebec. From there they traveled by train to Whitewater, Wisconsin. Gulbrand had two half-brothers, Kristin and Torger, who lived there. They had emigrated from Norway 1-2 years earlier.

In 1856, Gulbrand acquired a team of horses and a lumber wagon from Knute Nelson, a prominent citizen who would later become a US senator for the state of Wisconsin. With a number of families, Gulbrand and his family moved to Granby Township, Nicollet County, Minnesota Territory. Gulbrand claimed 160 acres and immediately built a log house with a sod roof. This was later replaced with a roomy frame home. Two daughters were born after they settled in Minnesota: Pauline and Maria.

Anna and daughter Maria died in 1860. Gulbrand, now using the Americanized name Gilbert Peterson, remarried in 1862 to Gunild (Julia) Knutsdtr Reierson. Gunild brought her 4 children into the family: Emile, Knute, Henry, and Helen. Gilbert and Gunild had two more daughters, Annie and Mary.

Gilbert died on April 17, 1901.

Peter G. Peterson, Gilbert's oldest, enlisted in the army in 1861 and served in Company B, 4th Minnesota Infantry Regiment. In 1863, he re-enlisted for two more years of service. In 1868, Peter G. married Carrie Christopherson. They had seven children: Anna, Theodore, Clara, Emma, Alfred, Alice and Oscar.

The original Pederson homestead has remained in the family since 1856. Gudbrand's granddaughter Alice Peterson and her husband Gottfried Nelson bought the farm from Gudbrand's son Peter. The Nelsons' son Thorild and his wife Ardith Wentzel purchased the original homestead in 1965. Their son Karlen and his wife Michelle Metzger purchased the farm site from Thorild and Ardith in 2002, and are the fifth generation to raise their children there.

Bukkøy, Jørgen Jonsson

Jørund Jonsson Bukkøy was born in 1787 on the Roholt farm in Vraadal, Telemark. He was the son of Leiv Jonsson Roholt and Anne Jørundsdtr Øy. He married Gro Jørundsdtr Krintolen in 1819. They lived on the Krintolen farm until about 1825 when they moved to Bukkøy. They had 8 children together. Gro died in 1852 and in 1853 Jorgen left for America with his daughter Else.

Jorgen settled in Houston County, Minnesota Territory. At various times he farmed in Mound Prairie, Sheldon and Money Creek Townships. He married a second time to Tone Olsdotter Vraa, a widow with 4 children from Vrådal, who had come to the US in 1851. They had one daughter, Cornelia, baptized Gunild in 1857, who later became Mrs. Charles Solberg. Jorgen was a member of the Houston Norwegian Evangelical Lutheran Church (Stone Church) and his death is recorded in their records as the 19th of March, 1883. Jorgen is listed as George Johnson and J. J. Bukoi in some records. In the censuses he consistently gives his age as 10 years younger than he was. Jørgen's obituary states his age as 88, but Jorgen was actually 96 years old when he died.

Jorgen and Gro had 8 children: Anne (1819-1903) and her husband Gjermund Jonsson Juve emigrated in 1858. They started out in Houston County, moved to Trempealeau County, Wisconsin, and finally settled in Jackson County, Minnesota. The family took the surname Johnson. They had 6 children.

Aleth (1821-1891) and her husband Halvor Halvorson Eikhom emigrated in 1867. They spent about a year in Houston County and then moved to West Heron Lake Township in Jackson County. The family took the surname Halvorson. They had 8 children.

Salve & Sigrid (Bukkøy) Schibsted

Sigrid (1835-1932) immigrated to Houston County in 1858 and married Salve E. Schibsted. They left Houston in 1879, took a farm in Viding Township in Clay County, Minnesota, and later moved to Perley in Norman County. They had 9 children.

Jon (1824-1872) and his wife Anne Knutsdtr emigrated in 1857. They started out in Houston County and then moved to Weimer Township in Jackson County about 1868. The family took the surname Buckeye. They had 9 children.

Jorgen (1826-1919) emigrated between 1854 and 1857. He served as a Union soldier in the Civil War. He started out in Houston County and moved to Jackson County about 1869. He never married. Jorgen appears in records as George Johnson or George J. Buckeye.

Abraham (1830-1908) also emigrated between 1854 and 1857 and served as a Union soldier in the Civil War. He started out in Houston County and moved to Jackson County about 1869. He and his wife Ragnhild Olsdotter Timrud had 5 children. Their children used the names Johnson and Buckeye.

Susanne (1832-1880) and her husband Anders Nielsen Kiil emigrated in 1866. They started out in Houston County but soon moved to Weimer Township in Jackson County. The family took the name Nelson. They had 8 children.

Else (1838-1853?) left Vraadal with her father in 1853. It is believed she died at sea.

Ellis, John and Ingeborg Torgrimsdtr

Johannes Ellefson Sauerlie was born April 25, 1821, in Heddal, Telemark. His parents were Ellef Stenerson Sauerlie and Guri Svenungsdtr Bamle. Johannes immigrated to the Muskego Settlement in Wisconsin in 1847.

Ingeborg Torgrimsdtr Moen was also born in Heddal on May 2, 1820, to Torgrim and Thone Moen. She emigrated in 1847. Johannes and Ingeborg were married and living in Vernon Township, Waukesha County, Wisconsin, at the time of the 1850 Census. They are listed as John and Ingeborg Ellefson. Their oldest children, Yank, Taurine (Tone), and Johanna were born in Wisconsin. In 1852, they moved to Jefferson Prairie, Iowa, where twins Edwin and Eldraine were born.

Ole, Julia, Guri and Anna were all born in Minnesota Territory after the family moved to Fillmore County. Yank, Johanna, Eldraine and Guri died as infants or young children.

"John Ellis" and his family were among the first settlers in Harmony Township in 1854 and he received a land patent for 160 acres in section 23 on April 2, 1857. "Johannes Elefson Sauerlie" was a charter member of Greenfield Lutheran Church in Harmony. He died August 6, 1897 on his farm in Harmony and Ingeborg died on November 19, 1900. Both are buried in Greenfield Lutheran Church Cemetery.

Emmons, Henry Gundersen and Kjersti Larsdtr

Helge Gundersen was born October 16, 1828, in Eggedal, Buskerud County, Norway. His parents were Gunder Sorensen and Kristi Helgesdtr.

In 1850, at the age of 22, Henry (Helge) Gundersen Emmons left Eggedal and crossed the Atlantic on a voyage that took thirteen weeks. His destination was Jefferson Prairie, Wisconsin.

Three years after Henry left Norway, in 1853, Henry's future bride, 18 year old Kjersti (Christi) Larson left Hadeland, Norway, and arrived at Jefferson Prairie.

She was the daughter of Lars Tostensen and Kjersti Mikkelsdtr and was born July 16, 1835.

Henry and Kjersti were married on April 19, 1854, in Clinton Township, Rock County, Wisconsin. Having heard about the opportunities in Minnesota Territory, the couple left Wisconsin in 1856 with their little son, George, who had been born March 28, 1855. All of their belongings were loaded into a wagon drawn by oxen.

After six weeks of driving and camping out nights, they arrived in Nunda Township, Freeborn County. Here Henry acquired 160 acres by pre-emption. They were only the second family to settle in Nunda Township. Their son Lewis, born December 30, 1856, was the first white child born in the township and the second white child born in Freeborn County. The farm where Henry and Kjersti lived eventually became the village of Emmons.

Henry died October 2, 1909, just a few weeks before his 81st birthday. Kjersti died less than five months later, on February 21, 1910. They are buried in Oak Lawn Cemetery, a mile west of the village that bears their name.

Engen, Ole Nilson and Margit Pedersdtr Rotneim

Ole Nilson Engen was born October 14, 1806. He was the son of Nils Myre and Sigri Brenna. Margit Pedersdtr Rotneim was born June 14, 1812, and was the daughter of Peder and Sara Sarabyne Rotneim. Ole and Margit had ten children: Nils, Sigri, Peder, Ole Oleson, Kjerste, Arne, Sarah, Helge, Ole, and Margit.

The family left Nes, Hallingdal in April of 1857 and came to America on the boat *Familien* from Drammen. Their youngest child, Margit, was just 6 months old. They landed in Quebec in late May and traveled by boat to Montreal and across the Great Lakes, took a train to Prairie du Chien and another boat to Brownsville, Minnesota Territory. They were set ashore with all their belongings, not knowing exactly where to go, with the river on one side and hills and woods on the other. They left their belongings on the shore and started west on foot. They found their way to Caledonia, a distance of about 15 miles. Farmers they met on the road agreed to take their belongings to Spring Grove, and Iver Kinneberg from Wilmington offered them a place to spend their first night in Minnesota Territory. The next morning Gunvald Tyrebakken came with oxen and brought them to his home outside Spring Grove.

Ole and Margit homesteaded and lived out their lives in Wilmington Township, Houston County. Ole died October 11, 1891 and Margit died June 6, 1894. They are buried in Old Wilmington Lutheran Cemetery.

Enger, Elling Peterson Sr.

Back: Hjalmer, Peter, Elling, Jr., Edward, Aase Sofie
Front: Elling Sr., Lina, Anna Lee Ellingsdtr, Ingeri Ostensdtr (Anna's mother)

Photo taken at Hanley Falls, Yellow Medicine County, c. 1890

Elling Pedersen Enger was born September 26, 1836, on the Enger farm in Eggedal, Buskerud County, Norway. His parents were Peder Ellingsen Enger and Aase Ellevsdtr Enger Oygarden. Elling was the first member of his family to come to America. He arrived in Houston County in 1854. His parents and siblings joined him in 1861.

In 1865, he married Anne Lee Ellingsdtr Bergsundeie. She was born on the Bergsund farm in Ringerike on May 21, 1845, the daughter of Elling Fredrikssen Ringerud and Ingrid Ostensdtr. Anne and her widowed mother came to America in 1861.

The family relocated to Yellow Medicine County, where Elling died on May 31, 1900 at Hanley Falls. Anne died on August 1, 1928 in Granite Falls.

Erickson, Halvor and Kari Overland

Halvor Erickson, the sixth child of Erick and Ingeborg (Ulsness) Overland, was born October 27, 1829, near Seljord, Telemark, Norway. He came to America when he was 21 years old and joined his old neighbors at the Skoponong parish settlement in Wisconsin. He joined the Overland party that relocated to Iowa in 1853. Halvor and Ole Overland explored land in Minnesota Territory, wintered in Calmar, Iowa, and in 1854 became the first settlers in Norway Township, Fillmore County.

Kari Overland and Halvor Erickson were the first couple to be married in the Highland Prairie Settlement. The marriage took place in Decorah, Iowa, with

Pastor William Painter officiating. They homesteaded on the farm directly north of the Highland Prairie Lutheran Church, where they lived out their lives. Halvor died May 3, 1904, and Kari on November 20, 1914.

Nine children were born to Halvor and Kari: Erik, who died young; Bella, who married Teman Evenson and had seven children; John, who married Thea Overland and had three children before he died, then Thea married John's brother Steinar and they had seven more children; Tilla married Lars Jensen and had twelve children; Lena married Ole Benson and had three children; Hans died in infancy; Ole married Annette Ness and had two children, remarried after her death and he and Adelle Anderson had two more children; and Carl, who married Tina Ukkestad and had ten children.

Halvor & Kari with Carl, Ole & Lena

Gaasedelen, Ole Knudsen

At the turn of the 19th century, the first husband of Ragndi Nilsdtr Wangensteen was involved in a property dispute with a neighbor, Ove Flaten. Her husband stabbed and killed the neighbor. Nearby military personnel knew Ove's killer because he was also in the military, and they alerted the authorities. He was arrested, tried, and sentenced to death. The *bygeboker* call him Torkel Kvaale. He evidently lived on the Gaasedelen farm since he was also known by the name Gaasedelen.

A neighbor farmer named Knud Knudsen Leirol married the widowed Ragndi Wangensteen in 1805. Ole Knudsen was born June 30, 1827. He had eight other siblings: Ingebjorg, Knut, Nils, Endre, Jon, Lars, Boye, and Ove. They were all born on the Gaasedelen farm.

In 1850, Ole Knudsen Gaasedelen signed out of the Vang, Valdres parish with a large group of his neighbors. Traveling as a group likely assured that there would be enough food and goods for everyone during the multi-month ocean crossing. Sharing the struggles and working together increased the group's chances for success when they establishing their new homes in America. Many of the same names that appeared in the minister's book in Vang can also be found on the passenger list for the brig *Ørnen* that sailed from Bergen, captained by Nicolai Jahn.

The ship arrived in New York on July 12, 1850. Ole eventually made his way to Minnesota Territory, where he settled with other Valdrisers in Holden Township. They named their Norwegian Lutheran congregation Vang Church, after their home in Norway. This still active church is in rural Kenyon, Minnesota. The Ellingboe family, which is well represented in the Vang Church Cemetery, also appeared on the ship's logs of the Brig Ørnen.

Ole endured the rigorous life of a pioneer farmer, and worked his homestead for the rest of his life. On June 13, 1861, he married Karen Olsdtr Kvam. She was born on September 15, 1836, in Vang. Ole and Karen lost three infants and one son, Ole, at the age of 30. Five children survived to live normal life spans: Rangdi (born in 1862); Sara/Sissel (1865); Knut (1867), the oldest son who took over the farm; Nils (1871), who moved to Minneapolis; and Peder Edward "Pete" (1876), who moved to California.

Karen died on November 11, 1877. Ole lived another 13 years, and died at the age of 62 on January 16, 1890. The Gaasedelens are buried in the Vang Lutheran Church Cemetery.

Interestingly, there is a connection between the Gaasedelen name and the Vang Rune Stone. According to Harald Boe, a resident of Vang in Valdres, the Vang Stone was discovered on or near the Gaasedelen farm. The runic writing along the side of the stone says "Gaas's sons raised this stone after Gunnar their brother's son." The more ancient form of the Gaasedelen name is "Gaasdeilde." Both names mean "Gaas's part or division." This probably means Gaas's part of another piece of property, possibly the North Boe farm. The Vang Stone dates to the time when Norway converted to Christianity 1,000 years ago, and is a notable part of Norwegian history and Gaasedelen family lore. This family/farm name is no longer found in Norway. By the early 20th Century, the farm name had been changed to Steinvoll (stony field).

Garnaas, Bjorn Olesen Sata and Sidsel Nilsdtr Nubgaard

Bjorn Olesen was born November 25, 1798, on the Sata farm in Hallingdal, Norway. Sidsel Nilsdtr Nubgaard was born March 13, 1803, on the Nubgaarden farm in Hallingdal. The couple was married on April 27, 1825, at Aal in Buskerud County.

The family moved to the Garnaas farm, located high above the Hallingdal Valley in Nes in 1833. In 1853, Bjorn, then fifty-five years old, and Sidsel, age fifty, decided to emigrate to America with their four sons and three daughters: Ole, Nils, Hans, Mari, Engebret, Guri and Kari. They left Drammen and entered the U.S. through the port of New York, going on to Milwaukee and Luther Valley, Wisconsin.

The family likely spent the winter with friends who had emigrated earlier. In the spring, Bjorn and his sons Ole and Nels walked across Wisconsin and into Iowa.

They then went north into Minnesota Territory, which was just being surveyed. Bjorn and his sons came to what is now Newburg Township in Fillmore County and found land with good sources of water. They went to the land office in Brownsville and filed their claim on September 7, 1854. The patent was issued on October 15, 1855, to Bear Oleson (another name used by Bjorn Garnaas).

The History of Garness Trinity Congregation reports that "They brought with them a strong heritage in the Lutheran Church in Norway. The Bible, hymnbook, and catechism used in their homes were a source of comfort and inspiration as the early settlers experienced the hardships and struggles of pioneer life." Because there was no church building, it was necessary to meet in homes and often the meetings took place in the home of Bjorn Garnaas. Bjorn died on July 25, 1868 on his farm outside Mabel, Minnesota. Sidsel died on March 10, 1883.

Ole B. Garnaas purchased his father Bjorn's farm and donated the land on which the Garness Trinity Lutheran Church was built. He also donated the land for the church cemetery where Bjorn and Sidsel, along with many of their descendants, were laid to rest.

Bjorn is the Norwegian word for bear, and so Bearson is an anglicized version of the patronymic Bjornson. One of the members of the family that chose to use the anglicized surname was Bjorn's son Engebret (1839-1915). He married Gunhild Syversdtr Krosshaug (1844-1910). After 40 years of married life, they sold their farm near Mabel and homesteaded in Kermott, North Dakota, where they are buried. It is thought that the reason they moved at such an advanced age was to help ease the pain of losing six children in fifteen years.

Garvik, Erik Knudson

Erik Knudson Garvik was born February 14, 1810, in Vestre Slidre, Valdres, Oppland *fylke* (county), Norway, to parents Knud Einarson Robøle and wife Marit Eriksdatter. He married Barbro Torgersdatter Faar on October 12, 1834. Barbro was born August 31, 1812, in Vestre Slidre, Valdres, Oppland, Norway, to parents Torger Erikson Faar and wife Gietru Nilsdatter Kaarstad. After marriage the family farmed at a couple places in Vestre Slidre, but came to America in 1851. They took the ship *Emanuel* which departed from Bergen, Norway. They first lived at the Koshkonong settlement in Wisconsin. Here their two youngest children were born. Erik and Barbro were parents of eight children: Marit, Knut, Torger, Erick, Marit, Nils, Gjertine, Ingebret.

Erik brought his family to Minnesota Territory in 1857. He purchased land and farmed in Section 2, Vernon Township, Dodge County. He was one of the organizers of St. Olaf Church in 1863, and signed its Articles of Incorporation as 'Erik Knudsen Garvig'. The church was built on land Erik gave the congregation for that purpose. The children sold the balance of the farmland, which was just south of the church, about 1885 to Hellek Aakre.

Erik died July 2, 1880, in Dodge County. Barbro died December 1, 1883. Both are buried at West St. Olaf Lutheran Church Cemetery. Their graves lie just south of the church on the land Erik amd Barbro once owned. The surname on their tombstone is "Knudson"; however the inscribed birth and death dates are grossly in error.

Gilbertson, Gilbert & Beret Ellingsdtr

Gilbert and Berit Gilbertson

Gulbrand Gulbrandsen (Gilbert Gilbertson) was born October 23, 1842, on one of the Thomle farms in Nordre Land, Oppland County, Norway. He came to America with his parents, Gulbrand Gulbrandsen and Astri Andersdtr Kassenborg in 1850. The family settled in Yucatan Township, Houston County, in 1853. He chose to use Gilbertson as his surname in America.

Gilbert married Mary Thorvildsdtr Kilane on March 10, 1862, in the Houston Church parsonage which was located in Fillmore County. Mary died July 13, 1863, at the age of 19 years. She is buried in the Houston Stone Church cemetery, rural Houston County, beside her mother-in-law, Astri Andersdtr Kassenborg.

Gilbert enlisted in the Union Army on March 20, 1865, in Rochester, Minnesota. He served as a private in Company F of the First Minnesota Volunteer Infantry. He was hospitalized at Burkeville, Virginia, approximately 45 miles from Appomattox when General Lee surrendered to General Grant there. The official records do not list him as wounded in action, so it can be surmised that he had an ailment of some sort. He was mustered out on July 28, 1865, from Mower Army Hospital, Philadelphia, Pennsylvania.

On March 9, 1866, Gilbert married Berit Ellingsdtr Bergsundeie, also at the church parsonage in Fillmore County. She was born in Aadalen, Ringerike, Buskerud County, Norway. Her parents were Elling Fredrikssen Ringerud and Ingeri Østensdtr. Elling drowned in the flood of 1860, and Berit came to America with her mother and sister in 1861.

Four of Gilbert and Berit's children were born in Houston County: Martin, Gilbert Elias, Inger Augusta and Lena.

In 1876 Gilbert moved his family to Wood Lake Township in the Yellow Medicine River Valley, Yellow Medicine County, northeast of Hanley Falls, Minnesota. Two more daughters were born: Laura Emilie (August 8 1882-June 18 1883) and Laura Galine (January 2 1884-September 27 1884) Both are buried in the Hanley Falls West Cemetery.

A newspaper clipping from the Granite Falls Tribune of September 7, 1897, tells a harrowing story:

> G.E. Gilbertson, living near Hanley, while driving home Wednesday night met with an experience he will not soon forget. As he drew near the Great Northern trestle bridge just out of town, two men who had been hiding, jumped into the road and called him to stop and at the same time made a grab for the horses' heads with the intention of stopping the rig, but quick as a flash Mr. Gilbertson whipped up the horses throwing the would-be road agents to the ground. Seeing that they were foiled in their plans they pulled out their revolvers and sent several bullets after the buggy, three of which went through the top, which was lowered, one of them passing through Mr. Gilbertson's hat in its flight. It so happened that the driver was sitiing in the center of the seat and the bullets passed on both sides of him.

It appears that Gilbert was not only resourceful but probably a little lucky as well! Gilbert died September 25, 1901, and Berit followed on December 11, 1904. Both are buried in the Hanley Falls East Cemetery.

Gilbert's son Martin was born in 1866. He married Hannah Gunderson and had two daughters who survived to adulthood. After Hannah's death, Martin married Helen Wolstad. Martin and Helen added two more children to the family.

Gilbert Elias, born in 1869, and his wife Ella Johnson had nine children.

Inger Augusta, born in 1873, married Ole Hardy and had three children.

Lena was born in 1873. She died at age 25, unmarried.

Grasdalen, Lars Olson and Ragnhild Moen

Lars Olson Grasdalen was born September 14, 1823, on Nappegaard (gaard means farm), Grasdalen, in Tinn, Telemark. His father was Ole Olsen Grasdalen.

Lars married Anne Høljesdtr on November 7, 1845. She was born on the Vastvedt farm in 1815, the daughter of Hølje Halvorsen. The two of them were living on Nappegaarden in Hovind parish at the time of their wedding. Lars

Photo of Lars and Ragnhild

and Anne had two children: Ingeborg, born June 4, 1847; and Ole, born December 14, 1849.

The family emigrated from Grasdalen (Gras valley) in 1852 and settled near Muskego, Wisconsin. Anna and the two children died during the Cholera Epidemic.

Lars remarried. Ragnhild Gisledtr Moen was born in Sigdal, Norway on April 6, 1834, to Gislie Moen and his wife Jåråm Ellingson. In 1856 Lars and Ragnhild moved to Manchester, Freeborn County, Minnesota Territory. Together they had 9 children.

Lars died April 16, 1897 and Ragnhild died on March 17, 1909.

Grønsten, Hans Johnsen & Kari Kjerstine Eich

Hans Johnsen was born on the Grønsten farm in Holla, Telemark, Norway, on May 26, 1819. He was baptized on May 30th in Holden Church. He married Karen Kjerstine Eich on September 8, 1842. She was born on September 19, 1816. They made their home on Grønsten, where along with farming, Hans was a successful spinning wheel maker. Their son John was born in 1842, and daughter Anne Marie and a twin sister (who did not survive) was born three years later.

Hans, Kari, and their two children left Norway for America on May 17, 1846, sailing first to Le Havre, France. They crossed the Atlantic on the sailing ship *Bowditch*, landing in New York on August 8. They made their way to Wisconsin and settled in Whitewater, where their daughter Anne Marie died during an epidemic. Two sons, James and Nels, were born in Wisconsin.

In 1856 the family moved to Canisteo Township, Dodge County, Minnesota Territory. Their daughter Ingeborg was born in their log cabin in 1858.

Church services were often held in their home. Hans not only developed his farm from the wilderness, he provided essential blacksmithing and carpentry to the community. He was especially interested in education and schools.

After 5 years, Hans built a bigger log home and increased his holdings to 360 acres. He was part of the effort that erected East St. Olaf church, and built the church's pews.

In 1881, Nels and his three sons resettled in Dakota Territory. After Kari's death, Hans remarried and had two more children: Inga Kinstad Groves and Johnny. Their mother died when they were very young, and Inga was adopted by the Kinstad family.

Hans spent his later years living with his children. He died in 1909 at his son Jens' home in Colorado.

Grover, Tarje Aslaksen and Geline Gulbrandsdtr Kassenborg

Aslak Tarjeisen died in February of 1846, and in May of the same year his widow Kristi Olavsdtr Lien (1796-1867) and her children Ole (1823-1891), Tarje (1830-

1895), Tone (1827-1889) and Aase (1833-1910) emigrated from the Graver farm in Fyresdal, Telemark. The *Flyvende Fisk* brought them to Le Havre, France, where they boarded a cotton packet ship, the *Ancona*, bound for New Orleans. They arrived in Louisiana on November 3rd.

Kristi and her children then traveled up the Mississippi. Ole and Tarje found day labor when the riverboat stopped to load and unload. More than once, they found themselves working beside slaves on the levees. Tarje's recollections of how the slaves were treated, and their gracious kindness to the two young Norwegian boys, have been passed down through the generations.

The journey continued up the Illinois River to La Salle, and the family rested at Elling Eielson's meeting house in the Fox River Settlement. They arrived at Kristi's brother Aslak Lee's farm in Deerfield Township, Dane County, Wisconsin, in December, 1846. Kristi and her children spent the next half dozen years in the Koshkonong Settlement. In the 1850 Wisconsin census, the family is listed under the surname "Aslackson."

Tarje, his brother, mother and younger sister moved to Houston County, Minnesota Territory, about 1853. He is listed in an early county history as clerk of the Stone Church. The 1857 Territorial Census lists him as a merchant and hotel manager in Houston. "Terry Grover" married Geline Gilbertson on June 6, 1857. She was born in Land *kommune*, Oppland County, Norway, and came to America in 1850 with her parents Gulbrand Gulbrandsen and Astri Andersdtr, and younger brothers Andreas and Gulbrand.

Back: Gustav, Edward, Alexander, Christian; Front: Elise, Tarje holding Tilde, Geline holding Otto, and Mary   photo about 1880

Tarje and Geline began farming in earnest shortly thereafter, and built a home on the Sheldon Township farm for which Tarje received a land patent in 1857. Tarje and Geline's children Gustav, Alexander, Edward, Christian, Mary and Elise were born in Houston County.

In 1874 Tarje moved his family to Moland Township, Clay County. Two more children, Tilde and Otto, were born. Tarje was active in church and community affairs. Our Saviour's (Concordia) Congregation held its first service in the Grover living room on November 12, 1874. Tarje was an enumerator for the 1880, 1885, and 1890 censuses and was involved in organizing and later served on the Clay County Commission. He was active in Republican politics throughout his life.

Gus and Edward never married. Alex married Pauline Kroshus. Christian married Elsie Bergland and, upon her death, Tone Dole. Elise married Louis Olson of Lake Park, Minnesota. Tilde married Andrew Sandwick and relocated to Oregon, where they were eventually joined by Otto and his wife Hulda Niklasen. Mary was struck by paralysis in her late teens and never married.

Tarje died March 14, 1895 and Geline died May 23, 1909. They are buried in Concordia Lutheran Cemetery, rural Glyndon, Minnesota.

Gubberud, Gulbrand

Gulbrand Andersen Gubberud was born on December 5, 1827 in Hedalen, Valdres, Norway. He was the son of Anders Øestensen and Kjersti Gudbrandsdtr, who bought the Gubberud farm in Bagn parish in 1844. Gulbrand was the first to come to America in 1852. He landed in Quebec and made his way to Dane County, Wisconsin, and then La Crosse, Wisconsin, where he saved enough money to arrange for other of his siblings to make the trip. His brother Øesten arrived the following year.

In 1854, Gulbrand and Øesten pre-empted claims in Wilmington Township, Houston County in the settlement known as "Norwegian Ridge." The rest of the Gubberud family made the trip from Norway to America in 1854, and Anders claimed acreage right next to Gulbrand's.

The young girl who became his wife, Malene Skiftun, was born November 8, 1838 in Hjelmeland, Stavanger, Norway. She came to America in 1850 with her parents, Ole Gudmundsen and Sissela Johnsdtr Skiftun. Her parents were struck down by cholera on the trip from Quebec to Wisconsin, and Malene was raised by her older sisters. Because there was no pastor in Spring Grove yet, she and Gulbrand traveled to LaCrosse, Wisconsin, for their marriage on August 1, 1856.

Gulbrand and Malene had fifteen children: Christine was born in 1857. She was followed by Inger, Anders, Gustav, Johan, Gunhild, Sorine, Elias, Ole, Thina, Anna Julia, Sophia, Edwin, and Sigrid. Anna Josephine, the youngest, was born in 1885.

Gulbrand died on March 18, 1898 in Spring Grove. His wife Malene died on October 9, 1931, at the home of her daughter Anna Rustad in Kindred, North Dakota.

Gulbrandsen, Ole and Birgit Reiersdtr

Ole Gulbrandson was born on January 22, 1831, in Nes, Hallingdal, Norway. His parents were Gulbrand Olsen and Ragnhild Gulbrandsdtr Hilde. He arrived in the United States on June 30, 1852 on the bark *Richard Cobden.* He married Birgit Reiersdtr in Wisconsin. She was born in Rollag Parish, Numedal, on June 3, 1836, the daughter of Reier Reiersen and Aslaug Simonsdtr. Their son, Gilbert, was born December 20, 1855, in Wisconsin.

In the Territorial Census of 1857, Ole, Betsey, and Gilbert Gilbertson were living in Rock Dell Township, Olmsted County, Minnesota Territory. Their first home was a room dug into a hillside, covered with timbers. The closest market was fifty miles away on the Mississippi River at Winona. The difficult journey took 4-5 days, and there were steep hills and streams to be crossed.

Ole and Birgit's son Elmer died in 1911 and their grandson Harold came to live with them. Harold was required to work hard, with a full slate of chores before and after school. He recalled two incidents:

Ole often enjoyed a cup or two of good cheer. On one occasion, he was "relaxing" on the front porch when he saw a neighbor driving past with his team of horses. Ole wanted to give him a friendly wave; he stood up and removed his cap and began waving it in the air. Unfortunately, Ole waved so vigorously that he lost his balance and fell off the porch! He landed in a heap on the ground. Harold began laughing; Ole did not find the situation quite so funny, and began scolding the young boy. Berit rescued her grandson and escorted him into the house, leaving Ole to regain his dignity without an audience.

Ole was returning from a neighbor in his wagon when his team was spooked and began to run. Ole was unable to control them, and eventually the wagon tipped over, trapping him underneath. The team ran to the barn, which alerted Harold that something had happened. He began searching and found the overturned wagon. He saw smoke rising through the floorboards and upon further investigation found Ole, still trapped underneath, smoking his pipe. Harold could not move the wagon alone, so he went for help. The wagon was set aright and Ole was freed, none the worse for the accident.

Several photos of Ole in his later years show a little man with a round face and a full head of hair reaching past his ears. He was a mischievous character who did not take life too seriously.

Birgit died December 16, 1920, and Ole passed away on April 3, 1923. They are buried in the East St. Olaf Lutheran Church Cemetery.

Gullickson, John and Marit

John Gullickson was born April 14, 1813, in Valdres, Norway. His wife Marit (Margaret) Knudsdtr was born in Hallingdal in 1814. They left Norway with their sons John and Knud from the port of Christiania on the ship *Incognito* and arrived in New York on August 30, 1851. Their first home was in Rock County, Wisconsin. In 1854, they made the three week journey by ox-driven covered wagon to Amherst Township, Fillmore County, Minnesota Territory. Two more children, Gilbert (1854-1927); and Anna, Mrs. Christian Dunham, (1857-1927), were born in Minnesota Territory.

Marit died on March 3, 1891, and is buried in Ellestad Lutheran Church Cemetery. John died in 1894.

Gulmon, Egel E. and Aaste Tovsdtr

Egel E Gulmon was born November 7, 1809, in Manheim, Seljord, Telemark. He was the son of Egel Eivindson Manheim and Ragnhild Knudsdtr Kvanbekk. He married Aaste Tovsdtr in Seljord on November 23, 1841. Their children Egil G., Thomas, Ragnild, Alice, and Gunnild were born in Norway.

Egel brought his family to America on the ship *Vesta* in 1851. They signed out of the parish on June 16, sailed from Langesund on July 5, and arrived in New York on September 2. The Gulmons first settled in Dane County, Wisconsin where their son Even was born. In 1855, Egel joined a group that relocated to "Greenfield Center," Harmony Township in Fillmore County, Minnesota Territory. Daughter Sarah was born there in 1856. Egel and Aaste lived the rest of their lives on their farm in Harmony. Egel died on August 13, 1880, and his wife Aaste died October 2, 1891.

Gulmon, Egil G. and Anne Lawrence

Egil G. Gulmon was born on October 13, 1841 on Leifjel Mountain, Manheim farm, Seljord, Telemark. He came to America with his parents, Egel and Aaste Gulmon, and siblings in 1851 and moved with them to Minnesota Territory in 1855. He married a young widow named Anne Lawrence on May 7, 1870.

Anne was born on September 28, 1846, in Telemark. Her father, Aslak Lavrantson, brought his wife, Aase Torgrimsdtr Hasleberg and their children to America from Seljord about 1850. After spending a few years in Wisconsin, the Lawrence family moved to Fillmore County, Minnesota Territory, in 1856.

In June of 1870, Egil and Anne were the first settlers in Norman Township, Yellow Medicine County. Later they migrated to Barnes County, North Dakota where Egil died on April 22, 1905. Anne died June 4, 1927 at Sanborn, North Dakota.

Gunderson, Bjorn & Helge Christophersdtr

Bjorn Gunderson (1827-1912) emigrated from the Enderud farm in Krødsherad, Buskerud, Norway with his parents, Gunder Bjørnsen & Kari Ingebrethsdtr, and siblings, Engebrit and Sigrid, on the ship *Emilie* in 1842. The family made their first home in the Muskego Settlement in Wisconsin. In 1850, they moved to Washington Prairie, Winnishiek County, Iowa.

Helge Christophersdtr (1829-1910) was the daughter of Kristoffer Olsen Kopseng and Gunhild Larsdtr Kodalen. She emigrated on her own from the Kopseng farm in Buskerud in 1849 on the ship *Drafna*. She and Bjorn were married April 17, 1852. Their first two children, Kari and Engebrit, were born in Iowa; their son Gunder was born on their homestead outside Peterson in Fillmore County, Minnesota Territory, in 1857.

"Bjorgov Gunderson" received a land patent for their farm on April 2, 1857. Beginning with the 1857 Territorial Census, Bjorn is listed as Ben Benson and Helge is listed variously as Helge, Helen, or Harriet. According to the 1880 Census, their other children were Gunhild, Christopher, Knut, twins Bernt and Ole, Anne Maria, Helen, and Sophia. The family at various times also used the surnames Gunderson, Endru, and Enderud. "Bjorn and Helge Endru" are listed as members of Highland Prairie Church on the pioneer stone in the park surrounding the church in rural Peterson, Minnesota.

Ben was not only a successful farmer, but also a sought after Hardanger fiddler. He passed along his love of music, and his considerable talent, to many of his children and grandchildren.

Gunderson, Martin Theodore O.

Martin Theodore O. Gunderson was born February 4, 1846, in Røyken, Buskerud, Norway. His father, Osmund (Asmund) Gundersen was born July 11, 1807, and his mother, Maren Gjertsdtr Klemetsrud, was born in April of 1805 at Røyken. Osmund and Maren had three sons: Gjert "George" who emigrated by himself in 1854; and Gunder O. and Martin T. O., who emigrated with their parents and their grandmother Anne Karine Tostensdtr Kjos on August 4, 1856.

The family settled in Minnesota Territory. George spent some time working as a blacksmith in McGregor, Iowa, but he also farmed in Minnesota, as did his parents and his brother Martin. Martin relocated for a few years to Marshall County, but moved back to Freeborn County. Gunder eventually moved out west.

Martin served in the Civil War from November 1, 1861, to December 7, 1863. He was a private in Company M, First Regiment, Minnesota Mounted Rangers. He saw service against the Indians after the massacre of the white settlers at New Ulm, Minnesota.

Martin married Anna Pauline Berg on December 19, 1879, in Hayward, Freeborn County. She was born October 5, 1829, on the Danielsrud farm in Vestre Toten, Norway. She didn't immigrate until May 31, 1878.

Martin and Anna had ten children: John Arnt, Emma Melvina (Mrs. Henry Earl), Amanda Theodora (Mrs. Albert Gullickson), Alma (Mrs. Edwin Thompson), Henry Edwin, George Oscar (died as an infant), George Oscar, Hilda (Mrs. Peter Borgeson), William Leonard, and Viola Rosalind (Mrs. Clyde Hammel). Martin's brother Gunder married Anne Knatvold.

Martin's granddaughter Luetta Earl Ernst recalled "...I remember Grandpa's beard, for when I was a small fry I used to stay with my grandparents a lot ... and Grandpa had a nice long white beard. I used to sit on his knee at night and braid it and the first thing in the morning, unbraid it...I also remember that Grandpa had a lot of pigeons in the back of the house. When he fed them they would sit on his head, shoulders, and arms...I have lots of happy memories of Grandpa."

Osmund and Marin are buried in the Oakland Midway Church cemetery. Martin Gunderson died May 21, 1920, at the Soldier's Home Hospital in Minneapolis; his wife Anna died October 8, 1929, in Sioux City, Iowa.

Back Row: George, Hilda, Alma, William Leonard, and Amanda; Front Row: John, Martin, Viola, Anna and Emma

Gunderson, Targe

Targe Gunderson (Gunnarson, Findreng, Sinnes, Flatland) was born in 1789 and spent the majority of his years in the small valley of Vrådal in West Telemark, Norway. He grew up on the Flatland farm with his parents.

Targe raised a family of nine children with his first wife on the Upper Sinnes farm. He left for the United States in 1852 from the Findreng farm with his second family: wife, Thone Kragness (Kråkenes) (1820-1909), and children Ole (1845), Anne (1847-1898), and Tollef (1851). They settled first in the Koshkonong settlement in Dane County, Wisconsin, and came to Houston County, Minnesota Territory, in 1854.

After first using the farm name Findreng as his surname, Targe anglicized his patronymic, Gunnarsson, to Gunderson. After establishing residence he qualified for a land patent in 1857, which was signed by President James Buchanan. He and Thone had two more children: Andrew (1857) and Dagne (1861-1937).

The Findrengs settled in Badger Valley, where they were surrounded by Thone's parents and five of her siblings. When Targe died in 1873, Ole (1845-1931) was old enough to take over the farm. Ole married Thone Morken (1844-1927). In 1902, he rented the farm and moved to Houston village where he sold grave monuments. Ole and Thone had no children, so they adopted Benhard as a baby. Later Ben was a mail carrier out of Houston, and married Bertha Jenson.

Tollef Findreng (1851-1916) married Anna Kragness (1865-1946), who was a daughter of Levi and Sarah Kragness, and they also settled in Badger Valley and were neighbors to Andrew Findreng. Andrew (1857-1927) married Anna Dahle (1865-1946), a daughter of Hans and Engebor Nelson Dahle. These two couples were married on the same day and were each other's attendants. Tollef and Anna had no children.

In 1907, Andrew bought the Findreng farm, and it remained in the family for 98 years. He and Anna had seven children: Tilde, Helma, Emma, Theodore, Dorothy, Olice, and Anton. Tilde married Viggo Olson whose father Martin owned the farm (now the Wayne Olson farm) where all the Findreng children were born before moving back to the home farm in Badger. Emma married Martin Eskar. Dorothy married Arvid Swenson and they were the parents of Lloyd Swenson. Olice married Julius Twaiten, and Anton married Evelyn Norskog. When Andrew and Anna, Helma, and Theodore, moved to Houston, Anton took over the Findreng farm. Later Emma and Martin Eskar rented the farm. In 1937, Dorothy and Arvid Swenson bought the farm and lived there 14 years.

Andrew died at the age of 70, and Anna died at age 81. They were both buried at the Stone Church Cemetery. All of the Findrengs, and several Dahle relatives, were life-time members of that church in rural Houston County. Targe, his son Ole, and Hans Dahle helped build the Stone Church; they hauled stone to the building site from a nearby quarry.

Guttormson, Guttorm

Guttorm Guttormson was born in Øino, Gol, Hallingdal, in 1829. He came to America in 1849, settling first in Wisconsin. He joined others in exploring Houston County in Minnesota Territory. In the spring of 1853, Mikkel Sinnes, Aamund Sanden, and Guttorm climbed a high hill on the east side of the Badger

Valley and each of them picked out the site of his homestead. In the early years, Guttorm "shared" his acreage in Section 7, Sheldon Township, with 300 Indians who spent part of the year camped on it. They were not hostile, and when he brought most of the land under cultivation, the Indians moved on without incident. At the time, however, the situation was a great source of consternation for Guttorm and many of his neighbors.

Guttorm was an early and leading member of Houston's Stone Church. He was also active in establishing and supporting the local school.

His wife Liv died shortly after they arrived in Minnesota, and Guttorm remarried. He and Belle (Ingeborg) A. Lee had six children. Their son Ole took over the home farm and their son John homesteaded near Grafton North Dakota, where he and his family lived for 26 years. In 1903 John (not shown in this family picture) took land in Saskatchewan, Canada, and moved his family to that province in 1907.

Guttorm died on April 9, 1904 and is buried in the Stone Church Cemetery, Houston County.

Photo of the Guttormson family courtesy Houston County Historical Society

Halvorson, Ellev and Dordi Dale

In 1856, Dordi Gunnarsdtr Dale and Ellev Halvorson were married in Fillmore County and settled on what is now Section 12, Norway Township. Near neighbors were Dordi's brothers Gunnar and Aslak, later joined by another brother, Anders.

Ellev had emigrated as a teen-ager with his family from Hjartdal, Telemark, in 1847. Dordi was in her early 20's when she emigrated from the Seljord area of Telemark to join other family members in America in 1854.

Ellev served in Company E of the 4th Minnesota Infantry in the Civil War. Family tradition is that he was captured and spent several months in the infamous Andersonville prison.

Dordi had considerable experience as a midwife in the Rushford area.

Six children, all girls, survived to maturity. The two oldest daughters followed the migration of the times to northwestern Minnesota. Helge married Lars Sand.

After farming in that area they moved to Rivercourse, Alberta, Canada. Helene married Johannes Lade of Fosston, Minnesota, and spent the rest of her life there. Ellen, the youngest daughter, married Olaf Jacobson of Rushford. Around 1917-1918, the Jacobsons moved to eastern Alberta where Helge was already established. Anne, Tilla, and Bergine worked as hired girls, cooks, and seamstresses in Minneapolis, northwestern Minnesota, and in nearby Rushford. In this way each earned enough for clothing and spending money while one of them was always at home to help their parents.

Ellev died in 1911. Dordi died in 1917. In 1944 the farm was sold to a grandson of the pioneers, Kent A. Jacobson. He still owns his grandparents' homestead.

Haraldson, Aase Aslaksdtr

Aase Aslaksdtr Nusvig was born on June 28, 1833, in Fyresdal, Telemark, Norway. She was baptized at Moland church on September 22, 1833.

She came to America in 1846 from the Graver farm with her widowed mother Kristi Grover, sister Tone, and brothers Ole and Tarje. They lived with Kristi's brother, Aslak Lee, in the Koshkonong settlement in Dane County, Wisconsin until

about 1852. At that time, the Lees and her sister Tone moved to Iowa. Aase went with her brothers and mother to Houston County, Minnesota Territory. Kristi and Aase remained in Minnesota until about 1860, when they moved to Iowa to live with Tone and her husband.

Aase married Torjus Haraldson on January 4, 1861, in the Shell Rock Congregation of Worth County, Iowa. They maintained their membership in this church, although they lived just across the border in Round Prairie, Freeborn County, Minnesota.

Torjus served in the Army beginning in 1864, and participated in some of the most important battles of the Civil War. In 1912, he told this story: "In July 1865, we were discharged and got our wages at Fort Snelling, Minnesota. I bought the gun I had used from the government. As I was on my way home, I would shoot now and then, as I was so happy just going home. My shots frightened my wife, who thought we were Indians, and she hid in the cornfield until she knew it was safe to come home!"

The family sold the Freeborn County farm and spent 4 years near Bristol, Iowa. The family then purchased land in Lyon County, Minnesota. They moved to Clay County, and finally settled in what would become Pennington County.

Aase and Torjus had six children: Aslak, born February 14, 1862 and died that same year; Aslak (Alek), born November 3, 1863; Anna, born November 17, 1867; Harald, born July 27, 1869; Kristian, born April 15, 1872 and died in 1876; Edvin (Edwin), born June 12, 1874.

Aase died on November 14, 1910. Torjus died October 13, 1921. They are buried in Greenwood Cemetery, Thief River Falls, Minnesota.

Hefte, Ole Olson (*Gofa* Ole)

Ole Olson Hefte was born in 1794 in Reinli, Valdres, Norway. His parents were Ola (Froysak) Brekke and Ingeborg Torsteinsdtr. He served as a soldier, fought the Swedes in 1814, and was still listed as a soldier when he married Ingrid Oldsdtr Kinneberg (born 1795) on March 25, 1819. Her parents were Ola Ivarson Kinneberg and Gunhild Endresdtr Steinsrud. *Gofa* (Grandpa) Ole and Ingrid became the titled owners of the tiny Hefte farm in Gol, Hallingdal, on February 22, 1820.

Their daughter Ingeborg and her husband Knut immigrated to America in 1851. In 1853 *Gofa* Ole and his wife Ingrid, sons Ole (*Storre* Ole) and his wife Ingri; Ole ("Lame Ole"); Nils, and daughter Bergit, joined other families from Gol who left for America. Sadly, Ole's wife Ingrid died on the voyage and was buried at sea.

The group took the train from New York to Chicago in 1853, and spent a brief time in the Fox River Settlement in Illinois before taking a riverboat to Brownsville, Minnesota Territory. They then made the thirty mile trek from Brownsville to Wilmington Township, Houston County over land.

Gofa Ole lived with his son, *Storre* Ole, for the rest of his life. He and his sons were charter members of Wilmington Lutheran Congregation in 1855, and *Gofa* Ole served as a church trustee for many years. His widowed daughter Gunhild Grangard Grant brought her children to America in 1870.

Ole died on December 11, 1881, and is buried in Old Wilmington Lutheran Cemetery in Houston County.

Hefte, Ole Olson (*Storre* Ole)

Ole Olson Hefte was born on the Hefte farm in November of 1828 in Hallingdal, Norway. He was the oldest son of *Gofa* Ole Hefte and his wife Ingrid. *Storre* (Big) Ole immigrated with his parents and siblings in 1853. He was accompanied by his wife Ingri Blekstad, who died in 1856 when their daughter Guri was born. He married Sigri Engen, who was born March 17, 1836 in Norway,  daughter of Ole and Margit Engen. Their oldest son, Ole N., was born in 1861, followed by Inger (1862), Olaus (1865), Ingeborg (1867), Margit (1869) and Nels (1872). Their daughter Sarah was born in 1875 and died of cholera in December, 1892. Ole and Sigri's youngest daughter, Theoline, was born in 1879.

Ole built a sturdy log cabin on his first 40 acre tract of land, and over the years worked hard and was able to expand his farm to a total of 200 acres. He served on the committee that built Wilmington Lutheran Church and went on to hold a number of offices in that congregation. He died at age 65, on April 22, 1896. Sigri died March 3, 1904. They are both buried in Old Wilmington Lutheran Cemetery in Houston County.

Hjermstad, Lars Sorenson

Lars Sorensen Hjermstad was born April 9, 1835, in Stange, Norway. His parents were Soren Larsen Gjermstad and Kjersti Ingebretsdtr Vethammer. Lars was their oldest child and had the following siblings: Ingebret, Anne Louise, Eline Mathea, Maren, Rikka, and Syverin. They lived on the family farm, but in 1850 Gjermstad went through bankruptcy and the family decided to immigrate to the United States. Lars' brother Syverin died during the family's voyage to America. Lars' father Soren died just a year or so after the family settled in Rock River, Wisconsin. On July 12, 1854, Lars married Bergithe Gundersdtr Homme at Rock River. The family moved to Fillmore County, Minnesota Territory, where Lars and Bergithe's first son, Soren, was born on July 15, 1855. Their second son, Gunder, was born at Wanamingo, Goodhue County, on March 21, 1857. According to the 1857 Territorial Census, Lars' sister Anne Louise was living with the family at that time. Lars and Bergithe (Betsey) had three more children, all born in Wanamingo: Edward, born January 28, 1859; Anne Marie, born July 25, 1860; and Bernt. Lars' wife Bergithe died giving birth to Bernt on May 5, 1863. Bernt survived just over 4 months; he died September 14, 1863. Lars became a widower at 28, with 5 small children in his charge.

Anne Olsdtr Overbo, born September 14, 1833, emigrated from Solvorn, Norway, to Cherry Grove, Minnesota, in 1862 with her four-year-old son Einar. By 1864 Anne was working for Lars Hjermstad; they were married on January 8, 1865. Their oldest son Olaus was born September 16, 1865. He was followed by Ragnhild Caroline, born June 8, 1867; Emma Bertilde, born April 3, 1869; and Albert Louis, born March 20, 1871.

Lars was only 43 years old when he died on October 9, 1877. The farm he purchased stayed in the family for four generations.

Holtan, Hans Hanson

Hans H. Holtan was born in Norway on December 14, 1820. His parents were Hans H. and Gunhild Veum Holtan. He traveled to Le Havre, France, and crossed the Atlantic on the *Louis Phillippe*, arriving in New York on August 21, 1845. He made his way west, settling in what was then the tiny village of Chicago.

Hans married Aslaug (Aline) Svenungsdtr on July 4, 1848. In 1849, the couple moved to Belvidere, Illinois, and the following year to Portage City, Wisconsin. In 1851 he bought a farm on what was known as the "Indian Land" about six miles from Portage City.

In the spring of 1856, Hans claimed land in Section 17 of Wanamingo Township, Goodhue County, Minnesota Territory. He fell ill and sold that claim. It took a few years for him to recover from this unidentified illness, but he then purchased another farm in Wanamingo Township, adding land until it exceeded 400 acres in size. He built a fine home on his farm in the late 1870's.

Mr. Holtan was a leading citizen in Goodhue County. He held a number of elected positions in his township and in Goodhue County. He was also elected, and was honored to serve as the area's representative in the first general assembly of Minnesota (the state's first legislative session).

Hans and Aline had two children: Hans, who was born in Illinois and died in Red Wing, Minnesota in 1873; and Samuel, who was born in Wisconsin. Aline died on August 12, 1855.

Hans married for the second time on October 31, 1857. Hans and his second wife, Anna Maria Pedersdtr Rygh, had seven children: twins Peder and Gunnil Cornelia; Andrew; twins Henry and Christina (Christina died as an infant); a son Charley, who died as a child; and a second daughter named Christina, who lived to adulthood. Anna died January 13, 1876.

Sophia J. Moslet became Hans' third wife on July 11, 1877. She was born in 1854 in Norway and came to America in 1867. Their children included Anna Maria (Mary), Hans, John, Louise, and Hilda.

Hans died on his farm at the age of 83 on September 8, 1904. He and his wives Anna and Sophia, and many of their descendants, are buried in Aspelund Immanuel Cemetery.

Humble, Lars Larsen Sr. and Anne Cathrine Jensdtr

Lars Larsen (Sr.) was born in Norway on April 16, 1817, on the Skjerven farm. His birth occurred in the Jevnaker *kommune* (district) of Oppland County. Oppland is the home of Lillehammer (site of the 1994 Winter Olympics). Records show that Lars had three older brothers: Ole, Gulbrand, and Kristoffer. By the year 1819, Lars' parents had moved east from Oppland to the neighboring county of Akerhus. Here they found work on the Homble farm. Shortly thereafter, Lars' mother brought a fifth son into the world on September 18, 1819. His name was Olavus.

Lars was confirmed in his local parish in 1831. At the age of 25, Lars married Anne Cathrine Jensdtr. Her family lived at Stenegaard (meaning "stony farm"). Members of her parents' family who later came to the United States used Stensgaard as a surname. Anne Cathrine's birth date was July 16, 1821. Lars and Anne Cathrine were married on April 4, 1842, in Nannestad Parish.

Lars and Anne Cathrine worked on the Homble farm for around ten years before they immigrated to America. During this time, Anne Cathrine brought six children into the world. Two of their children died at a young age: a first-born son as an infant, and Ingeborg Marie at the age of four.

On July 5, 1852, Lars and Cathrine left Norway with their four surviving children: Karen, Lars (Jr.), Marthea, and Ingeborg Marie. It is significant to note that though he was a second-born son, Lars (Jr.) was given the name of his first-born predecessor. This was the customary thing to do in Norway.

In America the Humble family wanted to acquire some of the land that had become available for homesteaders. They first went to the Koshkonong Settlement near the present-day city of Madison, Wisconsin. This was a stopover point for many of the Norwegian immigrants coming to the Midwest. After five years in Wisconsin the family moved to the Territory of Minnesota in 1857. Here they settled in what was to become Norway Township in Fillmore County. On the 20th of September, 1860, Lars Sr. was granted a land patent from the United States government for 160 acres of land in Section 13 of Township 103 (Norway Township).

In 1889 the Humble family moved to a new farm when Lars' son (L. L. Humble, Jr.) purchased a farmstead in Section 15. Lars Sr. lived with his son until he passed away in 1907.

Lars Sr. and his wife had 11 children. At his funeral only four of them remained: Karen Englestad of Minneapolis; Mrs. John Peterson of Streator, Illinois; Mrs. Andrew Christianson of Minneapolis; and John Humble of Washington State. Many of his children passed away from causes that would not be a problem today – pneumonia and tuberculosis, to name two. His son L. L. Humble became prominent in Fillmore County affairs; he ran for county treasurer at the age of 22. At death, Lars Senior was 90 years old (very old for a man at that time in history).

Huset, Ole Olsen

Ole Olsen Huset, son of Ole Olsen Huset and Anne Halvorsdtr Jøntvet, was born in Holla, Telemark, on July 15, 1820. He married Kirsten Maria Christensdtr Stenstadvalen on August 25, 1842. She was the daughter of Christen Andreas Jensen Stenstadvalen and Kari Thorsdtr Ytterbøe of Holla, and was born on May 4, 1825.

The family left Porsgrunn on the ship *Salvator* on May 2, 1844, and arrived in New York on July 5th. Traveling in the party were Ole's brother Halvor Olsen Huset, born February 3, 1824, his aunt, Lisbeth Olsdtr Huset, born September 19, 1786, and Ole and Anne's young son, Ole Olsen Huset, born November 27, 1842.

The family made their first home in the Koshkonong Settlement in Dane County, Wisconsin where Karen, Christen, Anne Kirstine, Marie and Maren were born. The family moved to Holden Township, Goodhue County, Minnesota Territory, in 1855.

Ole served as a musician in Company D, Minnesota Third Infantry, during the Civil War and died of illness at Memphis, Tennessee, in 1863. His remains were returned to Minnesota, where he was buried in Holden Ceemtery.

That same year, his son Ole married Kirsten Holman, who was born in Drangedal, Telemark. In 1868, Ole and Kirsten moved to Pope County, Minnesota, where they lived for eight years. During that time Ole served as a justice of the peace and a town clerk. In 1878 the family returned to Goodhue County, where Ole built a good farm and continued to serve as a justice of the peace. He was also elected to the Minnesota legislature.

Ole and Kirsten's children were Lauritz, Lettie, Maria, Caroline, Anna, and Carl.

Ole died on May 27, 1891. His mother Kirsten Christensdtr Huset died in Stearns County, Minnesota, on August 2, 1897. His wife Kirsten died sometime after 1900.

Ingulfsland, Herbjorn Nilsson

Herbjorn Nilsson Ingulfsland (1805-1885) along with his wife Aagot Øysteinsdtr Boen (1808-1887) and their four children: Aase (1832-1895), Øystein (1833-1912), Aagot (1836-?), and Nils (1840-1931), and Herbjorn's mother-in-law Aasne Jonsdtr Ingulfsland Boen (1779-?) left their homeland in Tinn, Telemark, Norway to come to America in May of 1842. They left Drammen, Norway on the schooner *Ellida*, and arrived in New York on August 8. Of the 63 passengers on the journey, 43 were from Tinn, Telemark.

The passengers were in miserable condition upon arriving in America. Eight passengers had died during the crossing, and thirty were so sick they had to be taken to the hospital. It is believed that the disease was a mixture of cholera and typhoid fever.

Herbjorn and his family located eighteen miles west of Milwaukee in Waukesha County, Wisconsin, where they remained for twelve years. Shortly after arriving, Aagot gave birth to their fifth child, Ausne (1843-1937). In 1847 their sixth child was born, Bergit (1847-1920). The Ingulfsland family was now complete.

In the summer of 1854, Herbjorn and his family joined other Norwegians in relocating to Harmony Township, Fillmore County, Minnesota Territory. They were among the first group of Norwegians to settle this area. Herbjorn purchased a claim of 160 acres in section 24, for which he paid the government $200.

That same year Herbjorn erected a log cabin. He and his sons broke, cleared, and grubbed the land and followed general farming for many years. In 1864, a frame house was built on the homestead.

Herbjorn, along with his sons, Oystein and Nils, were 1856 charter members of the Greenfield Lutheran Church – their names are inscribed on its memorial monument.

The Ingulfsland family later changed its name to Nelson. Herbjorn and Aagot lived the remainder of their lives in Harmony on the family homestead. Many of their descendants are buried with them in Greenfield Lutheran Church Cemetery.

Iverson, Christian and Bartha Housker

Christian Iverson was born in 1828 on the island of Rennesøy, north of Stavanger, Norway. The same year, his future wife Bartha Housker was born on the neighboring island of Finnøy. He immigrated to the U. S. in 1854. She came with her entire family in 1856.

By 1857 Christian and Bartha had married and were charter members of what is now Scheie Lutheran Church in Preble Township, Fillmore County. Children soon followed: Andreas (Andrew) C. (1857-1935); Edward (1859-1953); twins Syvert Christian (1861-1945) and Daniel C. (1861-1943); Ellen Marie (1863-1934); Christopher (1865-1961); and Børre (Ben) Christian (1868-1934).

Bartha passed away in 1903, Christian in 1906. In his obituary in the Rushford Star Republican, it says, "Mr. Iverson was loved and respected by all who knew him." Christian and Bartha are buried together in the Scheie Lutheran Church Cemetery. As of 2008, they have over 400 descendants spanning 7 generations.

Jellum, Jacob Johnsen and Cecilia Eivindsdtr

Jacob Johnsen Jellum was born to Jon Jacobsen Jellum and Kari Stenersdtr Kleiv on September 25, 1831, at Eggedal, Buskerud County, Norway. He came to America in 1852 with his sister, Ingeborg Johnsdtr Jellum.

Jacob married Sissel Eivindsdtr Grønvoll in 1855. She was born April 1, 1826, in Eggedal, Buskerud, Norway. Her parents were Eivind Kopsengeie and Berit Jonsdtr.

Jacob and Cecilia's oldest daughter Kari was born July 21 and baptized September 14, 1856, in Holden Church in Goodhue County.

Records indicate Jacob and his wife relocated to Wheeling Township, Rice County, in 1856. "Jacob Johnson" received a land patent for his farm in Section 4 on June 10, 1858.

Jacob and Cecilia (Sissel) added five more children to the family after their move to Rice County: John, born June 22, 1858; Berit, June 19, 1861; Even, February 1, 1864; Ingebor, July 22, 1866, and Kristina, June 4, 1870.

Jacob died in his home on March 25, 1897. This touching tribute was part of his obituary, published in the *Decorah Posten* on August 20, 1897 (translated from original Norwegian): "The deceased belonged to Valley Grove Congregation of the Norwegian Synod and for many years has been the congregation's janitor. The congregation, with its pastor, N. N. Quammen, will always remember the deceased as one of the quiet servants in the area, who was ever willing to use his ability to build up the congregation and the wider church body."

According to the 1905 Census, Cecilia was living with her son Even and his family in Wheeling Township, Rice County, when she died October 25, 1905. Both Jacob and Cecilia are buried at Valley Grove Church Cemetery in Rice County.

Johnson, Thomas Lommen

Thomas L. Johnson, a pioneer pastor of the Norwegian Synod, was born April 27, 1837, in Vestre Slidre, Valdres, Norway. He was the youngest of nine children born to Jorend and Jon Anfinson Lommen. His parents died when he was a child.

In 1851 he accompanied his older brothers to Dane County, Wisconsin, USA. The next year they relocated to Spring Grove, Minnesota Territory, where his brothers Peder and Jon purchased farms. For several years he made his home with them. According to *Recollections of Pastor N. Brandt*, in 1852 Thomas walked from Spring Grove to attend Rev. N. Brandt's services south of Decorah, Iowa. This was a distance of about 35 miles one way.

Thomas decided to study for the ministry. Accordingly he attended Concordia College, St. Louis, Missouri, from 1859-1860. He was a student at Concordia Seminary, Fort Wayne, Indiana from 1860-1861. To complete his education, he returned to St. Louis and Concordia Seminary where he earned his C. T. degree in 1863. On June 17, 1863, Thomas was ordained in the ministry at St. Louis, Missouri.

Just a week later, on June 24, 1863, he married Miss Maren Sohlgaard of Wisconsin. She was the daughter of the treasurer of Kongsberg silver mine in Norway. She was born in Norway on May 4, 1836. Mrs. Johnson was a musician who had brought her own piano with her to America.

On August 6, 1863, Pastor Johnson was installed as resident pastor of St. Peter and Swan Lake parishes near Norseland in Nicollet County, Minnesota. The 48 members of the congregation subscribed $181 for his annual salary, raising a total of $328.75. He also served as a missionary pastor in seventeen counties in Central Minnesota. These counties were Nicollet, Sibley, Faribault, Jackson, Carver, Brown, McLeod, Meeker, Yellow Medicine, Kandiyohi, Stearns, Chippewa, Pope, Blue Earth, Grand and Douglas. In this extensive area he established numerous congregations. He lived at Norseland throughout his pastorate. According to H. J. Holland, he baptized 55 children at Norway Lake, Minnesota, in three days. From *Missionary Pastors in Minnesota*. "For 43 years, 1863-1906, this all-time great among home missionary pastors carried the message of salvation to people in 17 counties in Minnesota. He did not live to see it all, but in 1927 that territory was served by

50 pastors in the former Norwegian Synod." In later years, he was relieved of some of his strenuous duties as pioneer pastor.

Pastor Johnson and wife were the parents of eight children; three daughters and one son grew to maturity. Anna married Emil B. Olson; Inga married Pastor Axel Bergh; Thora became the wife of Pastor John Dahle. Pastor and Mrs. Johnson's only son, Gotthard, died of a heart attack when he was a senior at Robbinsdale Theological Seminary.

Pastor Thomas Johnson died suddenly of a heart attack at Norseland on April 19, 1906. His wife Maren preceded him in death, passing away on March 30, 1898. Both are interred in St. Peter's Cemetery at Norseland, Minnesota.

In over 30 years of service at St. Peter's, he baptized 681 children, confirmed 511, married 100 couples, buried 217, and conducted 1, 268 services. He was very much loved by the members of his congregations. The young people of St. Peter congregation installed a memorial picture window in his honor.

Johnson, Tosten Lommen

Tosten Lommen Johnson was born July 18, 1834, at the Lommen farm in Vestre Slidre, Valdres, Norway. At age seven, he was sent to Sogndal to live with his married sister Ingeborg because both of his parents had died.

He served an apprenticeship as a blacksmith before coming to America with his brothers Peter, John, and Thomas, in 1851. They spent some time in Dane County, Wisconsin, before moving to Minnesota Territory. According to O. N. Nelson in his book *History of Scandinavians in the United States*, Tosten and his brother Peter were the first Valdresers in Minnesota, arriving in Houston County in 1851.

Although he lived in Minnesota, Tosten actually spent most of his first years in Iowa working on farms in the summer and attending school in the winter. He spent one year at Upper Iowa University in Fayette.

In 1856 Tosten homesteaded a farm near Spring Grove in Black Hammer Township. He worked hard to improve the land and built a house. He also taught English in the county schools.

While visiting his neighbor, Ole Borjum, Tosten met Ole's sister, Thora Gjesme, from Aurland. Thora and Tosten were married on March 3, 1860, and raised a family of 4 boys and 4 girls: John, born in 1862; Embrick, 1863; Tosten, 1865; twins Maria and Ole, 1867; Maria, 1870; Jane, 1872; and Gertrude, who was born in 1877.

During the Civil War, Tosten was the captain of a volunteer company that drilled in Houston County. He joined the regular army on October 1, 1864, and served in

Company D of the First Minnesota Heavy Artillery. He was discharged at Nashville, Tennessee, on June 20, 1865. He often said that "being discharged at the close of the Civil War without any wounds was the chief success I had in life."

Tosten Lommen Johnson was a leader in his church and community. He was a church trustee, town chairman, town clerk, and was appointed to the State Board of Equalization for several terms. He was elected as a representative of Houston County to the Minnesota state legislature and served from 1869 to 1874. Tosten went on to be elected to the Minnesota State Senate, serving from 1887 to 1890. According to Governor Eberhard's report, "Tosten Johnson was the first Norwegian to serve in the Minnesota Legislature."

In 1909, three years after Tosten's wife died, Tosten sold the farm and went to live with his daughters Jane and Gertrude, at Climax in northwestern Minnesota, where he resided until his death on April 24, 1914.

Tosten was a man of stalwart build, 5'10" tall, with blue eyes and light hair (per military records). He possessed a commanding personality and although he was not a fluent public speaker, he could say a great deal in very few words. Tosten was a deep thinker and a man of excellent judgement and integrity with a keen sense of humor. He was highly respected by all who knew him.

Johnsrud, Hovel Peterson

The original log house and outbuildings and the new home and barn built by Olaus appear in this photo of the Johnsrud farmstead taken c. 1900.

Hovel Peterson Johnsrud was born March 3, 1818, in Gran parish, Hadeland, Norway. He married Mary Larsdtr of Oslo, who was born March 28, 1823, on Christmas Day, 1848. They lived the next four years on a cotter (tenant) place with their oldest daughter, Maren. The family boarded the bark *Richard Cobden* in Christiania, Norway, on March 5, 1852. Packed with provisions and allotted 2 feet by 7 feet each, they arrived in New York 57 days later.

Traveling by canal boat and ox cart, they initially settled in Paint Creek, Iowa. They operated a farm and drove oxen. Hovel was a tall broad-shouldered pioneer who also swung a cradle to cut grain for 50 cents per day. Son Lars was born in Paint Creek. Two years later, in 1854, Hovel's family moved to the present site of the Johnsrud farmstead, 4 miles southeast of Spring Grove, Minnesota. They first lived in a dugout and later built a log house on the 120 acres acquired in 1855 for $1.25/acre. In 1873 they purchased an additional 120 acres. Hovel raised various crops and animals, and was known as a champion rail splitter. Hovel's family grew by four (Peter, Martha, Olaus, Theoline) while in Spring Grove. In 1876, his son Lars married and took possession of 110 acres, and in 1886 son Olaus married and took over the remaining acreage from Hovel. Hovel and Mary remained in the log house and son Olaus built a large brick house 100 feet away in 1896. The couple enjoyed their remaining years on the farm, until Hovel died on February 4, 1904. Mary then moved to her daughter's home in Sisseton, South Dakota where she died on May 9, 1905. The Spring Grove farm remains in the family, passing from Olaus to his son Harold, to present owner Harlan Johnsrud.

Jordgrav, Mikkel (Michael) and Taran Anundsdtr

Mikkel Jordgrav was born September 8, 1829, to Kittel Olavson Jordgrav and Margit Mikkelsdtr Øygarden on the Jordgrav tenant farm in the Kviteseid Parish of Telemark.

Mikkel, the oldest child, was fourteen when he immigrated in 1843 with his parents, younger siblings Ellen Marie and Kari, and several aunts and uncles. They made the nine-week journey from Le Havre to New York on the sailing ship *Tecumseh*. The total fare on this cargo ship was $13 per person. They were the first group from the Kviteseid Parish who dared make the journey to far off America, which in those days was considered a dangerous undertaking.

From New York they continued by canal boat to Buffalo and through the Great Lakes to their final destination, Milwaukee, Wisconsin Territory. Since most land there was taken, they continued with oxen and wagon westward and began clearing and breaking land in what would become the Skoponong Settlement. Kittel, Mikkel's father, was one of the founders of the Skoponong Church, which was located just a few miles southeast of Palmyra.

Mikkel married Taran Anundsdtr Hjamdal, who was born May 15, 1832. She emigrated from Telemark with her siblings and parents, Anund Erikson Hjamdal and Liv Olavsdtr, in 1844.

After their first daughter, Lena, was baptized on June 11, 1854, they moved settled with relatives on Highland Prairie in Fillmore County. Mikkel and Ta. secured 80 acres in section 22, Norway Township.

Mikkel's farming years were interrupted when he was drafted on May 31, 1864, into Minnesota's Second Infantry, Company K. He was thirty-four years old when he marched off to fight in the Civil War, leaving his wife and five children to run the farm. Mikkel arrived in Atlanta just in time to join General Sherman's "March to the Sea." After camping during the winter months in Savannah, the army continued through the Carolinas, to Goldsboro, Raleigh, Richmond, and Washington; and finally from Washington to Louisville, Kentucky. He was mustered out of the service when the war ended, on July 11, 1865. We will never know what this Norwegian farmer experienced during that year; there have been no letters or reports found by the family.

Sometime between 1875 and 1879, Mikkel and Taran moved to Yellow Medicine County and bought a farm east of Porter. They farmed and raised eleven surviving children: Ole, Kittel, Amelia Helene, Andreas, Lena, Carl, Karina Marget, Gustav Julius, Christian, Mary, and Clara. Two children, Lena and Marget Karine, died young.

Taran died on February 21, 1892, and Mikkel died on June 25, 1910. They are buried at Bethel Lutheran Cemetery west of Porter.

Juvrud, Ole Olsen and Martha Axelsdtr Iverson

Ole Olsen Juvrud and Martha Axelsdtr Iverson, Norwegian immigrants, were pioneers in Territorial Minnesota. They arrived in Rice County on July 10, 1855.

Ole Olsen, from the Enger farm in Ringerike (Buskerud) Norway, was born May 28, 1823. Later he adopted the surname Juvrud, for a farm near Enger. The *Christiane* sailed from Drammen, Norway, on May 17, 1851. Ole was one of eleven passengers from four neighboring families. After an 8-week voyage, they landed in New York City on July 10. They traveled up the Hudson River, through the Erie Canal, and across the Great Lakes to Milwaukee.

Martha Axelsdtr Iverson was born October 6, 1837, in the Voss District of western Norway. Her family came to America on the *Kong Sverre* which left Bergen, Norway on June 1, 1844, and arrived in New York on August 2. They first settled in Jordan Township, Wisconsin. Martha's parents, Axel and Ingeborg, had two more daughters in America: Synneva (1844) and Anna (1847). Axel Iverson died at Wiota in 1847 at the age of 45.

Ole and Martha Juvrud, with the Ole Hanson Korsdalen and Elling Olson Strand families, left for Minnesota Territory June 8, 1855. The group traveled by oxen and covered wagon and arrived at Fox Lake in Rice County on July 10. They were attracted to this area by the woods and water, a lake that held a number of fish, and fertile land for farming. Ole and Martha's daughter Oline was born two months after they arrived.

In 1856 Martha's sister Synneva and husband Gulleck Olson relocated to Fox Lake and, in 1863, their mother Ingeborg and step-father Erik Anderson Uggen came, bringing their two year old granddaughter, Karoline Iverson (her parents and two siblings died of consumption in Wisconsin).

Ole Juvrud secured 80 acres of land on June 1, 1861. He acquired the property through an assignment from Samuel Garland, a veteran of the War of 1812. The title was granted under the provisions of the Bounty Lands legislation. After the War of 1812, the United States Congress enacted legislation rewarding military service by entitling veterans to claim public domain lands in the northwest and western territories. After 1842 the veteran could redeem his warrant for public lands in Minnesota. Warrants could be assigned or sold to other individuals.

Martha died on October 18, 1880 (age 47) and Ole Olsen Juvrud died August 19, 1904 (age 81). These pioneers are buried in the cemetery at Fox Lake. Their daughter Inger Haugen described them as religious, neat, trustworthy and honest. Ole and Martha had 11 children and 53 grandchildren. These early pioneers to Minnesota were farmers, merchants, and teachers, assimilating into the culture of this new country while ever mindful of their Norwegian heritage. They helped found churches, schools, and towns while enduring the hardships, disease and injuries which took loved ones. In time, the next generation would relocate elsewhere in Minnesota, and are heavily represented in Leaf Lake Township, Otter Tail County, and Fern Township, Hubbard County, where many of their descendants can be found today.

Kassenborg, Andreas and Tone Olsdtr Kragnes

Andreas Gulbrandson (A. G.) Kassenborg was born December 1, 1836, in Nordre Land *kommune* (township), Oppland County, Norway. He was the son of Gulbrand G. and Astri Kassenborg. Andreas immigrated with his family to the United States in 1850. He recalled to his son Edward that the water supply was exhausted on the voyage and it caused great suffering.

After spending 3 years in Rock County, Wisconsin, the family moved to Houston County in Minnesota Territory. A. G. married Tone Kragnes, daughter of Ole Aanundson and Kari Kragnes, in 1857, in Houston County. The couple farmed in Yucatan Township.

Andreas made two trips to the Red River Valley, in 1869 and 1871, before joining other Houston County families who left to settle near the Buffalo River in Clay County in 1876. On the trip by covered wagon the families encountered familiar hardships – no roads or bridges, illness, accidents, nervous encounters with Indians, and the ever-present company of Minnesota's voracious mosquitoes.

A. G. built a successful farming operation of 1,000 acres in Clay County and was also involved in the local business community. He built the historic and recently renovated Kassenborg Block at the corner of Main Avenue and Fourth Street in downtown Moorhead. A. G. was an active member of Concordia Lutheran Church, was elected a township officer and school board member, and served as one of the first trustees of Concordia College in Moorhead.

A. G. and Tone were the parents of eight children: Anne Karine (Juve, Bergland) was born in 1858 and died in 1945; Mina Augusta (Morken), 1860-1937; Gilbert Olaus, who never married, (1863-1918); Anne Marie (Moe), 1866-1946; Edward Ludwig (1868-1957); Eliza A. (Olness), 1871-1950; Julia Ogena (Tvedten), 1874-1922; and Ingeborg Maline, born in 1876 and died in 1901.

From the newspaper, the *Moorhead Independent*: "A. G. Kassenborg has been one of the most successful of the early settlers along the Buffalo River. Mr. Kassenborg's farm is a beautiful tract of land, lying along the Buffalo River. He has always raised fine crops and at the World's Exposition in Chicago in 1893, received the first premium for the best oats exhibited. He also has a number of black walnut and fruit trees. His machinery is up-to-date. He grinds feed for his stock. He also raises concord grapes. His temper is seldom ruffled and he is very respected in the community..."

A. G. died September 28, 1913. Tone died May 17, 1921. Both are buried in Concordia Lutheran Church Cemetery, rural Glyndon, Minnesota.

Kassenborg, Gulbrand and Astri Andersdtr

Gulbrand Gulbrandsen Kassenborg was born on February 10, 1808, on the Kølbu farm, a *husmanplass* (sub-farm) of Nedre Skjærstein in Sør Aurdal, Valdres. His parents were Gulbrand Gulbrandsen Braker and Liv Knutsdtr Haug. "Gulbrand Gulbrandsen Skjærsteneie" was christened March 17, 1811, at Bagn Church. In 1818 the family moved to one of the Thomle farms in Nordre Land, possibly either Kasenborg or Nøss.

On October 19, 1833, Gulbrand returned to Bagn Church to marry Astri Andersdtr Skjærstein. She was born October 12, 1806. At the time of their wedding, Astri's parents, Anders Julsen Skjærstein (born Solbjør) and Anne Isaksdtr Sørum, owned the farm Kølbu that Gulbrand's family left in 1818. Gulbrand and Astri had three children: Gelina Andrine, Andreas Gulbrandsen, and Gulbrand Gulbrandsen.

In 1850, Gulbrand brought his family to America using the surname Thomleie. They settled first in Rock County, Wisconsin, and in 1854 moved to Yucatan Township, Houston County. The log cabin built by the family when they arrived in Houston County has been refurbished and still occupies its original site. Martin Ulvestad reported in his book *Nordmændene i Amerika*: "Guttorm Guttormsen Øino from Rotnem in Gol, Hallingdal; Ole Evensen Dølehus from Hemsedal; along with the Stutelien brothers and G. G. Kassenborg from Valdres, were the first white settlers on the South Fork (Root River); but at that time the area was full of drunken Indians. They discovered that they were not hostile, nevertheless, they had constant fear of them."

The land patent for the Kassenborg farm in Section 13 of Yucatan Township was issued to Gilbert Gilbertson on January 15, 1858. Valued as a blacksmith, Gulbrand was also a successful farmer known for his intelligence and business sense. Astri, who died in 1871, is buried in Stone Church Cemetery, Houston.

A severe flood on the Root River in 1866 killed 30 settlers and may have contributed to the family's decision to relocate. In 1874, Gulbrand moved with his daughter Geline and her husband to Moland Township, Clay County. Here he lived out his days, teaching his grandsons the art of being a blacksmith using the old anvil he had brought with him from Norway. Andreas joined his sister and father in what became known as the Buffalo River Settlement in 1875. Son Gilbert (who used the patronymic Gilbertson as his surname) resettled his family on the Yellow Medicine River in Yellow Medicine County.

Gulbrand died August 5, 1888, and is buried in Concordia Lutheran Church Cemetery, rural Glyndon, Minnesota.

Kinneberg, Ivar Pederson

Ivar Pederson Kinneberg was born at Kinneberbraaten in Gol, Hallingdal, Norway in 1818. He married Barbo Lostegaard in 1842. Five children were born in Norway but three of them died. In 1852, Ivar and Barbo emigrated with their two surviving children. They sailed from Drammen on the Norwegian bark *Drafna*, a sail ship, and landed in New York on July 16, 1852. In an interview with Barbro printed in a history of pioneers, she told of being so seasick on the voyage of six weeks that she was unable to eat and thought she would never see America. Facing them when they got to New York was another long journey of four to six weeks. They finally arrived in Rock Run, Illinois, 18 weeks after leaving Norway! For four years they lived with the Endre Trehus family. The Buxengard family and the Kinnebergs lived with the Trehus family until, in 1856, they went by oxen and covered wagon to Wilmington Township. Ivar purchased the present farm (shown in 1995 in the photo) for $5 an acre, paying $90 down with seven percent interest on the balance. Ivar and Barbo achieved their goal of a farm in America!

Because this was school land, the couple was often called "Ivar and Barbro Skoleland." The farm was sold to their son, Nels, and passed down through the generations from Nels to Nelvin to Glenn, who still lives on the original Kinneberg homestead.

Knutson, Ole

Ole Knutson, son of Knud Engebriktsen and Berit Larsdtr, was born September 27, 1846, in Eggedal Parish, Buskerud County, Norway. After his father passed away his mother sold the farm and immigrated to America in 1853 with five of her six children; Ole was just seven years old when he left Norway. The family settled first in Wisconsin, and then moved to Hartland Township, Freeborn County, Minnesota Territory

Ole & Nickolene Knutson

in 1857. Ole married Nickolene Gustine Hallum at Hartland in October, 1869. She was born in Hurdalen, Norway on September 25, 1853.

The Knutsons lived on the farm near Hartland and raised fourteen children.

In 1906, the family moved to Colorado and settled on a homestead near Genoa. They were early and active members of Genoa Lutheran Church. In 1911, they migrated to Tacoma, Washington, and returned to Hartland before re-establishing themselves in Colorado in 1916.

Ole died in Colorado on May 11, 1922. He was laid to rest in Genoa Lutheran Church Cemetery. Nickolene continued to live in Colorado until 1938, when her daughter, Julia Grasdalen, convinced her to return to Minnesota with her after a visit. She died shortly after her return, on August 17, 1938. Nickolene was buried in the West Lutheran Church Cemetery.

Kragnes, Aanund Ole

A O and Oline Kragnes, wedding photo 1877

Aanund Olesen Kråkenes was born in 1845 in Telemark, Norway. He was the son of Ole Aanundson and Kari Mikkelsdtr. The family left Norway in 1853, immigrating to Skuren, Wisconsin. In 1854, Ole pre-empted land in Houston County, Minnesota Territory.

A. O. married Ingeborg Lee in 1866, after he returned from the Civil War. They had two sons and a daughter: Gilbert, Ole Emanuel, and Karoline.

Aanund's father Ole died in 1873, and Aanund relocated to the Red River Valley, taking land in what would become Kragnes Township (named in his honor) in Clay County, Minnesota. For a short period of time he shared a log cabin with Torgrim Morken on his adjoining homestead. In 1875, A. O.'s wife and children and his widowed mother Kari joined him. Tragically, Ingeborg died that fall, on September 2, 1875, after giving birth to another child who died a year later.

Aanund remarried in 1877. Oline Studlien's family had also come to the Red River Valley from Houston County, where she was born in 1863. Isabelle, Oliver, Bernhard, Clarence, Luther, and Alvin were added to the family.

Aanund found success in Clay County. His land holdings expanded in both Kragnes and Morken Townships. He played an active role in township affairs,

Concordia Lutheran Church, and he was an early benefactor of Concordia College, Moorhead. Not only the township, but also the village of Kragnes was named after him.

Aanund Ole Kragnes died on March 27, 1912, and Oline died on November 30, 1937. Aanund, his wives, and many of their descendants are buried in Concordia Lutheran Church Cemetery, rural Glyndon, Minnesota. His descendants still live on the home place and in the surrounding area.

Kragnes, Ole Aanundson and Kari Mikkelsdtr

Ole Aanundson Kragnes was born June 10, 1800, in Fyresdal, Telemark. He married Kari Mikkelsdtr Holte (born 1809 in Kviteseid, Telemark) in 1827 in Vrådal. The family left the Kråkenes farm in Telemark in 1853 and immigrated to the United States. Their first stop was Iowa County, Wisconsin. One year later the family moved to the Badger Valley in Houston County, Minnesota Territory. Ole farmed in Houston County until his death on December 19, 1873. He is buried in the Stone Church Cemetery.

Kari Kragnes purchased her own land when she moved from Houston County to the Buffalo River Settlement with her children and others in 1875. She died on May 5, 1883, and is buried in the Concordia Church Cemetery, rural Glyndon.

Ole and Kari raised four children: Gunhild (Juve), Anne (Sannes), Tone (Kassenborg) and Aanund Ole (A. O.).

Kroshus, Anders Pedersen

Anders Pedersen Kroshus signed out of his church parish for America on June 11, 1850. He left the Røisumsmoen farm in Tingelstad, Hadeland, Norway, and came to Muskego, Wisconsin. Anders found work at Putman's saw mill. The first year, along with his room and board, he received $6.00 a month, the second he received $11.00, and the third, $16.00 each month. Four months into his fourth year, he was making $24 a month. They offered him $30 a month to remain, but he had saved nearly all he had earned, and decided it was time to start farming.

He met Thurine Haakaanes and fell in love. Her parents were Ole Gjermundson Haakenes and Mari Kittelsdtr Stensrud, who had come to Muskego from Tinn, Telemark, in 1840. Thurine's parents died in the cholera epidemic, which left Thurine an orphan responsible for the care of five younger siblings. Turi was just 18 years old.

Soon after Anders and Turi fell in love, he purchased a pair of oxen and a wagon and went westward alone. After three weeks he came to the farm owned by John

Anderson Kroshus or Stensrud about 2 miles south of Spring Grove. Anders Pedersen purchased the farm from John Kroshus for $150. In the old Norwegian tradition, he took the name Kroshus from the farm and became known as Anders Pedersen Kroshus. He stayed at his new place that winter doing some necessary work. The next spring he sold his oxen to Engebret Bensen Enderud, and walked back to Muskego, a distance of about 250 miles.

Upon his return to Muskego, Andrew married Thurine. He then purchased a team of oxen and a wagon and, in company with Mikkel Walhus, went back to Spring Grove where Anders and Thurine built themselves a home. When Anders died on November 12, 1882, he owned 313 acres of good land with many good buildings. Thurine died in February, 1916.

Today Anders' great-grandson Fred Kroshus and his family are still living on the land that Anders purchased.

Krosshaug, Sjur Hermannsen & Helge Olsdtr Høgset

Sjur (Syver) Hermannsen Krosshaug was born December 28, 1811 to Herman Nielsen Krydshoug and Gunild Syversdtr. Helge Olsdtr Høgset, daughter of Ole Torkelsen Høiset and Borgil Hermansdtr, was born February 24, 1812. Both families lived in Hallingdal, Norway.

Sjur and Helge were married October 15, 1844, in Aal, Buskerud. They left Norway in 1849 on the ship *Drafna,* with their children Gunhild (1844-1910) and Herman (born December 14, 1846). Their first residence was in the Luther Valley Settlement, Rock County, Wisconsin. In 1850, they relocated to the Paint Creek Settlement, Allamakee County, Iowa.

In the 1857 census the Krosshaugs are documented as farmers in Wilmington Township (T-101-N & R-6-W), Houston County, Minnesota Territory. They later moved to Mabel in Fillmore County. Syver and Helge were both buried in the Garness Trinity Lutheran Cemetery in rural Mabel, Minnesota.

In 1861, their daughter Gunhild Syversdtr Krosshaug married Engebret Bjørnsen Garnaas Bearson (1839-1915) from Newburg Township, Fillmore County.

Kvernodden, Nels N and Christiane Johnson

Nels Nelson Kvernodden was born September 5, 1849, in Wisconsin to Nels Tolvsen Kvernodden and Maria Olsdatter Vale, immigrants in 1844 from Holla, Telemark, Norway. The family moved before 1857 to Goodhue County, Minnesota. Nels spent the rest of his life in Goodhue and Rice counties.

Nels had an early start in the grocery story business when, as a single man, he worked in a store in Norway, Minnesota. Norway was in Goodhue County very close to the Rice County line; it is now a ghost town.

On November 5, 1875, in the Holden Church, Goodhue County, Nels married Christiana Martine Johnson who had also emigrated from Telemark. She was born September 25, 1853, in Brevik, Telemark, Norway, and came to the United States in June of 1871 destined for Chicago with her sister, sister's husband and two children. Family records indicate she lived in Chicago several years before moving to Goodhue County, Minnesota. Christiana/Christiane was known in America as Jenny or Annie, and sometimes Martina or Tina.

In 1875 Nels and Christiana established the Moland store in the south eastern corner (Section 36) of Rice County, which came to include a post office where Nels was the postmaster. The store was sold to Hagan O. Naeseth in 1879, and Naeseth sold the store to Nels' brother-in-law Peter Lund in 1881.

Nels, Christiana, and their family then moved to Faribault where they had a grocery store located on 10th Street between Main and Elm. Their residence was on the southwest corner of Main and 10th.

By 1895, grocer Nels with his wife and eight children had moved to Eklund where he established a general store. Nels was again commissioned as a postmaster in 1897. The children attended school at District #21. In 1905, the post office was discontinued when rural mail delivery began. The store was taken over by Nels' daughter Mabel and her husband, so it stayed in the family. The store is now (2008) a family home.

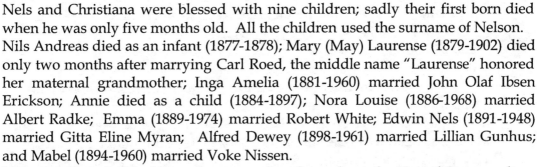

A newspaper article in the family file commemorates their service: "the Eklund store, serv[ed] the folks of that entire area with a smiling congeniality which has won for them hundreds of staunch friends."

Nels was living in Eklund when he died in 1921, at the age of 71. The Kvernodden graves are in the Eklund Cemetery, Walcott Township, Rice County, just north and a bit west of the Eklund Store intersection.

Nels and Christiana were blessed with nine children; sadly their first born died when he was only five months old. All the children used the surname of Nelson.

Nils Andreas died as an infant (1877-1878); Mary (May) Laurense (1879-1902) died only two months after marrying Carl Roed, the middle name "Laurense" honored her maternal grandmother; Inga Amelia (1881-1960) married John Olaf Ibsen Erickson; Annie died as a child (1884-1897); Nora Louise (1886-1968) married Albert Radke; Emma (1889-1974) married Robert White; Edwin Nels (1891-1948) married Gitta Eline Myran; Alfred Dewey (1898-1961) married Lillian Gunhus; and Mabel (1894-1960) married Voke Nissen.

Nels and Christiana's descendants now live throughout the United States and are proud of their Norwegian pioneer immigrant ancestry.

Kvernodden, Nels T and Maria Olsdtr Vale

Nels Tolvsen Kvernodden was born April 25, 1813, on the Kvernodden farm in Holla, Telemark, Norway. He was the oldest of 12 children born to Tolv Knudsen and Inger Nielsdtr. His wife, Maria Olsdtr Vale, was born in February of 1812 on the Hvale farm in Rommenæs Annex, Holden, Telemark. She was the daughter of Ole Jonson Vale and Anne Andersdtr Lunde.

Nels and Maria were married in Holla, Telemark, on November 13, 1835. Four children were born in Telemark: Tolef (1836-1903), Inger (1838-1874), Ole (1840-1927), and Nels (1842).

The family came to America on the bark *Salvator* in 1844, leaving from Porsgrunn, Telemark. They joined Maria's brother and sister, John and Anne Torine, who had immigrated to Sugar Creek, Walworth County, Wisconsin, in 1843. Marie's parents also emigrated from Holla and settled in the same area.

In Sugar Creek, Nels and Maria added three more children to the family: Anna (1846-1940), a second Nels (1849-1921), and John (1852-1915). The Kvernodden and Vale families were early, active members of the Sugar Creek Lutheran Church. Nels owned land and farmed near the church.

They continued farming after moving to Goodhue County, Minnesota Territory, in 1857 and were instrumental in establishing the Holden Lutheran Church. A service was held in their home on September 16, 1857. Nels and Maria are buried at Holden Lutheran Cemetery.

Nels' and Maria's oldest son Tolef (Tolif) used the patronymic Nelson as his surname. He married Anne Marie Johnsdtr. They had seven children. Inger (1838-1874) married Ole Larsen Soredahl. Ole married Mette Hoen and had four daughters. Anna and her husband Peter Foss Lund also had four daughters. Nels N. and his wife Christiane Johnson had nine children. John married Sigri Nybro and had seven children.

Larson, Enoch

Enoch Larson was born February 6, 1833, in Friestad, Klepp, Rogaland, Norway. His parents were Lars and Mette Friestad. He came directly to Houston County, Minnesota Territory, from Stavanger in 1854. He was accompanied by his mother, Metta Osmundsdtr, and a nephew, Lars Johannesen Friestad. Enoch's older brother died in 1853 and his wife remarried. Enoch was unhappy with the way his nephew's new stepfather treated him, so he took responsibility for Lars and brought him to America. Metta returned to Norway after two years.

Enoch married Karen Mathea Hansdtr Melbyeie on October 1, 1867. She arrived in Houston County in the summer of 1867 from Nannestad Parish, Akershus. Just a month later, after renting for thirteen years, Enoch purchased the southwest quarter of the southwest quarter of Section 33, Township 104, Range 7 (Yucatan

Township, Houston County) on Nov. 1, 1867, for $500. Four daughters were born on the Yucatan farm.

In 1873, Enoch became the first Norwegian settler in Dueul County (South Dakota) when he moved his family to Dakota Territory. His homestead document was filed on February 1, 1882. When the county was organized in 1878, he served as its first treasurer. In May of 1877, Bethlehem Lutheran Church was organized at his home. Before the church building was erected, the congregation met first in the Larson home and then at the Larson School.

Enoch died on July 17, 1887, at the age of fifty-four. His wife Karen died in 1918. They are buried in Bethlehem Cemetery, Astoria, South Dakota.

Lee (Lie), Berit Jonsdtr Lommen

Berit Lommen was born March 1, 1816, in Vestre Slidre in the Valdres Valley of Norway. She was the first child of Jon Anfinson Lommen and Jorend Gjermundsdtr. In 1845, Berit married Knud Lee (Lie). Three children were born to this union: Jorend, Anne and John. Very little is known about their life in Norway.

In 1856 or 1857 Berit, Knud, and the children immigrated to America. They left Norway on a small sailship. After 13 weeks on the ocean, they landed at Quebec, Canada. They made their way to Spring Grove, Minnesota Territory, where some of Berit's brothers had settled. The Lees lived in Spring Grove for about 12 years. A son, Ole, was born July 19, 1859.

Berit's husband Knud died July 10, 1869. He is buried in the church cemetery at Spring Grove. On May 31, 1870, Berit Lee and her children joined a caravan of covered wagons going to Grant County, Minnesota, where homesteads were still available. They located near Barrett, Minnesota, and experienced both the joys and hardships of pioneer life.

Berit was an active church worker in her new community. She was instrumental in organizing the Ladies Aid of Emmanuel Congregation near Barrett, and was hostess of its first meeting in October, 1870.

Mrs. Lee died on July 11, 1894, at her home. She was buried in Lien Cemetery near Barrett, Minnesota.

Lia (Lea), Hans Gunnarson and Aaste Anundsdtr

Hans, oldest child of Gunnar Hanson Fjågesund and his second wife Karen Kristine Olavsdtr Lia, was born August 19, 1820, on the *Middtigard* Fjågesund farm in the Kviteseid Parish, Telemark. Hans had two younger siblings: Olav, born in 1826; and Ingebjørg, born in 1829.

Hans was thirteen when his mother died and fifteen when his father died. Since Hans, Olav, and Ingebjørg all took the name Lia (shown in the US Census and on ship lists), it is presumed that they went to live with their grandfather, Olav Tronsson and their step-grandmother on the Lia farm, a small farm under the Fjågesund farm in Kviteseid.

At age twenty-nine, Hans emigrated; he sailed from Kragerø on the *Columbus* on May 22, 1851. He spent a year working in Wisconsin, where his brother and sister joined him the following year. They first settled in Skoponong in Walworth County, Wisconsin. Here Hans met Aaste Anundsdtr Hjamdal, who had immigrated in 1844 with her parents, Anund Erikson Hjamdal and Liv Olavsdtr. Hans and Aaste were married on January 23, 1852.

In June of 1854, Hans and Aaste moved to Minnesota Territory along with Hans' brother Olav and other people from Telemark. They settled on the "Waterless Prairie" (Highland Prairie). Hans homesteaded 160 acres in section 18, Norway Township, Fillmore County. His younger brother Olav secured neighboring farm land.

Indians tore down the first logs, but Hans remained determined to build a home for his family. He built a twelve foot square log home which still stands on the Lea farm. Aaste and Hans had to endure hard times during their child-rearing years. In addition to building a new home in a new country, four of their children died at a young age.

Hans and Aaste had eleven children: Gunder Andrias (December 10, 1852-August 2, 1864); Albert (March 27, 1854-June 22, 1891); Ole (September 10, 1856-May 10, 1936); Karen Kristine (May 26, 1858-September 7, 1940); Lena (September 5, 1860-May 15, 1929); Gunnill Annette (May 18, 1862-September 12, 1863); Andrias (March 25, 1864-July 7, 1866); a second Gunder Andreas (February 9, 1866-March

13, 1858); a second Gunnil Annette (February 22, 1870-May 9, 1957); Hans Magnus (born November 22, 1871); and Dorthia (August 27 1874-March 7, 1876). Their youngest son, Hans Magnus, enlisted for three years in the Army in 1905; he disappeared while serving at Camp McKinley in Honolulu, Hawaii.

Norway Township was home for Hans and Aaste for forty-six years. Hans was not only a great farmer, but also a skilled carpenter. After they had lived in the little cabin for several years, Hans built a log addition, larger than the original cabin, and this structure is part of the present farmhouse. The small cabin was moved to a different location on the farm some years later. It provided shelter for many who needed a temporary home. Hans and Aaste courageously built a home and future for their children in America. Hopefully, their descendants will treasure their ancestors' vision and strong will to better themselves.

Hans died on September 22, 1900 at the age of eighty. Two years later Aaste died at the age of seventy-two. They are buried in Highland Cemetery, Fillmore County.

Lie, Johannes Botolvson and Ingeborg Pedersdtr Otterness

Johannes Botolvson Ytre Lie and his wife, Ingeborg Pedersdtr Otterness came from Aurland, Norway, with four children: Randi, Johannes, Botolv, and Anna in 1854. The family first spent time in the town of Rio in Columbia County, Wisconsin, where Peroline was born on May 10, 1855, at Bonnet Prairie. The family relocated to Leon Township, Goodhue County, Minnesota Territory, near the present Urland Church and the village of Hader, Minnesota. Their daughter Christina was born on their Minnesota farm on August 16, 1857. Kari followed on May 24, 1860.

A brief biography of Johannes described him as a charter member of both Holden Lutheran Church and Urland Lutheran Church. The Holden Church records show that Randi was confirmed there in 1860. All family members are also listed on that record.

The family eventually grew to include ten children. Five of the children remained in Goodhue County and southeastern Minnesota, while four moved to the border areas of Minnesota and North and South Dakota. One daughter, Peroline, married Andrew Hagen and moved to Birch Hills, Saskatchewan, Canada, in 1903.

Anna Johannesdtr Lie (Lee) married Soren Hanson Underdahl. He immigrated to America in 1866. They were married on December 16, 1873, in Goodhue County. They had three children: Johan, Ellen Marie, and Stena. The family lived near the Urland Church until Anna died July 5, 1882, as a result of a farm animal incident. The children most likely stayed with Soren and his parents in Sogn until he remarried. Soren and Ostena Stondahl were married December 13, 1888. Family stories report that Ellen then stayed with Aunt Mary and Botolv Lee for some time.

Ellen married Samuel Olaus Aslakson on July 4, 1895. They lived on Sam's parents' (Sven and Liv Aslakson) homestead. Sam began farming with Sven about 1885 and later inherited the farm. Sam and Ellen had nine children. Joseph Edvin was born at the Minneola farm on October 15, 1903. *See Johannes Ytre Lie, page 173*

Lommen, Gjermund Johnson

Gjermund J. Lommen was born in Vestre Slidre, Valdres, Norway, on December 21, 1824. His parents were Jon Anfinson Lommen and Jorend Gjermundsdtr. He grew to manhood in Norway. In his youth, he learned the blacksmith trade from his brother-in-law in Sogndal, Norway.

In 1849 he immigrated to Dane County, Wisconsin, where he worked in the pine woods for about four years. At that time roof shingles were cut with a hatchet from a large block of wood; wages for this work ranged from 70 cents to $1.00 per day. Gjermund was an ambitious worker who split shingles until late at night, thus earning $1.50 per day. His fellow workers called him the "shingle-making machine."

Gjermund moved to Houston County, Minnesota Territory, in the summer of 1853. He bought land in sections 7 and 18 of Wilmington Township. He was the first Norwegian to settle there. A log cabin was erected and other improvements made to establish a home. Much of the land was covered with timber that had to be cut to provide fields for cultivation.

On November 15, 1856, Gjermund married Aagot L. Olson of Decorah, Iowa. The young people worked hard to develop their farm. Before long the farm was provided with comfortable buildings and productive fields.

Gjermund and Aagot were the parents of eight children. Three daughters grew to maturity: Marit, Sigrid, and Ingeborg.

The Lommen family was hospitable and generous. Gjermund frequently baned money to others for passage to America. Often times his loans were not paid back. Gjermund and Aagot also furnished newcomers with many necessities until they were able to establish homes of their own.

Though strict in his home, Gjermund was just, and quick to forget an injustice. He was honest and straight-forward. Without hypocrisy he expressed his opinion regardless of whether it was to a preacher or the hired man. On one occasion he and the hired man were stacking cornstalks. Gjermund walked on his knees as he put the bundles in place. Big Kristofer pitched the bundles bottom first, hitting Gjermund in the head, arms, and back. Finally Gjermund jumped to his feet and exclaimed, "If you want to kill me, do it in a decent manner, and not this way." Big Kristofer then pitched carefully, but spoke no more that day.

The first Lutheran service in Wilmington Township was held in Gjermund's cabin in 1855. Pastor V. Koren officiated. Gjermund and his wife were active in the organization of Trinity Congregation at Spring Grove. They supported it generously.

Aagot, Gjermund's wife, died April 14, 1893, at the age of 64. Interment was in the Trinity Lutheran Church Cemetery. Gjermund J. Lommen died at his home on November 1, 1902. He was also buried in Trinity Cemetery, Spring Grove.

Lommen, Jon Johnson

Jon Johnson Lommen, one of those intrepid pioneers who laid the foundations of prosperity in Houston County, Minnesota, was born in Valdres, Norway, on November 18, 1831. He grew to manhood in his native land, and at the age of thirteen lost both of his parents. After that, he had little chance for schooling as he had to support himself. One of his brothers, Gjermund, who immigrated to the United States in 1849, sent home a favorable report of this country, especially about Wisconsin. Jon and his brothers Peder, Tosten, and Thomas joined Gjermund in Wisconsin in 1851.

The first year after Jon arrived was spent in the Wisconsin pineries. Then in 1852, he and his brothers relocated to Spring Grove Township, Houston County, Minnesota Territory, where he bought a tract of land two miles northwest of what is now the town of Spring Grove.

On June 20, 1855, he married Marit Oldsdtr Ristey. The ceremony was performed in Knute Kieland's first log hut. This marriage, the second to be celebrated in the township, resulted in the birth of four children: John, Jorend, Ole, and Marit. Jon's wife Marit died April 24, 1867. The following year, on April 5th, Mr. Lommen married Kasperinde Erickson Oium, who was also of Norwegian parentage. Of this marriage six more children were born: Martin, Edward, Peter, Anton, Tosten, and Johanna. Johanna became the wife of Alfred B. Halvorsen, and resided on a farm adjoining the old homestead.

Mr. Lommen toiled with determination to improve and develop his farm. He broke the land, worked to bring it into good condition, and erected solid buildings on his farm. His early years on the place were full of hard work with little immediate compensation, but he waged a successful battle with the forces of nature and in time obtained its mastery. He resided on his farm until 1903, when he felt it was time to retire. He sold the farm to his son Peter, and moved with his wife to Spring Grove, where they lived the rest of their lives.

Lommen, Peder Jonson

Peder Jonson Lommen, one of the first settlers in the township of Spring Grove, Minnesota, was born in Valdres, Norway, on the 24th of September, 1822. He was the first son and fourth child of a family of nine born to Jorend Gjermundsdtr and Jon Anfinson Lommen.

Peder and all but his two youngest brothers took the surname Lommen from the name of the area in which they lived. Tosten and Thomas used their patronymic, Johnson, as their surname in America.

In the 1840's and 1850's, an "America Fever" was experienced by a great number of Norwegians. Times were hard. Because of the extreme poverty and lack of hope that they could better their lot, many joined groups who left their homeland. Among these were Peder Lommen, his wife, and two daughters, Jorend and Marit. They left Vestre Slidre, Valdres, in 1851 and sailed on an Atlantic sloop. After eleven weeks on the ocean they reached New York. From there they went to Wisconsin. After working for a time in the pineries, they came to Minnesota Territory, where Peder Lommen homesteaded. He took a claim in Section 3 of Spring Grove Township where he lived until his death in 1889.

Peder was married twice and was the father of eleven children. His first wife was Jorend Olson Riste, who was the mother of Jorend, Marit, John, Elizabeth, Ole, Tosten, and Jorgen (George). She died in childbirth when George was born. Peder and Jorend's son John P. Lommen was said to be the first male child ("*gutte barn*") born of Norwegian parents in Minnesota Territory. The first Houston County History states that he was the first white child born in Houston County.

Peder's second wife was Maria Arntson who was the mother of Christian, Andrew, Sigrid and Ingeborg (Belle).

The descendants of Peder Lommen honor his memory for the part he and his family played in the development of Houston County, Minnesota. He was a stern man, industrious and God-fearing. He passed away in 1889 at the age of 67 years, but lives affectionately in the memory of his descendants.

Lundby, Anders Larsen and Marte Maria

In August of 1854, a group of emigrants left Hurdal, Akershus, Norway, bound for America. Included in their number were Anders Larsen Lundby (b. 1799), his wife Marte Marie Olsdtr Ruud (1813), and their children Marte (1835), Lars (1837), Anne (1839), Ole (1842), Birthe (1844), Inge (1846), Hans (1848) and Laura (1851).

Also traveling with them were their newly married daughter Ingeborg (1834) and her husband, Hans C. Gullickson Rud.

After nearly two months' travel on the sailing ship *Fædres Minde*, a steamboat, and the train, via Quebec, Montreal, Detroit, Chicago, and Milwaukee, they arrived at Racine County, Wisconsin. The Lundbys lived in the Muskego settlement for three years. During this time three of their children – Ingeborg, Inge, and Hans – died and a son, a second Hans, was born.

In 1857 the Lundby family moved to Bloomfield Township, Fillmore County, Minnesota Territory. They made the trip by oxcart. Anders purchased a farm, and another child, Johan Andreas, was born that same spring. Their daughter Marte married Hans Gullickson, her sister Ingeborg's widower.

Only four years later Anders died at the age of 61. Marte died in 1887. Both are buried at the old Bloomfield Cemetery, northeast of the present town of Ostrander, Minnesota. Many descendants live in southeastern Minnesota, while others now can be found in northwestern Minnesota, Montana, California, and many other states.

Six of Anders & Marte's children (from left to right): Anne Katrine Hatlestad (1839-1907), Lars Osterud (1837-1907), J. Andreas Lundby (1857-1939), Hans Lundby (1854-1927), Ole Anderson Lundby (1842-1915), and Martha O. Gullickson (1835-1913).

Lunde, Christian Peterson

Christian Pederson was born on May 16, 1835, to Karen Knudsdtr Jørandlien and Peder Jensen Bratlien at Torpa, Nordre Land *kommune* (township), Oppland *Fylke* (county), Norway. Karen and Peder were not married, but in October 1835, when Christian was 5 months old, his mother married Johannes Stenersen Lunde. Eight more children were born to the family. Christian used the Lunde farm name; he was apparently adopted by Johannes Stenersen.

Christian was just thirteen years old when he left Norway. He sailed on the bark *Fremad* from Drammen, and arrived in New York on August 25, 1848 with his maternal uncle, Ole Knudsen Gaarder and his wife Kari.

Christian settled first in the Rock Run, Illinois, Settlement and in 1854 joined his uncle in Allamakee County, Iowa.

After making a claim on Section 26 in Minneola Township, Goodhue County, Minnesota in 1855, Christian began to build a life for himself in America. On March 19, 1859 he married Hilda L. Swenson, a native of Sweden, whose father had died in Sweden and mother had died after their arrival in America in 1850. Together the couple had eight children, of whom Caroline, Matilda, Edwin, Josephine, Carl A., and William (Wilhelm) survived to adulthood.

Christian Peterson was deeply interested in the Norwegian Lutheran Church. He attended the first worship service of what would eventually become Land Lutheran Church on Sunday, June 25, 1855 and was one of the original signers of its Articles of Incorporation. He went on to serve many years as a trustee. The church was named after the area many of the congregation came from in Norway. As one of the nine members of the Building Committee, Christian pledged to be responsible for financing the church and parsonage.

He also served as both supervisor and chairman of the township board, and as a member of the school board. His home was often a stopping place for the influx of Norwegians that were to follow, including five of his eight half-brothers and sisters and their families.

Christian died on May 16, 1904 and is buried in the Land Church Cemetery at Zumbrota.

Melbostad, Anders P. and Sigrid E.

Standing: Lars, Edward, Peter, Carrie, Emma & Martha
Seated: Anders & Sigrid Melbostad

Anders P. Melbostad was born September 23, 1827 and his wife Siri on April 10, 1830, both in Gran, Hadeland. She was living at Granseiet, and he on the Melbostad farm in Gran. They were old friends in Norway and came over within a few weeks of each other in 1854.

In Norway his name was Anders Pederson and at some point in America he adopted the farm name Melbostad and used the first letter of his patronymic, Pederson, as his middle initial. His name has also been found listed as Andrew P. Peterson and various misspellings of Melbostad. Siri's name has also been found as Sigrid Lynne, Sigrid E., and Siri Ellingsdtr.

The Melbostads followed a Northwest path through the Midwest, a path many immigrants traveled. They first came to Muskego, Wisconsin, a Norwegian settlement in southeastern Wisconsin, where they were married.

They lived in Muskego until 1858, and then moved to a farm in Eureka Township, Dakota County, Minnesota Territory. They had six children and lived there for twenty-four years, until 1882 when they moved to another farm in Humboldt Township in Clay County, Minnesota.

In 1900, Anders retired from farming and moved into a small home in Barnesville, Minnesota. He died August 21, 1907 in Barnesville; Siri preceded him in death, passing away on September 06, 1905. They are buried in the Melbostad plot in the Norwegian Evangelical Lutheran Cemetery in Wolverton (now called Faith Lutheran). Their names on the headstone are Anders P and Sigrid E Melbostad.

Their son Lars settled in Forest Lake and all of his children have also spent their entire lives in Minnesota.

Morem, Ole

Ole Morem (1832-1915) left his homeland of Tinn, Telemark, Norway, for America in 1852. He spent two years in Wisconsin before relocating to Fillmore County, Minnesota Territory in 1854-55.

Ole worked for John Jacobson, near Lenora in Canton Township, before purchasing his own farm on July 4, 1863. What became known as the "Morem farm" in Harmony Township was purchased from Ole's cousin John Johnson and his wife Mary for $200. Shortly after he purchased the farm, Ole married Aase Herbjørnsdtr Ingulfsland, who was the daughter of Herbjørn and Aagot Ingulfsland, who also immigrated from Tinn. Ole was a charter member of the Greenfield Lutheran Church – his name is inscribed on the monument honoring the congregation's earliest members.

Ole and Aase lived their entire lives on the Morem farm and raised their five children there: John (1864-1913), Henry (1866-1952), Austin (1868-1961), Ingaborg (1870-1877), and Gustie (1872-1947).

Ole and Aase Morem, along with many of their family, are buried in the Greenfield Lutheran Cemetery in Harmony Township, Fillmore County.

Næse, Ole Pedersen and Gjertrud Iversdtr

Ole Pedersen Næse was born March 27, 1821, and baptized on April 17 in Vik Parish of Arnafjord, Sogn, Norway. Gjertrud Iversdtr Næse was born on the same farm on April 7, 1830. Her parents were Iver and Dorthea Næse.

Both Ole Pedersen and Gjertrud Iversdtr (along with her parents) sailed from Bergen on April 30, 1845. It took 57 days reach New York on the ship *Albion*; they arrived on July 2, 1845. They all went overland from New York to the Koshkonong Settlement in Dane County, Wisconsin.

Ole and Gjertrud were married in the East Koshkonong Church by Rev. A. C. Preus on April 12, 1851. Their first two children were born in Wisconsin. Peder Pedersen was born May 27 and baptized on July 27, 1851. Anna Dortia Pedersen was born March 17, 1854, and baptized April 28.

The Næse family moved to Minnesota Territory in 1855. They made the trip by covered wagon, and took land in Holden Township, Goodhue County. They were early members of Holden Lutheran Church. When Urland Lutheran Church was organized in 1872, the family became members of that congregation and took an active role in the church community.

The first of the Pedersen children to be born in Minnesota was Iver, on July 7, 1856. Iver was followed by Johan Andrias, who was born December 2, 1858.

Pioneer life was difficult, and it took a special toll on young children. Anna Dortia and Iver were only seven when they died, Anna on January 5, 1862 and Iver on May 13, 1864. Johan died February 5, 1862 without reaching his fourth birthday. Following Norwegian tradition, a second Iver, born May 18, 1863 was named for his deceased brother. He was approaching his third birthday when he died on April 7, 1866. Anna Bertine was named for her deceased older sister, Anna Dortia. She was born June 28, 1870, and died before her first birthday, on May 6, 1871.

Ole and Gjertrud lived out their lives on their Leon Township farm. He died on March 30, 1909 and Gjertrud on May 5, 1918. Both are buried in Urland Lutheran Cemetery.

Four of their children lived to be adults:

Peder, who was born in Wisconsin, farmed in Leon Township until his death in May of 1925. He is buried in Urland Lutheran Cemetery.

Kristine Maline was born on September 5, 1862. She married Christopher Kristophersen Sandvig on June 19, 1896. She died in September of 1928 and is buried with her husband in Urland Lutheran Cemetery.

Johanne Pedersen was born January 28, 1867, and baptized March 31. She was confirmed on June 12, 1881, and married Andrew Larsen Flom on December 16, 1892. She died September 12, 1934, and is buried in Urland Cemetery.

Oliver was born March 31, 1872. He married twice. Oliver married Ellevine Hegvik on November 1, 1894. She died in 1906. In 1907, he married Josephine. Oliver died March 6, 1944.

Nelson, Evar and Aase Olsdtr Frygne

Evar (Iver) Nelson was born in Kirstiansand, Norway, on July 22, 1815. His parents were Nils Anderson and Marthe Thorsdtr. Evar left Kristiansand for Le Havre, France, and from there traveled on the ship *Magnolia* to New Orleans, landing on November 17, 1845. The voyage took 19 weeks.

Evar settled in Wisconsin. He served 5 years in the American Army from 1847-1852. The Mexican-American War was fought during this time and he received a pension as a result of his service.

After returning from the Army, Evar settled in Fillmore County, Minnesota Territory. In 1855, he married Aase (Esther) Olsdtr Frygne. She was born on March 12, 1829, in Numedal, Buskerud County, Norway. Evar and Aase's first six children - Martha (1856-1930), Nicholas (1859-1940), Anna (1861-1951), Thomas (1864-1933), and Caroline (1867-1953) - were born in Fillmore County.

Evar and Aase sold their land and moved their family to Yellow Medicine County by covered wagon. Three years later, they relocated to Lyon County. Sons Henry (1870-1953) and Iver, Jr. (1873-1964) were born in western Minnesota.

Aase died Jun 12, 1889, and Evar on June 20, 1895. They are buried in Christ Lutheran Cemetery, just west of Cottonwood, Minnesota.

Nelson, Knud

Knud Nelson was born September 3, 1822. His parents were Nels Ekabot and Sarah Neutsen Nelson. Knud immigrated to America in 1852. He landed at the port of Quebec and made his way to Dane County, Wisconsin, where he stayed for two years. In 1854, Knud moved to the Minnesota Territory. He pre-empted 120 acres in Section 7, Frankford Township in Mower County, later doubling his holdings to 240 acres. He was quite successful, involved in Republican politics, and considered to be one of the prominent men of the community. Knud was an early member of Bear Creek Lutheran Church in Grand Meadow, Minnesota.

Knud and his wife Julia (Jul) had eight children: Sarah, Julia, Emma, Nils, Bertine, Julius, Olava, and Alex.

Nord Strand, Knud Bendixsen & Ragnild Olsdtr

Knud Bendixsen Nord Strand (1824-1898) and his wife Ragnild Olsdtr Nord Strand (1827-1909) were raised in the Valdres Valley in Norway. Church records show that Knud relocated to Bergen in 1842. In 1848, the couple was married in Svennes, Nord-Aurdal, Oppland. Knud and Ragnild immigrated that same year on the ship *Augusta*, departing Bergen on May 6 and arriving in New York on June 27. They settled in Koshkonong settlement, Dane County, Wisconsin.

Knud and Ragnild came to Minnesota Territory in 1854. In the 1857 territorial census, they were documented as farmers in Preston Township (T-102-N & R-10-W), Fillmore County. Their daughter Caroline Bendickson (1863-1933), was baptized at Union Prairie, and married Mikkel Knudson (1852-1893) of Amherst Township, Fillmore County in 1875.

Ragnild, despite being bedridden for 21 years suffering from rheumatism, remained bright and cheerful to the last. Knud and Ragnild are both buried in the Henrytown Lutheran Cemetery in rural Harmony, Minnesota.

Norman, Nels O., Brynild and Ole

The Nels O. Norman Family
Standing: Albertina, Christina, Ole N. & Anna
Seated: Nels O. & Christine Lofthus Norman

Ola Nielsen Selland and Anna Strksdtr Jordalen-Giljarhus, along with sons Niels, Ole, Brynild and daughter Anna, emigrated from Vossestrand Norway. The ship *Virgo* left Bergen on May 10th and arrived in New York on June 24, 1853. The family used the surname Tweite on the ship, having lived for a time on the farm of that name. The family proceeded to Nicollet County, Minnesota, and settled in Lake Prairie Township in the spring of 1854. They were among the earliest settlers in what would come to be known as the Norseland Settlement. The census of 1857 shows the family using Nelson as a surname. They would later change it to Norman.

The three sons were actively engaged in the uprising of 1862, probably in the defense of New Ulm, according to family lore. All three are listed on the roster of the Lake Prairie Rangers, although no actual dates of participation are available. Nels is listed as a member of the St. Peter Frontier Guards from the 19th through the 26th of August, 1862. Nels and Ole are listed on the roster of the Scandianvian Guards starting on August 27 for a period of 21 days. Ole then joined the 1st Regiment of Minnesota Mounted Rangers October 11th, 1862, and was discharged 11 April 1863, using the name Ole Olesen. He subsequently joined Company B, 2nd Regiment Minnesota Volunteer Cavalry from December 10, 1863 through December 1, 1865, serving in Sibley's campaigns into Dakota Territory. Researcher and author Charles F. Flandrau expresses great difficulty in acquiring complete and accurate rosters of the citizen soldiers involved, therefore there are undoubtedly omissions of names and errors in spelling.

An interesting sidelight to the tragedy of the period which has circulated through the family by word of mouth was recently discovered in print. Columnist Edward N. Vernon's column "Along Side Roads and Highways" in the July 6th, 1928 issue of the *Montevideo News* reported as follows: "Mr. Norman Senior (Ole N. Norman, the son in the picture) had an interesting story to tell of early pioneer days, which time and space prevent recording in detail. He told of the experiences of his grandfathers Norman and Lofthus, who were defenders of New Ulm in the Indian massacre of 1862. How Grandma Lofthus who was alone with her babe at home and in time a neighbor came over and told her of the coming of the Indians and the necessity to flee for their lives. No wagon being available, this neighbor hitched his yoke of oxen to the Lofthus sleigh, although it was the month of August, and with his wife and child and Mrs. Lofthus and her baby drove the sixteen miles to St. Peter and safety."

Ohnstad, Rognald Johnson

Rognald Johnson Ohnstad was born on the Ohnstad gård in Aurland, Sogn, Norway, on February 18, 1832, to Johannes Olsen Ohnstad (1804-1880) and Kristine Olsdtr (Ohnstad) (1808-1884). In the spring of 1853, he made the seven week voyage from Bergen to America. He spent several days in New York after his arrival on July 4th. From there, he traveled to Dane County, Wisconsin, where he hired out to a farmer for a month. He and a friend from the old country then spent two years in Chicago.

Rognald saved enough money to send for his parents and siblings, including Brita (Larson) (1833-), Ole (1836-1913), Ole Andreas (1838-?), Jon (1841-1864?), Inger (Peterson-Thinglum) (1843-1924), Ingeborg (1846- ?), and Botolv (1851-1911). Two children, Botolv and Marta, died before they left Norway.

In the fall of 1855, Rognald went to Red Wing, Minnesota Territory. He filed on land in Section 20 of Leon Township before returning to Chicago. The next spring he and his family moved to his claim.

He married Martha Ottum, born in 1839 to Iver Jensson Berge and Gurina Carlsdtr (Ytrefjornen). Martha had emigrated in 1856 from the Luster fjord north of the Sognefjord. They had five children: Christine (Edstrom) (1859-1948), Joseph (1861-1861), Anna Marie (Melhus) (1863-1908), Johanna (1865-1872) and Josephine (Ramstad) (1867-1935).

Martha died in 1869, and Rognald's sister Inger took on the job of caring for the house and his children. Rognhald had known his second wife, Petrine Olsdtr Otterness, in Norway. They added seven children to the family: Joseph (1874-1958), Ingeborg/Hannah (Torgerson) (1876-1956), Tosten (1879-1940), Adolph (1884-1942), Peter Andreas (1887-1960), Rensa (1890-1892), and Robert/Clarence (1894-1948).

Rognald's land holdings in Leon and Warsaw Townships would eventually grow to 700 acres. He also bought land in the Bismarck, North Dakota area, although he never farmed there. Rognald was a pioneer member of Holden Lutheran Church, and was one of three who signed the Articles of Incorporation for Urland Lutheran Church in 1872. Along with holding offices in that congregation, he served as a township supervisor. He assisted in the founding of St. Olaf College in Northfield and sent three of his sons to school there.

The Ohnstads lived in a large seven bedroom house, which is still in existence. Rognald had a will that said the farm could not be sold during the lifetime of his wife Petrine. She lived to be 97 years old, so although her son Clarence had farmed the land all his life his son Raymond bought it from the heirs and still owns the property.

The obituary in the Cannon Falls Beacon read: "Rognald Ohnstad was a strong and healthy man until the last few years of his life when an attack of la grippe seemed to weaken him to such an extent that his health was not restored, and besides this old age crept on and he gradually grew weaker until about ten days before his death when he went to bed from where he never arose. He died April 18, 1914 at the ripe old age of 82 years, 2 month, and 16 days."

Oleson, Andrew and Martha

According to Norwegian churchbooks, Martha and Andrew (Anund) Oleson, along with children Ole, Bertha, Albert and Johanna emigrated on May 10, 1853, from upper Telemark, Norway. They traveled from Chicago by train and boat to Reed's Landing, Minnesota Territory, on the Mississippi River.

Andrew and Martha built a log cabin on a homestead in Minneiska Township, Wabasha County, in what would become the village of Weaver. They then bought and worked a farm for twelve years before repurchasing and returning to their log cabin in Weaver.

Martha and Andrew's daughters Eliza and Anna were born while Minnesota was still a territory. Mary Edna, Martha, Hattie, Amelia, Caroline, and Edna Madelia arrived later.

Andrew earned his living in winter cutting cord wood for the steamboats on the Mississippi River. He left home early in the morning carrying his cold lunch, and walked the 3 ½ miles to Minneiska. He returned from that river landing each night, often with soiled laundry from the ships' captains for Martha to wash.

Andrew and Martha were friendly with the Indians in the area. Martha helped them with many of their problems; she even assisted in the birth of their children. In return, the Indians helped her with the birth of one of her children. Many of the Indians whom Andrew and Martha had befriended took part in the Indian uprising of the 1860's around New Ulm, Mankato, and St. Peter. When Andrew and Martha traveled to Mankato, they saw the Indian prisoners sitting around the square. When the Indians saw their white friends, they hid their faces. The prisoners were later hung.

An excerpt from the book *History of Wabasha County*, compiled by Dr. L. H. Bunnell and published in Chicago by H. H. Hill Publishers in 1884 says, "Weaver village was laid out in 1871. William Weaver and a man by the name of Dodge were the proprietors. The town was named after the former gentleman, and stands on sections 29 and 30 of Minneiska Township. In the summer of 1851* Andrew Olson immigrated to this section with his family, took a claim and erected a house, the first in this vicinity. Soon after, two brothers, George and Christopher Abbott, and in 1857 William Weaver arrived from New York State and opened up a farm on the north side of which a part of the town now stands. As soon as the village was laid out a post office was established, with W. H. Hopkins as postmaster. At present writing, Weaver contains a store, hotel, butcher shop, blacksmith shop and two warehouses."

Martha, Edna and Andrew Oleson – 1876

Andrew died April 2, 1883. Martha moved to Plainview, Minnesota where she lived with her daughter Caroline and her husband, Louis O. Sundquist, until her death on August 16, 1916. Andrew and Martha are buried in Greenwood Cemetery outside Weaver, Minnesota.

* *The Wabasha County history offers an earlier date of arrival for the Olesons than Norwegian church records show as the date of their departure.*

Oleson, Thore and Margarette Stephensdtr

Thore Oleson was born April 5, 1807, to Ole Thorerson and Anne Hansdtr at Tingelstad, upper Alm farm, in Gran, Oppland County, Norway. He was an only child, baptized April 12, 1807, at the old Tingelstad Church. On November 27, 1827, he married Margarette Stephensdtr, who was born April 24, 1803, to Stephen and Kirstie Olsdtr Klovstadeie, Gran. In 1830, he was *husmannfolk* (a tenant farmer) at Tingelstad.

Thore and Margarette were blessed with six children: Ole was born October 3, 1827; Stephen, born August 16, 1830; Anne, born December 12, 1834; Hans, born September 4, 1838; Karl, born March 15, 1842; and Christine, born October 6, 1845. They were all baptized at the old Tingelstad Church.

On May 28, 1850, their oldest son, Ole, immigrated to America on the ship *Vesta*. The plan was that he would earn enough money to bring the rest of the family to America to build a better life.

Thore and Margarette's daughter Anne died January 25, 1854, at Tingelstad. Later that same year, on April 15, the rest of the family signed out of their church parish for that better life in America. Thore and Margrethe Oleson with their children Stephen, Hans, Karl, and Kirsti, joined Ole in Minnesota Territory, where the family settled on a homestead in Eureka Township near the town of Farmington, Dakota County.

All four sons served in the Civil War; Karl died. Thore and Margarette lived on their Minnesota homestead until their deaths in 1864 and 1869, respectively. They are buried at Highview Christiana Church cemetery in Dakota County.

Olson, William and Anna

William Olson was born in Norway on December 2, 1826. He came to America in 1849 and spent about 6 months in Summit, Waukesha County, Wisconsin, before moving to Lake Mills, Jefferson County, Wisconsin, where he lived until 1855. At that time he married Anna Olson, a recent immigrant from Norway, and they moved to Leon Township, Goodhue County where he built a fine farm of 180 acres.

William was Leon township treasurer for many years, and held other offices in his church and community. His children were Lewis J., Oliver, Christine, Isabella, Caroline, William Jr, George and Lovise.

Omsrud, Kari and Thord

Thord and Kari Omsrud immigrated to America in 1852 from Hedalen, Valdres. They spent some time in Wisconsin before settling in Linden township (later Lake Hanska Township), Brown County in 1857.

Opsal, Nels Danielson and Ragnild Halvorsdtr Røste

Nels Danielson Opsal was born on April 28, 1817, in Lier, Norway. His parents were Daniel Nilsen and Helle Hansdtr Schustad. In 1847, he married Ragnild Halvorsdtr Røste. She was born to Halvor Olsen and Anne Aslesdtr on Christmas Day, 1820, in Norderhov. In 1855, Nels, Ragnild, and their three small children left Norway for Rock County, Wisconsin.

Two years later, the family joined a small group of Norwegian immigrants bound for Meeker County, Minnesota Territory. They arrived in the summer of 1857 and settled in Acton Township. The children began attending school in 1860, when the county's first English school was established. Nels joined other Norwegian immigrants in organizing the St. Johannes Congregation of Meeker and surrounding counties, later known as Ness Norwegian Evangelical Lutheran Church. In 1868, he was one of the founders of the Arndahl Norwegian-Danish Lutheran congregation.

On August 17, 1862, five settlers were killed by a small group of Indians just four miles from the Danielson cabin. This was the trigger of what would become known as the Sioux Uprising of 1862. Nels was one of a small group of settlers

who rushed to the scene of the tragedy. Following burial of the victims at Ness Cemetery, the family gathered supplies and hastened to the county seat at Forest City. The Danielsons took shelter in a small cabin, and Nels joined other citizens in forming a "Home Guard."

In early September, the Home Guard built a stockade in just a single day to provide security for some 240 settlers. Hours after the stockade was completed, a band of warriors approached the village, and were surprised and disappointed to come upon the newly constructed stockade walls. They did not attack, but burned several buildings, including the cabin the Danielsons had so recently vacated. When the family returned to Acton, their cabin was in shambles and their possessions strewn in the woods.

In 1863, Nels homesteaded 160 acres of land a short distance to the south, becoming one of the first residents in the least settled area of Meeker County. Nels erected a cabin and barn and cleared land. The first year he planted hay, harvesting enough to feed 50 head of cattle through the winter. By 1870, nearly half of the 160 acres was improved and he owned horses, milk cows, oxen, cattle, sheep and swine.

On July 9, 1870, Nels died of pneumonia. A portion of Acton was later separately organized and named Danielson Township in his honor. His wife Ragnild remained on the homestead until her death on March 18, 1898. Nels and Ragnild Danielson are buried at the Arndahl Cemetery.

The seven Danielson children were Anne Helena (1847-1904), Maren (1849-1912), Daniel (1853-1949), Hans (1855-1939), Henry (1858-1908), Lena (1860-1862), and Anton (1862-1948).

Nels and Ragnild Danielson were quintessential Norwegian pioneer farmers who left their homeland in search of a better life. Enduring hardships, they persevered with courage and faith to establish their family in Minnesota. Hundreds of descendants are a tribute to these triumphant immigrants.

Orton, Cornelius Knute

Cornelius Knute Orton was born in 1846 in Dane County, Wisconsin. His parents were Knute Ole and Anne Knutsdatter Hovland. In 1853, the family moved to Iowa and in 1857 to Fillmore County, Minnesota. Cornelius grew to manhood in Fillmore County and married his wife Augusta Westling in La Crosse, Wisconsin, on June 1, 1869. She was born in Sweden on November 9, 1851, came to America as a young child, and grew to womanhood in Wabasha County.

In 1871, C. K. and Augusta moved to Big Stone County. He took 160 acres on which the town that bears his name, Ortonville, was founded. Cornelius Orton both helped organize Big Stone County and served as chairman of the board of county commissioners. He was mayor of Ortonville and its first postmaster. He was president of Orton's Bank, served as a director of the Fargo Southern Railroad, and was a large stockholder in the Big Stone Lake Navigation Company.

Cornelius and Augusta had six children: Clara Alice Janette, born February 19, 1872; Clark Walter, born March 7, 1874; Mary Adella, born March 15, 1876; Carl

Edward, born October 2, 1877; Nell, born August 20, 1879; and Dwight Wesley, born April 8, 1881.

C. K. Orton died at his home on December 24, 1890.

Orton, Knute Ole and Anna Knutsdtr Hovland

Knute Ole Orton was born July 12, 1812 on the Skjerdal farm in Aurland, Sogn og Fjordane, Norway and died in 1879, in Ortonville, Minnesota. He married Anna Knutsdtr Hovland on March 19, 1837, in Lærdal, Norway. Anna was born August 7, 1819, on the Hovland farm in Ardal, Sogn og Fjordane and died October 3, 1887, in Ortonville, Minnesota.

Knute's father, Ole Knutson Skjerdal, preceded him to the USA in 1843 on the sailship *Juno* unescorted by any family member. Knute followed in 1844. He and his wife, two daughters, Cornelia and Anna, and one son, Ole, sailed on the *Juno* from Bergen in April and arrived in New York on St. John's Eve, June 23rd, 1844. The crossing took only 5 weeks and 3 days - a record for fast sailing! His name was changed from Knut Olsson Aaretun when he emigrated.

From New York City, the party went by canal boat up the Hudson River to Buffalo, New York, arriving on July 4th. They then crossed the Great Lakes on a steamboat that arrived in Milwaukee at the end of July. The family continued on to Koshkonong via Muskego. They farmed at Koshkonong until they purchased a farm in Norway Township, Racine County, Wisconsin in 1847.

In 1853, Knute and his family moved to Winneshiek County, Iowa, and settled in Carrolton Township, Fillmore County, Minnesota about 1856. The first Lutheran church meeting in that township was held in the Orton home that same year. Knute built the township's first sawmill on the north branch of the Root River in 1857. It had a reciprocating-type saw. In 1858, it was destroyed by a flood. Rebuilt in 1860, it again washed away and the mill was then demolished. Knute was the organizer and, as director, one of the first three officers of school district #49. In 1858, the first English speaking school was held in the Orton home.

In 1874, Knute and Anna moved to Ortonville in Big Stone County in western Minnesota to join their son and town founder, Cornelius K. Orton. They built their home where the Whetstone River enters the Minnesota River.

Anna was one of those pioneer women with a knowledge of practical nursing. One family member was shot in the arm with an arrow by an Indian being pursued to recover stolen horses. She successfully treated the wound with tobacco leaves and honey. She served as a midwife and was often called upon to help with sick neighbors.

Otterness, Guttorm Pederson and Marta Larsdtr Ytre Lie

Guttorm Pederson Otterness was born in 1831 in Aurland, Norway. He was thirty years old when he sailed to America from Bergen, Norway on the *Augusta*. His name was the third entry on the passenger list. When he arrived on June 29, 1853, he went to Koshkonong, Wisconsin, and then to Spring Grove, Minnesota, where he had relatives. In Spring Grove, there was very little good land still available. Guttorm's sister Ingeborg lived in Goodhue County; on December 17, 1856, he paid $170.00 for 160 acres in Leon Township.

Guttorm married Marta Larsdtr Ytre Lie on June 06, 1859. Marta was born May 7, 1832, in Aurland, Norway. Her parents were Lars Oddsen and Marta Knutsdtr Ytre Lie. She came to America with her parents and brothers, Odd and Lars.

Guttorm and Marta had eight children: Peder (1860-1933), Lars (1861-1948), Johanne (1863-?), Anna (1865-1924), Erik (1868-1902), Odd/Edward G. (1870-1954), Nels (1876-1905) and Ingeborg (1872-1873). Guttorm was a genial, hard-working man. The family's first home was a log house. They cleared the land and pulled stumps with oxen. It was a very tedious process. Guttorm would eventually add 160 acres of land to his holdings and build a comfortable frame house with shutters and a white picket fence.

Wheat was the main crop, but the nearest market was over twenty miles away in Red Wing. In the early years, when it was cold and the roads were icy, local Indian children would grab the wagons and slide along behind.

Guttorm was active in his community. He helped build a log school house in 1857, and in 1872 was one of the founders of Urland Lutheran Church. Guttorm ran a post office in his house before there were any towns that had one. He had a big, black safe that was handed down through the family and a desk that he used for business purposes.

Marta stepped on a nail and her foot became infected. Gangrene developed. The doctors recommended amputation, but she did not want to be a burden to her family and would not let them cut off her leg. As a result, she died on November 19, 1881.

Odd (Edward) was ten years old when his mother died. He said it was a very sad time for all the family. Guttorm placed this loving tribute on her tombstone:

> Farewell, my dear wife, with you I lived happily
> but with sorrow I now grieve your passing. I
> think God for the children you gave us. Peace be
> with your dust. Blessed be your memory.

Guttorm never married again and lived until December 26, 1905. In his old age, he used a cane. Toward the end of his life, he developed a terrible indigestion problem. The doctor was called in and poked a hole in his stomach to try to relieve the pressure. At the time, some thought he may have died of a burst appendix. Guttorm was seventy three years old. He and Marta and many of their descendants are buried in Urland Lutheran Church Cemetery.

Otterness, Odd Larsen

Odd and Randi Otterness and their family: Back row: Lars, Benjamin, Ellen. Front row: Lawrence, Odd Otterness, Eddie, Randi Otterness, Ingeborg, and Jensine

Odd Larsen Otterness was born in Aurland, Sognefjord, Norway. His parents were Lars Oddsen Otterness and Marta Knutsdtr, both born on the Ytre Lie *gård* (farm). Odd was baptized and confirmed in the Vangen Church in Aurland, Norway. Odd, his parents, brother Lars and sister Marta came to America in 1857. The family settled in Leon Township, Goodhue County, with one of his brothers who had come two years previously. Odd lived with his parents for seven years until he bought his own property.

In 1866, Odd married Randi Olsdatter Berekvam. She was born in 1843 to Ole Olsen Berekvam and Inga Eriksdtr (Tunselle) of Aurland, Norway. Randi, her parents, and two siblings, Brita and Jens, immigrated to America in 1860. Three other siblings had immigrated earlier - Ole in 1854, followed by Erik and Kari in 1857.

Odd and Randi had eleven children born to them: Anne Jensine (1866-1898), Lars Olaus (1870-1931), Ellen Martini (1872-1931), Benjamin Sivert (1874-1960), Lawrence Oliver (1876-1963), Ingeborg Rebekke (1878-1918), Eddie E. (1880-1919),

Odd (stillborn in 1880), Carl Edward (1882-1882), and twins Gurina E.(1885-1885) and Irvina Petrina (1885-1885).

Odd was a robust man who led a long and healthy life. He may have had a stroke about three years before he died, and it is proof of his tough constitution that he was able to recover to some extent. He was confined to his bed for only the last two days of his life.

Odd, Randi and many of their descendants are buried in the Urland Church Cemetery.

Ottun, Nels Jenson

Nels Ottun was born February 25, 1843, and came to America with his parents and siblings in 1850 from the Sogn og Fjordane district of western Norway. His parents were Jens Nilsen and Ollegaard Nilsdtr Talle and his siblings were Peder, Jacob, Inger, Caroline, and Susanna. They lived in Wisconsin until the spring of 1854, when the family claimed land in Wanamingo Township, Goodhue County, Minnesota Territory. In 1861, Nels went to college in Decorah and after two years came back home where he was a teacher for a dozen years. In 1873, Nels was elected to the 16th General Assembly of Minnesota and was re-elected to a second term. He also served as a justice of the peace, town clerk, and held many other local government offices.

Nels married Ellen Lovise Munkhaugen in 1861. Their children were Petrine, Julius, Elgerine, and Jens. Ellen died on October 21, 1877. He and his second wife Oline Loftness were married November 21, 1878, at Red Wing. Their children included Ellen, Guro, Marianna, Inger, Susan, Anna, Berent and Berta. The family moved to Custer County, Nebraska, in about 1882.

Nels died on October 12, 1905 in Custer County. Oline died in 1933 in Round Valley, Nebraska.

Overland, Johannes and Tone

Johannes Olson Overland was the seventh of nine children born to Olav Knutsen Overland and Bergit Tovsdtr. He was born in 1799. In 1823, he married Tone Olsdatter Kilen also born in 1799. They homesteaded on Overland, Heimistogu, where all of their children were born: Ole, Gunil, Britt, Kari, Knud, Guro, Steinar, and Anne Overland. This farm is located between Kviteseid and Seljord in the Brokefjell Mountain area of Telemark. In 1851, Johannes and Tone, along with six of their children, packed their belongings and left Kviteseid, journeying to Kragero, Norway. Their oldest son Ole had gone to America in 1848 and daughter Gunil and her husband Aamund Berland remained in Norway. On July 12, 1851, the family departed on the ship *Columbus* with 165 passengers, making the trip to America in seven weeks.

Arrangements had been made for them to stay on the parish farm of Pastor A. C. Preus for two months. They lived at the Skoponong Settlement in Walworth County, Wisconsin, until 1853 when they set out northwest through Prairie du Chien to Calmar, Iowa.

Land and a spring were found in Fillmore County. In 1854, claims were filed in Norway Township and homes built. Highland Prairie Lutheran Church was organized. Land was given for the church, parsonage, and church park in this beautiful setting.

Johannes and Tone remained in Norway Township for the rest of their lives. Johannes died October 24, 1882, and Tone died September 18, 1877. Both are buried at the Highland Prairie Cemetery.

Overland, Ole and Gunil

Ole Overland was the oldest of eight children born to Johannes and Tone Overland. In 1848, he set off for America to join his future mother-in-law; an aunt, Kari Rue; and relatives who had emigrated in 1843. They were the first settlers near the borders of Jefferson and Walworth counties in Wisconsin, southeast of the large Koshkonong Settlement in Dane County.

There is reason to believe that Ole went back to Norway to marry his cousin, Gunil Franson Rue, and returned to Wisconsin in 1849. Their two oldest children, Frans and John, were born there.

In 1853, the family went to Winnishiek County, Iowa, together with his parents and family and other relatives, and Halvor Erickson. Ole and Halvor Erickson, his future brother-in-law, went north into Minnesota to try to locate land where they could all settle. Finding a spring and land, they returned to winter near Calmar, Iowa.

In the spring of 1854 the men returned to what would become sections 15 and 16 of Norway Township, where they built a log home. Ole and Halvor then went back to Iowa to get the family.

Seven children were born to Ole and Gunil: Frans married Mary Groshong and had nine children; John married Gunloug Rorhelle and had ten children; Ole married Beta Myrhagen and had eleven children; Hans died at age 14; Kari died in infancy; Elias married Martha Flattum and had three children who survived; and

Thea married John Erickson with whom she had three children and, after his death, she married his brother Steinar and they had seven more children.
Gunil died March 1, 1881. Ole died November 27, 1890. Ole had remarried after Gunil's death and his second wife, Signe Overland Rorhelle, died May 21, 1891.

Pedersen, Christen and Mari Sørensdtr

Christen Pedersen was born on Brenna, Dvergsten farm, in Gran, Norway, on December 11, 1821. His parents were Peder Carstensen and Johanne Torgersdtr. He married Anne Larsdtr on March 3, 1843. They came to America with daughters Johanne, Anne, and Birthe, in 1851. The family lived in Koshkonong where Anne Larsdtr died in 1853. Christen then married Mari Sørensdtr, who was born in Buskerud County, Norway, on February 1, 1831. Their son Søren was born in Wisconsin, and Anne was born in Minnesota Territory after the family settled in New Brighton, Ramsey County, in 1856.

Christen was a farmer in New Brighton until he retired. He and Mari then moved to St. Paul. He died in 1883. Mari died in 1914.

Ramstad, Ole Anderson & Ragne Hansdtr

Ole and Ragnhild Ramstad Family
Front: Anna, Elizabeth, Randi
Middle: Bertha, Ole Ragnhild, Maren
Back: William, Oscar, Joseph

Ole Anderson Ramstad was born May 15, 1827, on the Ramstad *gård* (farm), Fetsund, Norway to Anders Amundsen and Berte Marie Olsdtr. Along with farming, Ole was a business man and ran the near-by store called Pynten, later Nanson, in the Sogn Valley, The store is now on the historical register.

On June 24, 1853, he married Ragne Hansdotter Valsenger. She was born in 1832 on the Hvalsenga *gård* to Hans Andersen and Berte Vexelsdtr. She was brought up by her grandparents because her mother died when she was very young.

In 1854, Ole and Ragne took the six week voyage from Oslo to New York City. Rationing was necessary and the trip was filled with hardships. They first settled in Dane County, Wisconsin, and then moved to Stoughton, Wisconsin. In 1858, they traveled to Goodhue County, Minnesota, in a covered wagon with Kristen Eggen and Gulbrand Nilsen. They crossed the Mississippi River at Dubuque, Iowa, with an ox team and homesteaded in section 6 of Wanamingo Township, Goodhue County.

Ole was a kind, jovial man with a whole lot of common sense. Being one of the pioneers he had to endure all the hardships that fell to their lot, but he and his wife were economical and hard working and they prospered.

Granddaughter Marie (Langemo) Voxland recalled: Grandma Ragnhild was bed-redden for quite some time. Aunt Maren stayed at home to care for Ole and Ragne in their older years. Other aunts, especially Anna, came home to help care for their parents.

Nine of their thirteen children survived. Maren, who never married, died in the Cannon Falls Sanatorium at the age of seventy-seven. Bertha, (Mrs. Aslak Breidall) died in St. Paul at eighty-eight. Anders was killed by lightning on the home farm in 1891 at age 33. William's farm was on the northeast corner of the same section as his father; he died in 1939 at 79 years old (that farm is now owned by grandson Gary Esterby). Anna (Mrs. Carl Jahr) lived in Bemidji and died in 1950 at 88 years old. Joseph married Sarah Borstad Peterson, lived in Seattle and died in 1955 at 86 years old. Elizabeth (Mrs. Ernest Meyers) lived in Beach, North Dakota, and died in 1958 at 86 years old. Randi, (Mrs. Jørgen Langemo) lived in Kenyon, and died in 1928 at 53 years old. (Hans) Oscar, who lived on the Ramstad homestead, died in 1962 at 85. Four children, Hans, Hansine, Joseph, and a second Hansine all died very young.

Ragnhild had remarkably good health until she was stricken with heart failure about five years before she died. Her condition declined steadily, and in the last two years of her life she could not walk without assistance.

Ole was in good health until shortly before his unexpected death. His obituary described him as a "kind, jovial man with a whole lot of common sense."

Ragnhild died in 1909, and Ole in 1910. They were both buried at Holden Cemetery. All of the children but Elizabeth and Joseph were buried at Holden Church Cemetery.

Rekanes, Ole Mikkelson & Birgith Kittelsdtr Dompendal

Ole Mikkelson was born March 10, 1810, to Mikkel Gunnelvson Rolegheta and Helga Olavsdtr Ulsnes in Flaabygd, Telemark. The family lived on the Rekanes farm under the Nes farm in Flaabygd. Ole married Birgith Kittelsdtr Dompendal on November 20, 1834, in the Flaabygd Church. She was born February 14, 1813, to Kittel Kittelson Dompendal and Birgith Olsdtr, who lived on the tenant farm Dompendal under the Flom farm in Flaabygd.

Birth and Ole had seven children, six of them born before the family emigrated. Helga (born 1835), Mikkel (1838), Birgit (1842), Kittel (1845), Helene, and Ingeborg (1851). Anne, the youngest, was born in Wisconsin in 1854.

The family emigrated from Flaabygd, Telemark, in 1853. They settled first in Walworth County, Wisconsin, but in 1855 they came to Fillmore County, Minnesota Territory, with several of Ole's brothers and other people from Flaabygd. All but one of Birgith's siblings also came to America. Birgith's parents also immigrated but her mother never arrived in Minnesota, so it is uncertain if she died during the trip or in Wisconsin during the family's short stay there. Birgith's oldest brother, Kittel Kittelson Haugen, remained in Telemark.

Ole and Birgith settled on a prairie which the locals called *griserumpen* (pig tail prairie) in Holt Township, Fillmore County. Three adult children settled and farmed near their parents: Mikkel (Michael), who married Margit (Margaret) Lone from Tuddal; Kittel, married to Sevine; and their youngest daughter Anne, who married Mikkel (Michael) Hanson.

No records have been found confirming where Ole Mikkelson died. Records show that Birgith (Betsy) died a widow on July 11, 1877 in Rushford Township in Fillmore County. Since Birgith's daughter, Ingeborg (Isabel, married to Charles Gunderson) is the only child who lived in Rushford, it is possible she died while living with her daughter.

Richardson, Thrond & Gunvor Halvorsdtr Vindlaus

Gunvor Halvorsdtr Vindlaus was born May 14, 1808, in Lårdal, Telemark. She married Ole Drengson Kleppo on July 1, 1828, in Lårdal. He died June 2, 1837, in Lårdal.

Ole and Gunvor had five children, only one of whom, Aasne Olsdtr, born November 20, 1831, in Lårdal, survived.

On April 16, 1838, Gunvor Halvorsdtr remarried in Lårdal. Her second husband, Thrond/Tron Rikardson was born June 24, 1809, also in Lårdal.

Thrond and Gunvor had five children, but only two survived: Rannei/Rachael, born October 7, 1839 in Lårdal; and Ole, born November 15, 1846 in Lårdal.

Thrond and Gunvor and their children emigrated June 15, 1850. They sailed from Kragerø on the ship *Colon*, arriving in New York on August 12, 1850. They went first to Koshkonong, Wisconsin. Sometime between 1852 and 1854, they moved to Six Mile Grove, Nevada Township, Mower County, in Minnesota Territory. From *De Norske Settlementers Historie* by Hjalmar Rued Holand (1908), translated by Nettie Brown:

> "Because of the abundance of wild life, Six Mile Grove was a favored place for the Indians. Across the field from Thrond Kleppo was an Indian camp. The two tribes conversed with each other on very friendly terms. The little red 'papooses' mumbled Indian and the

white talked 'Telemark' and between them they patched together a mutual understanding that served well for all kinds of tricks and mischief.

The Indian women were very poor in preparing food. Besides the half-burned meat, the main part of their food was a kind of 'hoe-cake'. This was made by emptying a corn batter into the ashes, where it immediately changed to a stone-hard lump that was heavy as lead. When Mrs. Kleppo not only let them bake their batter in her oven, but also revealed to them the secret of 'saleratus' (baking soda) there was great joy. Immediately the Indians were off to town to buy great quantities of saleratus packages and mixed corn batter with it in great quantities. They baked and ate with great greed.

After that nothing the Indians could do for the Kleppo family was enough. They brought the fattest venison, the heaviest blankets for their beds, embroidered moccasins for the children and the most colorful calico available for Mrs. Kleppo.

In Kleppo's yard stands a tree assumed to be the largest in all the Northwest. It is an elm, 35 feet in circumference. One of the branches is three feet in diameter fifteen feet from the trunk. The majestic top shades about one-half acre. In the shade of this mighty tree, Pastor Clausen held his first congregational meetings."

The Six Mile Grove Lutheran Church was organized in the shade of this great elm tree November 19, 1859. The tree was struck by lightning many times and finally had to be taken down.

In 1939, a monument was erected on the spot to commemorate the "Great Elm Tree." The bronze plate reads:

> In this yard under the Great Elm Six Mile Grove Luth. Church was organized Nov. 19, 1859

Inscribed in the cement base, "This boulder was once in the rock garden of Mrs. J. Muller Eggen, deceased in 1888." Mrs. J. Muller Eggen was the wife of a pioneer pastor.

Gunvor and Thrond lived out their lives in Six Mile Grove and are buried in the church cemetery. Thrond died August 28, 1882; Gunvor died September 16, 1883.

Ringdahl, Mathias Pedersen

Ringdahl Farm in Pine Island, Township, Goodhue County

Mathias Pedersen was born on January 30, 1829, in Fåberg, Gudbrandsdal Valley, Norway. His parents were Peder and Cari Nedre Rindal. In 1849, he and his mother immigrated to Wisconsin, where they stayed until 1851. Mathias was one of the first settlers in Red Wing in 1851. He spent a year in St. Paul before returning to Red Wing for two years.

On November 11, 1854, he married Ingeborg (Isabel) Olsdtr Ommelstadsæteren, who had been born in Land, Oppland County, Norway on March 24, 1825. They traveled to Paint Creek, Iowa, where Pastor Koren performed the ceremony. He was the closest Norwegian Lutheran minister at that time.

Ingeborg had immigrated to America in 1849 and settled on Rock Prairie, Rock County, Wisconsin. She worked in Rockton, Platteville, Mineral Point and Beloit in Wisconsin, then in Galena, Illinois, and in Allmakee County, Iowa. In 1852, she moved to St. Paul, Minnesota Territory. The next year she moved to Red Wing where she met her future husband.

In 1855, Mathias and Ingeborg claimed land in Pine Island Township, Goodhue County. They were reported to be the first Norwegian married couple (and Ingeborg the first woman) to settle in the county. That same year, Pastor Nils Brandt held the first Norwegian church service in Goodhue County in the Ringdahl home. Their valuable farm grew to 240 acres, with good fields and sturdy buildings.

Three of their seven children survived to adulthood: Caroline who was born June 5, 1857; Peter, born February 10, 1861; and Olive, born March 14, 1869. They suffered the loss of four of their children – Ole (1859-1869), Gustav (1862-1864), Gusta (1865-1877) and Melvin (1872-1879).

Matthias died on November 17, 1884. His widow Ingeborg died on November 26, 1919. Both are buried in Lands Lutheran Cemetery.

Rotegard, Knute & Barbro

Knudt (Knute) left the beautiful mountain valley farm near Nesbyen, Norway, in 1852 with his wife Kari and two sons, Ole and Nels. They arrived in Wisconsin a few weeks later and settled in Rock County. Kari died and Knute later married Barbro. In 1856 they all left in a wagon train of 8 families and went to Waseca County in Minnesota Territory, near a lake later called St. Olaf Lake. According to the Steele-Waseca County history published in 1887: "With them were 12 yoke of cattle, 30 cows, about 50 head of young cattle, and about $600 in gold. Each took 160 acres of land." They started planting corn, but it was eaten by blackbirds and gophers. They had two years of bad luck, and survived only because of all the fish in the lake and in the LeSueur River.

Knute and Barbro had one son, Carl Olavus, born in 1863. Knute's brother Ole Rotegard also came from Norway and settled next door. The two brothers were in the group that founded the LeSeuer River Lutheran Church. The first schoolhouse was built on Ole's land and called Rotegard School.

Knute died in 1878. Barbro made her home with Carl, his wife Hannah, and their 5 children who stayed on the land until Carl's death in 1896. Carl and Hannah's third son, Bernard Rotegard, lived in New Richland, the nearest town, his entire life.

Rukke, Knud Olson

Rukke farmstead in Mower County – original barn

Knud Olson Rukke was born February 2, 1812, in Nes, Hallingdal, Buskerud County, Norway. His parents were Ole Thorsen

Tollefsgardie and Joran Christiansdtr Gire. Ole was born in 1777 in Gislerud, Fla, Hallingdal, and Joran was born March 1, 1775 in Rukkedal, Nes Hallingdal.

Knud married Else Halvorsdtr Klemstads Prestegaardeie in Norderov, Norway, on April 14, 1839. She was born May 9, 1815, in Norderhov, Hollingdal, to Halvor Nielsen Wilhelmstad and Inger Ellingsdtr Prestegaardeie. Knud and Else had four children born in Norway, but only one son, Halvor survived. They immigrated on April 1, 1851, listing 'America' as their destination. The ship *Incognito* departed from Christiania with Knud, Else and Halvor aboard, and arrived in New York on August 30, 1851.

Later that year, Else gave birth to a daughter in Wisconsin. She was named Jorand, after one of her siblings who had died in Norway. In 1852, Ole was born giving Knud and Else great promise in the new land.

Knud farmed well and after a few years, he and his brother Christian learned of the opportunity to purchase more acreage in Minnesota. They sold their land in Primrose, Wisconsin, at a profit and began their journey with cattle, sheep and oxen, through St. Ansgar, Iowa, and then north into Minnesota Territory.

They arrived in the Blooming Prairie area in July of 1855 and found shelter with a neighbor. Knud built a mud roofed cave home into the hillside. This would be their home until the actual purchase of the land. Knud bought 160 acres of land next to Christian. He built his home and red barn on another 37 acre parcel in Section 31 of Udolpho Township, Mower County.

Knud was a charter member of Red Oak Grove Lutheran Church and was instrumental in establishing its cemetery and the development of the Corning Creamery. He worked hard, raised hard-working Christian children, and died at the age of 55 on April 6, 1867. Else lived to see the dawn of the 20th century, and spent the last years of her life living with her children.

Rukke, Sever Knutson

Sever Knutson Rukke, son of Knud and Else Rukke, was born in his parents' home in Udolpho Township, Mower County, Minnesota Territory, in March of 1856. He married Clara Thompson on January 10, 1885, in Austin, Minnesota. She was born in 1869. They had 8 chiildren, only 4 of whom lived to adulthood. In the late 1890's, Sever moved to North Dakota and worked as a farm hand on a number of farms. He and Clara divorced. She died in 1941 in Roseau County. Sever is believed to have died in North Dakota in the 1930's.

Rygh, Torger O. & Torbjor Andersdtr

Torger was born in Norway in 1808, and Torbjor in 1812. They brought their family to America in 1845. They lived in Chicago, Illinois, until 1856 when the family moved to Wanamingo Township, Goodhue County. When they retired, Torger turned their farm over to his son and namesake Torger. Torger and Torbjor lived with him and his family for the rest of their lives. Torger died February 6, 1885 and Torbjor died in 1886. They are both buried in Holden Lutheran Cemetery.

Sæthre, Tron Christenson

The family of Tron Christenson Sæthre moved to Minnesota Territory in the spring of 1854. Hjalmar Rued Holand's 1908 book *De Norske Settlementers Historie* mentions the family arriving in Olmsted County, along with four other families. They were the very first Norwegian pioneers to arrive in what would become the Rock Dell -East St. Olaf Settlement.

Tron Christenson Sæthre was born June 12, 1817, in Sigdal, Buskerud, Norway, to Christen Anderson Øvestad and his wife Kari Tovsdatter. Tron married Sønnøv Olsdatter Halvorseth on December 27, 1840, at the Holmen Church in Sigdal, Norway. Sønnøv was born May 3, 1822, in Sigdal, Buskerud, Norway, to parents Ole Ingebretson Halvorseth and wife Marthe Schartum.

After their marriage, Tron and Sønnøv lived on the farm Horgesætra in Sigdal. The farm was forested; it had hilly terrain and very poor soil. It could not support the family and they immigrated to America in 1852. The Sæthre family first settled at the Koshkonong settlement in Dane County, Wisconsin. They resided there two years before relocating to Rock Dell Township in Olmsted County, where Tron claimed 160 acres of land in Section 25.

Tron and Sønnøv were the parents of eleven children; seven born in Norway, one born in Wisconsin, and three born in Minnesota. Only five lived into adulthood: Kari, Marthe, Christie, Christen, and Maria, and just three lived normal life spans. The two oldest daughters died from complications of childbirth.

In 1875, Tron and Sønnøv turned title of their farm over to their eldest daughter and her family, but they continued to reside on the property for another 20 years. Sønnøv died June 14, 1895, in Rock Dell, Minnesota. After her death, Tron moved in with his son Christen. He died September 17, 1904.

Sønnøv and Tron are buried at the East St. Olaf Lutheran Church Cemetery in Rock Dell, Minnesota. No photos exist of the couple. East St. Olaf Church records show that Tron was active in the congregation's beginnings. Otherwise the couple appears to have lived a quiet life of farming, with no other findings noted. Their uniquely shaped gravestone still stands. Along with dates on the stone, written in Norwegian is "born in Sigdal" and the bible verse "Eternal are those who die in the Lord".

Sævre, Knud Knudsen

Knud was born in Nes, Buskerud (Hallingdal), Norway on December 23, 1818. He left Norway in 1846 and settled in Luther Valley, Rock County, Wisconsin. On March 30, 1851, Knud married Gunhild Guttormsdtr Syversrud, who had emigrated from Nes in 1848. Their sons Carl and Mikkel were born in Wisconsin. In May 1853, Knud and his family joined the largest party of Norwegian land-lookers ever to embark on an expedition of its kind. Pastor C. L. Clausen, on behalf of the 40 men and their families, purchased no fewer than 44 wagons for the 300-mile caravan to St. Ansgar, Iowa. They found the creeks of northeast Iowa in flood stage, so three scouts broke away from the wagon train and headed north into Minnesota Territory to seek out the highest ridges they could find.

The Knud Knudsen Sævre family was the first to settle in what later became Strung-Out-Town or Stringtown (later renamed Amherst) in Fillmore County, Minnesota Territory. Knud constructed a 12x14 log cabin on his 160 acre farm and received his land title on September 7, 1854. He served as the first Justice of the Peace in Amherst. Knud and Gunhild had eleven children, six of whom lived to adulthood, and are buried in the Elstad Lutheran Church Cemetery in Fillmore County.

The Knudsens opened their home to many pioneers in the early years, and the farm is still owned by their descendants. It passed from Knud and Gunhild to their son Mikkel, to Mikkel's son Henry, and to his daughter, Charlotte and her husband Sylvan Nelson. At the Minnesota State Fair on August 25, 2008, the Knudson farm was recognized as a Sesquicentennial Farm, one of the oldest in Minnesota with continuous family ownership.

Sampson, Ole and Mary

Ole O. Sampson was born June 17, 1826, in Norway. He was born on a farm that was referred to as Bjondal. The location of the farm is not known, but Bjondal translates as "River Valley." When he was young, he attended school and assisted his folks  on the farm until he was fifteen years of age, after which he worked out by the month for two years at farming. At the age of seventeen he started learning the trade of stonemasonry, working for three years for the Government. He was then drafted and served two years in the Norwegian military. In 1851 he came to American, landing at New York. He immediately started west, going to Columbia County, Wisconsin, where he worked for one year. The summer of 1852 and 1853 he worked as a stonemason in Chicago. The winter of 1852 he went to the state of Mississippi and worked on a boat on the Mississippi River. The winter of 1853 he lived in Boone County, Illinois.

In January of 1854, Ole Sampson married Mary Christopherson in Chicago, Illinois. When he met Mary and how she got to Chicago is not known. Mary was born in Norway on July 18, 1831. According to the 1900 Census, she also came to America in 1851.

Ole and Mary traveled by ox cart to what is now Mower County in the Minnesota Territory. The trip took four weeks, as they took their time and camped along the way. They arrived in June of 1854 and settled on the northeast quarter of Section 19 of Nevada Township. Ole built a small 10 x 12 shanty and covered it with bark and sod. He stayed one year and then moved to the southeast quarter of Section 30, Nevada Township. He lived there one year under a shed covered with wild hay. The shed had no walls; Ole turned his wagon box on its side to shelter his bed. In the fall he built a good log house. After a year he moved to the northeast quarter of Section 33, Nevada Township, where he erected a good log house; Ole and Mary lived there for 25 years. In 1880-1881 he built a large frame home about 80 feet west of the old log home which he finished off beautifully. He also built a large frame barn and granary and devoted his time to raising grain and livestock.

Ole put his talent as a stonemason to good use and was instrumental in building the Six Mile Grove Lutheran Church in Nevada Township. The church is still in use today.

Ole and Mary had nine children between 1854 and 1873: Anna, 1854; Julia, 1855; Christina, 1858; Christopher (Chris), 1860; Kirstin (Jessie), 1862; Molina, 1864; Andrena, 1868; Sven, 1871, and Hans, 1873.

Sateren, Johannes Olsen and Anne Marie Engebretsdtr

Johannes Olsen Ommelstadsæteren was born June 4, 1822, in Torpa, Land  *commune*, Oppland County, Norway. He was one of seven children born to Ole Larson Skogstad Ommelstadsæteren and Gubjor Martea Larsdtr Stuve. His siblings were Lars, Ingeborg, Christian, Halvor, Tosten, and Ole. The children were raised in a puritanical atmosphere because the family was caught up in the early 19th Century Haugian religious movement.

Johannes and sister Ingeborg made the journey to America together. They left home and began their trek to Drammen on foot. Chests containing their provisions and few belongings were loaded on wagons. The emigrants walked or rowed down the fjord. After a few days they reached Drammen, but they were delayed three weeks waiting for the bark *Benedicte* to sail. During the wait, they added to their food supply in case of an extended voyage. Soon after leaving port, the ship had to return to Drammen for repairs. The *Benedicte* finally left Drammen on June 8, 1849, and arrived in New York on August 22. During the 9 ½ week voyage, the ship encountered stormy weather that sent waves washing over the deck.

The captain accompanied the immigrants up the Hudson to Albany where they transferred to canal boats towed on the Erie Canal to Buffalo. Here they found passage aboard a steamboat carrying cholera patients, many of whom died, for the trip across the Great Lakes.

Upon arriving at Milwaukee, Wisconsin, Johannes and Ingeborg joined a family journeying with an oxcart carrying a mother and daughter with cholera. The child died and was buried en route.

Johannes spent four years traveling until he married Anne Maria Engebretsdtr Rudd on November 19, 1853, in Lansing, Iowa. Anne was the daughter of Engebret Johannesen Helgerudsveom and Marte Hansdatter Bjørkeeie, born April 17, 1831, in Loeng Nordsinni, Norway. Anne emigrated from Norway in 1851 on the bark *Sjofna*. She arrived in New York on July 21st of that year.

Johannes and Anne had eleven children: Gunhild (Julia) Mathia, Oluf, Maria, Edvard (Edward), Caroline, Hanna Olava, Joseph Albert, Lise (Lizzie), Inger Mathia, Adolph and Benjamin Otto (Bennie).

Gunhild was born April 9, 1855, in Lansing, Iowa. She was just nine weeks old when Johannes and Anne Maria moved to Minnesota Territory, settling a mile west of Zumbrota in Goodhue County. Johannes' sister Ingeborg and her husband Mathias Ringdahl were also living in the area.

Johannes was active in the religious and political affairs of the community. On June 25, 1855, the family attended the first Norwegian religious service on record in the area. It was conducted by Rev. Nils O. Brandt at the Ringdahl home. In 1867, Johannes signed the Articles of Incorporation for Lands Church and held the first two meetings of the building committee in his home. He had a passion for founding churches; he often left his family and joined missions to Oregon to help establish churches there.

In May, 1877, the family moved from Minnesota to Cuming County, Nebraska, by covered wagon. Their youngest child, Benjamin, was born in the wagon during that journey.

Johannes died April 12, 1907, in Zumbrota, Goodhue County, and was buried in Lands Cemetery. His wife Anne Maria died March 22, 1909 in Dawes County, Nebraska, and is buried in Antelope Cemetery.

The puritanical Haugian influence filtered down the generations. Her granddaughter remembers Gunhild's daughter Lena Hansen drinking Postum and playing Rook.

Selland, Ola Nielsen & Anna Styrksdtr Jordalen-Giljarhus

Ola Nielsen Selland was born about 1812 in Voss, Norway. He married Anna Styrkvårsdtr Jordalen on April 12, 1841 in Voss. She was born in 1813. They had 4 children: Niels, Ole, Brynild, and Anna.

Ole, Anna, and their children left Vossestrand, Norway May 10, 1853, on the ship *Virgo* and arrived in New York on June 24th. The family can be found in the ship's passenger lists with the surname Tweite. They settled in what would become the Norseland Settlement, Lake Prairie Township, Nicollet County, Minnesota Territory, in June of 1854. Ola and Anna lived out their lives in Nicollet County. Ola died on September 13, 1890, and Anna in 1899.

Sevareid, Erik Eriksen

Erik Eriksen Sevareid was born on the Sevareid farm in Kyrping, Norway, on November 3, 1835. His parents were Erik Eriksen Sevareid (1792-1851) and Ingeborg Tollevsdtr (1792-1853). He was the third son to carry that name; the first two Eriks died as infants.

Erik came to America in 1854, settling first in Illinois. He pre-empted a claim in Wanamingo Township, Goodhue County, in 1856. He returned to Illinois for a time. He married Maria Vinje in August, 1861; she died on August 28, 1870. Erik and Maria had five children: Osmund, Ingeborg and Elias lived to adulthood. Two sons named Elias were young children when they died.

Erik married for the second time on November 24, 1874, to Carolina Krogstrum. They had 9 more children: Martin, Pauline, Vier, Marie, Adolph, Alfred, Mathilda, Ephrian, and Tabitha.

Erik died on March 5, 1892. Carolina died May 15, 1913. Erik, his wives, and many of their descendants are buried in the Holden Lutheran Church Cemetery.

Sigurdsen, John

John Sigurdsen was born in 1894 in Vinje, Telemark, to Sigurd Jonsen and Gunnile Torbiornsdtr. On December 28, 1818, he married Tårånd Torjusdtr. Tårånd was born April 17, 1796, to Torjus Olsen and Torbjor Nerisdtr in Vinje. The couple had eight children: Torjus, Sigurd, Gunild, Bergit, Albert, Torbjorn (Thomas), John, and Ole.

Sigurd and his family came to America in 1845, settling in Dane County, Wisconsin Territory. John and Tårånd and their other five sons joined them in 1850 and spent five years in Dane County, Wisconsin. In 1855, John and Tårånd took land in what would become Section 19 of Iosco Township in Waseca County,

Minnesota Territory. John was the first Norwegian to settle there. He was a founding member of North Waseca Lutheran Church in 1858. Succeeding generations have played an active role in the congregation and descendants, including his great-great-granddaughter Delores (Jackson) Srp, are members today. The church celebrated its sesquicentennial on October 19, 2008.

John died in 1864 and his wife Tårånd died in January of 1881.

John's oldest daughter Gunhild was born December 18, 1824. She was already married when her parents came to America. She and her husband, Jacob Jackson, immigrated and settled in Blooming Grove Township, Waseca County, in 1862. She was the oldest person in Minnesota when she died on January 16, 1930, at the age of 106. According to the local paper's front page story of the celebration of her 100th Birthday, Gunhild was in excellent health and had not been sick in thirty years. Mrs. Jackson credited her longevity to "plenty of fresh air, regular meals, regular hours for sleep and plenty of out door exercise…."

Gunhild Sigurdsdtr Jackson

Skaro, Askrim Knudsen

Askrim Skaro was born June 4, 1829, in Hol, Hallingdal, Buskerud, Norway. His parents were Knud Ellingsen and Guro Eriksdtr Skaro. He immigrated at age 19, sailing on the sailing ship *Tricolor* from Christiania. The ship arrived in New York on July 25, 1846.

During the Mexican War, Askrim served as a private in the army and was stationed at Fort Snelling from 1847 to 1852. In 1852, he staked a claim in Oshawa Township near St. Peter, Minnesota Territory, and put his efforts toward building a successful farm. On September 15, 1857, he married Theodora Laumann. Their son Joseph was born in 1858.

In July of 1858, about 50 men organized a militia company dubbed "The St. Peter Guards," with Askrim as its captain. In June of 1861 the company was ordered to Fort Snelling and became Minnesota's 2nd Infantry, Company E. Captain Skaro led his men against the Sioux from July 5, 1861, until March 20, 1862 when he resigned because of illness.

On August 31, 1862, Skaro again raised a company and they were assigned to Minnesota's 9th Infantry, as Company D. At four o'clock on the afternoon of December 16, 1864, Captain Skaro led his company in a charge of Confederate lines during the Battle of Nashville. He was felled by a bullet through his right breast. The history of Minnesota's 9th regiment reports that Captain Skaro was a "brave and gallant officer" and a "thorough soldier, greatly loved by his men."

Askrim Skaro was buried in Green Hill Cemetery, St. Peter, Minnesota. His wife and their children Joseph, Edwin, Clara and Alvah eventually relocated, first to Amo Township, Cottonwood County, and then to Minneapolis.

Stabeck, Ingebor Kittelsdtr

Ingebor Kittelsdtr Stabeck was born at the Stabeck *gård* (farm), Rollag, Numedal, Norway on March 10, 1833. Her father was Kittel Tostenson Stabeck, who was born January 26, 1799. Her mother was Marit Christophersdtr Gaaseberg from Flesberg, Numedal. The couple had four children: Tosten Kittelson, Ingebor Kittelsdtr, Torgen Kittelsdtr, and Christopher Kittelson. They sold the Stabeck farm in 1842 and moved to Muggeberg in Sandsvær where they lived until 1850. In that year they immigrated as a family to America, arriving in New York City on July 8, 1850.

The family traveled up the Hudson and then on a canal boat to Buffalo, and from there they took a small steamboat to Milwaukee. A young relative met them and drove them by horse-drawn wagon the long distance to Rock Run, in Winnebago County, Illinois.

The family arrived at the home of Ingebor's uncle, Clemet Stabeck, on August 3, 1850. Clemet and his wife Live had come to America on the sailing vessel *Amelia* in 1830. They founded the Norwegian settlement at Rock Run in 1839.

Ingebor's family was adventurous. Her Uncle Clemet and brother Tosten Stabeck joined others who left Rock Run in 1852 to seek their fortunes in the California Goldrush.

On March 8, 1856, Ingebor married Halvor Knudson Volstad in Rock Run. The same year she moved with him to the Six Mile Grove settlement near Lyle, Minnesota Territory, and established the family home. There she spent the rest of her years as a devoted wife and help mate to her husband. The couple had six children: Knud, Knut, Marie (Mary), Kittel (Charles), Gunhild (Julie), and Henry Johan.

From her obituary in the *Lyle Tribune*, March 6, 1914: "Of her death it is sufficient to say that it was as her life – peaceful and quiet. After an illness of 5 days, with double pneumonia, she fell asleep in the full assurance of a child of God going to serve her Master in a new and greater life on February 27, 1914, on the farm where they had settled. She was a devoted and faithful Christian, one whose daily lot it was to serve others, but to her this was not a burden but a pleasure and she deserves to be remembered as one who not only knew the teachings of Christ but used every means in her power to fulfill them."

Ingebor Stabeck Volstad is buried with her husband at the Six Mile Grove Cemetery, Lyle, Minnesota.

Strenge, Even and Karen Olson

Daughter Emma with Karen and Even Strenge in front of their homestead c. 1905

Even Strenge was born May 19, 1827, at Sandsvær, Norway. His parents died when he was quite young and he was raised by other families. He married Karen Maria Ellefsdtr on June 3, 1853.

They left Norway on the ship *Heste Maria* from the port of Drammen with their infant son, Olaves, in 1854. There were about 100 passengers on board, and during a 72-hour period of stormy weather the men were enlisted to move barrels down in the hold to stabilize the ship. They landed in Quebec, Canada, and took barges to New York State. They then made their way to Rock County, Wisconsin, where they joined other immigrants from Sandsvær. Their daughter Maren (May) was born in Wisconsin in 1855.

In June of 1856 the Strenges joined a band of settlers from Rock Prairie who made the journey to Minnesota Territory and became the first settlers in what would become New Richland Township, Waseca County.

Even cleared and built up a successful farm in Section 14 of the township. Karen was a valuable community member in her own right, who served as a mid-wife and doctor in the pioneer settlement. She knew the old Norwegian cures. She was recognized as a great story teller with a vivid imagination, and the settlers would often gather at her home in the early morning to listen to her tales. She had a loom and made cloth, and made wine for the church.

Seven children were born after Even and Karen settled in Minnesota. Edward was born in 1857, followed by Georgina (1859), John (1861-1899), Henry (1863-1937), Severt (1866), Joseph (1868), and Emma (1872-1864). John died in the Spanish-American War and Georgina, Maren, and Severt fell victim to tuberculosis as young adults. Emma cared for both of her parents in their declining years, and then took care of her brother, Olaves. Henry also stayed in Waseca County, while Joseph and Edward moved elsewhere.

Even died June 14, 1906 and Karen passed away on September 21, 1917. They are buried in the Le Seuer River Lutheran Church Cemetery.

Strenge, Olaves

Olaves (Olaus) Strenge was born in Sansvær, Norway, on April 21, 1953. He was a year old when his parents, Even and Karen Strenge, brought him to America. The family was part of the first band of Norwegian settlers to pre-empt land in New Richland Township, Wadena County, Minnesota Territory, in 1856.

In his prime, Olaves was said to be the strongest man in Waseca County. He never married, and was blind for the last 46 years of his life. He passed away on December 11, 1927, and is buried with his parents in Le Seuer Lutheran Church Cemetery.

Swenson, Christian and Kari Olsdtr

Christen Svennungsen was born in Norway on July 29, 1818, on the Hvilen farm in the Bø district of Telemark County. He was confirmed at the church in Lunde parish. Christen had five younger siblings: Marthe, Aslaug, Thomas, and twins, Ole and Kittil. As the oldest, Christen was named after his father's father following the custom of the time.

On May 10, 1845, Christen married Kari Olsdtr from the Nordskoug farm in Lunde Parish. Her birth date was recorded as November 4, 1815. After working on tenant farms for seven years, the young couple decided to immigrate to America. America offered them a greater opportunity to acquire a farm of their own. By the time of their departure on May 21, 1852, they had two children. Ole Christensen was born on August 29, 1847; and Kari was born in 1849. The couples' oldest son Svening died at the age of four while the family was still in Norway.

The young family left Telemark and went by ship to America. In America, they first resided in Jefferson County, Wisconsin. While there a third son named Sveinung was born in 1852. Shortly thereafter they moved on to Washington Prairie just outside Decorah, Iowa. In Iowa a fourth son, Kittil (later called Charlie), was born in 1853. Still without land of their own, they moved north into the Territory of Minnesota in 1857. They settled on Highland Prairie in what would become part of Norway Township in Fillmore County. By this

Kari Olsdtr Swenson

time Christen had anglicized his name and was known as Christian Swenson.

On September 19, 1860, Christian Swenson was granted a land patent by the U. S. government for 3 pieces of property totaling 160 acres. This land was located in sections 5, 8, and 9 of Norway Township. One of the stipulations associated with pre-emption claims was that the land be improved and include a cabin at least 12' by 12.' This property would eventually be passed on to Christen and Kari's son Ole C. Swenson.

Farm work in the early days was labor intensive. It involved not only putting up log farm buildings but also clearing land to make it tillable. The farm implements were transported by oxen. The nearest market was located in Winona, about 25 miles away. They hauled their produce there using oxen and a crude wooden-wheeled wagon called a "*kubberulle.*" This was very slow and presented problems during the winter. The family farm eventually grew to about 600 acres, which made it one of the larger farms in Norway Township.

Two of Christian's sons moved to Portland, North Dakota. Sveining homesteaded and Charlie ran the grocery store in Portland. Christian's oldest living son, Ole C., remained on the family farm and helped his dad with farm work. All of Christan and Kari's sons married and had children. Christian's daughter Kari died in Fillmore County at the age of 14. Christian passed away in 1876. His wife Kari died in 1888.

Swenson, Swen Sr.

Swen Swenson, Senior (Svein Sveinsen Rudningen) was born February 12, 1808, in Hol, Hallingdal, Norway. His wife, Guri Sandersdtr Slettemoen was born February 12, 1812, in the same district. They immigrated with their six sons, Swen Jr., Sander, Lars, Ole, Paul and Tolleiv, and their daughter Kristi in 1857. Tolleiv, the youngest son, died on the voyage to America and was buried at sea. The family joined Swen's brother, Lars Sveinsen Rudningen, who lived in the Norseland Settlement near St. Peter, Minnesota Territory. The following year Swen Senior homesteaded land in New Sweden Township, five miles west of his brother.

During the Indian uprising of 1862, the family sought refuge in St. Peter for several weeks. Two sons, Sander and Lars, served in the Civil War. Swen Senior was a charter member of the Norseland Lutheran Church in Norseland. Swen Senior and Guri died, in 1878 and 1903 respectively, and are buried in Norseland Lutheran Cemetery.

Swen Junior homesteaded land near his father. Swen Junior was a progressive farmer, active in community and church affairs. He helped establish the first creameries in the county, established one of the first herds of registered Holstein cattle in Minnesota, served in the 1888 session of the Minnesota House of Representatives, and on the New Sweden Town Board. Swen Junior was an early member of Norseland Lutheran Church and was its first parochial school teacher. Many of his descendants still reside in the Norseland/New Sweden communities.

Thorson, Amund & Margit Germundsdtr

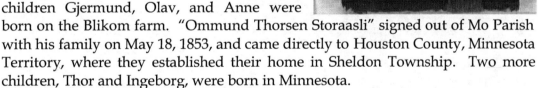
Amund and his second wife, Margit Germundsdtr

Ommund Torsen was born December 26, 1799, in Kviteseid, Telemark, Norway. His parents were Tor Aanundsen and Sissel Sveinsdtr. He married Anne Knutsdtr N. Tveiten (1797-1837) in 1824. They had three children while living on the Barskor farm in Skåfsa: Sissel, Thor and Margit. Only Sissel survived to adulthood. She immigrated with her husband Mikkel Hegland and their children Kristi, Torger, and Thor, to Fillmore County in 1861.

Amund married Margit Germundsdtr N. Storaasli in 1840 in Mo, Telemark. Their children Gjermund, Olav, and Anne were born on the Blikom farm. "Ommund Thorsen Storaasli" signed out of Mo Parish with his family on May 18, 1853, and came directly to Houston County, Minnesota Territory, where they established their home in Sheldon Township. Two more children, Thor and Ingeborg, were born in Minnesota.

Amund died in 1873. He is buried in the Stone Church Cemetery in Houston County. Some of Amund's children and grandchildren eventually settled in Polk County in northwestern Minnesota. Descendants of Amund now live all over the United States.

Tuve, Gulbrand Olesen

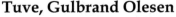

In 1854, Gulbrand O. Tuve (Tuff) followed his older brother Ole Oleson from their barren and poor farm in the Valdres Valley, Oppland County, Norway, to Minnesota Territory. The farm named Tuff was never meant to support ten children. Gulbrand came first to Wisconsin and then soon to Fillmore County. He was 26 years old. Ole's farm was the first stop for the rest of his five brothers, and became the "old Home" that reminded them of the hills and valleys of Valdres. Living conditions were primitive, and the weather more severe than back in Norway, but the pioneers were optimistic and the land fruitful.

Two years after arriving, Gulbrand met the widowed Torbjor and her little 4-year-old daughter. Torbjor Aanundsdtr had come to the US in 1851 from a properous farm with several buildings in Aust-Agder, Bygland. In fact, there was some doubt about the match given her higher social standing – clearly, an Old World idea. In 1856, the young couple walked 30 miles to be married by Pastor V. Koren in Decorah, Iowa, who was the closest Lutheran pastor. Their daughter Rangdi was born in 1857, and three more children were born in Fillmore County.

For a time, the five brothers lived in Fillmore County and gathered to share celebrations and to assist one another. They had come separately from Norway and slowly they drifted apart as their interests shifted. Gulbrand and Torbjor moved to Winnishiek County, Iowa, near Decorah in 1867. They built a log home on good farmland. Today this home, built of 16-inch oak logs, is being reconstructed on a nearby farm. Gulbrand became a lay preacher and Torbjor was absorbed by her home life. Torbjor died in 1901 at the age of 81, and Gulbrand in 1906.

The experience of being pioneers in Minnesota was not well-recorded by the Tuves. The work was apparently hard, but for most of the first generation, religion played a central role. They do not seem to have left Norway for religious freedom, but the religious choices they found here among the Norwegian language churches gave them new direction and purpose, and shaped their lives. While they learned some English, Norwegian was spoken at home and early lessons and prayers were in Norwegian. Torbjor told the 1900 census that she did not speak Enlgish, though she must have known some to shop in nearby Decorah.

One wonders what the comparison between the home life of 1850 Norway and 1850 Minnesota might be. For Gulbrand and Torbjor the answer was worse at first, then about the same for much of their lives. However, for their children there opened real opportunity. Their youngest son Anthony, born in Minnesota in 1864, continued his education beyond grammar school and was elected president of Augustana College at the age of 26. He, the son of an immigrant farmer, really was in the Land of Opportunity!

Tveito, Aslaug Jacobsdtr Einong

The first Telemark girl who "stood as a bride" in America, still lives. She is Aslaug Einong, who was married to Hans Tveito from Tinn. She and her sister, Anne, who "got" John Molee, were married in Even Hegg's barn in Muskego in 1843 by (Rev. C.L.) Clausen the first year he was a pastor here in this country. (See *Telesoga* No. 1, Page 9)

Aslaug, or Mrs. Tveito, is now 86 years old, but has been in good health. She lives in Lake Mills (Iowa). Hans Tveito died in middle age (at age 50). As everyone knows he was a *kjempekar* (giant man) and his sons were big as well, but *skjotfeige* like their father. Only Torgrim is still alive, but Aslaug is still around too.

It is almost unbelievable that the first Telemark girl who "stood as a bride" here in America is still alive. Much water has run into the sea since 1843, and there are not so few Telemark girls either, who have stood as brides in America since that time!

Source: 'The First Telemark Bride in America" An article from *Telesoga* No. 7-8, March-May 1911, translated by Jim Skree

Granddaughter Mamie Kittleson's description of Aslaug included the following: "She was a smart woman and an excellent manager. She was *very* particular and her home was spotless. She had a good philosophy on life and good judgement. She was up and around till a week before she died of pneumonia in 1913."

Tveito, Hans Torgrimson

Hans Torgrimson Tveito was born on the Berge farm in Vestfjordalen, Tinn, Telemark, on October 12, 1815. His parents were Ase Hansdtr Berge and Torgrim Halvorsen Tveito. Hans' father died in February of 1820, and his mother died in childbirth the following month. Income from the Berge farm helped defray the expense incurred by those who then raised Hans and his brother, but he always felt he was a guest and not a member of these families.

Hans gained fame when he lifted a large boulder that now sits in front of the Tinn museum. A bronze plate bears the inscription *"Denne stein er lyft av konfirmant Hans Tveito (Sterke Hans) f. 1818-Død I USA 1870"* Translation: "This stone was lifted by confirmand Hans Tveito (Strong Hans) born 1818 –died in the USA in 1870." His legend grew with fantastic tales of amazing feats of strength, among them: As a child, Hans kicked a pail of water over the roof of the family cottage; he picked up a cannon and handled it like a rifle; and he stepped over a fence with a calf under each arm. Even his emigration to America generated a story about Hans' fight with a tiger while in Le Havre de Grace, France!

In 1853, the *Argo* was delayed at the port of Le Havre for repairs and, to assure a full complement of passengers, the captain lowered his fare to eight dollars – about a quarter of the usual price. Hans accepted the deal, and it cost another eight dollars to make the trip to Wisconsin. Hans arrived in Muskego on August 15, 1843.

On Easter Sunday, April 7, 1844, Hans married Aslaug Einong. Her father had recently died, and so they took responsibility for some of her younger siblings. While living in Wisconsin, the couple had five children of their own: Torgrim (Thomas), Jacob, Annie, Aase, and Oscar.

Aslaug's brother John settled in Houston County in Minnesota Territory, and in 1855 Hans and Aslaug followed him. Poor roads (or no roads at all) made the 300 mile journey by covered wagon difficult. When they finally reached Minnesota, Hans acquired forty acres a mile west of Spring Grove and within six months added an adjacent 120 acres. Three more children were added to the family: Isabelle, and twins John and Clara.

Hans died on February 10, 1866. Aslaug was left to manage their farm and raise their youngest children on her own. By 1870, she had sold the Spring Grove farm and moved the family to Iowa. Aslaug died on July 16, 1913.

Hans is laid to rest at Trinity Lutheran Church in Spring Grove. Aslaug is buried in Salem Lutheran Church's North Cemetery in Lake Mills, Iowa.

Uggen, Oline Juvrud

Oline Juvrud was born September 13, 1855, shortly after her parents, Ole and Martha Juvrud, arrived in Rice County Minnesota Territory. She was the first

Anders and Oline Uggen – 1874

white child born in Forest Township. On November 24, 1874, Oline married Anders Uggen. According to the history of Forest Township in *The History of Rice and Steele Counties*, ©1910, "…The girl grew to womanhood, was married and lived with her husband and a large family of children on the identical spot where the wagon stood when the birth occurred." Oline Juvrud Uggen died in 1889.

The following account of the Uggen farm's brush with the James gang was written by Sally Taflin, daughter of Mary Annette (Uggen) Hagen:

"Anders Uggen was a farmer – he had cattle and horses but raising good horses was what he liked best. In September of 1876 the Jesse James gang raided the First National Bank at Northfield which was a few miles to the north of the farm …Some of the gang escaped and headed south out of town. They stopped at Grandpa Uggen's farm and Jesse asked permission to water their horses. He didn't realize that Grandpa Uggen recognized them. He told him they could – he was afraid they'd take his horses, of which he was very proud. They watered their horses and went on their way."

Ulen, Ole and Torgun Olsen

Ole Ulen Family
Back: Anna (Mrs. Halvor Burtness), Gunhild (Mrs. Arne Evans), and Randi (Mrs. Ole Asleson)
Front: Ole and Torgun

Ole Olson, born in Flaa, Hallingdal, Norway, on April 18, 1818, and his wife Torgun, born July 5, 1818, farmed a small cottage allotment named "Ulen."

In the spring of 1851, Ole and Torgun, with their daughters Anna, Gunhild, and Randi, left that home behind and set out to create a new life in America. Following the same route as most pioneers of that time, Ole Ulen first settled in Rock Prairie in southern Wisconsin where they farmed for one year.

In 1852, the Ulen family relocated to section 26 in the southern part of Spring Grove Township in Minnesota Territory. Ole and Torgun became parents of a baby girl in February 1853 who sadly did not survive beyond infancy. Ole was listed as a member of the first Lutheran congregation in Spring Grove in 1853. Oldest daughter Anna married Halvor Burtness there in 1866.

During those early years in southern Minnesota, a Sioux Indian uprising threatened the pioneers. Hundreds of settlers lost their lives. In 1866, Ole packed up the family and led a team of oxen into Iowa's Winneshiek County. They farmed on "Looking Glass Prairie" just across the Minnesota-Iowa border. Ole and Torgun's second daughter, Gunhild, married Arne Evans in 1870 in the Big Canoe Lutheran Church of rural Decorah.

In 1871, Ole, Torgun, and Randi, accompanied by Gunhild and her husband Arne Evans, spent five weeks on a journey that brought them to Lake Park in Becker County, Minnesota. Ole then set out alone to find a good place to build their home. Ole likely spent his first winter alone in a dugout built into the side of a cliff overlooking the Wild Rice River about 20 miles north and west of Lake Park. The following year his family joined him. Torgun gave birth to another daughter, Rachel, who lived only about three years. Their living conditions improved when Ole built a fine 18' x 26' cabin. The nearest towns were Hawley and Lake Park and it took a hearty man about two days for the round trip, often returning with a sack of flour on his back. Ole Ulen must have made those trips countless times.

Daughter Randi married Ole Asleson at Lake Park in 1874, and they lived there until 1878 when they, too, joined her parents along the Wild Rice River. In 1881, daughters Anna and her husband Halvor and Gunhild and her husband Arne Evans moved to the Ulen area.

Ole Ulen was a highly respected man and was elected to several positions of responsibility. He was among the group of men who organized Hallingdal Norwegian Evangelical Lutheran Church on October 6, 1876. The church name was later changed to Ulen. Ole was one of the first trustees of the congregation and was a member of the committee that decided to erect a church building in 1883.

In June of 1881, Clay County Commissioners chose to name the newly constituted township after its first settler, Ole Ulen. In 1886, the village of Ulen was also named after Ole.

Ole Ulen passed away in January of 1890, at the age of 73. His wife Torgun died in February of 1893.

Vaaler, Christopher Larson

Christopher Larson Vaaler was born in Eidsvold, Norway, on October 9, 1824. He was the youngest son of Halvor Olsen Vaaler and Marie Larsdtr. He came to America in 1853 and spent a short time in Rock Prairie, Wisconsin, before moving to Fillmore County, Minnesota Territory. He began farming in Section 12 of Spring Grove Township, Houston County, before the land was available for purchase. (The government had to complete its survey before it could issue land patents.)

Since he had been a tree feller in Norway, Christopher made short work of building a log cabin before clearing and developing the farmland on his claim. He purchased 40 acres from the government in Section 12 of Spring Grove Township on April 2, 1857 using his patronymic, "Christopher Larson." Through diligence and hard work, his holdings would expand to 200 acres.

There were many Indians in the area in those early days who came and went as they pleased without causing any harm. One day, Christopher was hewing logs for a new building using a large old-fashioned broad ax. It became dull, so he went into his cabin to grind it. He wasn't aware that a passing Indian had already gone into the cabin to warm himself. When Christopher appeared in the cabin doorway holding such a large ax, the Indian assumed that it would be used against him. The Indian raced out of the house. Running at full speed he was out of sight in a moment!

On April 11, 1855, Christopher married Ragnhild Johnsdtr Flåberg, who was born in Solar, Norway, in 1822. They had five children: Olaus, born in 1856, would eventually take over the home farm; Kaarn, born in 1858, married Christ Steneroden and settled in Red Wing, Minnesota; Bernard, born in 1862, moved to California and was a railroad worker; Johan was born in 1861 and died in 1865; and Christopher, who died a day after his birth in January of 1864. Ragnhild also died as the result of Christopher's birth.

In these early times, a man with young children could not delay finding a helpmate. Christopher's second wife, Martha, gave birth to their first daughter, Helena, in 1865. Rosalia, born in 1866, married Gust Gubrud and settled in Bagley, Minnesota. Karl, born in 1868, became a prosperous farmer in Fillmore County. Christopher and Martha's youngest child, Ludwig, was born in 1870 and died in 1888.

Christopher worked on his farm until his death on December 28, 1888. He and other family members are buried in Old Trinity Lutheran Cemetery, Spring Grove.

Vethammer, Kjersti Ingebretsdtr

Kjersti Ingebretsdtr Vethammer was born February 17, 1809 in Stange, Norway. Her parents were Ingebret Olsen Vethammer and Mari Mikkesldtr Ile. On October 27, 1834, she married Soren Larsen (Gjermstad) in Stange. They had seven children: Lars, born April 9, 1835; Ingebret, born March 1, 1837; Anne Louise, born September 4, 1839; Eline Mathea, born April 4, 1842; Maren, born March 22, 1844; Rikka, born April 29, 1846; and Syverin, born February 8, 1848.

Soren and Kjersti owned the Gjermstad farm but in 1850 the farm went through bankruptcy and the family immigrated to America. Syverin, age 18 months, died on the journey across the Atlantic. The family went to Rock River, Wisconsin, and Soren died about a year later.

In 1854, the oldest son, Lars, married Bergithe Homme. They were in Fillmore County, Minnesota when their oldest son Soren was born in 1855. They can then be found in Goodhue County in 1857, when Gunder was born.

In the 1857 Minnesota Territorial Census, Kjersti (spelled Christina, 59 years old) is listed in Goodhue County with her daughters Rikka (spelled Rebecca, 12 years old) and Ellen, 18 years old. Anne Louise, 18 years old, is living with her brother Lars – he and Bergithe probably needed help with their young family!

Kjersti died in 1893 and is buried at the Holden Church in rural Kenyon, Minnesota.

Volstad, Halvor Knudsen

Halvor Knudsen was born September 29. 1826, at the Volstad farm in Drangedal, Telemark, Norway, to Knut Gunleikson Volstad and Gunhild Halvo Gautefall. In 1853, he immigrated through Quebec, Canada to Chicago. He spent only three weeks in Chicago before moving to Rock Run, Winnebago County, Illinois, where he found employment on a farm for $10.00 per month.

He married Ingebor Kittelsdatter Stabeck on March 8, 1856. The newlyweds made the twenty-one day journey by horse and wagon to Lyle, Mower County, Minnesota Territory. They brought two pair of oxen and a wagon filled with their household goods.

Halvor had been to Mower County the previous summer. He had claimed the east half of the southeast quarter, and the west half of the southwest quarter of Section 30, Nevada Township. Halvor did not have money to formally register the land for another four or five years. His holdings would eventually include 274 acres of good farmland in Iowa.

Halvor had prepared a log cabin for their arrival, and the virgin land was covered mostly with grubs. He cleared 60 acres, erected a good house and a large frame barn.

He raised his first wheat in 1860, but harvested only enough for his family's own use. In 1861, he brought his wheat to market at McGregor, a distance of 125 miles, and received fifty cents a bushel. In *Den Norske Settlementers Historie*, Hjalmar Rued Holand tells the following story, "As the distance to market was far, and as prices for farm produce before the Civil War were low, trips to market were few and far between and never once to grind grain. Gunder Stabbestad and Halvor Volstad (from Drangedal) drove a heaping load of wheat to market, hoping it would bring enough to buy provisions to carry them through the winter. When they reached McGregor (Iowa), the price of wheat was so low that, after paying their hotel expenses, they had just enough for a barrel of salt. This they sawed in two and, on the way home, each man sat on his own half-barrel of salt."

Halvor was one of the founders of Six Mile Grove Norwegian Lutheran congregation and helped erect the church building. In 1906, Halvor and the Gunder, Knut, and Charles Volstad families purchased the Methodist church and formed the Mission Church. In 1937, the property was donated to the Christian Missionary Alliance Church.

He and Ingebor had five children – Knut, Marie (Mary), Kittell (Charlie), Gunhild (Julia), and Henry Johan.

Halvor died February 1, 1912. The *Lyle Tribune* reported on his death as follows: "Although the deceased started out in active life with many handicaps he forged his way to better conditions by ceaseless toil and untiring devotion to his calling. As a pioneer he experienced all the ups and downs which made up the life of that honored class, all the time improving every opportunity which he had by getting familiar with the laws, customs and language of the country of his adoption. His neighbors showed their appreciation of his efforts by electing him to various public offices. He has served as a member of the town board of supervisors, and in 1878 represented the district in the State Legislature under Governor Pillsbury. While he never was a politician in the sense of following politics for office or gain, he always took an active interest in his duties as a citizen and for the past twenty-five years he warmly championed the cause of temperance and prohibition..."

Halvor's brothers Gullik (Peter), Kittel (Charlie), Knut, and Gunder also came to America.

Winjum, Jens Ellingsen and Anna Olsdtr Otternes

Jens E. Winjum was born in 1829 on Dyrdal, a subfarm of the Vinjum farm in Aurland, Sogn, Norway. His parents were Elling Larsen Vinjum and Kari Jensdtr. In 1849, Jens married Anna Olsdtr Otternes. The Otternes farm was a few miles down the fjord from Vinjum. Anna was born in 1826 to Ole Olsen Skjerdal Otternes ("*Sme-Ola*") and Ingeborg Guttormsdtr Otternes.

In 1851, Jens and Anna emigrated along with Anna's siblings, Guttorm and Mari. The Winjums arrived in America with heavy hearts, having lost 3 daughters. Two died in Norway, and an infant daughter died on the boat that carried them across Lake Michigan. They buried this daughter in Milwaukee after the boat docked and before continuing on to the Koshkonong settlement for the winter.

In the spring of 1852, Jens and Anna moved to the Washington Prairie Settlement near Decorah, Iowa, where their son Elling was born. Anna's brother Jens Olsen Otternes, his wife Marta, and their children emigrated from Norway that same year.

Jens and Anna relocated to Minnesota Territory in 1853. They were joined by Anna's siblings Guttorm, Mari, Jens, and their families, and the Knud and Martha

Ike family. These pioneers were among the first settlers in Black Hammer Township area of Houston County. Jens and Anna were founding members of Faith Lutheran Church of Black Hammer.

Jens Ellingsen Winjum died in 1918. Anna Olsdtr Otternes Winjum outlived all of her siblings, passing away in 1923 at the age of 97.

Jens and Anna raised 7 children. Three children went on to pioneer in South Dakota: Marie and Botolf and their families remained there, Ole returned. Four of the Winjum children married and remained in Houston County. There would eventually be 3 adjacent Winjum farms in Black Hammer, and all remain in descendants' families to this day.

Ytre Lie, Johannes and Ingeborg

Johannes Botolvson was born on the Ytre Lie farm in Aurland, Norway, on August 2, 1818. His parents were Botolv Kristensen and Randi Jonsdtr. He married Ingeborg Pedersdtr in 1844, and they came to America in 1854.

After spending time in Wisconsin, the family moved to Goodhue County and settled in Leon Township in 1856. Their youngest son, John J. Lee, was born in 1867 and grew to adulthood on the Leon Township farm.

Johannes died on May 15, 1900. Ingeborg died in 1906. *See Johannes Lie, pages 127-128*

Ytre Lie, Lars Oddsen and Marta Knutsdtr

Marta Knutsdtr was born in 1796 to Knut Larsen Turli (1740-1803) and his wife, Ingeborg Larsdtr Veum (1756-1825). She and her first husband, Anders Oddsen Otternes (1796-1827), had four children: Lars, Ingeborg, Knute, and Anna.

After Anders' death, Marte married Lars Oddsen and he moved to the Otterness farm. Lars was born April 22, 1803, on the Ytre Lie farm. His parents were Odd Amundson Ytre Lie (1763-1811) and Martha Sjursdtr Midje (1762-1835).

Lars and Marta had three children: Anders, Marta, and Odd. Marta's son Knut immigrated to America in 1850 at age 25. Then in 1852, Marta's daughter, Ingeborg (age 30) came with her half brother, Anders (age 22). They probably joined other Aurlandings in Koshkonong, Wisconsin.

Lars and Marta brought their sons Odd and Lars and daughter Marta to America in 1857. They settled in Goodhue County, Minnesota Territory.

Lars died in 1867 and is buried in the Holden Lutheran Church Cemetery. Marta died in 1872, and was buried in Urland Lutheran Church during the first year of burials in that cemetery.

Section Three
Minnesota's Norwegian Century Pioneers

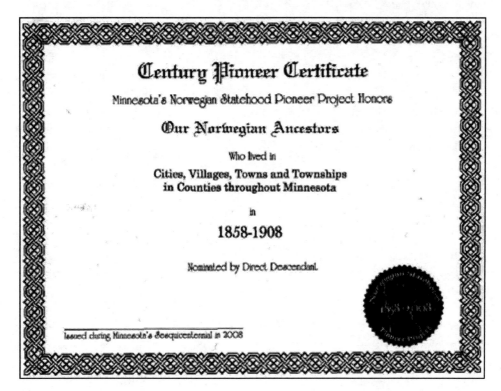

Most of Minnesota wasn't settled until after it became a state. Many towns in northern Minnesota weren't established until after the turn of the 20th Century. Tens of thousands of Norwegian-Minnesotans built farms and schools, started churches, opened businesses, helped organize local governments and were elected to public office in these new communities.

The project is proud to recognize the contributions of the Norwegians and Norwegian-Americans who lived in Minnesota before 1908. Only a handful of Norwegian Century Pioneers are recognized here - founders and farmers, pastors and civic leaders, and those who led quiet lives earning a living and raising their families – but they represent all of the Norwegian settlers who contributed to the culture and conscience of communities throughout the state.

Following the roster, a selection of stories illustrate the lives of – and challenges faced by – Minnesota's Norwegian Century Pioneers.

Norwegian Century Pioneers

Century Pioneer Name(s)	Year	County	Town/Township
Ødegaard Sven Aslakson & Liv P Valtvedt	1858	Goodhue	Minneola
Noem Petter Johnson & Anne Pedersdtr	1859	Fillmore	Holt
Bordsen Mari Aaker	1860	Goodhue	Holden
Dyreson Christen	1860	Goodhue	Minneola
Foss Andrew Brynildsen	1860	Houston	Spring Grove
Orton August Ludvig	1861	Fillmore	Lanesboro
Hegland Mikkel Tarjeisen & Sissel Amundsdtr	1861	Fillmore	Norway
Vinjum Nils Olsen	1861	Houston	Black Hammer
Aarbak Gunnlaug (Julia) Hansdtr	1861	Houston	Houston
Evensen Aad	1861	Houston	Sheldon
Enger Peder Ellingson & Aase Ellevesdtr	1861	Houston	Sheldon
Grover Edward Gilbert	1861	Houston	Sheldon
Enger Ingrid Østensdtr	1861	Houston	Spring Grove
Stangeland Elias & Gurine Einong	1861	Olmsted	Rock Dell
Olson Peter	1862	Carver	Carver
Gunderson Gunil (Benson)	1862	Fillmore	Rushford
Ulland Andrew Oleson	1862	Freeborn	Moscow
Jackson Jacob & Gunhild	1862	Waseca	Blooming Grove
Jenson Michael	1863	Nicollet	Bernadotte
Jacobson John	1864	Fillmore	Newburg
Dahlen Anna Christina	1864	Fillmore	Newburg
Olson Gilbert Monserud	1864	Fillmore	Newburg
Grover Christian Alfred	1864	Houston	Sheldon
Pedersen Berta Serine	1865	Fillmore	Newburg
Erickson Erick & Inga	1865	Freeborn	Bath
Enger Elling & Anne Ellingsdtr	1865	Houston	Spring Grove
Bratsberg Halvor Tolvssen	1865	Jackson	Des Moines
Stall Oliver & Helga Hanson	1865	Jackson	Des Moines
Olsen Mathias & Martha	1865	Nicollet	Lake Prairie
Sundby Theodor A & Anne M Holmlie	1866	Dodge	Westfield
Gundersen Olaus	1866	Freeborn	Hayward
Tokerud Elene Olsdatter	1866	Freeborn	Hayward
Swenson Peter & Ingri Andersen	1866	Freeborn	Newry
Flatten Targe Olson	1866	Houston	Sheldon
Anderson Anton Julius	1866	Jackson	Rost
Gilbertson Ole & Guri (Julia) Peterson	1866	Pope	Barsness
Aaberg Albert Peterson	1866	Pope	Gilchrist
Anderson Joseph & Ingri	1866	Pope	Gilchrist
Olson Dorothea Fuglehaug	1866	Pope	Gilchrist

Norwegian Century Pioneers

Century Pioneer Name(s)	Year	County	Town/Township
Olson Thor & Olia	1866	Pope	Gilchrist
Peterson Ole & Guri (Julia) Thorson	1866	Pope	Gilchrist
Peterson Peter	1866	Pope	Gilchrist
Suckstorff Hans & Lena Peterson	1866	Pope	Gilchrist
Thorson Peter	1866	Pope	Gilchrist
Thorson Erick (Isaac) & Jorund (Jan) Haldorson	1866	Pope	Rolling Forks
Thorson Ole & Maria (Minnie)	1866	Pope	Rolling Forks
Thorson Tory & Olina Norderhus	1866	Pope	Rolling Forks
Thorson Oley & Betsy Dokkebakken	1866	Swift	Camp Lake
Botten Hans Johnsen	1867	Brown	Linden
Hanson Ole & Mari Sanden	1867	Fillmore	Canton
Harstad Tollef A & Margit	1867	Fillmore	Harmony
Ramsey Bottolf Pederson & Gertrud Mikkelsdtr	1867	Fillmore	Pilot Mound
Griffin Oliver (Ole) Gullickson & Berthe Bjerke	1867	Houston	Money Creek
Larson Karen Hanson	1867	Houston	Yucatan
Anderson Gust & Lena	1867	Jackson	Rost
Halvorson Belle (Ingeborg Halvorsdtr)	1867	Jackson	Rost
Eikhom Halvor H & Aleth J Bukkøy	1867	Jackson	West Heron Lake
Spigedalen Johannes Mikkelsen & Mina Holte	1867	Otter Tail	Oscar
Eriksen Martin & Eli Pedersdtr	1867	Sherburne	Santiago
Martin Ole	1867	Sherburne	Santiago
Paulsen Ole & Marthe Andersen	1868	Brown	Hanska
Teigen Hans & Marie	1868	Brown	Linden
Hanson Helen (Mrs Peter Olson)	1868	Carver	Carver
Olsen Peter & Oline Christophersen	1868	Dakota	Hastings
Evensen Adeline	1868	Houston	Sheldon
Elstad Anna Hogstad	1868	Renville	Camp
Hogstad Anna Martha Melhus	1868	Renville	Camp
Hogstad John O	1868	Renville	Camp
Hogstad John Peder & Oline (Lena)	1868	Renville	Camp
Hogstad Ole Pedersen	1868	Renville	Camp
Mutta Halvor & Anna	1868	Renville	Hawk Creek
Sagnes Hans Sønsteby & Berthe	1868	Renville	Hawk Creek
Kanten Iver Halvorsen & Anne Gulbrandsdtr	1869	Chippewa	Tunsberg
Larsen Anders	1869	Douglas	Belle River
Hasleiet Kittel (Charles)	1869	Fillmore	Holt
Hasleiet Thor Kittilson & Gunhild Nielsdtr	1869	Fillmore	Holt
Opsal Rasmus Rasmusson	1869	Fillmore	Holt
Rasmusson Knud	1869	Fillmore	Holt

Norwegian Century Pioneers

Century Pioneer Name(s)	Year	County	Town/Township
Runestad Rasmus Olson & Anne Serine Opsal	1869	Fillmore	Holt
Bjerke Karine Christensdtr	1869	Fillmore	Rushford
Narumshagen Johannes Martinson	1869	Fillmore	Rushford
Gjermundson Ole & Ingeborg	1869	Goodhue	Cherry Grove
Bredeson John	1869	Kandiyohi	Kandiyohi
Peterson Bernt & Otilde	1869	Nicollet	New Sweden
Boe Peter Aslagson (Olson)	1869	Pope	Gilchrist
Thortvedt Olav & Thone	1870	Clay	Moland
Anderson Ole	1870	Douglas	Belle River
Garnaas Kittel O	1870	Fillmore	Newburg
Olsen Amund & Bertha Jennison	1870	Murray	Mason
Kittelson Hans & Bertha Bustul	1870	Otter Tail	Erhards Grove
Lee Berge & Olina Anderson	1870	Otter Tail	Tordensjold
Elstad John H	1870	Renville	Camp
Hogstad Peder O	1870	Renville	Camp
Otterness Edward	1871	Goodhue	Leon
Larson Josephine	1871	Houston	Yucatan
Peterson Martin	1871	Pope	Rolling Forks
Peterson Ole & Enge	1871	Pope	Rolling Forks
Hagen Bersvend & Karen	1871	Renville	Sacred Heart
Berge Aanund & Thone Olsen	1872	Houston	Yucatan
Johnson Olaus & Elen Anna	1872	Murray	Leeds
Jacobson Ole & Olena Peterson	1872	Renville	Camp
Olson Elise Andrea Grover	1873	Houston	Sheldon
Grover Tarje A & Geline Kassenborg	1874	Clay	Moland
Roundal Knute & Aslaug Thimrud	1875	Clay	Flowing
Kragnes Aanund Ole	1875	Clay	Kragnes
Sandwick Tilde Grover	1875	Clay	Moland
Kassenborg Andreas G & Tone Kragnes	1875	Clay	Oakport
Anderson Andrew & Martha Christopherson	1875	Douglas	Belle River
Johnson Nils & Anne Jakobsdtr	1875	Fillmore	Arendahl
Martinson Johannes & Karine Bjerke	1875	Fillmore	Peterson
Bollie Julia	1875	Goodhue	Kenyon
Larson Erik & Tolline Johnson	1875	Goodhue	Prairie Island
Soine Ole & Gertrude Elton	1875	Renville	Hawk Creek
Stone Hans Olsen	1875	Stevens	Rendsville
Olson Sigvald & Kate	1876	Kandiyohi	Harrison
Rolfson Asben S (Asbjørn)	1876	Mower	Dexter
Sagnes, Jr Hans & Marie Mutta	1876	Renville	Ericson

Norwegian Century Pioneers

Century Pioneer Name(s)		Year	County	Town/Township
Elandson	Christ & Karen Enden	1877	Brown	Allsin
Christopherson	Rachel (Ragnhild Hansdtr)	1877	Dakota	Hastings
Grover	Otto Julius	1878	Clay	Moland
Torgersrud	Hans Olson	1878	Grant	Gorton
Ellson	Ellef & Rena Hansdtr	1878	Grant	Norcross
Kroshus	Halvor Anderson & Kjersti	1878	Norman	Mary
Mickelsen	Mathias & Marie	1878	Ramsey	St Paul
Gaare	John O	1879	Clay	Viding
Stras	Theador E & Ingeborg Kleven	1879	Otter Tail	Oscar
Thompson	Petrina Pedersdtr	1879	Swift	Benson
Helgedalen	Nels & Anne Hanson	1880	Clay	Goose Prairie
Espeland	Osten & Aslaug Boen	1880	Clay	Morken
Christopherson	Michael & Anna Olsen	1880	Dakota	Hastings
Mork	Einar Torgerson	1880	Fillmore	Pilot Mound
Mork	Torger Erickson & Marte P Vollum	1880	Fillmore	Pilot Mound
Larsen	Hans & Anna Marie Wahl	1880	Otter Tail	Erhards Grove
Korssjoen	Bernt P & Oline	1880	Otter Tail	Folden
Korssjoen	Marit O	1880	Otter Tail	Folden
Kulberg	Ole P & Malene	1880	Otter Tail	Nidaros
Johnson	Ludvig	1880	Polk	Halstad
Botten	Ole & Julia	1880	Stearns	North Fork
Kolsrud	Ole Knudssen	1880	Stearns	North Fork
Trostheim	Gunhild Pedersdtr	1880	Stearns	North Fork
Solberg	Knut Knutson & Aashild Haugen	1880	Yellow Medicine	Clarkfield
Storbo	Theodor P & Berit J	1881	Otter Tail	Folden
Hogstad	Johanna Marie Olsen	1881	Renville	Bandon
Olsen	Osalf (Aasulf)	1881	Renville	Bandon
Olsen	Susanna Jambakkmyra	1881	Renville	Bandon
Soine	Ole & Gertrude Elton	1881	Renville	Maynard
Kvernodden	Inga Amelia Nelson	1881	Rice	Faribault
Rogness	Knute Nelson & Kari Engebretson	1881	Rock	Vienna
Anderson	Isak	1881	Sherburne	Santiago
Haakenstad	Halvor Pedersen & Sophia A Olson	1882	Fillmore	Canton
Johnson	Peder & Ingeborg Wahl	1882	Otter Tail	Erhards Grove
Wahl	Anders & Berthe Syversen	1882	Otter Tail	Erhards Grove
Strass	Carl Johan	1882	Otter Tail	Fergus Falls
Langhei	Ole O	1882	Polk	Bygland
Gunderson	Knudt	1882	Renville	Bandon
Bekkerus	Askild T & Tone Kleven	1883	Clay	Moland

Norwegian Century Pioneers

Century Pioneer Name(s)		Year	County	Town/Township
Nelson	Carl & Petra Finsand	1883	Freeborn	Albert Lea
Golden	H I & Andrina Swanson	1883	Marshall	Warren
Langejoen	Peder & Gertrude Jordet	1883	Otter Tail	St Olaf
Hole	Johan C	1883	Polk	King
Dybsand	Anton	1883	Renville	Sacred Heart
Graff	Caroline	1883	Stevens	Stevens County
Grover	Alexander & Pauline Kroshus	1884	Clay	Moland
Loe	John O	1884	Lyon	Lucas
Hauger	Gustaf B	1884	Polk	Winger
Johannssen	Mikkel & Mallin	1884	Ramsey	St Paul
Alm	Hans Oleson	1885	Chippewa	Tunsberg
Branno	Iver & Olava	1885	Houston	Wilmington
Kroshus	Albert	1885	Norman	Mary
Wahl	Syver & Anne Marie Swenson	1885	Otter Tail	Erhards Grove
Bekkerus	Theodore	1886	Clay	Moland
Grover	Clarence	1886	Norman	Mary
Sandwick	Andrew	1887	Clay	Moland
Hanson	Johan & Karn Alitta	1887	Kandiyohi	Norway Lake
Jergenson	Berger & Ingri	1887	Pope	Rolling Forks
Rekstad	Erik & Martia	1888	Chippewa	Grace
Alm	Ole Erickson & Johanne Hansdtr	1888	Chippewa	Tunsberg
Loe	Jerdine Eikeland	1888	Lyon	Lucas
Moe	John & Mary Olesdtr	1889	Chippewa	Montevideo
Grover	Elmer T J	1889	Clay	Moland
Hagen	Hans J	1889	Yellow Medicine	Sandnes
Alm	Iver Herman	1890	Chippewa	Tunsberg
Strandheim	Gunvor Larsdatter	1891	Dodge	Hayfield
Paulson	Benhart Martin	1891	Marshall	Big Woods
Branno	Iver & Olava	1892	Fillmore	Canton
Morck	Conrad Deitlef	1892	Hennepin	Minneapolis
Alm	Oscar	1893	Chippewa	Tunsberg
Alm	Erick Oleson & Lisa Martinsdtr	1893	Chippewa	Watson
Christopherson	Ragnhild (Rachel) Hanson	1893	Dakota	Hastings
Knutson	Arne & Gjertrud	1893	Roseau	Pinecreek
Erickson	Carl (Charles) Edvardsen	1894	Rice	Richland
Erickson	John Olaf Ibsen	1894	Rice	Richland
Skjenstad	Martha Oline (Lena)	1894	Rice	Richland
Johnson	Peder & Ingeborg Wahl	1895	Clay	Moorhead
Golden	Harold N	1895	Marshall	City of Warren

Norwegian Century Pioneers

Century Pioneer Name(s)		Year	County	Town/Township
Johnson	Andrew & Mary	1895	Otter Tail	Elizabeth
Bakken	Simon & Karen Wahl	1895	Otter Tail	Maplewood
Hanson	Clara	1895	Otter Tail	Pelican Rapids
Hanson	Johan & Karn Alitta	1895	Pope	Gilchrist
Akre	Cora Angeline Aslakson	1896	Goodhue	Cannon Falls
Hagen	Rev Ole Jacobson & Johanna Engen	1896	Murray	Slayton
Johnson	Mabel Isabel	1896	Polk	Fertile
Stangeland	Simon & Gunhild Kørnbo	1897	Beltrami	Turtle Lake
Gunderson	Asborg Olsen Våsjo	1897	Renville	Bandon
Sumstad	Anton O	1898	Grant	Pelican Lake
Olson	John & Oline Olsdtr	1898	Morrison	Cushing
Hegland	Allette	1898	Polk	Brandsvold
Hegland	Sophie	1898	Polk	Brandsvold
Hegland	Thor Mikkelsen & Lina Berge	1898	Polk	Brandsvold
Enger	Edward Ellingson & Hannah Larson	1898	Yellow Medicine	Hanley Falls
Hegland	Anton	1899	Polk	Brandsvold
Enger	William Delander	1899	Yellow Medicine	Hanley Falls
Knutson	Andreas & Anna	1900	Crow Wing	Pequot
Wahl	Edward	1900	Otter Tail	Fergus Falls
Hegland	George Carlton	1900	Polk	Brandsvold
Olsen	Finbo	1900	Renville	Bandon
Olsen	Ole	1900	Renville	Bandon
Hogstad	Josephine	1900	Renville	Franklin
Larson	Martin & Mathea Ellson	1900	Yellow Medicine	Hanley Falls
Svensrud	Evan & Randi	1901	Morrison	Cushing
Thoreson	Eddie	1901	Polk	Climax
Jordahl	Clara Bertina	1902	Polk	Tynsid
Paulsen	Tilde Petrine Vaage	1903	Brown	Lake Hanska
Orton	Albert George	1903	Big Stone	Ortonville
Orton	August Ludvig	1903	Big Stone	Ortonville
Hegland	Lorentz	1903	Polk	Brandsvold
Okland	Engel	1904	Hennepin	Minneapolis
Erickson	Michael & Anna Johnson	1905	Goodhue	Red Wing
Hegland	Alfred	1905	Polk	Brandsvold
Anderson	Andrew & Karen Christopherson	1906	Ramsey	St Paul
Hogstad	Clara	1906	Renville	Franklin
Haugo	Hazel Syverson	1907	Becker	Walworth
Johnson	Fritz	1907	Grant	Erdahl

An American Adventure
based on the biography of Andras (Andrew) Foss
from "The History of Houston County Minnesota," edited by Franklyn Curtiss-Wedge and published by H. C. Cooper, Winona MN 1919, page 519-522

    Andrew Brynildsen Foss was not only a pioneer of Houston County, but also a gold seeker in California in the thrilling and romantic days of the early 1850's. He was born near Bergen, Norway on April 24, 1826. There were few opportunities for him in his native country, so he turned his eyes toward America as the land of opportunity. In May, 1849, the twenty-three year old left Norway on a voyage of seven weeks and four days to New York. He arrived on the 4th of July. From that city he went by railroad to Albany, from Albany to Buffalo by the Erie Canal, and from Buffalo by way of the Great Lakes to Milwaukee. By the time he arrived in Milwaukee he was out of money, so he set out on foot for Janesville, where his cousin lived. Twenty two miles into his walk, he arrived at a little place named Georgeville where he met an Irish farmer named Joseph Lennon.

    Lennon offered Andrew fifty cents a day for two weeks work in his hay fields, and he quickly agreed. After eleven days, Andrew' hands were so blistered from the use of the scythe that he was unable to do any more. Although he had but two days more to serve to make up the half month, the farmer meanly refused to pay him anything, so he went on his way penniless.

    Andrew finally reached Janesville. His cousin was a bricklayer and hired him to mix mortar and carry the hod (a box with a long pole handle used to carry mortar) for one dollar a day. During the following winter, when mason work was out of the question, he took on whatever work he could to cover his board and lodging. In the spring of 1850 he found work on the farm of Levi St. John near Janesville, earning ten dollars a month wages, and remained until the fall. He then went to Plattville, Wisconsin, where he found work with another cousin who was a contractor.

    During the winter of 1850-51 he met an American just returned from California, who told wonderful stories about the recent discoveries of gold. These stories left a strong impression on Foss and his cousin, Mons K. Foss, was equally enthralled with the possibilities offered by such an adventure. They joined forces with five Americans to form a traveling party. Each member contributed $100 to the expedition. They packed two wagons and began the journey with five yoke of oxen in April of 1851. The journey began without incident and although some Indians were encountered, they gave the party no trouble. When they reached the desert 300 miles east of the Rocky Mountains, they traded their oxen for mules and crossed it in four days and nights. They stopped in Salt Lake City to resupply and traveled through the Mormon Pass over the Rockies. While on this part of the journey some Indian guides joined the party without invitation. The travelers had heard stories that made them a little nervous, but after a day and night the Indians disappeared and they saw no more of them. Two of the company rode ahead of the others. This resulted in the only casualty they suffered on the journey, when one of the two was shot. They often encountered bands of Indians numbering 500 or more, and occasionally they joined other caravans of emigrants and accompanied them for a while until for choice or by accident they separated. On June 10 they reached the Rockies, and soon after arrived at their destination, Hangtown, California, which would eventually take on the more civilized name of Placerville.

At Hangtown Mr. Foss and his cousin hired out to mine for four dollars a day and board, working there and at Cold Springs until the spring of 1852. Then with his cousin he spent some time prospecting in the vicinity of Hangtown without much success. Deciding that a change of location might change their luck, they set out for Sacramento. Upon arriving there, they continued up the Sacramento River by steamer to Marysville, a mining town, and from there to Parker's Bar, another camp three miles above, where there were rich diggings. They bought a share in a mine for two hundred dollars. Soon afterwards Andrew Foss, as one of a company of sixteen equal partners, moved forty miles north and bought his share in another mine for a one hundred dollar investment. To accomplish their operations successfully they built a dam and flume to turn the water so they could search for gold in the river bed below. This flume was 400 feet long and was covered with canvas. It was late in the fall when it was finished, so they were able to do but two weeks' mining before the rainy season set in. The work netted each man only six dollars a day, an amount which, considering the fearfully high price of all necessities, was insignificant. To save themselves from further losses and months of weary waiting, they sold their works to some Chinamen for $2,000. Almost as soon as this transaction was complete the rains came on with such violence that everything was washed away and the Chinamen completely ruined.

Andrew lost all his money in a "freezeout" game and returned to Parker's Bar, poor in pocket but rich in experience. His cousin had established a miner's boarding house there, but neither of the young men were successful in Parker's Bar. They set out for Downeyville, forty miles from Sacramento, where they found the mining poor. By this time the young Mr. Foss had discovered that it was not easy for him to acquire sudden wealth, and made up his mind to return to Wisconsin and seek it by the slower but surer method of agriculture.

He and his cousin made their way to San Francisco, and three weeks later they were able to set sail for New Orleans. The first leg of their journey cost $150 each, steerage. The eight day trip down the coast brought them to Acapulco, where they took on supplies, and then, after another eight days, they were landed in Nicaragua. They crossed the Isthmus partly on mule back and partly by boat journey across Lake Nicaragua, the mule hire costing them $5 apiece. On this part of the journey they had to traverse the river from the lake until they reached the rapids, where they made a portage, went by a steamer which they found below to the second rapids, then made another portage and took a second steamer to the eastern coast, where they boarded a Gulf steamer and in three days found them in New Orleans.

The next stage of their journey was made up the Mississippi River to St. Louis, the fare being $12 apiece. They then proceeded to Dubuque, where they crossed the river to New Galena, Illinois, and from there traveled on foot to Janesville, which place they reached just three years after leaving it. In the fall of 1853 Andrew and Mons walked from Janesville to McGregor Iowa, and then pressed on to Decorah. At Locust Prairie, Iowa, Andrew bought 160 acres of wild land on which he built a shack and some straw sheds, and began to make improvements, leading a bachelor's life.

On June 20, 1855, he married Anna Solberg, daughter of Andros and Gerhardt Solberg of Spring Grove Township, Houston County, Minnesota Territory. Mr. Solberg died, and Andrew and Anna sold the Iowa farm and bought her parents' homestead in Section 32. Andrew and Anna raised their eleven children on the farm, increasing its size to 340 acres. In 1887, they built a two-story brick home on West Main Street in the village of Spring Grove, where the couple lived out their lives.

Mr. Foss was active in Spring Grove community affairs. He was one of the founders of the Spring Grove congregation of the Norwegian Evangelical Lutheran church and for several years served as a trustee. The Foss children included Barbara, Mrs. N. H. Nelson, Mabel, Minnesota; Germa, Mrs. Thorvold Doely, Elbow Lake, Minnesota; Johana, Mrs. C. M. Warms of Winnishiek County, Iowa; Brady, Cuba; Albert, Spring Grove; Martha, Mrs. T. A. Kroshus; Peter, on the family's original homestead; Julia, Mrs. Anton Waihus of Winnishiek County; Edward, Spring Grove; Anna Sophia, Mrs. Frank Joerg, Spring Grove; and Leander, Robinson, North Dakota.

War Comes to Norwegian Grove
By Gene Estensen

This article is dedicated to the memory of Ole Østensen Bøen (later Ole Estensen) and Astrid Johnsdatter, the author's great great grandparents. They left Tinn, Telemark, Norway in 1851 and worked their way across America before settling at Norwegian Grove, New Sweden Township, Nicollet County, Minnesota Territory. Torstein Østensen Bøen was Ole's older brother. Both were Minnesota Territorial Pioneers and citizen soldiers in the Scandinavian Guard of Nicollet County. Their families survived the Sioux Uprising of 1862.

The Minnesota River begins its journey to the Mississippi in west-central Minnesota. It flows south and west then eventually turns sharply north and east toward St. Paul. At the sharp bend in the river is a natural crossing that the Sioux Indians (Dakota) called Oiyuwege, meaning "the place of the crossing". French explorers called it Traverse des Sioux, or "crossing place of the Sioux". For centuries the great buffalo herds migrated across the plains of present day Minnesota and crossed the Minnesota River at Traverse des Sioux. This spot became a crossroads and meeting place for people of many cultures. A town named St. Peter grew near this historical crossroads. To the west, the Great Plains was the home of the Sioux Indians and for centuries they lived in harmony with the buffalo and other wildlife. However, to the east were the pioneers from Scandinavia and Germany and they were pressing ever westward onto the plains. The two cultures clashed in southern Minnesota Territory and violence flared up in 1862 resulting in the loss of life of nearly 1,000 settlers and Indians. In twenty Minnesota counties, bands of Sioux warriors swept down on isolated farms and settlements, killing the men, capturing women and children, and burning or plundering property.[i] About thirty persons were killed in Nicollet County.[ii] This is the story of Norwegian territorial pioneers in one county (Nicollet) and one township (New Sweden) that got caught up in the war. The letters written to Norway from Nicollet County, and translated for this article, describe the terror that filled the Minnesota River Valley.

In 1851, at Traverse des Sioux, the Sioux Indians ceded 24 million acres of tribal land to the U.S. Government. This land was opened to settlement in 1853, leaving 7,000 Sioux living on a narrow reservation of two million acres along the Minnesota River. In 1858, the Sioux ceded an additional one million acres of land. At the same time the government tried to turn the nomadic Sioux into farmers.[iii] This divided the Sioux into two groups, those that took on the ways of the whites, and those that remained faithful to traditional tribal ways. This division would impact life in Minnesota Territory and the outcome of the Sioux Uprising.

Before Minnesota became a state, and just as settlement in southern Minnesota was allowed for the first time, a wagon train moved slowly westward from the Norwegian settlement of Muskego in Wisconsin. In the year 1854,[iv] after a journey of seven weeks, the families of Norwegians Torstein Østensen Bøen of Tinn, Telemark,

Johan Tollefson of Totten, and Lars Svenson Rodning of Hallingdal (a single man) crossed the Minnesota River at the Traverse des Sioux. They climbed the far shore and settled near what is now St. Peter in Nicollet County. They settled this area and it became known as the Norseland Settlement.[v] Torstein Østensen settled at Scandian Grove in Lake Prairie Township. About a year later, on October 7, 1855 a group of Swedes joined him at Scandian Grove. Andrew Thorson of this group would write, "It was a beautiful fall season. During the winter we lived among Indians who were numerous in our woods. Four or five Norwegian farmers were living in the vicinity. We were the first Swedes at this place".[vi] Thorson reported that the Swedes spent the first winter in a house that stood on some land "now occupied by Annexstad" (Author, this would be the Torstein Østensen Bøen farm). The next year, on June 17, 1856, Ole Østensen Bøen and family from Tinn, Telemark, Norway joined his brother Torstein at Nicollet County. Accompanied by Gunder Nereson and Swenke Torgerson, they settled near a grove in the northern part of what is now New Sweden Township and named the area "Norwegian Grove".[vii]

"There are no towns or railroads in this township, but the domain has a wonderful fertility and is known far and near as being one of the best improved among the banner townships of the county and state. Its people, largely Scandinavians, are the true type of men and women who fear not to do and to dare. They have developed this six-mile square tract of Nicollet county in a manner that would put to blush many an older and fairer looking country, by nature, than was this when they first set their plowshares to the tough prairie sod in the fifties and sixties."[viii]

As cultures clashed and tensions mounted between the Indians and Territorial Pioneers it was decided that the U.S. Government would build a fort in Nicollet County to protect the early settlers on the Great Plains. In 1853, the U.S. military started construction of Fort Ridgely near the southern border of the new Indian reservation and northwest of the German settlement of New Ulm. The fort was designed to keep peace as settlers poured into the former Sioux lands. It was substantially completed by 1855. This fort would play a great role in the war to come. With the protection offered by the fort, settlers poured into the Minnesota River Valley. By 1858, when Minnesota became a state, thirty-one families resided at Norseland.

Pioneer C. C. Nelson found mostly Indians when he came to what is now New Sweden Township in 1858. "We lived among the Indians four years. They visited us frequently and occasionally stayed all night and we accommodated them the best we could, although we didn't find them very pleasant or agreeable. However, we tried not to cross them for fear they would attack us at any time."[ix]

By 1862 the Sioux were near starvation. Food and clothing were on hand in a warehouse at the Indian Agency near the present town of Redwood Falls, but had not been distributed.[x] To make matters worse, the customary payment date to the Sioux from the Congress of the United States was missed by two months. Now the Sioux would desperately try to drive the white people out of the land given up in the Treaty of

Traverse des Sioux in 1851. War broke out on August 17, 1862 when a small band of Indians shot and killed four or five settlers in Meeker County, near Acton. A war council was held the following day under the leadership of Little Crow, Chief of the Mdewakanton Santee Sioux, and the decision was made to go to war. Little Crow had been to Washington, D.C. in 1854 thus knew of the vast number of white people to the east. He gave an impassioned speech to his followers:

"We are only little herds of buffaloes left scattered; the great herds that once covered the prairies are no more. See! The white men are like the locusts when they fly so thick that the whole sky is a snowstorm. You may kill one – two – ten; yes, as many as the leaves in the forest yonder, and their brothers will not miss them. Kill one – two – ten, and ten times ten will come to kill you. Count your fingers all day long and white men with guns in their hands will come faster than you can count……….Braves, you are little children – you are fools. You will die like the rabbits when the hungry wolves hunt them in the Hard Moon (January). Ta-o-ya-te-du-ta is not a coward; he will die with you."[xi]

The war soon spread across the entire Minnesota frontier. Major battles were fought at Fort Ridgely and at New Ulm in Nicollet County. Life and death struggles occurred in the townships like New Sweden.

Dr. Asa W. Daniels wrote in his Reminiscences[xii] "The news of the Indian Uprising reached St. Peter during the night of Monday, the 18th of August". Dr. Daniels went north and west on Tuesday (toward Norwegian Grove) to warn the settlers and on his return found "the refugees were already pouring in, and by noon the village became crowded with men, women, and children. Some had been attacked on the way, and bore their wounded with them. All were in the most pitiful condition, having in their haste taken little clothing, and no provisions".

The war reached New Sweden Township on August 23, 1862. A band of Sioux warriors moved from south to north through the township, through the farms of many Swedes and directly to the Norwegians at Norwegian Grove. Sections 18, 8, and 4 saw the most destruction. Before the approaching Indians, the Larson and Carlson families fled in terror in a horse-drawn wagon. As they approached a curve in the road at Norwegian Grove, they appeared to be doomed. The Sioux warriors took a short cut across the prairie to get ahead of the Larson team. They would have succeeded if it had not been for a strong built rail fence. The Indians turned back and began to search for the Erik Johnson (Swedish) family who had abandoned their wagon. Years later, at the age of 73, in 1920, Inger Johnson Holmquist wrote her story about the encounter at Norwegian Grove:

"It was on the 23rd of August that the Indians murdered my mother and brother. I was 14 years old. We met the Indians. Father turned and drove to the end of the pasture. There he stopped while we jumped off the wagon and hid in the grass. The Indians took our horses and were pursuing my brother and a neighbor. They shot a neighbor boy, John Solomonson through the wrist. Then they came and found mother, one brother Pehr, twelve years old, one brother 10 months old, and myself. They shot mother in the chest. The last words she said were 'Lord Jesus, receive my soul'. Then they kicked my twelve-year-old brother and told him to get up. Then they kicked me and said get up. I was in a trance and could hear and feel, but could not move or see. They asked my brother if I was dead. Do not remember his answer."[xiii] The Indians took Pehr and led him away. It appeared that they intended to kidnap him but he refused to go so they shot him dead. After a long day, night came and Inger heard her baby brother crying. She found her mother dead and the baby crying in her arms. They hid through the night. Inger's father later returned and found Inger and the baby hiding under a haycock.

Herman Solomenson later recalled an incident regarding the fence at Norwegian Grove. "This fence was close to a Norwegian settler's home. The wife, hearing the noise, picked up a small child and ran outdoors to see what was going on. She came face to face with the Indians who did not molest her".[xiv] (Author: There were four Norwegian families at Norwegian Grove. I will always wonder if this woman was my great-great-grandmother Astrid Johnsdatter Bøen, wife of Ole Østensen Bøen. The child could have been Østen, age 6, or Nils, age 4).

The next day soldiers came out from St. Peter and were unable to find anyone at New Sweden; they had fled to St. Peter or the Scandian Lutheran Church. The Indians had burned several houses. They belonged to the Swedes Carl Nelson, Pehr Carlson, Swen Benson, John Johnson, and Lars Solomenson. In addition, losing their houses and their grain were Pehr Benson, Peter M. Fritioff, Joran Johnson, Erik Johnson, J. Larson, Johannes Ecklund, and Lars Solomenson.

One settler, E. O. in St. Peter, wrote his family in Stavanger, Norway on September 9, 1862:

"I will now describe everything to you as thoroughly as I am able, and as far as my heart, which is trembling with fear, will allow me. That which I suspected and wrote about in my last letter has come about. The Indians have begun attacking the farmers. They have already killed a great many people, and many are mutilated in the cruelest manner. Tomahawks and knives have already claimed many victims. Children, less able to defend themselves, are usually burned alive or hanged in the trees, and destruction moves from house to house. The Indians burn everything on their way - houses, hay, grain, and so on. Even if I describe the horror in the strongest possible language, my description would fall short of reality. These troubles have now lasted for about two weeks, and every day larger numbers of settlers come into St. Peter to protect their lives from the raging Indians. They crowd themselves together in large stone houses for protection, and the misery is so great that imagination could not depict it in darker colors. A few persons have their hands and feet burned off. May I never again have to see such terrible sights."[xv]

Scandinavian farmers quickly united to secure their defense. "All the settlers in that neighborhood, and the western part of New Sweden, gathered to work on a stockade. They decided to put up sod walls. The wall was built six feet in height. Their stockade stood there many years". The settlers formed groups of citizen soldiers to protect themselves. They gave themselves names like the Le Sueur Tigers, St. Peter Guards, and the Scandinavian Guards of Nicollet County. Also, soldiers rushed from St. Paul to defend the counties of southern Minnesota. An experienced Norwegian-American soldier, originally from Hol in Hallingdal, by the name of Askrim Skaro trained the group named the Scandinavian Guard of Nicollet County. Skaro went on to become a Civil War hero and was killed at the Battle of Nashville. The Scandinavian Guard of Nicollet County was organized in Nicollet County, Minnesota on the 27th day of August 1862. Gustaf A. Stark became their captain and they patrolled the prairie around Nicollet County for three weeks. He was later killed by the Sioux. Below is an excerpt from a second letter to Norway, from St. Peter, Minnesota, dated September 9, 1862 and translated by the Vesterheim staff for this article:

" ----- But here in our neighborhood we have not seen any of those appalling things, thank God. But about 300 miles west of here there have been terrible murders and atrocities– the worst the world has ever seen. For we have talked to people from that area and also seen letters, written in a grieving state of mind so that it makes it hard to even talk about how the Indians had rampaged. They don't do like other warring powers; they go from one farm to the next, committing atrocities against women and men, wives and children, and they came like thieves and murderers, taking with them everything they could, and what they couldn't take, they set on fire, such as hay stacks, wheat stacks, buildings, and fences, and they didn't kill like other murderers; they would take young and old and bang them against a wall, leaving them half dead in a pool of blood, and others they would take and attach to fences and buildings, and others again they would stab with spears and knives in the outer part of the limbs. I heard of a child who had been stabbed 11 times and still lived for a while, and 12 miles from here there is a girl who was able to escape, but her husband and children were killed there on the farm, and she had to witness it. She also was knocked down by a couple of heavy blows and was left on the farm, half dead, along with her smallest child, and when she came to again, she set out with her little child who had been lying by her side and had also been hurt and was half dead. You can imagine what kind of misery that poor woman has to suffer through, losing both her husband and her children, and there are many more who are going through hardships equally terrifying. Young and attractive girls were herded together and had to go along from one camp to another, and you can just imagine what kind of misery and grief those poor girls had to go through, having to be with such people, because they were just like wild animals, and their faces were red, black, and blue, and I must tell you that they have had a tremendous effect, and the reason for it is that people didn't know a thing until they were coming over them, and secondly because all soldiers have gone south to fight against the southern powers, and consequently they had a good opportunity to advance before people had time to get together. But then the soldiers came, and they received the same gifts back as they had been handing out earlier, and they deserved nothing better. On the 2nd day of Christmas 39 Indians were hanged, and the ropes were made so that they all had to give up the ghost at the same moment, and 600 are in prison for life, tied together two and two with iron chains. This curse against humanity took place in August and September. But for a while now, the Indians have been completely quiet. However, in the south there have been great battles with casualties as high as 20,000 in one battle --------- neither the North nor the South has been winning ------------. May God be with you, that is the wish of your sister,

Author: Helga Knudsdatter left Tinn, Telemark for America in 1843 with her brother Ole. Helga was born February 18, 1817 and was the daughter of Knut Olsen Heggtveit and Aase Halvorsdatter Gøystdal).[xvi]

Many of the Sioux were peace loving. Today, a statue stands at Morton, Minnesota to honor the memory of John Other Day, Anpetu-Tokeka, and four other "faithful Indians" that were instrumental in saving the lives of white settlers. They were:

Indian Name	Translation	American 'nickname'
Am-pa-tu To-ki-cha	Other Day	John Other Day
Mah-za-koo-te-manne	Iron that shoots walking	Little Paul
To-wan-e-ta-ton	Face Of the village	Lorenzo Lawrence
A-nah-waug-manne	Walked alongside	Simon
Mah-kah-ta He-i-ya-win	Traveling on the ground	Mary Crooks

Other Day was a full-blooded Sioux who lived on a farm and grew crops. He heard of the Sioux's plan to attack New Ulm and began to protect a group of settlers. Other Day stood guard all night outside a warehouse that hid 62 settlers. The settlers heard the cries and whoops of the Indians throughout the night. The next day Other Day led the group on a three-day journey out of harms way. One can only imagine what might have happened if all of the Sioux were united in their desire to rid their ancestral homeland of white settlers.

The uprising was short in duration, lasting only a few weeks. Some four hundred and twenty-five Sioux were arraigned for criminal trial. A military commission convened for the trial. "All ages, from boys of fifteen to infirm old men, were represented".[xvii] Those who pled "guilty" soon had their cases disposed of. The others took some time but in the end three hundred and three were sentenced to be hung, and twenty to imprisonment. President Abraham Lincoln later reduced the number to be hung to thirty-nine, then thirty-eight. The execution was carried out on the 26th of December 1862. The thirty-eight were hanged at Mankato, Minnesota. A. P. Connolly described the execution.[xviii] The condemned Sioux climbed the stairs

Monument at execution site in Mankato

to the large execution platform. "They kept up a mournful wail and occasionally there would be a piercing scream" until the moment of execution came. The cutting of the rope was assigned to William J. Daly of Lake Shetek who had three children killed and his wife and two children captured. All 38 were hanged at one time, the largest public execution in American history.

The Sioux wars continued, off and on, for nearly thirty years as the Sioux were pressed ever westward. On June 25, 1876, near the Little Big Horn River, General George Armstrong Custer was killed in a battle between the U.S. Army's seventh cavalry, guided by Crow and Arikara scouts, and several bands of Lakota Sioux, Cheyenne, and Arapaho. Then, on December 29, 1890, at the massacre of Wounded Knee the great Sioux wars ended, as did a way of life. In his old age, Black Elk (1863-1950), also known as Hehaka Sapa, looked back on this day: "I did not know then how much was ended. When I look back now from this high hill of my old age, I can still see the butchered women and children lying heaped and scattered along the crooked gulch as plain as when I saw them with eyes still young. And I can see that something else died there in the bloody mud, and was buried in the blizzard. A people's dream died there. It was a beautiful dream... The nation's hoop is broken and scattered. There is no center any longer, and the sacred tree is dead."[xix]

Thus it was on the Great Plains as one culture made way for another. The swarms of Scandinavians and Germans moved ever westward. A boy living near the rim of the Dakota country long remembered the pageant of pioneer caravans that passed on their way westward. "We watched the schooners come up from the south," he wrote many years later, "zigzagging up the tortuous trail like ships beating up against the wind. Slowly they drew nearer - sometimes one, sometimes five or six in a fleet. Out to the road we went to watch them pass, and it was the only event of interest from one day to another. Usually the woman was sitting at the front driving the team, and beside her or peeking out of the front opening were a flock of dirty, tousled, tow-headed children. Often she held a small baby in her arms. Behind followed a small herd of cattle or horses driven by the man and the boys on foot, for the rate of travel was a walk". Sometimes the travelers would stop. "They told us where they came from, Fillmore or Goodhue County in Minnesota, or Wisconsin, or Iowa......... " Slowly the wagons passed on, the children now peeking from the opening in the rear, the schooner receding into the distance, very much like a real ship plowing its way over a trackless sea and then disappearing below the horizon."[xx]

----

i   "Sioux Terror on the Prairie", Kachuba, John B., in America's Civil War, p. 34.
ii History of Nicollet and LeSueur Counties, Gresham, Wm G., p. 140.
iii "Sioux Terror on the Prairie", Kachuba, John B., in America's Civil War, p. 30.
iv Saint Peter Tribune, June 27, 1906, Obituary of Torstein Østensen states that he came to Minnesota Territory in 1854.
v   Nordmandene i Amerika, Ulvestad, Martin (v.1 1903).

vi   Scandian Grove, A New Look, Johnson, Emeroy, 1980, p. 24.
vii   History of Nicollet and LeSueur Counties, Gresham, Wm G., p. 166.
viii   History of Nicollet and LeSueur Counties, Gresham, Wm G., p. 168.
ix   "New Sweden Township, Nicollet County, History of the Early Pioneers of this Neighborhood, Nelson, C.C., 1926.
x   Scandian Grove, A New Look, Johnson, Emeroy, 1980, p. 31.
xi   Through Dakota Eyes, Edited by Gary Anderson and Alan Woolworth, 1988, p. 40.
xii   Microfilm HKR-170, Minnesota Historical Society Collection, V15. Reminiscences of the Little Crow Uprising.
xiii   Microfilm HKR-170, Minnesota Historical Society Collection, V15. Reminiscence of August 23, 1862 Dakota Indian attack on New Sweden Township.
xiv   Scandian Grove, A New Look, Johnson, Emeroy, 1980, p. 35.
xv   The Promise of America, Lovoll, Odd, p. 130.
xvi   Translated for Author from Tinns Emigrasjons Historie, Svalestuen, Andres A., p. 158.
xvii   Dakota War-Hoop, McConkey, Harriet, B., p. 249.
xviii Microfilm HKR-170, Minnesota Historical Society Collection, V15.A thrilling narrative of the Minnesota Massacre and the Sioux War of 1862.
xix   Web site of Virtualmuseumofhistory.com
xx   "Sod Houses and Prairie Schooners," Minnesota History, 12:155-156 (June 1933) and reprinted in Norwegian Migration to America, Blegen, Theodore C. 1940

Christian Ahlness Leaves Norway
By Joel Botten, Jr.

This article is comprised of selections from Ahlness' autobiography entitled "Recollections of an Emigrant," reprinted by Jay Patterson, 1977. It is not often that a pioneer takes the time to write the story of his or her life from childhood through the "sunset years". Christian Pedersen Ahlness was one such man. He conquered the English language and wrote his autobiography containing 400 pages of adventures, trials, tribulations, joys and sorrows. The Alnes (as spelled in Norway) farm from which he emigrated is located on the shores of Lake Mjøsa in the Feiring annex in Hurdal parish, Akerhus County. It lies immediately south of Østre Toten, Norway.

One afternoon Christian met his boyhood friend Jorgen Flesvig on the road. Jorgen told him of his emigration plans and asked Christian to join him on this journey to America. Jorgen offered to pay his passage and Christian was immediately excited about the possibility.

Christian was restless and felt he should be independent of his parents. He had been a successful small sailboat builder in the neighborhood and had applied to various schools for further education. Boys with families of more influence received preference for more schooling and he would soon have to serve in the military assisting Denmark in their war with Germany. His parents thought he was joking when he announced his sudden decision, but soon preparations were being made for his departure the next day.

Christian wrote:

The next morning bright and early, I set out for my friend's home to inform him that I should be glad to avail myself of the offer he had made me. It was a fine spring morning and Sunday. Every object that met my senses appeared to remonstrate with me and to have me desist from my purpose. Even the birds in the treetops seemed to think it their duty to impress on my mind how beautiful a country we had and what a fool I must be to think of leaving it. 'But', says I, 'You yourselves, many of you at least, have been away from here during the long, cold winter enjoying yourselves under a foreign sky, why should not I?

Arriving at my friend's home, I found many of his and my friends there to bid us farewell and it was late in the afternoon before I could get away. On my way home others of my relatives and acquaintances were called upon for a parting handshake and it was already dark when I got home. Here a whole company of the young people in the neighborhood had assembled for a final frolic and to bid me goodbye and God-speed, some of them declaring it could be their intention to see me again in the far off America. They left at last and we were alone. Mother insisted on my sleeping in the best bed in the house, but I could not sleep, my heart was too full, Morning came and with it the stern reality; the parting of our ways. Mother and sister were looking over my belongings giving them the parting touches. Many a tear fell upon their hands while stitching, mending and packing away my clothes into an iron bound chest which henceforth it would be for me to take care of.

Oh, how little did I understand all that was being done for me in those my last hours of my last morning of the last day at home under their loving care, and never should I fully learn to appreciate it until another whom I loved and who loved me, would take their places.

I shall not attempt to describe the parting scene, it being too sacred to my memory. Impossible to relate through the medium of any material instrument, it is spiritual and in that sense we are not parted yet; the ties are still intact. My father's parting words are yet so vividly impressed on my mind and proved to be of so much prophetic semblance that they deserve to be recorded. Standing at the threshold he turned to me with these words: 'WHEREVER YOU GO AND WHATEVER MAY MEET YOU, DO NOT LET ANYONE TURN YOU AWAY FROM THE TRUTH AS YOU HAVE LEARNED IT IN YOUR CATECHISM HERE AT HOME.' Many a time, when doubt and disbelief have been met with, these few, simple words spoken by my dear, venerable, old father, have next to God, been my strongest support.

Followed by nearly the whole household, we are now going down the oft trodden path to the landing where my boat lies, drawn up on the sandy beach. Soon the boat is launched, my things stowed in, pushed off from the shore and out on the unknown future, carrying me along with it. The lake was as smooth as a mirror and the trees along the shore, the fields, the farms and mountains in the background were plainly reflected in the deep, still water below. It was as if we were floating in mid air; the blue sky below as well as above; what a beautiful picture, but, vanishing like the scenes of childhood behind me.

This was, perhaps, the last time my eyes should feast upon its beauty. To be sure, I had promised to come back in a couple of years, but fortunately the future is hidden from the picture. The wild cherries on the shore were just beginning to bud and their delicious fragrance was wafted like a healing nectar into my aching heart, but could not comfort it; the wound was too deep and too fresh.

Christian and Jorgen Flesvig rowed down the lake to Eidsvoll where they stayed overnight and the next day boarded a train for Christiania (Oslo). In the city, they were greeted by a "horde of ragamuffins" ready to take advantage of their obvious inexperience. Here they were detained two weeks; at times feeling very much like returning home. They were finally able to acquire steamer steerage tickets for seventy specidalers each. They would travel to America via Hull and Liverpool, England and Quebec and Montreal, Canada.

In Hull, England their boarding house was near the wharf where they had to ward off the overtures of young prostitutes. After a week's time, the two boarded the ship *Damascus* which proceeded onto the open sea. Christian wrote:

The voyage across the Atlantic was only a repetition of our experiences in crossing the North Sea (referring to the fact that so many became horribly seasick). A jolly lot of

Irish emigrants were taken on board at some place in the Irish Sea, which made the already overcrowded steerage still more uncomfortable. The fare consisted mostly of potatoes and half boiled meat, hard tack and black tea, with plum pudding on Sundays. The pudding was intended for an extra delicacy, but when we happened to take notice of how it was prepared our appetite for it was considerably lessened. They were 'messing' the ingredients of the pudding in a little cabin on the forward deck, whether by kneading it with their hands or by treading it with their feet, we could not see, but when the bags were full they would throw the little bags out of the window and onto the dirty deck, where others who stood ready, would kick them by their toes and heels, playing regular football with the bags, over to the cooks cabin which was quite afar distance off. But when it was ready for distribution there was a scramble for that pudding which was ludicrous to behold.

Traveling through dense fog, their ship finally arrived in Quebec, Canada. Christian and Jorgen had railroad tickets through to Chicago, but the tickets did not include food. The train was made up of cattle cars with simple wooden benches on which to sit. They were about to board when two English boys, with whom they had become acquainted, literally grabbed them back and, later in the evening, they were able to board a regular train with good accommodations. In Montreal, after buying dinner, they had but fifty cents between them with a long train ride to Chicago still before them. A hard lump of cheese was their only sustenance. They took turns chewing on it for two days and three nights. Their silver half dollar proved to be somewhat "magic", when, after disembarking in Chicago, they were able to buy a loaf of bread and get the same amount in paper change, silver having greater value than the paper money.

The two, being new to Chicago, reasoned that finding a Norwegian church might afford them some assistance since neither one spoke English and they were in need of work. The church found, they were refreshed to hear a sermon in Norwegian and looked forward to the end of the service when they were sure they would be recognized as new arrivals and offered help. To their surprise, most were speaking English and neither of them could understand a word. Christian wrote, "Apparently they were all 'Yankees' now and not one of them paid the least attention to us."

It was a German boarding house keeper who rescued the two from the streets by leading them to his place of business where they were given food and lodging. This arrangement continued until they found work and were able to pay. Of this Christian recorded: "Our thankfulness to that German was more than we were able to express in words, but we promised ourselves that we would never forget it, and I never have, and I never will?

Jorgen and Christian found work in the Chicago brick yards where they were given room and board and wages of $2.00 per day. It was dirty and strenuous work in the hot, July sun. Their necks became covered with blisters.

On a rainy day when they could not work, Christian was lying down on his bunk. Whether asleep or awake, he recalled the incident as follows: "I was laying down on our bunk, which was close to the door and of course my thoughts were with my people at home, when the door opened slowly and turning my eyes in that direction whom should I see coming through the door but my dear, old father. He was dressed in his nightgown and coming close up to me, embraced me and said: 'I have come here only for to see you once more, as I shall never see you again'. Those were his words which I distinctly heard and understood and in my bewilderment tried to hold him in my arms, but lo! and he was gone."

Months later Christian received a letter which told of his father's death on the very date and time of his appearance to Christian in the brick yard bunkhouse. Tired of the brick yards, Jorgen and Christian decided to cross Lake Michigan and find work in the lumber camps. Not getting paid without protest, they left there and made their way to LaCrosse, Wisconsin.

Christian was intent on looking up his fellow countrymen, the Ourens. John Ouren's parents, the Jens Ourens, were living at Coon Prairie, Wisconsin. Jens was a blacksmith and also farmed forty acres.

Arriving at Coon Prairie, Christian was just in time for the marriage of Jen's Ouren's oldest daughter to Ole P. Sigstadstoe (later known as Ole P. Olson), from Fron, Gudbrandsdalen. Ole had served in the celebrated 15th Wisconsin regiment under Colonel Hegg, from its organization, until he was promoted to the rank of 2nd Lieutenant.

Jens Ouren informed Christian that his son, John, could use help in his blacksmith shop which was located on a public road three miles from Greenfield at Richland Prairie; address, Lenora , in Amherst township, Fillmore county, near Rushford and Harmony, Minnesota. This suited Christian well and he decided to go there immediately.

John Ouren was married to Johanna Nielsdatter Smedbyhagen. Her mother, Anna Gullicksdatter Helle, lived with the Ourens. Johanna's sister, Tonette Nielsdatter Smebyhagen, soon arrived with her brother, Jens Nielson Smebyhagen, another sister, Theolina Nielsdatter Smebyhagen and a nephew, Martin Anderson. Christian Ahlness soon married Tonette and began farming on the present (year 2000) Donovan Brink farm on county road 19 southeast of Preston, Minnesota.

With an adventurous spirit and hopes to homestead new land, Jens Ouren sold his farm near Coon Prairie and announced his intention to go west. Jens and his son, John, went exploring in western Minnesota and returned intent on moving the family to an area near Granite Falls, Minnesota The Bent Erickson and Ole Miller families joined them. (It is probable the Borre Evensons also came with this group or followed soon after.) Christian Ahlness and a fellow named Halvor were engaged to drive extra wagons for the move.

In Christian Ahlness' autobiography, he described these several families' journey west. Their route took them from Fillmore County through Olmstead, Steele, Waseca, Blue Earth, Brown and Redwood counties and into unorganized and unsettled areas of what is now Yellow Medicine and Lac Que Parle counties of Minnesota. On the 4th of July 1868, they reached Redwood Falls and continued thirty additional miles to the claims staked by Jens and John Ouren. The area had beautiful rolling hills and good stands of timber, but the mosquitoes were so bad they had to "dress" the horses with sheaves of long grass to protect them from the pesky insects. The horses, Christian wrote: "appeared as moving haystacks". At night they would wrap themselves in blankets, "...but the 'song of the mosquito in our ears would give us the creeps', which was almost as bad as the sting and there was no rest for us," wrote Christian.

To add to their concern with the region, they camped on a site preferred by the Indians and one day a ragged band came and pitched teepees right next to them. Christian and two other men had been off exploring and upon their return could not find their loved ones and were filled with fear until they found their party camped in another spot. The frightened campers described the arrival of the Indians: "You can hardly realize what we felt when a whole cavalcade of Indians appeared in view, bearing directly down upon us. The noise and racket they made was something fearful; something which was enough in itself to scare the wits out of us. Their outriders on their ponies first came up to reconnoiter; then a long train of carts, which had never been greased, loaded with women and children, dogs innumerable, kettles, tent poles and muskets sticking out everywhere. You need not smile at us for becoming alarmed." The Ouren party soon learned these Indians were members of a friendly tribe who had been left to roam over the prairies. Destitute and subdued, they were thankful for any little crumbs the settlers could give them.

Mosquitoes and the possibility of more Indians being in the area, caused the Ouren party to turn back. They eventually arrived at crossroads about three miles south of New Ulm. Here Christian Ahlness and the other hired driver, Halvor, continued east, back to Fillmore county, while the Ourens made a right turn south on an old wagon trail. This brought them to the west shore of Linden Lake. Jens Ouren bought the farm of John Armstrong who had been killed by the Indians shortly after the beginning of the Dakota Conflict. Here the older members of the party lived in a log cabin while Jens' sons, John and Mads, purchased adjoining land and fashioned dugouts as their first dwellings.

It was not long before Christian and Tonette Ahlness, Tonette's sister Theolina, brother Jens Nelson(Nilsen-Smebyhagen in Norway) and little Martin Anderson (son of another sister, Christina Nilsdatter Smebyhagen and Andrew Anderson Fjeldhaug who remained in Norway for a few more years) decided to migrate west. They "sold out" in Fillmore County and joined the Ourens in Linden, Brown County, Minnesota in the year 1869.

The Ahlness party camped in the timber of Jens Ouren's farm until Christian and his family settled on one of the last Homestead Act tracts, part of which is the present Lake Hanska cemetery west of the city of Hanska, Minnesota. Here Christian Ahlness built a dugout of some distinction near a small slough or lake. Ole Synsteby described it as, "...one of the finest dugouts I have ever seen." (Under the Homestead Act land that was "proved up" for five years could be gotten free of charge. Land could also be purchased for $1.25 per acre, and, if proved up for 6 months, title was received.)

Theoline Nilsdatter Smebyhagen and little Martin Anderson lived with the Ahlnesses and the old grandmother, Anne Gulliksdatter, lived with the Ourens. Jens Nelson was 19 years of age when he arrived in Linden township of Brown County, Minnesota and, as Mrytle Wenberg, his granddaughter, wrote, "(Jens). ..became a farm hand for $8.00 per month plus food and a corner to sleep in." He eventually married Louisa Vislander and worked as a blacksmith with John Ouren in Madelia, Minnesota. He later worked for the railroad. The Nelsons' daughter, Nellie, married Fred Jensen. They moved to Hanska, Minnesota where they had a harness shop and motorcycle dealership in the former and now razed East Side Tavern building.

Pastor Nils Brandt's Travels in Minnesota in 1869
Contributed by Norwegian-American Genealogical Center & Naeseth Library

Pastor Nils O. Brandt, born in Vestre Slidre, Norway, in 1824 was educated for the ministry at the University of Christiania, where he graduated with high honors. In 1850, the Pastor J.W.C. Dietrichson, who had been pastor at Koshkonong in Dane County, Wisconsin, was visiting in Norway and persuaded Brandt, following his ordination, to immigrate to America, and minister to his fellow Norwegian immigrants. Brandt immigrated in 1851 and became an early pastor in the Rock River and Pine Lake areas of Jefferson and Waukesha Counties, Wisconsin, and from 1865-1882, was Professor at Luther College. Brandt was one of the six Norwegian pastors who organized the Norwegian Synod in 1853, and he served as vice-president of the Synod from 1857 to 1871. He also serving as co-editor and business manager of *Kirketidende*, the official organ of the Norwegian synod, from 1869-1878. During the 1850s and 1860, Brandt became known as the "traveling missionary" and is considered the first minister from Norway to step on land west of the Mississippi River. His pledge to the immigrants that the ministers of the Gospel were willing to follow no matter how far the farmers had wandered to find desirable land is well known among Norwegian-American scholars. In 1907, Pastor Adolf Bredesen interviewed Brandt, and a fascinating study of his mission trips during the years 1851-1855, including an 1855 trip to Goodhue and Houston Counties, Minnesota, is recorded in the 1907 edition of *Symra*. Nils O. Brandt died August 10, 1921, aged 97 years.

The following article was taken from portions of a six page hand-written Norwegian document authored by Brandt in 1909, and together with his original 1869 missionary notes, and lists of ministerial acts, records one of his many mission trips to Minnesota. These recollections by Brandt and his original notes were found among the papers of the late Gerhard B. Naeseth, 1913-1994, a great-grandson of Nils O. Brandt. These papers are now housed among the collections of the Norwegian American Genealogical Center and Naeseth Library in Madison, Wisconsin.

In the summer of 1869, I, Pastor Nils O. Brandt, who at that time was the pastor of the Decorah and Madison congregation [Winneshiek County, Iowa] and teacher at Luther College, made a mission trip to northern Minnesota. After first visiting Pastor Norman Johnsen's congregation at St. Peter, and dedicating the church, I went to St. Paul then to St. Cloud and stopped at the home of Gustav O. Hegg, originally from Winneshiek County, Iowa. Here I gave a sermon and communion to in the evening of July 20th, to four people. On July 22, I reached Osakis and on the following day gathered Norwegian families by the lake near the Danish farmer Søren Schmidt, his wife being Norwegian, and preached to them, and had sixteen who came to the altar for communion. That same evening I traveled to Alexandria and was the guest at the home of the Honorable L.K. Aaker, who had just had a visit of his wife's brother from Hardanger. In Alexandria the Aaker family was the only Norwegian. Aaker was very interested in the affairs of the church and suggested that we hold a gathering on his land while I was in the area. My colleagues Pastor Thomas Johnsen from near St. Peter, Minn., had at one time at least been up to that area, and Pastor Abraham Jakobsen from Decorah had traveled up there to attend to some churchly duties.

On July 25th, 1869, I gave a sermon in Evansville and seven people came to the altar, among them was Theodor Baardsen, who I knew from Luther College. On July 26th, I preached a sermon at Ole Sæther's at the western part of Pelican Lake, and two of Andrew Hansen's children were baptized namely, Louis, born March 22, 1867, and his sister, Anne Elise, born June 28, 1869. In addition, eighteen people came to the altar for communion. The following day I traveled to Otter Tail County, and on July 27th held a sermon at the home of Ole Estensen, where I baptized Mons Bottolfson's son, Carl Johan, who was born on February 22, 1869. In addition, twenty came to the altar for communion, and here I also held a burial service for two children of Lars Nilsen. On July 28th., I preached a sermon at the home of Engebret Risbrot and here baptized many children including Knudt Johnsen's daughter, Marta Oline, born June 28, 1869; Halvard Magnesen Berge's son, Henry Louis, born March 29, 1869; Peder Svensen Pennes' son, Samuel Andreas, born June 18,1869; Isak Thomasen's daughter, Ane Johanne,born November 18, 1868; Amund B. Larsen's son, Lewis Olai, born March 11, 1869; and Cornelius L. Aasnes's son, Edward Severin, born May 3, 1869. In addition, twenty two guests came to the altar for communion. On July 29, I held confirmation in the home of Aslak Johnsen for the following seven students: 1. Jakob Peter Olsen Hatling; 2. Christian Johannessen Dahl; 3. Edward Pedersen Grefseng; 4. Anders Eriksen Kjøsven; 5. Gustaf Pedersen Fougner; 6. Betsy Gurine Olsdatter Sether; 7. Dorthe Larsdatter Kopperud. Even with time being short, I met with the women of the congregation, and the same day held communion for the confimation class and also nineteen others, totaling twenty six that day. Also on the same day I held a burial for Carl Emil Knudsen, aged 4 ¾ years.

On the trip south to Douglas County, I stopped by Grant County in the home of the bride's parents and married on July 30th the bachelor Ole Peterson and maiden Anna Gundersen. On the same day I came to Thore

Evenson's, and on July 31st held a congregational meeting. The meeting dealt with considering what should be done to continue a pastor visiting in these parts. I reminded them of a similar search that the congregation from Norway Lake, had done a year ago, and they had got a Pastor from the Norwegian Synod. Those gathered were in agreement to find someone from the Norwegian Synod as soon as possible a permanent pastor.

In Holmes City several children from Otter Tail needed to be confirmed. Besides giving the sermon, I as Pastor had to take care of the children. On August 1st, I held sermon in Lewiston's house, baptized many children including, William Hansen's son Wilhelm Marius, born November 15, 1868; Knud Knudsen's daughter Maria, born November 8, 1868; Johannes Olsen's son, Ole Kornelius, born November 26, 1868; Lars Andersen's daughter, Antonette, born April 10, 1869; Johannes Olsen's son Ole Gunnerius, born November 26, 1868; Nils Nilsen's son, Knudt, born March 10, 1869; Carl Bruns daughter Emma, born March 19, 1869, and her twin sister Amalie; Carl Anders Josiassen's son Johan Theodor, born July 12, 1869, and Erik Eriksen's daughter Gustava, born April 5, 1869. Also on the same day and at the same place, fourteen guests came to the altar for communion. Earlier in the day, I held burial services for Even Fosli's son, Fingar, aged 23 years, who died July 6, 1869, and Ole, aged 5 ¾ years old, who died August 3, 1868. On August 2nd., 1868, I held a burial at Holmes City at the home of Tosten Solum. It was Tosten Sigurdsen's daughter, Margit, who had been born on January 11, 1869. The same day, I also baptized several children including Paul Nilsen's daughter, Siri, born October 1868, who had been originally baptized at home by Nils Paulsen on October 18th; John Nilsen's daughter, Sina, born October 27, 1868, and Roald Benson's daughter, Ida Marie, born November 22, 1868. At the same service there were sixteen who were confirmed.

On August 3rd I held a meeting the entire day with the confirmands and on August 4th, I held a sermon at Ole Mo's in Holmes City, and baptized Amos Johnsen's daughter Kari, born March 14, 1869, and Ole T. Aanderud's daughter Tine Hanna Bergitta, born November 15, 1868. On August 5th., I held a confirmation at Ole Mo's house, the largest in the area. The confirmands were: 1. Olaf Tostensen; 2. Martin Olsen; 3. Ole Olsen Mo; 4. Nils Abraham Thorsen; 5. Anne Amundsdatter Bjerkhagen; 6. Aaste Thorstensen; 7. Bergit Ingemunsdatter; 8. Ragnhild Pedersdatter; 9. Margit Olsdatter; 10. Emma Thoresdatter; 11. Synneva Kristofersdatter. On the same day it was necessary to travel to Ole Gudmundsen Molstad's home near Chippewa in Grant County where twenty-two took communion. On August 6th., I was back again at Ole Mo's and held a service, and held communion for both the confirmands and others, altogether forty-nine people. The following day I left for Pope County, and took with me, Even Fosli's son.

Following the communion, a custom of gift giving [offering] that for several years has been followed in the synod, was taken up for my work. Then the Bible verses were read by the confirmands among the people of the congregation, for I was unknown, and had spent little time with this group and had no responsibilities for the teaching of the confirmands. Confirmation for the young people both in Otter Tail and here; after such little preparation would normally be delayed unless they were newcomers from another congregation, where they had religious Lutheran schooling. However, among these religious parents and through their diligence, much has been done so that these confirmands had such good religious knowledge. (Among them in Otter Tail I noted one boy who had talked to his parents about attending Luther College, but the parents could not afford it. When the Pastor received contribution for the trip and for the school it was decided that the boy should come along and join Brandt to Decorah. But when the Pastor was ready to leave Douglas County, a message came that he could not come along. The money that the Pastor had collected was returned with permission to give it to another needy student.

On this trip I received many subscriptions to the church and to the New Testament for Communion use. I did not meet many old acquaintances among those living in Otter Tail and Douglas Counties, but those I met were friendly and loving. Mosquitoes are found in all settlements and are an irritant at night. If you do not have a mosquito net to cover your bed there will be no sleep.

Forty years have gone since this Mission trip took place. I remember the many I met with dear fondness, but I fear I will not meet them again on this earth.

Pastor Nils O. Brandt, 1909

This photograph of the interior of the Emaus Church, Osakis, Minnesota, was found among Brandt's 1869 papers. The church was not yet built, but on July 23-24, 1869, Pastor Brandt preached and held communion for sixteen parishioners.

To the Northwestern Frontier!
By Levi Thortvedt

Levi Thortvedt was a child when his family moved from the relative comfort of Houston County to the wilds of northwestern Minnesota. His recollections were originally published in the "Moorhead Daily News" as a 10-part serial beginning in February, 1938. The articles were combined and edited for publication here. Sketches by his daughter, Orabel, were published in her retelling of the same story in the "Fargo (ND) Forum" in 1942.

We left Fyresdal, Telemark, Norway in 1861. After a journey of 8 weeks, we landed in Quebec, Canada. We left there on the Canadian railroad and crossed the steam ferry at Detroit, Michigan, then by rail to Chicago. We stayed there two days with relatives. From there we went to La Crosse, Wisconsin, and on to Highland Prairie, along the south fork of the Root River. We lived there for 2 years and then bought land at Mound Prairie, Houston County, Minnesota. On May 18, 1870, our little band of Norwegians started for the Red River Valley.

This group of settlers consisted of 3 families, 4 single men, and an old man with a big mule and a single wagon. The leader of this little flock of home seekers was my father, Ola Gunderson Thortvedt. We were 6 in our family: father, mother (Thone Saangdal Thortvedt), Joraand, Thone, Signe, & myself, Leif Levi. We had 1 covered wagon drawn by a team of horses and the other by a team of oxen. We had 4 cows and a heifer, 2 yearling colts and 13 head of sheep. About 25 chickens were housed in lathe crates. Halvor Fendalstveit (Salveson) drove our team of oxen on one of father's wagons. The second family was Aanon (Gunderson) Gjeitsta, my  father's brother. There were also 6 in his family: himself, his wife Thone, and their 4 sons, Gunder, Gustav, John, and Andreas. They had an old team of oxen and 2 cows. The third family was Tarjei Skrei and his wife, Gunhild, and their only child, Signe. The Skreis left their home on Corn Creek, Houston County, driving their yoke of oxen. They also had 2 cows.

The single men were Ole Midgarden, Halvor Fendalsveit (Salveson), Ola Anderson and Tarjei Muhle. Tarjei Muhle had a yoke of steers and took some of Skrei's stuff in his wagon. Ole Midgarden drove Skrei's oxen, while he drove the cattle and sheep aided by Ola Anderson and sometimes by my sisters, Joraand and Thone.

At noon on May 18, 1870, we gathered outside of Houston. At 4:00 PM, we started for the "Unknown West." About 2 miles west of Houston near Cushen's Peak, we camped. We had trouble with the cattle - they wanted to go home! They scattered all over. Nearly all of us had to help gather the cattle around the wagons again, and a night shift was put to watch them.

The next morning, the cattle were all there. We had just started again, when an axle broke on the lead wagon. This was just the start of the 400-mile trip! A farmer on his way to Houston told my father that there was a good blacksmith living a half mile from there. He got the axle loose and put it on his shoulder and started off. In a couple of hours he was back with it welded so good that the welding could not be seen. As soon as the axle was on, we started again and camped 1 mile west of Rushford. On May 20th, we started to cross North Prairie. After camping overnight, we came to a high bluff and looked down at Chatfield. We stopped and wondered how to get down. We put rough locks on the rear of our wagons and finally got down and crossed a creek. We passed near a place called Marion and went northwest to Rochester in Olmsted County. This was a nice little town with fine stone buildings. It was Saturday and we inquired for a place to camp as we did not travel on Sunday. We were informed by a generous fellow that there was a good place 2 miles west of Rochester on a high knoll. We got the directions and found it. It was a fine elevation, gently rounded, with about 40 acres of prairie. There was plenty of water nearby. Everybody was well pleased with this magnificent camping ground. We could see all over the country by Rochester.

In the evening when the campfires were going for the supper cooking, I suddenly woke from my slumber to the lively sound of a violin. This was the first time I knew that there was a fiddler along with us! It was Tarjei Muhle sitting on the wagon pole playing waltzes, polkas, and cotillions. Tarjei Muhle's music made me feel good and livened up the whole party. We had our usual supper consisting of sweet milk mush and milk.

Sunday we stayed as the sheep and cattle needed rest and grass. Some of the boys went down to Rochester to spend part of the day. I will never forget this camping place where we could see for miles, especially to the east and to the south.

On May 23rd, we started slowly on our long, long journey. We got as far as Pine Island and camped about one-mile north of there. The next morning we moved on, passing Zumbrota. We camped at White Rock Creek. This road was very sandy and stony and ran around a wood covered bluff or hill. We reached Cannon Falls Wednesday night, crossed the Cannon River on a pontoon bridge and camped. This was the first pontoon bridge I had ever seen. Cannon Falls is a nice town.

By Thursday evening we had reached the Vermillion River and by Friday we were within 3 miles of St. Paul. On May 28th, we moved on towards St. Paul. The road was crooked and downhill and lay between the high bluff and the great Mississippi River on a very narrow stretch of land. Near St Paul we saw a few houses, some stores, and a blacksmith shop. This is what I suppose is now South St. Paul. We finally came to the great bridge over the Mississippi River. It was long and low down on the south side and very high on the north side.

St. Paul made quite a showing to me, lying on a high sandstone bluff. It looked yellowish with the monster buildings on the top of the bluff. It was a beautiful site. On the big river, two steamboats were at the docks, and one was steaming up the river towards the high bridge – I tell you it was a sight for me! We had to stop here a while and make arrangements to pay the toll. It cost 25 cents per wagon, 10 cents per head of cattle and 5 cents per head of sheep. Chickens in their crates went free.

Crossing the bridge we were right in the busy but narrow streets of St. Paul, with tall buildings on both sides. I wondered how we could get through here with all our contraptions, wagons and livestock. Luckily there were no street cars to be found in 1870. The people of St. Paul did not take much notice of us. Evidently it was not the first moving outfit that had passed through their streets. We got through in fine shape, although it seemed to take quite a while. We were now headed for St. Anthony, which was a little town on the northeast side of the Mississippi River, just across from Minneapolis.

The Mississippi with its rippling waters and swift current was shining against the glare of the sun. High buildings were seen on the other side of the river. This was Minneapolis. Somewhere along here we came to a wonderful scenic place with a bridge across a little stream, which seemed to be in an awful hurry to reach the Mississippi. A fine waterfall, about 20 feet high, was seen just below the bridge. The wagons were set to one side of the road while we inspected this magnificent waterfall. We went below the falls and looked up on it. The water dropped about 20 feet, perpendicular. It shivered and shone like silver! It looked something like Minnehaha, which I did see later. This was the first time I had ever seen a waterfall.

Well, the wagons started to move again and I had to leave this interesting and grand scenery. A mile or so north of St. Anthony we camped. On May 29th, we moved 3 or 4 miles to get a better camping place for the night. We found one with plenty of grass, water and fuel. It was raining a little. One of the little boys, John Aanonsen, became missing, and a general hunt was on. Thone, my sister, walked up the railroad track and met two men leading John, age five. These men had seen our party and assumed that this lost boy belonged to us. Thone brought him home to camp and the panic was over.

The next day we did not move because it was raining heavily, and on Tuesday the moving was very slow because of the muddy roads. We camped at Coon Creek. We passed through Anoka, crossed the Rum River and came within a couple of miles of Elk River village. Within the next 3 days we moved through Elk River, Baker Station and Cable Station. On June 4th, we got to East St. Cloud. Here were a few stores and a saloon. The door was open to the saloon. It was a lively place, with someone playing a fiddle.

Tarjei Muhle, our fiddler, asked what the name of the tune was. "Red River Jig" was the answer.

We crossed the Mississippi for the last time on our journey and reached St. Cloud. It was quite a place in 1870. It was the terminal for the Red River Cart Trains that brought furs and hides from the northwest. We saw these carts for the first time – there were about 50 of them.

On Sunday, the 5th, it was a typical June morning with fine sunshine and clear blue skies. Later the church bells began to ring and the people flocked to church. Mother asked us if we would like to go and we were willing. It was a big church with a high steeple. The door which faced north stood wide open. We looked in - it was decorated in brilliant colors. I don't think any of us got a word of the sermon, but we felt well repaid for our walk.

From St. Cloud our road lay in a southwesterly direction until we reached Richmond, then in a northwesterly direction, winding over a rolling prairie, with no trees to be seen. There were lots of strawberries on both sides! Wherever you looked, everybody was filling up on the finest berries in the world. We moved on slowly as there were some soft and bad places.

We moved along for several days on the prairie, with nothing of interest to be seen. On June 11, we reached Sauk Center. In this little town mother purchased a cast iron match holder, with two holders in one. We still have this relic!

It was here also that my uncle Aanon's dog went crazy and had to be shot. Later, the men went up town and met an old acquaintance, Tallef Flateland. I guess he was related to Ole Midgarden. This fellow had a lawyer's education and the party got a lot of information on seeking land. We learned that the next town west was Alexandria, the land office for the northwestern Minnesota.

We then came into a more wooded country. The road lay along the south end of Lake Osakis, the biggest lake I had ever seen. It was timbered all around and had fine graveled shores. We camped here and everybody praised this wonderful place, but had to leave it the next morning.

On June 14, we reached Alexandria. Here we saw the first "Blanket Indians" since we left Houston County. We had seen plenty of them there, but I think some of the women got a little nervous seeing these wild savages away out in the west. There were supposed to be thousands of them scattered all over the northwest. Here were 4 or 5 Indian teepees. I remember one tall old Indian with his red blanket over his shoulder, drunk as an English lord and very talkative. Some of the men had quite a talk with him.

We spent the next day in Alexandria, purchasing supplies as it was our last chance to buy certain articles. We bought utensils, stoves, axes, spades, grindstones, breaking plows, scythes, and whetstones. We also got the two inch augers so necessary for building of log cabins.

Here we met Ola Strandvold who was back to buy supplies. He had taken up a claim in the Red River Valley, about 2 miles south of the Hudson Bay post of Georgetown,

Minnesota. His claim was on the North Dakota side of the river. He gave us new enthusiasm, as now we had a leader who was acquainted with the roads and camping places. They went to the land office for information about maps, vacant, surveyed, and unsurveyed lands. The land office agent happened to be an old acquaintance of my mother's way back in Norway. He gave us all the information he could. Here was also the home of Knut Nelson, who became governor of Minnesota and later United States Senator, but we had not heard of him in those days.

With Ola Strandvold in the lead, we moved on the next day with much heavier loads. Roads were hilly and winding around small lakes, heavily wooded. We camped at Chippewa Station, near a little lake that we compared to one in Norway called *Rowdiest Vattern*. It was inspiring to father and mother.

We traveled through Evansville and came to Pelican Lake, where we made camp. Oh! What fine scenery! Our camp was about 30 or 40 feet above the lake, which is about a half mile across. It was wonderful to see three or four big white stones in the lake that shone like white pelicans. It was believed in our camp that these stones were the reason why it was so rightly called Pelican Lake. We spent a restful Sunday here. Our horses, cattle and sheep did not go far from camp as the short fine grass, mixed with wild prairie tea, suited them good enough. Tarjei Muhle played his fiddle for us and that added to my cheerfulness, too.

The next morning we moved on and camped at a place called Stony Brook for dinner. The air was full of those four winged "Devil's Needles" (*Ague Stinger* is the Norwegian name for them) with red, green, blue and silver bodies. While fording the Pomme-de-terre River, my Uncle Aanon got stuck. His oxen were old and poor. One more yoke of oxen was put on and the wagon came out. The station was on the west side of the river on a high knoll, with an old stockade fence around the unpainted buildings. It was kind of a lonesome sight.

We came to Lightning Lake and camped for the night. After a while two men with a pair of ponies on a double buggy came and camped nearby. After supper my father went over to them and they asked him where he was going. When he said, "The Red River Valley," they became very talkative as they both lived there. They said, "You are heading for the greatest farming country in the world." They described this land and it was the same description as Paul Hjelm Hanson and Ola Strandvold (now of our company) had given. Ole came over to them and shook hands as he knew them both. One was his close neighbor who lived the Minnesota side. His name was E. R. Hutchinson. The other was R. M. Probstfield who lived farther up the river also on the Minnesota side. They were old-timers in the Red River Valley. Hutchinson had worked for the Hudson Bay Company for 14 years, and Probstfield for 12 years. They were on a trip to St. Cloud for provisions.

On June 21st, we moved on in clear weather. The country was getting more level. We could see blue hills. It was what they call the Leaf Mountains in Ottertail County, about 20 miles away. Timber could be seen far to the east. Towards night we crossed the

Ottertail River on a toll ferry at Old Crossing. On a sharp bend of the river, there stood a long row of buildings - Stage Station.

A Red River cart train of about 40 carts came across. They were loaded with furs from Hudson Bay Company and headed for St. Paul. The Ottertail River is actually the Red River of the North, but is not called so until it has joined the Bois de Sioux at Breckenridge. Neither the Bois de Sioux nor the Ottertail have many trees along their banks, but after the junction with the Red River it is thickly wooded. It flows north to Winnipeg Lake and thence to Hudson Bay. At Breckenridge commences a valley that is 50 miles wide and 250 miles long, "the Great Red River Valley." When you get into the valley you don't think there is any valley about it, as the hills are so far away on either side that you can't see them. It is 25 miles to the hills on either side of the river.

We took the cut-off road that runs in a northwesterly direction. We are here on a nearly level prairie, with no trees to be seen. After a while a long thin bluish streak could be seen on the western horizon. It was the timber along the Red River. We finally reached the river north of Breckenridge and camped. The mosquitoes were very bad.

We moved on slowly, meeting Red River carts. We crossed Whiskey Creek and camped for the night. The timber along this creek extended far eastward. The water in the creek was the same color as whiskey. The mosquitoes were terrible and then it rained through the next day. Some of the men took a little walk south along the Red River on the Minnesota side and came to McCauleyville. There was one little store and a few other buildings. They crossed the river to Fort Abercrombie, North Dakota. There were 250 soldiers stationed here and this was a grand sight for the settlers up in this Indian country, far from civilization. There were many wagons standing around, and a lot of horses and cattle grazing. On June 26th, we moved along slowly in the mud and were just 25 miles south of Georgetown, Minnesota, the old Hudson Bay post.

After our usual Sunday stop, on June 28th, we moved along the Red River, or Pembina Trail. Every now and then we would meet Red River carts. It was a picturesque sight when you saw sometimes 90 or 100 of these carts loaded with furs, buffalo hides, deer hides, bear, beaver, mink, and muskrat skins. Either an ox or pony pulled the carts. The drivers were dressed in their buckskins with wide hats and long hair. They wore large tobacco pouches decorated with glass beads of all colors.

This old Red River trail has 3 or 4 roads, side by side, each with 3 deep ruts in the prairie – one for each wheel and one for the ox or pony in the center. Our horses would blow their noses in fear every time we met a cart train, because of the wild smell of the hides, the drivers and the dogs.

Towards evening it began to rain a little. Ola Strandvold, who was acquainted with this area, guided us to "Burbank's Hotel." It was an old log building, with a fairly good roof, but no doors or windows. The mosquitoes were the worst we had ever experienced. My mother made milk mush (*melke grod*), but when the pot was done, it was a stiff, rich mixture of sweet milk and mosquitoes. After 3 tries, Mother gave up and threw the milk mush away! She also threw the pot away and nearly hit a calf! We went to bed without supper. There must have been billions upon billions of mosquitoes. The next morning there was a layer of dead mosquitoes 6 or 7 inches thick around the ashes of the camp fire.

Photo of ox cart encampment – Courtesy Marshall-Duluth Genealogy

June 29th was a fine morning. A lot of Red River carts had come in the night and had camped close by. We moved slowly as the roads were real muddy and we were nearly to our destination. Late in the afternoon we came to a fine house of hewn logs, a stable, and a couple of other small buildings inside a fence, the home of R. M. Probstfield. Ola Strandvold said that Probstfield was one of those agreeable fellows we met at Lightning Lake in Wilkin County. We camped a little ways north on a point between the river and the big coulee. As we were having our supper a government wagon, hauling supplies to Forts Pembina & Totten came along and camped nearby.

On June 30th, we followed the trail northwards and reached the timber of the Buffalo River. It flows into the Red River at Georgetown. We turned off the trail and went due west to the Red River, two miles south of Georgetown. E. R. Hutchinson, the other man we met at Lightning Lake, had a little log cabin that stood south of the road that goes down to the river. There was a ferry there. The Hutchinson children came over and pointed at our flock of sheep - they had apparently never seen sheep before. We crossed the river on the ferry and were now in Dakota Territory. We had always heard that it was full of hostile Sioux Indians. We drove through big heavy timber with elm trees for about a quarter of a mile and then camped for the night by the river. Ola Strandvold had left us to return to his homestead, about two miles farther north.

"Land-picking" was the next on the program – for here was plenty of land – the whole of Dakota Territory. We stayed an entire week, taking long hikes to look at the land. One day one of my Uncle Aanon's oxen was missing, and after a while the old ox appeared on the Minnesota side of the wide, deep and muddy Red River. Ola Anderson, a good swimmer, crossed the river, and after a long tussle with the old ox, finally got him into the river. Ola followed closely to guide him. On the other side, men stood ready with long ropes to pull the ox out of the mud and up on the land. Father gave Ola a dollar for the good job he done.

They were not satisfied with the land in Dakota, so on July 3rd, we returned to Minnesota on the Hutchinson Ferry. We went south on the Red River Trail and camped at R. M. Probstfield's. He had just returned from St. Cloud and was out plowing his corn. He recognized our party. Father told him we were heading for Otter Tail County. "What's the matter with the land in Dakota?" asked Probstfield. Father said it was too low, with too much slough grass and even driftwood was found on the prairie.

"Well, if its higher land you want, I can tell you where you can find it," Probstfield said. He pointed over to the Buffalo River, the timber of which could be plainly seen. He also made the remark about the Buffalo River country being so high that Hudson Bay Company at Georgetown, during high floods, drove their cattle and horses a little ways up the Buffalo River because it stayed dry. Probstfield went on to say with considerable effect, "If the land on the Buffalo River does not suit you, you can just as well drive back to where you came from because you won't find land in the whole United States that will."

Well, father became very interested and asked him if they could get him to show them the land. "I can't," said Probstfield, "I have to plow my corn." "Well," said my father, "we will get somebody to plow the corn." "Well, can he plow straight?" asked Probstfield. Father then said they would put on two men to lead the horses and hold the plow. This was perfectly satisfactory to him. So after dinner Tarjei Muhle and Ola Midgarden offered to do the plowing. Jim, our big bay horse, was hitched to Probstfield's buggy, and father and Probstfield got in. Uncle Aanon rode old man Weum's mule Jerry, and the trio started for the Buffalo River.

"Now we will make for the south end of the heavy timber you see, over there," said Probstfield while pointing in a northeasterly direction to what was later known as "Kassenborg Point." When they got there they stopped in an area where the government had sold speculators land for 25 cents an acre to get money with which to carry on the Civil War. "Oh my," said father, "It is too bad that this land is 'speculator land' as this is the finest land we have seen." "Just wait a while and you will see just as fine land if not finer, when we come farther up the river," said Probstfield. "Now all the land south and east of here is unsurveyed as yet and you can take what you want."

At dusk, Father and Aanon returned to the camp. Father was thoroughly convinced that the land they had seen today was the finest and the most inducing for settlers to settle on in the whole state of Minnesota!

On July 9th, we started off good and early, with father in the lead, across the prairie to the Buffalo River at "Old Fish Place." We reached here about 1 o'clock - everybody stood dumbfounded and looked and looked on this wonderful land. The whole bend looked something like a field of tall barley, so high that you could not see the sheep.

One of the first things I did was to go to the river to see if it was deep enough. It is about 25 feet across and averages 4 feet deep of nice clear water. It is fed entirely by springs as we have found out later and it runs in a northwesterly direction until it hits the Red River at Georgetown. The river was full of catfish, pike, and pickerel, a fact which was quickly found out when a couple of the younger men had got out their fish lines and we had good, fat boiled catfish for our first dinner.

The afternoon was taken with leisure, but they made a little trip around. Tarjei Skrei, Halvor Salveson and Ola Midgarden went up the river till they came to a slough, which was later known as "Skrei slough." This place suited Tarjei fine, as here was plenty of hay and he was a cow man. The four single men in our company said "You people with families take first and we will find land nearby as close as we can."

The next morning some more skirmishing was done around to decide which claim to take, as there were plenty of them, absolutely free with the exception of the $14 filing charges for 160 acres. It was a little difficult to space themselves, because none of the party knew exactly how big a space 160 acres would take. There were no section or quarter stakes as the land was not surveyed.

On July 11th, the wagons began to spread out. Tarjei picked his claim just around the bend to the south, and Uncle Aanon over by the next point of the river north. It was commonly accepted that father was satisfied with the spot where the wagons and camp stood, and he certainly was - but a funny thing had happened. Father made a trip round the "*oddan*," as we called the bend, and what did he find? White spots here and there on the trees where the bark had been chopped off and on each was written "G. G. Weum." This was a surprise for father. This old man had been the tail end of the expedition all the time and had never been consulted about anything, and here he was the first one to pick, when a place to settle was found.

Early in the afternoon, Tarje Skrei came over to our wagon and was surprised to see that nothing was done in the way of settling down, and G. G. Weum's wagon still stood there. Tarjei said to father, "*Hos kan de ha seg, er du ikke fornogde ma dette landet, Olav?*" "*Jou de a eg,*" said father, "*med gamle Gunnar Veum ha tekje de.*" "*Mi jev gaen i gamle Veumen, me vi ha du I mitten, so har slipesteinen,*" said Tarje Skrei and thereupon asked my mother, "*Hor vil du ha stoge, Thone?*" (Translation) "What is the matter, Ola, ain't you satisfied with this land?" "Yes," said father, "but old man Weum has taken it." To which

211

Tarjei answered with vehemence, "We don't give the devil about old man Weum, we want you in the center because you have the grindstone." Then he asked mother where she wanted the house. She pointed to the spot where our house now stands. Tarjei drove the oxen and father the horses over there where they started to unloaded.

They found a big elm that stooped against the west, with wonderful thick foliage. If it rained, it barely got wet under the tree. Here they set the stove, the first thing to be unloaded. Under another elm, father put up his blacksmith bellows. He put up a stump for the anvil. This elm we called "*Bag almen,*" or bellows elm.

Our cooking and eating was in the shade of the stooping elm tree, and the sleeping was in the wagons that stood on the level prairie. Later, the wagons were moved in the thicket near the stove for shelter. The wagon box with the covering was taken off and set on the ground to sleep in. The first field was broken down in the "*oddan.*" I don't know how long it took them to do it, but it was broken. The homestead law called for five acres to be broken and shanty put up before it could be filed on. In this case the claims could not be filed because the land was not surveyed and consequently no description could be given.

From now on the full force was put on gathering hay. A hay rack had to be made. It was made from ash poles - young sapling elms were used to form the bows over the wheels, so that the hay would not rub on the wheels. Perpendicular stakes about three feet long were put on to hold the hay.

Ola Anderson was cutting with a scythe and he called to Thone and me to come and get some honey. He had found a bumble bee's nest in an old gopher hole. When we came, Ola was poking it with a stick to get the honey. Suddenly a big swarm of bees came right out of the hole. I jerked backwards and my back hit Ola's scythe. I became terribly scared. I thought my back was cut clear across and I was going to die, an awful feeling. Ola and Thone pulled off my shirt to see how big the cut was. "Ah, shaw," said Thone, "It is not quite one inch long." I got new life again and I knew I was not going to die. We got the honey. Thone and I went home where my mother dressed my wound.

When the haying was done and stacked, we needed to build a house. A little bridge was built over the river, so we could haul the logs home. Ole Midgarden, Tarjei Muhle and Halvor Fendalsveit helped to make it. We had to build smudge fires every evening to chase away the mosquitoes. They were worse when it rained. When Mother and my older sisters were milking, I used a bush from the willows, to try to keep the mosquitoes away from the cow my mother was milking. I managed to keep most of them off.

One day, I noticed a dark speck to the southwest on the prairie. Finally I saw it was a man. I ran and reported it to father. "Run up again," he said, "If he comes to you, you can tell him to come here." I did and the man was at my side. He asked where I lived and if we had bread and milk. I took him to our camp and told mother that he wanted food.

She started to prepare the meal and I took him to see father. It did not take long before there was a good conversation going on. Father asked him what his name was and what he was doing out here in the wilderness. "My name is Martin Wells, and I can give you some pretty good news. I am one of the locaters of the Northern Pacific railroad. You will have the railroad not more than two miles away," he said. This was great news for us pioneers. Mr. Wells ate before he returned to his own camp.

Father started to cut logs for the house. He had taken the extra work to hew them, shorter and shorter till it got to the ridge of the roof. Elm bark was placed on the logs for the roof. Prairie sod was broken up and cut with an ax into square chunks and pieced on the rough side of the bark roof. The sod was packed tight, so it made a water proof roof. A small upstairs was also in this house. The cabin had a door in the center of the south wall and a full window on the west. There was a half window on the north wall. The stove was placed on the east wall and the table stood close to the window on the east wall. A double deck bed was made from hewed basswood boards, 20 inches wide and 1 ½ inches thick. We called this bed the "*over seng*" (upper bed).

The next thing was to get up a stable. This was a long, low structure. It was made from round logs. Some big logs went into this stable. There was one long elm, 50 feet long, nice and straight. The oxen were next to the log and the horses on the lead, yet it was all they could do to pull it 20 or 30 feet at a time. The stable was built in two compartments and roofed with willow hay and sod. Then it was plastered with river mud. Now, when house and stables were built and all of the hay was home, only routine business went on day by day.

Turn-of-the Century Pioneers
Recollections of Charlotte Karine Stangeland Morsch, submitted by Alice Kirn

In 1897 my parents, Simon and Gunhild Stangland, left the prairies of Day County in South Dakota by covered wagon and came to the newly established town of Buena Vista, twelve miles north of Bemidji, Minnesota. They had with them three children: George, three years old; Hilda, eighteen months; and Sam, two months.

The trip took about two weeks and was very rough going. The distance was about 400 miles. They had a wagon load of furniture, all their household goods, and a cow tied on behind. From Park Rapids on, the roads were especially rough, just logging roads through the woods. At one very rough spot, the wagon tipped over, dumping everything to the ground. A heavy piece of furniture barely missed hitting the baby. The cow broke loose and ran off in the woods and they had quite a time finding her.

Life was very hard for my parents in the north country after living on the prairie. My dad did not go in for the big logging operations going on at that time in the area. He made his living by trapping, which he was very good at. He also had a small grocery store in their home, hauling the supplies from Park Rapids by horses. In addition, he was an amateur photographer. He took and developed his own pictures, using glass plates. He would travel for miles around, taking pictures for homesteaders for a small fee.

The forests were full of game, the lakes full of fish, and there was an abundance of wild berries; my mother canned hundreds of quarts. They raised a big garden.

While in Buena Vista, two more children were born: Gratia in 1899, and James in 1903. When things died down in Buena Vista, I think about 1904, my parents decided to go back to South Dakota and try farming again. This time they went by train. While in South Dakota, three more children were born: Elmer in 1905, William in 1908, and in 1910 I arrived on the scene, a tiny premature baby weighing in at one-and one-half pounds. For a long time they didn't think I was going to survive, but here I am, still going strong.

My folks farmed for seven years in South Dakota; then my dad had an urge to go back to Minnesota, this time to the Spring Lake area in Max Township, Itasca County, fifty miles east of Bemidji. They started back to Minnesota with eight children. I was just a year old, so I don't remember anything about that trip. My dad took an eighty-acre homestead at Spring Lake.

We lived at Spring Lake eleven years. During this period, in 1916, Edmund was born. Dad proved up on the two forties and then decided to sell out and move to Ontario, Canada. After almost three years in Ontario, my dad had a stroke. He passed away June 13, 1925. My mother, four brothers and I continued to live on the Canadian homestead for four more years. My mother never liked it in Ontario and wanted to move back to Minnesota where several of her children had established homes of their own.

In 1929, we moved back to Minnesota and I have been here ever since. Not far from our house was a huge mound where my brother thought would be a good place to dig a root cellar which we needed to store our vegetables for the winter.

One summer day Sam started digging and before the day was over he had uncovered seven human skeletons. They had been buried in a sitting position with their knees drawn up to their chests. Also in the mound was a lot of broken pottery; also one perfectly formed pot, exquisitely designed, which my brother later donated to a museum at Big Falls, Minnesota. For a small fee, we let the public come in to inspect the remains and view the burial site.

Archeologists came from Duluth and they decided the bones were at least 200 years old and had been from a huge race of people between seven and eight feet tall. It still remains a mystery who those huge people really were that roamed our land over two centuries ago.

Needless to say, no root cellar was ever built at that site.

*Gunhild with her four oldest children.
L to R: Hilda, Gratia, Sam and George*

Norwegian Fishermen on Lake Superior
by Iver Rommegen

In the 1870 US Census, only 242 Norwegians were counted in Duluth, but by 1900 the population had reached 7,500 people of Norwegian ancestry. Most of these were fishermen, and many more could be found in small fishing communities that spread up the North Shore of Lake Superior. In June of 1870, the *Duluth Minnesotian* newspaper reported that the freighter *St. Paul* had arrived in Duluth carrying 140 immigrants, most of them Norwegians.

The first Norwegian captain may have been L. O. Pedersen. He was born in Tromsø, Norway, and came to Duluth in 1869. He found work as a sailor on a Great Lakes sailing ship, and in 1871 became captain of the schooner *Charley of Beaver Bay*. He spent the summer season on the lake and attended Augsburg Seminary in Minneapolis during the winter. He was ordained as a Norwegian Lutheran minister in 1878.

There were many Scandinavian sea captains ported in Duluth and Superior, Wisconsin, but most of them seem to have been Danes and Swedes. Norwegians seemed more interested in developing family fishing ventures along the North Shore from Duluth to the Canadian border. Eventually there would be over 200 boat landings dotting the North Shore - at Knife River, Two Harbors, Tofte, Grand Marais, Grand Portage and Pigeon Point, and points in between. Many of the names along the lake recall the Norwegian pioneer fishermen. To name just two, Tofte was named for the Tofte family, whose fishing operations were substantial and very successful, and Claus C. Monker, a Norwegian homesteader and fisherman who made his home in Grand Marais and gave his name to Monker Lake.

The fishermen worked both in summer and in winter. The fishermen could use the same skills they had developed in Norway to fish Lake Superior, and the climate that less hardy groups found offensive reminded the Norwegians of their homes on the fjords. Sidewheel steamers running between Grand Marais and Duluth would bring supplies from Duluth and pick up fresh catch on the way back to the Twin Ports. In the winter, ice fisherman sent their catch to Duluth first in sleighs that ran along the lake shore, and eventually by truck. Their catch included herring, chubs, and trout.

In the early years, fishing was done from a 12' X 18' canoe-shaped boat called a skiff. Nets were set within a mile of the shoreline, but the tempestuous nature of Lake Superior could make even that short distance a danger when a gale blew up without much warning. Days were long, and even in summer it was often bone-chilling cold on the lake. The chance to match wits with nature and the challenge of finding a bountiful fishing spot made the long days, danger and drudgery worthwhile. Fishing the North Shore required vigilance, discipline and endurance. By both experience and temperament, Norwegians were perfect for the job.

Section Four
A Norwegian-Minnesotan Sesquicentennial Celebration
150 Years in the Making!

On Saturday, October 18, 2008, the Norwegian Statehood Pioneer Project sponsored a Celebration of our Norwegian-Minnesotan heritage in the ballroom at the Marriott – Mayo Clinic in Rochester, Minnesota.

A number of vendors and demonstrators provided an interesting variety of products – from books to jewelry, quilts to organizational information – in a "Norwegian Marketplace" from noon until 5.

At one o'clock, the afternoon program celebrated the Norwegian Statehood Pioneers who were in Minnesota when the state was born and paved the way for the waves of Norwegian immigrants that would follow. After the program, coffee and cookies were served.

A cash bar reception was held at 5 o'clock, with musical entertainment that set the mood for the banquet at 6 pm. A day of remembrance, pride and laughter came to an end with a photo of the descendants of the Statehood Pioneers who attended the banquet.

Afternoon Program
October 18
1:00 PM

Greeting
    Anne Sladky, Walker
    Norwegian Statehood Pioneer Project Coordinator
        Descendant of Bjorn & Helge Gunderson, Amund Thorsen, Gulbrand & Astri Kassenborg, and Tarje & Geline Grover

Master of Ceremonies
    Gary Olson, Rochester, President, Sons of Norway-Kristiania Lodge

Presentation of the Flags
Flag of the United States
    Staff Sergeant Ashley Goodwin, Granite Falls
        Served in Kuwait in 2005
        Descendant of Gulbrand & Astri Kassenborg
Flag of Norway
    Kjell Hoelstad, Moorhead and Oslo, Norway
        Vietnam Veteran (3 tours)
        Spouse of descendant of A. O. Kragnes
Flag of the State of Minnesota
    Allard Stevens, Granite Falls
        World War II Veteran
        Descendant of Gulbrand & Astri Kassenborg
Minnesota's Sesquicentennial Flag
    Jared Thoreson, Mazeppa
        Boy Scout Troup #78

National Anthem
    Elaine Nordlie, Dassel, Accompanist
        Descendant of Mikkel Kittelson Jordgrav & Taran Anundsdtr, Hans Gunnarson Lia & Aaste Anundsdtr, and Ole Mikkelson Rekanes & Birgith Kittelsdtr.

Pledge of Allegiance
    Members of Boy Scout Troop #78, Mazeppa

Reinlender Medley
Sørposten from Østfold, Adam Gjervert
Laurdagskveld på Vona from Sogn, Leiv Vonen
Styggen på Låven from Nord Trondelag, in the Hilmar tradition, O. Okasås
    John Berquist, Rochester

Keynote Address   "They're All Bound for Minnesota!"
    Dr. Odd Lovoll, Professor Emeritus, St. Olaf College, Northfield

Reinlender by Hilmar Alexandersen
    John Berquist, Rochester

Intermission

Remembering our Statehood Pioneers
    Ja, Vi Elsker (Norwegian National Anthem)
        Ole & Helge Gamme   Gran, Hadeland, Norway
    Call of the Roll
        Georgia Rosendahl, Spring Grove
            Descendant of Anders Pedersen Kroshus
        Jim Skree, Caledonia
            Descendant of Ole & Anna Kragnes, Anfinn & Martha Anfinnson, Ola & Helge Skree, and Knut & Sigrid Lønnegrav
    Reflection & Prayer
        Pastor Per Inge Vik, serving Mindekirken, Minneapolis, from Alesund, Norway
    Den Store, Hvite Flokke (Behold a Host)
        Pastor Vik
        Elaine Nordlie, Dassel, Accompanist

"Those Lutheran Ladies"
    Janet Letnes Martin, Hastings
    Suzann Nelson, Grand Rapids

Retire The Colors
    Ashley Goodwin, Kjell Hoelstad, Allard Stevens
    DeLos Olson, Rochester, Sesquicentennial Flag

"Hail, Minnesota!"
    Elaine Nordlie, Dassel, Accompanist

Reception & Banquet
October 18
5:00 PM

5:00-6:00 **Cash Bar Reception** with Cheese & Crackers
Entertainment by the Rochester Accordion Band

6:00 **Banquet**

> ## MENU
> Salmon with Dill Sauce *or* Herb Roasted Pork Loin
> White & Wild Rice   Roasted Redskin Potatoes
> with
> Garden Salad
> Raspberry Vinaigrette — Ranch Dressing
> Chef's Choice Vegetable
> Lefse
> Rommegrøt

7:00 **Program**
Sandra Hendrickson, Mistress of Ceremonies

Bunad Parade
Sandra Hendrickson   Evelith Kuecker
Elaine Nordlie   Kjell Nordlie
Sharon Haugo   Deb Nelson Gourley

Entertainment by Leroy Larson and the Minnesota Scandinavian Ensemble

"They're All Bound for Minnesota"
Keynote Address by Dr. Odd Lovoll, Professor Emeritus
St. Olaf College, Northfield

Odd S. Lovoll earned his doctorate in U.S. History, specializing in immigration history, at the University of Minnesota. He joined the faculty of St. Olaf College in 1971 and has been publications editor for the Norwegian-American Historical Association since 1980. In 1992 he was appointed to fill the King Olav V Chair in Scandinavian-American Studies. Since 1995 he has held an appointment at the University of Oslo and teaches there in the fall semester. In 1986 Lovoll was decorated by H.M. King Olav V with the Knight's Cross of the Royal Norwegian Order of Merit and in 1989 he was invited to occupy a seat in the history section of the Norwegian Academy of Science and Letters.

Thank you for the invitation to share with you my observations about the distinctive role played by Norwegians in Minnesota's historical path over the past 150 years or more. I extend my personal congratulations and best wishes as we mark the sesquicentennial of Minnesota, and today I most especially wish to commend and congratulate the Norwegian Statehood Pioneer Project on this celebratory commemoration of Norwegian-Minnesota heritage. Eleven *bygdelag*, the Genealogical Center in Madison, Wisconsin, and other interested individuals, with Anne Sladky as coordinator, organized the NSPP and initiated the awarding of Statehood Pioneer Plaques to direct descendants of Norwegian settlers who were in Minnesota at the time of its birth in 1858, and Century Certificates to recognize Norwegian pioneer ancestors who lived in the state before January 1, 1908. It is a most commendable and noble cause that deserves the gratitude of everyone of Norwegian descent in Minnesota and beyond. I extend warm congratulations to all recipients. Given the chronology adopted by the Recognition Program of the Project, I will for the most part limit my comments on the Norwegian American historical experience to the first fifty years of Minnesota's existence as a state with a brief look back to the territorial years. The legacy of the labors of the Norwegian pioneer settlers is today much in evidence in the high quality of life Minnesota offers its residents.

In a sense, of course, by recognizing the contributions of Norwegians to the development of the state and its institutions and culture we are in fact by extension celebrating immigrants from all parts of the world "Who Chose Minnesota," the title given the history of Minnesota's many ethnic groups published by the Minnesota Historical Society Press. A variety of national groups, many new arrivals, have created a noticeable cultural diversity that has greatly enriched Minnesota.

The heading of my address, "They're all bound for Minnesota" (*Aa allsamen ska dem reis te Minnesota*) is a quote from Carl G. O. Hansen's very personal account in his 1956 *My Minneapolis* and attributed to one of his schoolmates in his childhood in Trondheim, Norway, and as Hansen writes, indelibly implanted in his mind. Hansen asks the basic question why Minnesota and Minneapolis have had such an attraction to immigrants from Norway. He simply states that "those of us who have been Minnesotans, for a long time . . . are inclined to think that it was the most natural thing in the world for new arrivals to set their course for this particular spot." Having lived in Minnesota since 1971 I certainly see its attractions. We will, however, shortly say a bit more about causalities in the overseas exodus. Hansen proudly points out that "With the single exception of North Dakota with its much smaller population, no State in the Union and no American city of the first class have proportionately as many people of Norwegian blood." "I was impressed by this back in the old homeland," Hansen continues, "even before I was a teenager. This was at the beginning of the mass migration of Norwegians to America, in the early eighties of the [nineteenth] century, when in one year close to 30,000 Norwegians hied themselves off to America."

The year was 1882 and Carl Hansen was one of the emigrants that year. Arriving in Minneapolis, he was struck by how Norwegian the surroundings were. Hansen had come to an uncle and aunt, and "My aunt," he writes in *My Minneapolis*, "sent one of her children out to make purchases. Some things were to be bought at Haugen's, some at Tharaldsen's, and some at Olsen's & Bakke's." Norwegian was the language of both store clerks and customers. There were grocery stores, clothing establishments, furniture merchants, bakeries, and even a Norwegian funeral home. In this district Norwegian-language newspapers were printed and Norwegian social and cultural interests pursued.

Perhaps the question of how the immigrants adjusted to the new society in America has equal relevance to why they came in the first place. They, as we have just related, recreated much of the environment of home in their new location. For Hansen, as he professes, "the story of the Norwegian immigrants in Minnesota, especially in Minneapolis, is one that I intensely feel is a part of me." Clearly, Minneapolis became the place called home. We human beings possess a marvelous ability to accept and adjust to new challenges and situations. Yet, there was a price to pay. Minnesota looked nothing like the mountain valleys and fjord communities Norwegian immigrants had left. It has been claimed that we all carry within us a sense of place, the images of a geographical landscape engraved from childhood, regardless of distance from the place of birth. This sense of place provides belonging and comfort. The many *bygdelag*—"old home societies," if you will—that came into being in the early 1900s, each cultivated a specific geographical place and landscape in the old homeland. These societies, early on finding their main support in farming communities and small towns in the Upper Midwest, are surely well represented on this particular festive occasion. At the time of their founding, the *bygdelag* gave evidence of a measure of success in Norwegian farming communities that provided extra energy and time to nourish emotional ties to the immigrants' past and to recreate in a new environment the treasured local aspects of their cultural heritage.

May we claim that the challenge to the immigrants was to create a redefined sense of community and a shared identity based on the new landscape and place? Even though the immigrants could not in their hearts abandon the legacy of the dramatic scenery they had departed, they were undeniably a part of a process to make the new environment the place called home.

The immigrants had clearly come to a nation on the move. The earliest Norwegian immigrants to make their way to Minnesota arrived only a little over two decades after the landing of the small sloop *Restauration* in the port of New York on October 9, 1825, with the first boatload of Norwegian immigrants. The small group, numbering fifty-three, crew and passengers and a baby born in transit, in the manner of later arrivals, responded to the appeal of American freedom and opportunity.

Minnesota achieved territorial status the summer of 1849. Fewer than 4,000 residents, excluding Native Americans in the count, had found their way to Minnesota. The territory was basically a wilderness. The tireless chronicler of Norwegian settlement Hjalmar Rued Holand credits Nils Nilsen with being the first Norwegian settler in Minnesota; he arrived in the territorial capital of St. Paul, a village of at the most 900 citizens, in 1849. Nilsen was born on the farm Klegstad in Modum, in the County of Buskerud in 1830, and emigrated in 1849. After working as a stable boy in Stillwater for an Irishman by the name McCusick he became known as Nils McCusick. The first Norwegian woman settler was Ingeborg Levorsdatter Langeman, who came to St. Paul together with her brother Amund in 1850. They were immigrants from Hallingdal and had first come to the Rock Prairie settlement in southern Wisconsin before moving on to Minnesota. Ingeborg Langeman served as a maid in the residence of Governor Alexander Ramsey for one year. One might well imagine that she was present and even met the celebrated Swedish author and feminist Fredrika Bremer when she was a guest in the modest governor's mansion. Following her visit, Fredrika Bremer declared with clairvoyant prophesy that Minnesota would become a glorious new Scandinavia, claiming that "The climate, the situation, the character of the scenery agrees with our people better than that of any other of the American States, and none of them appear to me to have a greater or more beautiful future before them than Minnesota."

There is not time to discuss in detail early settlement. It is a story full of hardship as well as achievement, and for present generations also one of romance and adventure. Land and immigration were the two factors that propelled Minnesota's spectacular growth. In 1860, two years after statehood, the federal census lists more than 172,000 residents in the infant state. Nearly 12,000 were Norwegian, compared to only nine listed in the census a decade earlier. It was to a large extent a migration from the Norwegian countryside to agricultural settlements in America—a rural-to-rural movement. The 1860s, influenced by the Homestead Act of 1862, witnessed a great influx of land-seeking Norwegians to the state; by 1870, 49,569 residents of Norwegian blood lived in Minnesota; 68 percent of them had emigrated from Norway. Considering the ancestors to be honored, we might note that in 1910 Norwegian Americans were nearly 385,000 strong; the number of Norwegian-born that year reaching its peak, made up 27 percent of the total; combined the first and second generations accounted for 18.5 percent of Minnesota's population. Indeed, Norwegians had a visible presence in the North Star state.

Few had come directly from Norway. Guided by familial connections, they might have first come to kin in Iowa, Wisconsin, or Illinois before moving west. These settlements consisted to a large extent of people from the same Norwegian home community; the local Norwegian speech, traditions in food and social conventions, as well as a multitude of old-world sacred and profane customs were retained. One might consequently speak of Trønder settlements, Halling settlements, Nordfjord settlements, and a multitude of other rural gatherings of fellow *bygd* folk.

A rich folk life characterized the many agricultural settlements. Bonds of kinship were strengthened when kindred newcomers on their westward journey transited through older Norwegian settlements and also when these same communities gave up their youth to new settlements farther west. Each settlement acted both as a receiving station and as a mother colony for new farming communities, each which in turn might become a new point of departure. The process created a sense of solidarity and of belonging to a larger community.

Norwegians exhibited a special rural bond, a strong attachment to land and farming. They were the most rural of any major immigrant group who arrived in the nineteenth century; it was an attachment that was passed on to the next generation. We might agree with T.A. Hoverstad who in 1915 concluded emphatically that "the emigrants came to stay on the land," and "their children remain on their lands after them." They clearly resisted the pull of the city. Norwegian farmers settled in large numbers in the three major agricultural regions of the state; these were the hay and dairying counties in the southeast, corn and hog raising in the southwestern counties, and the spring wheat and small grain counties in western and northwestern Minnesota. Perhaps the greatest contribution made by Norwegian American farmers was their dedication to farming as a way of life. It is a determination that explains the persistence in later generations of a lifestyle associated with the family farm and traditional rural values.

Most Norwegian immigrants, wherever they hailed from in the homeland, embraced the Lutheran faith. We do not, of course, wish to overlook the religious pluralism of America. Norwegians did indeed respond to the message of other Christian faiths; there were converts to Methodist, Baptist, and Mormon faiths, though in the nineteenth century never in large numbers. Norwegian Lutheranism represented the dominant religious conviction, indeed to the extent that, as the Norwegian sociologist P.A. Munch described the situation in America, "it is virtually impossible to distinguish 'Lutheran' from Norwegian'." Small and large edifices, built with great sacrifice, dotted the landscape in regions of Norwegian settlement. Many of these rural places of worship, as their members in increasing numbers moved to a nearby small town or to a distant city, were torn down, the site now marked by a memorial. The Norwegian Lutheran church in America in its many conflicting manifestations became the immigrant community's central institution. In addition to its religious role, the church became the most important social institution established by Norwegians in America. "The church on the prairies and in the wood groves of the middle west," to cite one of my own earlier statements," provided an array of social activities; mutual support in time of need; comforting rituals associated with baptism, confirmation, marriage, and burial; and solemnity and a sense of security in unfamiliar surroundings."

The Lutheran church evinced a deep and abiding commitment to education, not only to pass on the Lutheran creed to new generations, but to prepare the young for life in America. There were the numerous congregational or Norwegian schools which convened the children for summer courses, the more ambitious academies or high schools, and there were the several colleges, some of these having been founded as academies. Three major educational institutions of higher learning in Minnesota bear witness to the deep-felt responsibility harbored by Norwegian pioneer settlers to provide educational opportunities for Norwegian youth. St. Olaf College, high on Manitou in Northfield, was started in 1874, the same year Augsburg College in Minneapolis began as a college division at Augsburg Seminary; Concordia College in Moorhead in the western part of the state dates its establishment from 1891. They all had modest beginnings. It required an enormous investment of time and resources, as well as dedication to the task ahead, to bring about the notable place these institutions of higher learning currently enjoy.

These colleges all cultivated a strong tradition of song. Directors like St. Olaf's F. Melius Christiansen lifted choral singing to new heights. A rich store of hymns strengthened congregational worship when Lutherans assembled. But Norwegian musical activity received its strength and inspiration just as much from a long tradition of folk music in all its variations and from the works of Norwegian composers. It was a cherished heritage cultivated early on by hundreds of male choirs later joined by women singing societies. The male quartet Lyren (The Lyre), organized in Minneapolis in 1869, introduced a statewide flourishing of male choirs and song festivals in the following decades. That same year, in 1869, Norwegians in Minneapolis were sufficiently secure of their place in America to celebrate *Syttende mai* — Norway's national holiday — for the first time. It was not a question of conflicting loyalties, but instead a demonstration of a mutually supportive and self-reinforcing allegiance to both American citizenship and ethnic adherence.

Their place in American society held paramount importance. Norwegians in Minnesota took part in civic life to higher degree than did other populations in the state. Until World War I eligible voters in Minnesota's Norwegian settlements showed voting records that exceeded the state average in voter turnout. Historian Kendrick Charles Babcock in 1914 claimed, "The Norwegian, of all men of the Northern lands, has the strongest liking for the political arena." Norwegian-language newspapers like *Nordisk Folkeblad* (Nordic People's Newspaper), started in Rochester in 1868, *Budstikken* (The Messenger), established in Minneapolis in 1873, and *Nordvesten* (The Northwest) begun in St. Paul in 1881, guided their compatriots to political party loyalty. Politicians of Norwegian birth and descent have exhibited great political skill and influence at the local, state, and national level; from the 1880s there was a pronounced advance to elected offices. Norwegian-born Knute Nelson exemplified the success possible in the American political system. He was the first Scandinavian American politician to attain national prominence; in 1892 he ascended to the governorship in Minnesota on the Republican ticket; from 1895 until his death in 1923 he served as United States senator. He became the object of great ethnic pride.

Finally let us return to Carl G. O. Hansen's beloved Twin Cities of Minneapolis and St. Paul. As historian John R. Jenswold stated, "In the 1890s the Twin Cities seemed to symbolize the promise of America, a new world where new cities sprang from the wilderness in a few years." By 1900 over 16,000 Norwegian immigrants lived in the two cities.. Norwegian-born men were employed in skilled, semiskilled, or unskilled blue-collar occupations; many worked in the expanding flour-milling, lumber, and construction industries. And there were the Norwegian men in business, education, law, medicine and politics. A maturing Norwegian American urban colony existed.

Minneapolis sheltered the Sons of Norway, organized in 1895 as a mutual aid society in north Minneapolis by eighteen young laboring men; similar societies emerged in small towns in the state. However, only the Sons of Norway expanded its influence both within and outside the United States as a major Norwegian American secular organization. Norwegian women played a major role in voluntary social service work of the churches. In Minneapolis both the Norwegian Christian Assistance Society, organized in 1892, and the Lutheran Charitable Society from 1893 owed their existence to Norwegian women who came to the aid of fellow Norwegians in need. The expanded congregational work of the church conducted by women included the deaconess cause. In 1888 a Norwegian deaconess hospital—the second in America after the one in Brooklyn—came into being. Benevolence enjoyed success. The Fairview Hospital emanated as well from the Norwegian community in Minneapolis; it was organized in 1906 in competition with the deaconess facility. In 1973 it became integrated into the large Fairview health care system through consolidation. The Norwegian American community with these and the many other Norwegian charitable institutions, including homes for the elderly, it instituted throughout the state reached a new and important stage in its development.

Norwegian Americans have clearly had a positive impact on the development of Minnesota's economic growth, political life, institutions, and culture. Some of us even regard Norwegian influence on "Speaking Minnesotan" a treasured contribution. A Norwegian ideal is of course modesty and reserve. Being boastful is totally unacceptable. Norwegians consequently respond to questions in the negative. In advising delegates to the Republican National Convention in St. Paul in September how to relate to Minnesota expressions, the *Minneapolis Star Tribune* gave the following example. "Not too bad" would be the invariable response to a question addressed to a native Minnesotan about living in Minnesota, which should be interpreted to mean, the newspaper insisted, "amazingly great!" Let us then today celebrate our amazingly great state. Again, my congratulations and best wishes.

On the Importance of Religion
Pastor Per Inge Vik
Mindekirken, Minneapolis

Thank you for inviting me to be part of this celebration of the 150 years of Minnesota statehood. The topic I was asked to give some remarks on, is the importance religion had for the first Norwegian pioneers.

One answer to the question is that we find two main reasons for Norwegians 150 years ago to emigrate to America. The one was to find work and make a living because "you can't eat fjords". The other main reason was religious. We know that a big percentage of those who emigrated, were persecuted for religious reasons by the authorities, the pastors of the state church included. Some Quakers coming from Stavanger were among them.

Either the pioneers came to Minnesota looking for religious freedom or they came from a main stream State Church background, they brought their faith, their Bibles and their Hymnals with them! To me it is amazing to see how huge an impact Hans Nielsen Hauge has had in this country. Those who belonged to the Hauge movement, stayed in the state church in Norway. But here they made their own Hauge Synod. In the beginning the pioneers gathered for prayers and worship in homes, and even in barns.

The density of churches in this country is one of the signs I see of the importance of religion. For sure, not all the Norwegian immigrants were religious active. But when Norwegians go abroad, something strange happens. We see it at the Norwegian Seaman's Churches scattered around the world, and we see it at Mindekirken in Minneapolis. Many Norwegians who were not so very church active in the Old Country, have become more active in their new country. The church for them became a home away from home. I think that by leaving your country, then your heritage, values you were brought up with, religion included, becomes even more important.

I do not know too much about the Norwegian pioneers here in Minnesota. But let me mention a parallel, my relatives in Saskatchewan in Canada. 5 of the 10 siblings of my paternal grandfather emigrated about 100 years ago from Syvde in Norway to Bulyea, Saskatchewan. They all married Norwegians, and had children. Now they count more than 100 people. One of the first things they did after they homesteaded, was to find a lot for a church, at the farm land of one of them. As soon as they had built their own houses, they started the project to build Norrøna Church, a replica of their home church. I visited this church a few years ago, and preached there. It was moving. I admire the pioneers, their courage, their faith, their energy, their determination to let the church be so important in their lives.

A Prayer of Remembrance
Pastor Vik

Let us pray,

Lord, triune God, we thank you for this great state of Minnesota and it's history.

We thank you especially today for the Norwegians that took the chance to leave their safe life in Norway and contributed to building this state. We honor their memory, and we thank you for their unselfish efforts, hard work and good skills.

Above all we thank you for your faithfulness to our peoples, both in Norway and Minnesota. Help this generation keep a strong contact over the Atlantic, and continue to build and develop the state of Minnesota so it may be the very best for generations to come.

                        In Jesus name we pray.   Amen

Photos from the "Norwegian Marketplace"

Don Olson, Wood Carvings

Vangie Krueger, Chip Carvings

Randy Trelstad's Uff Da! Gifts

Deb Nelson Gourley-Astri, My Astri Publishing

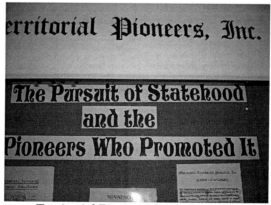

Minnesota Territorial Pioneers Sesquicentennial Display

Photos from the Afternoon Program

NSPP Coordinator, Anne Sladky

Master of Ceremonies, Gary Olson

Presentation of the Flags

John Berquist, Button Accordion

Dr. Odd S. Lovoll, Keynote Speaker

Ole & Helga Gamme, Norwegian Nat'l Anthem

More Photos from the Afternoon Program

Georgia Rosendahl & Jim Skree, Call of the Roll

Pastor Per Inge Vik, Reflection

"Lutheran Lady" Janet Martin

"Lutheran Lady" Suzann Nelson

Elaine Nordlie, Keyboard Accompanist

Descendants of Statehood Pioneers stand

Photos from the Reception and Banquet

Reception Entertainment: Rochester Accordion Band

Bunads!

Banquet Entertainment: LeRoy Larson and the Minnesota Scandinavian Ensemble

Mistress of Ceremonies, Sandra Hendrickson

Attendees

The following people attended the Celebration, based on reservation records. Additional tickets were sold at the door and those individuals may not be listed. Numbers in parenthesis indicate total number of tickets purchased by the named individual(s).

Photo of descendants of Statehood Pioneers taken after the evening banquet and program. Many more attended only the afternoon program.

Agrimson Arne
Anderson Paul
Anderson Verla (4)
Anderson Verlyn & Evonne
Bailey Betty
Benson Carolyn
Bergland Betty
Bjugan Oraine & Darleen
Boyer Rozalyn
Brattelid Ivan
Brodin Robert & Rosalie
Buche Helen & John
Burket Tom
Carlson Jean M
Cleveland Delores
Dalager Elaine
Delano Ann (2)
Eischens Richard & Paula
Fried Karen
Gamme Ole & Helga
Gilbertson Norma
Gillespie Douglas
Goodwin Ashley
Gourley Deb Nelson
Gunderson David
Gunderson Joann
Hagen Dick & Karen
Haglund Chris
Halbert Ralph & Mary
Hansing Ross & Virginia

Haugo John & Sharon
Hendrickson Sandra
Heusinkveld Jan
Hoelstad Kjell & Orpha
Horn Barbara
Janda Mark & Anne
Johnson Audrey H
Johnson Darlene
Johnson Deborah M
Johnson Mark
Johnsrud Harlan & Sandy
Jorstad Lois A (4)
Kinneberg Glenn (3)
Krueger Allen & Joyce
Kuecker Evelith
Leimbach Marian
Liebe Larry & Clare (5)
Linder Breanna
Linder Jessica
Linder Kim
Linder Sammy Jo
Lund Joel A
Marthaler Jean
Merten Sharon
Meyer Sandra & David
Miller Elsie (2)
Miller Marlene
Morben Pamela
Nelson Char

Ness Arnold
Nordlie Kjell & Elaine
Norland Ralph (2)
Norman David & Kay
Norman Dick & Gloria
Olson DeLos & Karen
Paulson Arthur
Pfeffer David
Reese Matt & Cheryl
Rosendahl Georgia
Schill Mildred
Schmitt Barb
Simonson John (2)
Skree Jim
Sladky Anne
Sorenson Marilyn
Sorum Dean & Carol
Spande Beverly
Srp Roy & Delores
Stevens Allard & Anne
Stevens Dennis & Judy
Studley Deborah M
Susag David
Swenson Lloyd & Ramona
Swenson Owen & Evie
Teigen Sylvia
Turner Sandra
Tweeten Geneva
Vigeland Dean
Ziesemer Gerald

Section Five
Minnesota's St. Olav Medal Winners

The St. Olav Medal is the highest honor bestowed on foreigners by the King of Norway. The award was instituted in 1939 by King Haakon VII. It recognizes "outstanding service rendered in connection with the spreading of information about Norway abroad and for strengthening the bonds between expatriate Norwegians and their home country."

Through the years, many Minnesotans have been honored by the king for their efforts in maintaining the connection between Norwegian-Americans and their ethnic home. Recipients of the St. Olav Medal include professionals and blue collar workers, those with advanced degrees and some with only an eighth grade education. What they have in common is their extraordinatry commitment to helping Americans find and maintain their historical connections to Norway, and their willingness to invest their personal time and effort in that quest. The strength of the Norwegian-American, and specifically the Norwegian-Minnesotan, community is in large part due to the unselfish efforts of these dedicated individuals.

Thanks to Astri Olsen at the Royal Norwegian Consulate in Minneapolis for providing this list of all of the recipients of the St. Olav Medal from Minnesota.

Name	City	Year
Karl G Andersen	Minneapolis	1939
J A Asgaard	Minneapolis	1939
Anna Theodora Fuhr	Duluth	1939
Clemens Granskov	Northfield	1939
Eric Bjarne Hauke	Minneapolis	1939
Oscar Hertsgaard	Minneapolis	1939
Engebreth Hobe	St Paul	1939
Johanne A Hobe	St Paul	1939
Christan Holm	Hibbing	1939
E W Humphrey	Moorhead	1939
Oakey Jackson	Northfield	1939
Leo Koll	Alexandria	1939
Fredrik Krohn	Minneapolis	1939
Raymond Lee	St Paul	1939
Henry Nycklemoe	Fergus Falls	1939

Name	City	Year
Herman Roe	Northfield	1939
Hanna G Stalland	St Paul	1939
Theodore Wold	Minneapolis	1939
Hjalmar Bjørnson	Minneapolis	1946
H C Caspersen	Minneapolis	1946
Benjamin Ross Eggan	Minneapolis	1946
Peter August Hovland	Minneapolis	1946
Herman Jorgensen	Minneapolis	1946
Jacob K Stefferud	Minneapolis	1946
Ole Hegedahl	Minneapolis	1947
Walter Ridder	St Paul	1947
Anna M Thykesen	Northfield	1947
Helen B Tormoen	Duluth	1947
Nat Finney	Minneapolis	1948
Esther Gulbrandson	Northfield	1948
Ellen Hammer	Minneapolis	1948
Branda Ueland	Minneapolis	1948
Josephine Brack	St Paul	1952
Borghild Dahl	Burnsville	1952
John K Daniels	Minneapolis	1952
Preston Martin Hegland	Northfield	1954
Hans M Jacobsen	Minneapolis	1954
Paul G Schmidt	Northfield	1954
Andrew Melgaard	Warren	1955
Ludvig Strauman	Minneapolis	1957
Signe Fossum Lillejord	Minneapolis	1959
Erling Stone	Minneapolis	1960
Marie Siqveland	Minneapolis	1961
Lorraine Carlson	Northfield	1962
Christian Christensen	Minneapolis	1962
Hilda Myhre Hanson	Minneapolis	1963
Ivar Aus	Minneapolis	1964
Nels Minne	Winona	1964
Pauline Farseth	Minneapolis	1965
Frances Kuross	Maldura	1965
Lawrence Molsather	Minneapolis	1965
Magne Smedvig	Minneapolis	1966
Hagbart Bue	Minneapolis	1968
Sverre Dalland	Minneapolis	1968
Erling Innvik	Decorah IA	1968
Jenny Alvilde Johnson	Minneapolis	1968
Hulda Aus	Minneapolis	1969
Bent Jarl Vanberg	Minneapolis	1969

Name	City	Year
Axel Valla	Minneapolis	1970
Einar Duvick	Minneapolis	1971
Eyvind Evans	Kasson	1971
Mikal Kartvedt	Duluth	1971
B E Mortensen	Minneapolis	1971
Leland Sateren	Minneapolis	1971
Elsie M Melby	Duluth	1972
Stella Brunsvold	Glen Lake	1975
Reidar Dittmann	Northfield	1977
Paul G Christiansen	Moorhead	1978
Estelle H Knudsen	Minneapolis	1980
Odell Bjerkness	Moorhead	1981
Lawrence Olav Hauge	Minneapolis	1981
Donald Padilla	Minneapolis	1981
Walter E Jacobson	New Brighton	1982
Kjell Bergh	Minneapolis	1983
Liviu Ciulen	Minneapolis	1983
Richard C Magnuson	St Paul	1983
Lois Rand	Minneapolis	1983
Ron D Smith	Minneapolis	1983
Hildegard M M Strom	Minneapolis	1983
Roy Eide	Minneapolis	1984
James J Johnson	Edina	1985
Carl Narvestad	Granite Falls	1990
Margaret Miller	Apple Valley	1993
Liv Dahl	Minneapolis	1995
Egil Almaas	Minneapolis	1996
Mary Johnson	Edina	1996
Orlyn A Kringstad	Minneapolis	1996
Marilyn Somdahl	Minneapolis	1996
Andrea Een	Northfield	2002
Lee Rokke	Minneapolis	2004
Verlyn Anderson	Moorhead	2007

Even before 1939, the King of Norway acknowledged the contributions of individual Norwegian-Americans in maintaining and enhancing relations between the Norwegian-American community and Norway. In 1915, King Haakon bestowed the Order of St. Olav, First Class, on Conrad Deitlef Morck of Minneapolis. Mr. Morck was a Norwegian immigrant who was very active in the Norwegian community and helped organize and was the first President of Nordlandslaget. Other Norwegian-Minnesotans were no doubt similarly honored, but we were unable to locate a comprehensive record of those recipients.

The announcement letter received by Mr. Morck from the Norwegian Consul in Minneapolis began "I have the honor to inform you that this consulate has received a diploma as well as decoration of St. Olav to be delivered to you...." His award diploma is shown below.

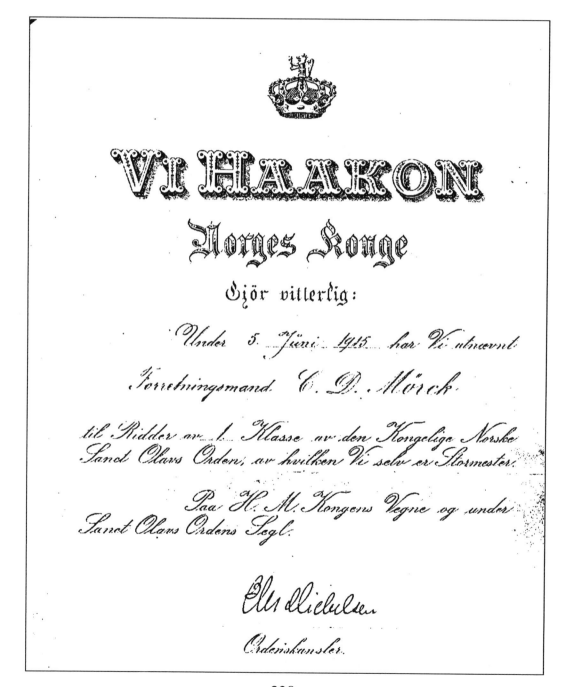

Section Six

Organizations that Participated in the Norwegian Statehood Pioneer Project

Bygdelags are community organizations that bring together descendants from approximately thirty specific areas of Norway. The project was supported directly by eleven of these organizations and the Norwegian-American Genealogical Center and Naeseth Library in Madison, Wisconsin. It could not have been successful without their involvement and support.

All of the project's files will eventually be housed at the Genealogical Center and available for genealogical research.

Hadeland Lag of America

Hadeland is located about an hour's drive northwest of Oslo and is comprised of the three southernmost *kommunes* (municipalities) in Oppland *Fylke* (county). Gran, site of the medieval Sister Churches and Stone House, includes the historical district of Brandbu; Jevnaker is home to the world famous Hadeland Glassworks; and Lunner has become a fast-growing suburb of Oslo.

Thomas Walby of Hudson, Wisconsin, was a salesman for the International Harvester Company. He encouraged *Hadelending* visitors to his venue on Machinery Hill at the Minnesota State Fair to return on Saturday afternoon for a meeting to organize a *bygdelag* (community organization) for Hadeland. As a result of his efforts, the Hadeland Lag of America was founded in St. Paul at the Minnesota State Fair on September 10, 1910. For several decades, its yearly *stevner* (gatherings) offered thousands of Hadeland immigrants and their descendants the opportunity to gather with their extended families, renew friendships, share news from their home district in Hadeland, and enjoy good food and fellowship in the tradition and dialect of the 'Old Country.'

After World War II, most of the immigrant settlers had passed on and the succeeding generations did not share a strong desire to maintain an active connection with their Hadeland roots. By the early 1970's, the Lag had only a handful of members and the annual gatherings were suspended.

Morgan Olson led the effort to reinvigorate the lag. A stevne was held on July 9-10, 1976, in Mayville, North Dakota, in conjunction with Landingslaget, which had also fallen on hard times. The focus turned to genealogy and renewed family contacts in Hadeland, and the lag once again began to grow. Over 500 individuals and families in the US, Canada, and Norway, are now members of the Hadeland Lag. It became a tax-exempt non-profit corporation in 2008.

Each summer, Hadeland Lag joins with Landingslaget, Numedalslag, Ringerike-Drammen Districts Lag, Sigdalslag, Telelaget, and Toten Lag in hosting a 7-Lag Stevne in varying locations in Iowa, Minnesota, North and South Dakota, and Wisconsin. An additional Hadeland Lag meeting is usually held on the third Saturday in October. Visits to Hadeland focus on connecting members with their ancestral farms and visiting historic landmarks. They take place every five years. During the trip scheduled for June of 2010, there will be a special celebration of the Lag's Centennial.

The *Brua* (bridge) is the Hadeland Lag's newsletter. It is published four times a year – in February, May, August and November. Along with the latest news about current activities, regular features include "Our Hadeland Ancestors" and "Recollections of Pioneer Times" which tell the stories of members' ancestors. Content submitted from Hadeland includes news from the Hadeland Folkemuseum, articles about the history and landmarks of Hadeland, and the popular "Hadeland Today" column.

In 2002, the Hadeland Lag entered into a formal relationship with Kontaktforum Hadeland-Amerika, an organization that combines the efforts of the historical societies in Gran, Lunner and Jevnaker to provide genealogical support for both Norwegian and foreign researchers, and offers a contact point for the Hadeland Lag in Norway. The goal of Kontaktforum's Emigrant Identification Project is to trace the more than 10,000 Norwegians who immigrated from Hadeland to the US and Canada between 1843 and 1930. As of January, 2009, over 8,600 emigrants had been identified.

The lag opened its website in 2002. The site offers information not only about membership and current activities, but also about points of interest in and the history of Hadeland, the lag's history, genealogical resources, and includes a special members-only area that provides detailed family research files and Kontaktforum's emigrant database.

Visit the Hadeland Lag on-line at
http://www.hadelandlag.org/   http://www.myspace.com/hadelandlag

2008-2009 Officers and Board Members
Jan Heusinkveld, President
Anne Sladky, Vice President & Webmaster
Norma Gilbertson, Secretary
David Pfeffer, Treasurer
David Gunderson, Genealogist
Verlyn Anderson, Editor of the *Brua*
Delores Cleveland, Past President
Carol Sorum, Membership Secretary
DeLos Olson
Anne Janda
Barb Schmitt

Emeritus Advisory Council
Ellef Erlien
Harriet Foss
Palmer Rockswold
Leslie Rogne
Robert Rosendahl
Dean Sorum

Kontakforum Hadeland-Amerika
Hadeland Lag: Ole P. Gamme, Leader
Gran Historical Society: Hans Næss
                         Kjell Myhre
Jevnaker Historical Society: Geir Arne Myrstuen
Lunner: Kirsten Heier Western
Harold Hvattum, Kontaktforum Treasurer

Hallinglag of America

Hallingdal is a rugged mountain valley in Norway, part of Buskerud County (fylke). Many people migrated from this valley coming to America and Canada, especially during the 1800's. The Hallinglag is an organization formed in 1907 by these immigrants and their descendants. The Hallinglag aims to preserve and promote the unique cultural heritage given to us by these pioneers.

The above paragraph appears in each issue of *Hallingen* - the magazine that keeps Hallinglag members up-to-date on lag happenings - and the message sums up why this group has actively pursued knowledge about its Norwegian heritage. The Hallinglag has published *Hallingen*, which was given that name in 1912, since 1908. The magazine is published quarterly, and is just one of the lag's many strengths. Although *Hallingen* was printed entirely in Norwegian for years, today only an occasional article is written in Norse. Each year the Lag sponsors a stevne (gathering) in the Upper Midwest that offers food for thought as well as excellent meals and entertainment. It is a great place to make friends, do a little genealogical research in our extensive genealogical library, and learn about the beautiful Norwegian valley that our immigrant ancestors left behind.

The lag's silk banner, shown at the top of this page, was made in Christiania and presented as a gift from Norwegian Hallings. The motif is from Hol, Norway and Hallingskarvet is in the background. A man and woman are looking to the west, toward North America. The woman's bunad is from Gol, the man's from Aal. Embroidered beneath the scene is *Lat oss inkje forfædrane gløyma* (Let Us Not Forget Our Forefathers), a line from an Ivar Aasen poem, that serves as the lag's motto.

In honor of its centennial year, Hallinglag published <u>People's History of the Hallinglag of America 1907-2007</u>. It offers a brief history of Hallingdal, a more detailed history of the Hallinglag, and a collection of biographies, photos and family histories contributed by its members. <u>People's History</u> was the proud recipient of a 2007 Minnesota State University-Moorhead Heritage Commission's G. K. Haukebo Award.

For more information about our *bygdelag* and membership information,
visit our website at:
http://www.fellesraad.com/hallinglag-home.htm

Landingslaget i Amerika

Landingslaget was founded in 1910 by a group of Norwegian settlers from the *bygd* (community) called Land in Oppland *fylke* (county) in south central Norway.

The communities of Nordre Land and Søndre Land (North and South Land) lie among the green slopes and valleys of central Norway about 100 miles north of Oslo. The more rugged northern portion is west of Lillehammer, the site of the 1994 Olympics. The southern part boasts the Randsfjorden, a scenic inland lake. Dokka and Hov are the delightful centers of the two respective *kommuner*.

Today, Land is a modern, thriving community with a mixture of agriculture and business - a very fine cross-section of Norwegian rural life. Over one hundred fifty years ago, thousands of individuals and families immigrated to America looking for new opportunities. In the 20th century, the children of Norwegian and American "cousins" are now re-establishing their ties.

Landingslaget is a *bygdelag* dedicated to the preservation of Norwegian cultural heritage and historical knowledge of one's roots and to the promotion of fellowship among those who share these interests. *Bygdelag* is a combination of two words: *bygd* implies a settlement where people share a common dialect and customs, and *lag* is an association or a group of people.

The lag publication, *Land-i-Amerika*, contains articles of genealogical and historical interest. It is mailed to members three times a year. Lag activities include the annual meeting (stevner), held in conjunction with six other lags, and visits to Land. The lag visited Land in 1989, 2000, and 2005 and plans to celebrate its centennial year with a visit in 2010.

To learn more, or for an application, visit http://www.landingslag.org

Scenes in Land today

Nordfjordlaget

Our "bride" surrounded by stevne goers

Imagine the emotions felt by immigrants who had left their homeland to go to America. It is not surprising that they wanted to be in contact with others who had done the same. In the early 1900's a group of immigrants from Nordfjord, on the west coast of Norway, decided they wanted to organize and in June, 1909 a preliminary organizational meeting was held at Como Park in St. Paul, Minnesota. Temporary officers were elected and a committee appointed to draw up a constitution and make arrangements for a constitutional meeting. That meeting was held in June of 1910. With one exception, meetings (stevner) have been held every year since, except during World War I and II. The constitution states "The purpose of this organization shall be to foster and preserve the cultural values of the emigrants from Nordfjord, Norway and their descendants." The stevner were popular events attended by hundreds of people, many coming long distances, having a chance to visit, hear news from Norway and renew friendships. Originally, and continuing until 1950, Norwegian was the language of each stevne. The stevner have been in various locations in Minnesota, North Dakota, South Dakota, Wisconsin, and Norway. Nordfjordlag now alternates between a one-day stevne/picnic one year followed by a two-day stevne the next.

A complete bridal costume with an ornate crown, was presented to the Nordfjordlag at the 1933 stevne in Fargo, North Dakota. The gown was made by the women in Nordfjord and the crown, belt and other ornaments were created by goldsmith M. J. Hestenes of Bergen. From an article written about the event, "...the gift was received not only with happiness, but with an enthusiasm which is seldom seen in the calm and restrained Norwegian character." The by-laws of the Nordfjordlag specifically designate the use of this treasured bridal costume. Traditionally, each stevne includes a *Bryllupsmarsj* (a bridal march or wedding procession) with a member of the lag wearing the bridal costume. On a Saturday afternoon at the 1949 stevne an actual wedding took place with the bride wearing the dress and crown. The presentation of the bridal couple and the bridal march are always a special part of the stevne.

Music is a popular part of each stevne and everyone joins in singing the old favorites. In 1940 Lars Gimmestad wrote the Nordfjordlagets Sang to commemorate the stevne. The translated final verse is "Bless this our gathering dear God, with friends and members dear, with richest blessings from on high to crown the coming year."

Close-up views of the bridal crown

If you are interested in learning more about your ancestors from the Nordfjord area, or just want to meet and enjoy fellowship with other descendants of the area, join us!

Nord Hedmark og Hedemarken Lag

Our Lag includes 16 kommuner in the three districts of Nord-Østerdal, Sør-Østerdal, and Hedemarken / Hamar: Alvdal, Elverum, Engerdal, Folldal, Hamar, Løten, Os, Rendalen, Ringsaker, Stange, Stor-Elvdal, Tolga, Trysil, Tynset, Vang, and Amot.

The Nord Hedmark og Hedemarken Lag was organized in 1995, and is an expanded revival of the former Østerdalslaget which was formed during its first stevne at Fergus Falls, Minnesota, on June 18, 1910 and dissolved in 1962. NHOH was granted tax exempt status by the IRS in 2008. Membership includes around 220 descendants and friends of immigrants from the three districts, with about 35% residing in Wisconsin and 23% in Minnesota. About 40% of the membership has roots in Ringsaker followed by Stange (15%) and Hamar (11%).

The lag offers limited genealogical research assistance. Our "Cousin finding" tradition uses a worksheet, ancestral farm names, and other information to help members find other members from their family trees.

The NHOH newsletter is published three times a year. Each newsletter includes stories of immigration and early pioneer life that have been provided by members and other sources. A "Seek and You May Find" section offers members an opportunity to request information about "lost" relatives. Upcoming events and e-mail addresses of genealogical resources in Norway and in the United States and any new genealogical resources acquired by the Lag are also published.

NHOH joins with Trønderlag and Gudbrandsdal Lag National to host an annual stevne. Members can make use of the lags' extensive genealogical holdings for research, and there is always great entertainment, interesting tours of local landmarks, and educational seminars covering research, genealogy, and history.

Gary Olson, who served as emcee of the Norwegian-Minnesotan Sesquicentennial Celebration's afternoon program, is a past president of Nord Hedmark og Hedemarken Lag.

For contact information or a membership form, visit http://www.nhohlag.org/

Opdalslag

The homeland of Norway was unable to support the steadily growing population. Census numbers from 1800 and after in Oppdal climbed so dramatically that it became necessary for many to say good-bye to friends and relatives and seek a new life in America. Many of them never returned. In 1865 there were 4500 inhabitants in Oppdal. Fifty years later the population had dropped to 3760. This decline was caused by the massive emigration.

The Opdalings settled primarily in two places in USA: Snohomish County in Washington, and on the prairies surrounding Sioux City, Iowa; Sioux Falls, Yankton, Volin, Irene, and Sinai, South Dakota.

Opdalsag was founded on the West Coast at a picnic in Woodland Park in Seattle, Washington on August 1, 1920. The Eastern Division of the Opdalslag was founded at Centerville, South Dakota on July 27, 1925.

The idea of collecting and publishing the stories of Norwegian American immigrants from Opdal arose at a meeting in Seattle, Washington, in the summer of 1920. Out of the second meeting came the first yearbook, or *årbok*, dated 1921-1922. For the next twenty years, the Opdalings published yearbooks that recorded events of note and included reports on the annual meetings, membership lists, and obituaries, histories and autobiographies of both those who immigrated and those who stayed in Norway.

All the volumes were written in Norwegian. Of the thirteen Yearbooks that were published between 1921 and 1941, five have been translated into English. Each volume includes fascinating histories and stories of the Opdalings' new lives in America as well as nostalgic remembrances of the homeland they left behind. The yearbooks are valuable research sources and copies can be found in the Library in Oppdal, Norway. Membership in Opdalslag started with 68 members in 1921-22, climbed to 248 in 1927 and reached 401 in 1931. Membership began to decline in 1933 (306) and in 1941 it had fallen to 239 members.

Activities were suspended during World War II and did not resume when the war ended. Sixty-one years after the original Opdalslag ceased to meet many Norwegian descendants showed enough interest in 2002 to re-organize the Opdalslag. Since that time, our membership has ranged from 120 – 140. We are fortunate to have seven members living in Oppdal, Norway who belong to our Lag.

The area that many of our forefathers settled when they emigrated from Oppdal in the 1800's was in Yankton, South Dakota and surrounding areas. The first official re-organized Opdalslag took place August 31 and September 1, 2002 in Yankton and Tondhjem Lutheran Church near Volin, South Dakota. The second, 2003 in Mission Hill and Vangen Lutheran Church in South Dakota. The third was held 2004 in Irene, South Dakota. The fourth, fifth, sixth and seventh Lags were held in Scandia Lutheran Church in Centerville, South Dakota. The eighth Lag will be held September 12 and 13, 2009 in Scandia.

Our Lag is a member of the Bygdelagenes Fellesraad. Visit their website at www.fellesraad.com for contact information and the latest news about Opdalslag. Our purpose is to support and promote the preservation of the Norwegian heritage in America in all its forms, particularly the heritage of the Norwegian settlers of the Northern Prairies and Plains, and to find and become acquainted with distant relatives.

Enoch Larson from Yucatan, Minnesota, was a Statehood Pioneer. His descendants belonging to Opdalslag are Lorraine Engelsgaard, Duane Engelsgaard, Mildred Schill and Evelith Kuecker. No other people from Opdalslag reported a Minnesota Statehood Pioneer.

Exterior & Interior of Oppdal Church in Norway

Ringerike-Drammen Districts Bygdelag

Predecessors of the present Ringerike-Drammen Districts Bygdelag were Ringerikslaget, organized in Albert Lea, Minnesota, June 7, 1916, and Modum og Eiker Laget, organized at the State Fairgrounds in St. Paul, Minnesota, June 6, 1925. People from these combined areas began meeting together in 1986. Some years later, the group voted to include all the unserved *kommuner* (communities) of eastern Buskerud *fylke* (county). The nine communities now represented by R-DD Lag include Ringerike, Hole, Modum, Øvre Eiker, Nedre Eiker, Drammen, Lier, Røyken and Hurum.

Historically, each *bygd* or rural community of Norway was somewhat isolated from neighboring communities so that their speech, dress, food customs, artistic and musical traditions and other folkways developed with distinct geographic variations. The immigrants remembered these social connections to ancestral home districts in Norway and wished to perpetuate them through their b*ygdelag* organizations in the United States and Canada.

Ringerike-Drammen Districts Lag invites emigrants and their descendants to join in preserving its cultural heritage in America. Members receive a quartely newsletter and they may use lag resources to trace ancestral roots. The goals of the lag are:
1. To cherish Norway, the land of our ancestors;
2. To discover and preserve knowledge about Buskerud – its arts and music, its people and history;
3. To establish and maintain friendships between Norwegians in lag areas and Americans;
4. To nurture and encourage activities that will benefit and honor R-DD Lag here and in Norway;
5. To provide opportunities to conduct genealogical research and attend classes related to family history.

6. To work with other Norwegian-American organizations.

Modern Norway Has an Ancient Past

The easternmost communities in Buskerud share a glorious history from ancient times. They include:
- .. An exciting archaeological find at Veien, near Hønefoss: a remnant of a 153-foot longhouse, dated from the period of Christ's birth!
- .. King Olav II spent his boyhood in Hole before he died in battle in 1030 and became Norway's patron saint.
- .. Hole was also the home of three other Kings of Norway: Halvdan Svarte, Sigurd Syr, and Harald Hardråde.
- .. The Blue Cobalt Mines (*Blaafarveværk*) of Modum, produced the cobalt that was use to create the blue color in the porcelain of the 1700s and the 1800s.
- .. Lier, home of St. Hallvard, a major producer or fruits and vegetables, is known as the breadbasket of Norway.
- .. Situated on Drammensfjord, Drammen has always been a major industrial port city and leading importer of cars.

R-DD is one of 28 active *bygdelag*. Its annual *stevne* (meeting) is usually in July with six other groups called the 7 Lag Stevne. It publishes a quarterly newsletter, the *BREV*, collects family histories, and owns detailed maps and various resource materials. Our web site, www.fellesraad.com/rdd-home gives more information.

To assist in keeping this rich, cultural heritage alive through membership or tax-deductible gifts, please contact Narv Somdahl, 5100 W. 102 St., Unit 209, Bloomington, Minnesota 55437. Phone 952-831-4409 or e-mail somdahl2@usfamily.net. Membership is currently just $10 per year or $25 for three years.

The port of Drammen today

Romerikslag

Bunad Parade at annual stevne

Romerikslaget i Amerika is a Norwegian-American association whose members have ancestral roots or present-day ties to the area that nearly surrounds Oslo, Norway, called Romerike. The Lag was founded in September 1990 to honor the unique culture of Romerike and to strengthen the bonds with the parishes of our ancestors. Since then we have come together each September or October for our festive annual stevne (gathering) which is held at varying locations in the Midwest. At the stevne, we enjoy a rich combination of presentations, films, music, and traditional foods. The stevne also gives us the opportunity to explore our roots. It is a good place for both beginning and experienced genealogists.

Telelaget

TELEFANEN
Fra telelaget i Norge til telelaget i Amerika
"No ser eg atter slike fjell og dalar"
—Vinje

The first Telemark emigrants left Tinn, Telemark, in 1837. By 1915, 44,000 *Telemarkings* had immigrated to America. A majority of these immigrants became farmers, settling mostly in the Midwest.

After the disunion with Sweden in 1905, there was a rise in patriotic pride among the Norwegians and shortly thereafter, immigrants were uniting to preserve and strengthen their cultural bonds. It was during this time that the *bygdelag* movement began.

The first meeting of Telelaget was held on January 16, 1907, at the Piries Hall in Fargo, North Dakota. There was a tone of urgency in this meeting as already seventy years had passed since the arrival of the first *Telemarkinger*. As Torkel Oftelie, co-founder, expressed it at the first *stevne* on June 25, 1907, "We must see to it that the Telers are not forgotten."

Telelaget began as a national society but later organized into several conveniently located regional groups to accommodate those traveling long distances to attend a *stevne*. In 1911 three state lag were formed: Iowa Telelag, Wisconsin Telelag, and Tinnsjølag in South Dakota. Later the following *lag* were formed: Wisconsin/Bandakslag in 1912, Minneapolis Telelag in 1914, Northwest (North Dakota) Telelaget in 1917, Rocky Mountain *Lag* in Montana in 1919, and finally the Red River Valley Telelag organizing in Climax, Minnesota, in 1928.

Most of the lag did not meet during World War I and many did not reconvene after the war. The larger, more active *lag* continued with the usual vigor until World War II, when activities ceased temporarily and many never reconvened. There were no national Telelag *stevner* between 1939-1948. The Northwest Telelag met in 1949 and convened annually through the 1950s, 1960s, and 1970s, but after the June 1977 *stevne* ceased to exist. The National Telelag made a serious attempt to continue but after 1953 failed to revive enough interest.

In 1979 a group of energetic officers met to revitalize the National Telelag. The first reorganizational meeting was held in Appleton, Minnesota, in June 1980, resulting in a very successful *stevne*. Since that time Telelaget has met for annual *stevner* either as a single lag or with other lag in various locations in the Midwest. During these years Telelaget has published four books, including a hundred-year history, and has maintained a web site. *Telesoga*, started by Torkel Oftelie in 1909, is published biannually. A newsletter, *TeleNews* is distributed several times a year. Also, during this time, Telelaget has sponsored four tours to Telemark, most recently in 2007, and enjoys a close relationship with friends and relatives in Norway.

Torkel Oftelie, co-founder, the first historian, and long-time editor of the *Telesoga* said, "We need to leave an impression. This nation is composed of many different people, like the rainbow with its distinct colors. Let there be a Norwegian color in the American rainbow." Torkel published 53 issues of the *Telesoga,* in which he documented names and stories of the early Telemark immigrants and their settlements. He left a huge impression and continues to be our inspiration.

Above: Telemark Canal
Left: Heddal Stave Church

Learn more about Telemark and the benefits of membership in Telelaget at
http://www.telelaget.com

Toten Lag

Toten Lag serves descendants of immigrants from the Gjøvik, West Toten, and East Toten *kommuner* (municipalities) of Oppland County, Norway, about 60 miles north of Oslo.

The lag was founded in 1910, and from its early focus on maintaining social connections among family and immigrants in North America, the lag's purpose has evolved into a more educational one, centered on providing expert assistance in genealogical research and educational resources, while still offering a unique opportunity to develop friendships with others whose families came from this part of Norway.

Membership privileges include an hour of free genealogical research in our extensive library with the Lag's genealogist, a subscription to our quarterly newsletter, and an invitation to attend the 7-Lag stevne, Toten Lag's annual get-together held in conjunction with six other bydgelags.

Toten was the dwelling place of some of the early Norwegian 'small-kings'. Tradition has it that the Alfstad farm was named after King Alf who lived there. Toten has never been a kingdom in itself, but rather a part of the Hadafylke small-kingdom which included Toten, Hadeland, Land and Romerike.

Harald Hvitbein conquered much of Hedemark, Vestfold and Toten, and died a violent death in Toten about the year 700. Halvdan Svarte defeated Øistein, king of Oplands, about the year 950. Halvdan was victorious in a second battle on the island of Helgøy in Mjøsa according to the saga. To show he was still a friend, Halvdan returned to Øistein half of Hedemark, taking for himself Toten and Land.

In Toten it was that the young ambitious Harald Haarfagre first met the proud Ragna Adilsdatter who gave him the inspiration to gather all Norway into one kingdom. It is said that she herself owned most of Toten, including Eina where she lived. Harald stayed in Opland much of one year and celebrated Christmas there. Before his death King Harald gave Toten to his sons by Snaefred, one of his several wives. The saga then has nothing to say of Toten until Olav Haraldson's time. An Opland king who warred against Olav lived then in Toten. Olav, the victor, traveled around the district to Christianize it about the year 1020.

In 1293 King Haakon Magnusson the elder gave Toten a charter, which included its appointment as a coach station, the beginning of Toten's coach-house business.

In the bloody Seven Years War of 1563-1570, during which the Swedes burned the cathedral at Hamar, Swedish military units traveled throughout Oplands to induce the people to pledge their loyalty to the Swedish King Erik the 14th. Once the Swedes had withdrawn to Aker farm near Hamar, the *bønder* farmers of Toten held their own meeting at which they pledged their allegiance to King Fredrik II of Denmark.

In 1795 Toten's population was 6,245 persons, distributed between 180 full farms and 362 husmannsplasser. At the beginning of the 13th century Stabohagen and Gudrudvolden were military drill fields and maneuver areas. Later Sukkestadsletten, then Fauchaldmoen and, still later, Storumsletten have served that need. Until 1756 Toten was a part of Akershus amt (county) but thereafter was part of Oplandenes amt. Oplandenes was later divided into Kristians amt and Hedemarkens amt, with Toten part of the former. Today, Toten is part of Oppland fylke.

from the 1921 Totenlag Yearbook translated by L. Opsahl

Toten Lag's Officers - 2008
Helen Buche, President
Peter Christianson, Vice President
George Olson, Secretary
Marie Brown, Treasurer
Millie Ardorfer, Genealogist
Donis McCallum, Membership
Karen Christianson, Toten Bulletin Editor
Ruth Christ, Webmaster

Directors
David Bauman   Helen Daniels
Eileen Gulbranson   Karen Mathison

Toten's Bunad (Traditional costume)

Trønderlag

Members of Trønderlag at the Centennial celebrated in Fergus Falls at the Tre Lag Stevne in 2008

Trønderlaget was established in 1908 in Fergus Falls, Minnesota, as an organization of descendants of immigrants from the Trøndelag (middle) region of Norway centered around Trondheim.

The symbol of Trønderlag of America is Nidaros Cathedral, the traditional site of the king's coronation, in Trondheim. The cathedral is said to have been built over the burial site of St. Olav, the Norwegian king who was killed at the Battle of Stiklestad in 1030. Work began on the cathedral around 1070, but the edifice wasn't completed until the beginning of the 14th century. The cathedral was ravaged by fire more than once; a fire in 1708 left only the stone walls intact. A major renovation begun in 1869 is responsible for the way the cathedral looks today.

In the earliest years of the Lag, the stevner (conventions) were well attended and membership reached over 2000. By the mid-1960's, interest in the organization had waned and it was disbanded. The lag was revived at a stevne in Dawson, Minnesota, in 1982. The group responsible for rekindling the Tronder spirit consisted of Agnes Boraas, Floyd and Selma Boraas, Irvin and Anna Kleven, Lowell and Bernice Oellien, Rudy and Bernice Prestholdt, Bervin and Arlene Skjei, Mildred Skurdahl, Ellsworth and Sylvia Smogard, Orvin and Josephine Larson, Selma Torstenson, and Berdeen and Mable Vaala. In 1999, the name was changed to "Trønderlag of America" and a new set of by-laws was approved.

Members enjoy receiving the newsletter, *Trønderlag Nyhete Brev*, three times a year. It includes information about current activities and genealogical and cultural articles that focus on Trønder heritage. An Årbok (yearbook) that includes both lag history and member/ancestor biogaphies was published in 2005 and in 2006. A third volume will be published shortly. An interesting and enjoyable trip to Trønderlag was shared by members in 2005, and another trip is being planned for 2010. Yearly stevner are held in conjunction with Gudbrandsdal Lag and the Nord Hedmark and Hedemarken Lag. These gatherings are held in Minnesota or surrounding states and in communities with strong ties to these areas of Norway. The extensive genealogical library is available to researchers attending each stevne, and its genealogist can assist members with look-ups and guidance throughout the year.

In 2008, these three lags sponsored a research trip to the LDS Genealogy Library in Salt Lake City. A week of classes and research in their facilities was well received. Another trip occurred in early 2009.

The Lag's purpose:

1. To aid in the preservation of Norwegian history, culture and heritage for coming generations by collecting and preparing historical information and data relative to immigration and settlement and to encourage research and writing of family, immigration and settlement histories.

2. To maintain communication and working relationships between the members of Trønderlag and other related organizations with Norwegian Heritage.

3. To develop and maintain a library of resources, such as bygdeboker (farm histories), Norwegian church and government records and other such genealogical information.

4. To maintain and enhance fellowship among the descendants of people from the Trøndelag area of Norway and to maintain a bond between Trønders in North America and Norway.

Norwegian-American Genealogical Center and Naeseth Library

Beginning in January 2007, following a nearly thirty-three year association with the Norwegian-American Museum, the Norwegian-American Genealogical Center and Naeseth Library became a completely independent organization. Chartered as a non-profit in the State of Wisconsin, the NAGC has its own corporate articles, bylaws, board of directors, and membership. The new name reflects its mission as America's foremost institution dedicated to collecting, preserving, and interpreting the resources for Norwegian and Norwegian-American genealogical research. The building and its library in Madison, Wisconsin, still carry the name Naeseth Library, in honor of the Center's founder, Gerhard B. Naeseth, and the Naeseth family's long involvement in the genealogical field.

Since it was established, the center has grown immensely. Experienced staff has helped tens of thousands of individuals—both by mail and in person—uncover their family histories. NAGC's research collection contains a wide range of materials dealing with families on both sides of the Atlantic. With nearly 5,000 reels of microfilmed Norwegian and Norwegian-American church records; Norwegian census records, 1801-1900; nearly 8,000 volumes of printed material such as family and local histories; thousands of pages of church record transcripts; passenger lists; obituaries; card files; topographic maps; and an extensive correspondence collection, the genealogical center has developed a fine research library. Gerhard Naeseth transcribed the names and dates from graves in over 800 cemeteries throughout the Midwest. NAGC's cemetery database, now containing over 325,000 names, is often an excellent source to begin a search. Naeseth especially concentrated his efforts on U. S. records that might list a birthplace, last residence in Norway, parents' names, or year of immigration to America. Some of the commonly used U. S. sources include Norwegian-American church records; vital records; county histories; and census records from 1850 to 1900. Center volunteers have prepared specialized indexes to the Norwegians in the 1900 U. S. census records, which are especially useful. Many years of microfilmed passenger lists and passenger list transcripts are among the Center's collections as well as microfilmed copies of the available emigrant lists for the Norwegian ports. In addition to microfilmed records, the NAGC holds one of the largest collections in the country of Norwegian local history and bygdebøker. The NAGC collection is complimented by the extensive collection of bygdebøker found at the University of Wisconsin – Memorial Library, just a few blocks from the NAGC.

	...alie		Ole Anders...	
	Gurine Amalie		Ole Andersen Bö	
	birth	Anne	Ole Andersen Bö	
	birth	Henry Olaus	Ole Andersen Bö	
.05	birth	John	Ole Andersen Bö	As
09.??	birth	Anders	Ole Andersen Böe	Aslau
8.12.20	birth	Kari	Ole Andersen Borren	Ingebo
50.02.24	birth	Anne Marie	Ole Andersen Borstad	Aslaug
866.10.25	birth	Ingeborg	Ole Andersen Brække	Eli Gjert
868.06.07	birth	Anne Severine	Ole Andersen Brække	Eli Gjerts
869.07.20	birth	Anne Severine	Ole Andersen Brække	Eli Gjerts
861.01.08	birth	Ingeborg	Ole Andersen Brække	Margit K
69.07.08	birth	Ingeborg	Ole Andersen Braekketo	Margit
0.04.02	birth	Margit	Ole Andersen Brækketoen	Thore
06.27	birth	Peroline	Ole Andersen Brakke	Eli
14	birth	Anders	Ole Andersen Bratvold	M
	birth	Julie Mathilde	Ole Andersen Bratvold	
	birth	Maria	Ole Andersen Bratvold	
	Helene		Ole Andersen Brek...	
	ders		Ole Anders...	

Excerpt from the Birth by Parent Name Database

In 2001 the organization established the Gerhard B. Naeseth Chair for Genealogical Research and Publication. In addition to his role as Executive Director of the NAGC, Blaine Hedberg is continuing as the Naeseth Chair Fellow, and has just completed the fifth volume of the series, *Norwegian Immigrants to the United States, A Biographical Directory 1825-1850*. These volumes together constitute one of the most important research and publication projects ever undertaken in support of Norwegian-American genealogy. To help complete this series he has put together some extensive databases documenting vital records of the Norwegians in the United States, especially for the years 1842-1880, including thousands of records from Minnesota.

The NAGC is fortunate to have an excellent and experienced research and support staff. Jerry Paulson, who interacts with so many researchers, is now the Center's director of research. The NAGC is open to the public from 10-5, Monday through Friday, appointments are encouraged. For additional information on our genealogical resources or membership in the NAGC, you may contact the Norwegian American Genealogical Center and Naeseth Library, 415 W. Main Street, Madison, WI 53703-3116. (608) 255-2224 or visit our website, www.nagcnl.org

Acknowledgements

The Norwegian Statehood Pioneer Project offers special thanks to the following:

Members of the Project's steering committee:
    David Gunderson, Fergus Falls   Jan Heusinkveld, Rochester
    Anne Janda, Bloomington   DeLos Olson, Rochester
    David Pfeffer, Maple Grove   Anne Sladky, Walker

Members of the participating organizations who accepted and reviewed Statehood Pioneer applications and helped promote the project and the celebration.

Gillespie's Sporting Goods of Rochester produced the project's Statehood Pioneer Plaques.

Hummingbird Press of Walker produced the Century Certificates and all of the Project's brochures and programs.

Kahler-Marriott Banquet Services, Rochester worked with us in planning and presenting the Norwegian-Minnesotan Sesquicentennial Celebration at the Marriott-Mayo Clinic.

Norwegian Stevner, Inc. provided the insurance umbrella that made the Celebration possible.

Vendors and demonstrators who helped make our Celebration's "Norwegian Marketplace" a success:

Astri, My Astri Publishing	Rosemaling Demonstration
www.astrimyastri.com	*Nordic Designs*
Card Making Demonstration	Rosemaling for Sale
Jo-Anne Larson	*Dean Vigeland*
Chip Carving Demonstration	Scandinavian Marketplace
Darwin & Vangie Krueger	*www.scandinavianmarket.com*
Christmas Ornaments & Mobiles	Toten Lag
The Engwalls of Huson MT	*Helen Buche*
Embroidered Apparel & Home Décor	Uff Da! Gifts
Judy Stevens	*www.uffda1.com*
Minnesota Territorial Pioneers, Inc.	Wood Carving Demonstration
www.mnterritorialpioneers.org	*Don Olson*

        Quilting for Sale
        Carol Vigeland

Read More About It...

If you are interested in learning more about the Norwegian immigrant experience, especially in Minnesota, Dr. Verlyn Anderson suggests the following:

Blegen, Theodore C. *Norwegian Migration to America, volume I: 1825-1860: volume II: The American Transition.* Minneapolis, Minnesota: University of Minnesota Press, 1931, 1940. (A classic of Norwegian immigration history.)

Drache, Hiram M. *The Challenge of the Prairie: Life and Times of Red River Pioneers.* Fargo, North Dakota: North Dakota Institute of Regional Studies, 1970.

Holmquist, June D., editor. *They Chose Minnesota: A Survey of the State's Ethnic Groups,* especially chapter 11, *The Norwegians* by Carlton C. Qualey and Jon A. Gjerde, pages 220-247. St. Paul: Minnesota Historical Society Press, 1981.

Keillor, Steven J. *Shaping Minnesota's Identity.* Lakeville, Minnesota: Pogo Press, 2008.

Lagerquist, L. DeAne. *In America the Men Milk the Cows: Factors of Gender, Ethnicity, and Religion in the Americanization of Norwegian-American Women.* Brooklyn, New York: Carlson Publishing, Inc. 1991.

Lovoll, Odd S. *Norwegians on the Prairie: Ethnicity and Development of the Country Town.* St. Paul: Minnesota Historical Society Press, 2007.

_____. *The Promise of America: A History of the Norwegian-American People,* revised edition, Minneapolis: University of Minnesota Press, 1999. (Dr. Lovoll's extensive 14-page bibliography on pages 351-364 will direct the interested readers to hundreds of additional Norwegian American books and articles.)

_____. *The Promise Fulfilled: A Portrait of Norwegian-Americans Today.* Minneapolis: University of Minnesota Press, 2007.

Muller, Chad. *Spring Grove: Minnesota's First Norwegian Settlement.* Charleston, South Carolina: Arcadia Publishing, 2002.

Nelson, E. Clifford and Eugene L. Fevold. *The Lutheran Church among Norwegian Americans,* 2 volumes, Minneapolis, Minnesota: Augsburg Publishing House, 1960.

Nelson, Marion, editor. *Norwegian Folk Art: The Migration of a Tradition.* New York: Abbeville Press, 1995.

Qualey, Carlton and Jon Gjerde. *Norwegians in Minnesota*. St. Paul: Minnesota Historical Society Press, 2002.

Rolvaag, Ole E. *Giants in the Earth: A Saga of the Prairie*. New York: Harper, 1927.
(The classic Norwegian-American immigrant novel. The story of this immigrant family continues in the following two novels: *Peder Victorious: A Tale of the Pioneers Twenty Years Later* and *Their Fathers' God*.)

A special note: The Norwegian-American Historical Association (NAHA), located at St. Olaf College, Northfield, Minnesota, was established in 1925 at the Centennial of the first Norwegian immigrants' arrival in the United States. NAHA has published nearly a hundred scholarly volumes related to the study of Norwegian immigration and settlement.

And On The Internet...

The editor suggests the following free websites catering specifically to Norwegian and Minnesotan internet surfers:

www.digitalarkivet.no   Census and church records from all over Norway, made available by the National Archives of Norway.

www.norwayheritage.com   Passenger lists, ship information, immigration accounts and general information about the Norwegian immigrant experience.

www.mnhs.org   Minnesota Historical Society website, includes searchable statewide birth and death indices, photo database, maps, place name information, and veterans grave index.

www.glorecords.blm.gov   Database of federal land patents issued between 1820 and 1908. Many land patent records include images of original patent documents.

www.naha.stolaf.edu   Searchable catalog of the holdings of the Norwegian-American Historical Association housed at St. Olaf College in Northfield, Minnesota. Complete transcripts or excerpts of many of their holdings can be accessed on-line.

www.dalbydata.com   A privately developed database that includes 875,000 Minnesota cemetery records, 26,000 Minnesota civil war veterans, plus other information with a special focus on Rice County and selected southern Minnesota areas.

Index of Names

In old Norway, the second name was a patronymic: Andersen/Anderson (son of Anders) or Andersdatter/Andersdotter (daughter of Anders). Throughout the book, the female patronymic uses the abbreviated suffix "-dtr." The third name was more like an address; it was the name of the farm on which the individual lived. When people moved, their third name changed.

For the Norwegians who immigrated to America, the notion of a surname as a family name was unfamiliar. Many used their own or their father's patronymic as their last name, others adopted a Norwegian farm name as their family name. As they adjusted to this new naming convention, some anglicized their Norwegian patronymic or farm name. As a result, Norwegian immigrants and their children might change their last name a number of times before settling on a permanent American surname. It wasn't unusual for parents and children to adopt different last names; in fact, surnames often differed among siblings.

Many of the articles and statehood biographies list only the first names of family members or friends. No assumptions can be made about their surnames, but individuals for whom only a first name is given are indexed by the last name of the biographical subject or parent.

To assist researchers in locating individuals of interest, the complete index is printed in last name order and then repeated in first name order beginning on page 282.

LAST NAME ORDER

Aaberg,Albert Peterson 176
Aaby,Aane 74
Aaby,Aaste 74
Aaby,Anders 52,74
Aaby,Anders Jonsen 74,76
Aaby,Aslak 51,74
Aaby,Aslak Anderson 74-75
Aaby,Gunhild Andersdtr 75
Aaby,Ingeborg 74
Aaby,Ingeborg Georgine Grønsten 50
Aaby,John 51,74
Aaby,Jøran 74
Aaby,Jul 74
Aaby,Nils 74
Aaby,Severin 74
Aabye,Torsten A 72
Aadnes,Peter 70
Aaker,Knud Saavesen 75
Aaker,L K 200
Aaker,Lars Knudson 75
Aakre,Hellek 91
Aamodt,Aslak Knudsen 39
Aamot,Aslak Knudsen 38
Aanderud,Ole T 201
Aanderud,Tine Hanna Bergitta 201
Aanonsen,John 205
Aanundsen,Tor 165
Aanundson,Ole 120
Aarbak,Gunnlaug Hansdtr 176
Aarbak,Julia Hansdtr 176
Aaretun,Knute Olsson 143
Aasen,Berthe Hansdtr 70

Aasen,Ivar 242
Aasnes,Cornelius L 200
Aasnes,Edward Severin 200
Abbott,Christopher 139
Abbott,George 139
Adilsdtr,Ragna 255
Adzlew,Boye Captain 74
Agrimson,Arne 234
Ahlness,Christian 193-198
Ahlness,Halvor 196,197
Ahlness,Tonette N Smebyhagen 197
Akre,Cora Angeline Aslakson 181
Alexandersen,Hilmar 220
Alf,King 255
Alm,Erick Oleson 180
Alm,Hans Oleson 180
Alm,Iver Herman 180
Alm,Johanne Hansdtr 180
Alm,Lisa Martinsdtr 180
Alm,Ole Erickson 180
Alm,Oscar 180
Almaas,Egil 237
Amundson,Anders 148
A-nah-wag-manne,Simon 190
Andersdtr,Astri 95
Andersen,Anne 33
Andersen,Antonette 201
Andersen,Gulbrand 76
Andersen,Hans 38
Andersen,Karl G 235
Andersen,Karoline Henrikke 76
Andersen,Kierstine 76

Andersen,Lars 201
Andersen,Ole 76
Andersen,Ragnhild 33,38
Anderson,Adelle 89
Anderson,Albert 76
Anderson,Anders 76
Anderson,Andrew 178,181
Anderson,Anton Julius 176
Anderson,Brothers 32
Anderson,Bruun 29
Anderson,Edwin 76
Anderson,Elling 75
Anderson,Emelie Dorthea 77
Anderson,Evonne 234
Anderson,Gunarius 76
Anderson,Gust 177
Anderson,Gustav Oscar 77
Anderson,Hans 33,148
Anderson,Henry Alfred 77
Anderson,Ingri 176
Anderson,Isabelle 76
Anderson,Isak 179
Anderson,John 76
Anderson,Joseph 176
Anderson,Karen Christopherson 181
Anderson,Lena 177
Anderson,Lewis 75
Anderson,Martha 76
Anderson,Martha Christopherson 178
Anderson,Martin 196-198
Anderson,Nils 135
Anderson,O W,Dr 39

Anderson,Ola 204,210,212
Anderson,Ole 178
Anderson,Ole P 70
Anderson,Paul 234
Anderson,Susan 76
Anderson,Thor 71
Anderson,Verla 234
Anderson,Verlyn 234,237,241
Anderson,Andrew 75
Anderson,Anne 75
Anderson,Cornelius 75
Anderson,John 75
Anderson,Lewis 75
Anderson,Nels 75
Anderson,Ole 75
Anderson,Susan 75
Anfinnson,Anfinn 220
Anfinnson,Martha 220
Annexstad 186
Appelen,Inger Olsdtr 77
Appelen,Ola Tostensen 77
Appelen,Thorstein Olsen 77
Applen,Albert 78
Applen,Ambjor 77
Applen,Arnold 78
Applen,Carl 78
Applen,Christian 78
Applen,Emma 77
Applen,Fremont 78
Applen,Henry 77
Applen,Inger 77
Applen,Ingman 78
Applen,Johnny 77
Applen,Knut77
Applen,Mabel 78
Applen,Maggie 77
Applen,Nellie 77
Applen,Ola Tostensen 77
Applen,Ole 77,78
Applen,Oline 78
Applen,Otto 77
Applen,Susan 77
Applen,Theodore 78
Applen,Tosten 77
Applen,Tudor 78
Ardorfer,Millie 256
Arntson,Maria 130
Asgaard,J A 235
Aslackson,Kristi 95
Aslaksdtr,Kristi 103
Aslaksdtr,Tone 103
Aslakson,Joseph Edvin 128
Aslakson,Liv 128
Aslakson,Ole 103
Aslakson,Peter S 78
Aslakson,Samuel Olaus 128
Aslakson,Sven 128
Aslakson,Tarje 103
Aslesdtr,Anne 141
Asleson,Ole169-170
Aus,Hulda 236

Aus,Ivar 236
Baardsen,Theodor 200
Babcock,Kendrick Charles 226
Bailey,Betty 234
Bakke,Greta 78
Bakke,Gunhild 78
Bakke,Hallstein Torson 78
Bakke,Hans 28
Bakke,Lena 78
Bakke,Mary 78
Bakke,Nils 78
Bakke,Ola 78
Bakke,Ole 78
Bakke,Peter 78
Bakke,Thor 78
Bakken,Guro 83
Bakken,John O 21
Bakken,Karen Wahl 181
Bakken,Simon 181
Bakkene,Barbro 83
Bakkene,Ingebor Jorgensdtr 83
Bakko,George 57
Bakko,Margit 56,57
Bakko,Ole 56,57
Bakko,Ole Jorgen 56
Bamle,Guri Svenungsdtr 86
Barskor,Amund 165
Bauman,David 256
Bearson,Engebret 91
Bearson,Engebret Bjørnsen Garnaas 122
Beaver,Wallace 49
Bekkerus,Askild T 179
Bekkerus,Theodore 180
Bekkerus,Tone Kleven 179
Bendickson,Caroline 135
Benson,Ben 99
Benson,Carolyn 234
Benson,Gunil 176
Benson,Ida Marie 201
Benson,Ole 89
Benson,Pehr 188
Benson,Roald 201
Benson,Swen 188
Berekvam,Amund 79
Berekvam,Andrew Botoh 79
Berekvam,Anna 79
Berekvam,Bertha 79
Berekvam,Botoh Andrew 79
Berekvam,Botolv Botolvsen 78
Berekvam,Botolv Johannesen 78
Berekvam,Brita 145
Berekvam,Brita Amundsdtr 79
Berekvam,Erik 145
Berekvam,Ingeborg 79
Berekvam,Iver 79
Berekvam,Jens 78,145
Berekvam,Johan 79
Berekvam,Johannes the elder 79
Berekvam,Johannes the younger 79
Berekvam,Karen 79
Berekvam,Kari 145

Berekvam,Martha 79
Berekvam,Ole 79,145
Berekvam,Ole Olsen 145
Berekvam,Randi Olsdtr 66,145
Berekvam,Torstein 78
Berg,Anna Pauline 100
Berg,Jonas Nelsen 38
Berg,Kirstenas 38
Berg,Ole Amundson 28
Berg,Ragnhild 38
Berg,Tollef Amundson 28
Bergan,Christian C 72
Berge,Aanund 178
Berge,Ase Hansdtr 167
Berge,Halvard Magnesen 200
Berge,Henry Louis 200
Berge,Iver Jensson 138
Berge,Thone Olsen 178
Bergetongen,Beret 79,80
Bergetongen,Elsa Marie 80
Bergetongen,Knute 79,80
Bergetongen,Ole 79
Bergetongen,Ragna 80
Bergh,Axel,Pastor 112
Bergh,Kjell 237
Bergkvam,Berekvam family 79
Bergland,Anne Kassenborg 117
Bergland,Betty 234
Bergland,Elsie 96
Bergman,Berekvam family 79
Bergo,Knud 28
Bergquam,Berekvam family 79
Bergrud,John Steingrimsen 71
Bergsundeie,Anna Lee Ellingsdtr 88
Bergsundeie,Berit Ellingsdtr 92
Berkvam,Berekvam family 79
Berland,Aamund 147
Berquist,John 220,231
Bjerke,Karine Christensdtr 178
Bjerkhagen,Anne Amundsdtr 201
Bjerkness,Odell 237
Bjertnes,Elling 71
Bjørkeie,Marte Hansdtr 158
Bjørnsen,Gunder 99
Bjørnson,Hjalmar 236
Bjugan,Darleen 234
Bjugan,Oraine 234
Bleikedammen,Dorthe Amundsdtr 76
Blekstad,Ingri 105
Blexerud,Anna 22
Blexerud,Nels Olsen 20
Blexrud,Christopher 81
Blexrud,Henry S 81
Blexrud,John H 81
Blexrud,Ole L 81
Blexrud,Ole Lewison 80
Blikom,Amund 165
Blixerud,Hans Johann 81
Blixerud,John 81
Blixerud,Knut O 80
Blixerud,Ole Lewison 80

Boe,Harald 90
Boe,Peter Aslagson 178
Boen,Aagot Oysteinsdtr 109
Boen,Aasne Jonsdtr Ingulfsland 109
Bøen,Aase 81
Bøen,Astrid 82
Bøen,Astrid Johnsdtr 188
Bøen,Astrid Jonsdtr 81,82
Bøen,Augusta 82
Bøen,Gunleik Jonsen 81
Bøen,John Østenson 81
Bøen,Jon Gunleikson 81
Bøen,Jon Olsen 81
Bøen,Louis 82
Bøen,Louise 82
Bøen,Nils 82,188
Bøen,Ole Østensen 186,188
Bøen,Ole Østenson 81,82
Bøen,Østen 188
Bøen,Østen Olsen 82
Bøen,Torstein 82
Bøen,Torstein Østensen 81,185,186
Bohn,Arne 33
Bollie,Julia 178
Booth,Walther S 33
Boraas,Agnes 257
Boraas,Floyd 257
Boraas,Selma 257
Bordsen,Mari Aaker 176
Borgesen,Peter Mrs 100
Borjum,Ole 112
Børtnes,Astri Herbrandsdtr 82
Bostwick,Mr 38
Bottelsen,Berekvam family 79
Botten,Hans Johnsen 177
Botten,Julia 179
Botten,Ole 179
Bottolfson,Carl Johan 200
Bottolfson,Mons 200
Bottolson,Berekvam family 79
Bow,Arthur 27
Boyer,Rozalyn 234
Braaten,Erik Erikson 71
Brack,Josephine 236
Braker,Gulbrand Gulbrandsen 118
Brandt,Nils,Rev 1,111,152,158,199-202
Branno,Iver 180
Branno,Olava 180
Bratlien,Peder Jensen 131
Bratsberg,Halvor Tolvssen 176
Brattelid,Ivan 234
Bredesen,Adolf,Pastor 199
Bredeson,John 178
Breidall,Aslak,Mrs 149
Brekke,Ola Froysak 104
Brekke,Ola Nilson 15
Bremer,Fredrika 224
Brenna,Sigri 87
Brink,Donovan 196
Brodin,Robert 234
Brodin,Rosalie 234

Brokken,Aase 82,83
Brokken,Amy 83
Brokken,Isabelle 83
Brokken,John 83
Brokken,Julia 83
Brokken,Ole 83
Brokken,Tallack W 82,83
Brokken,Thaddeus 83
Brokken,Tilda 83
Bronson,Carl 83,84
Bronson,Herbrand 83
Bronson,Ingebor 83,84
Bronson,Ingebor Jorgensdtr 83,84
Bronson,Jorgen 83,84
Bronson,Karine 84
Bronson,Knute 83,84
Bronson,Ole 83,84
Bronson,Ole Herbrandson 83,84
Bronson,Ragnild 83
Brown,Marie 256
Brown,Nettie 150
Bruflat,Erhard 34
Bruflat,Gullick Erhardson 34
Bruns,Amalie 201
Bruns,Carl 201
Bruns,Emma 201
Brunsvold,Stella 237
Brynsaas,Anne Maria Pedersdtr 84
Brynsaas,Gudbrand Pedersen 84
Brynsaas,Hanna 84
Brynsaas,Johanna 84
Brynsaas,Kristin 84
Brynsaas,Martha 84
Brynsaas,Martin 84
Brynsaas,Peter 84
Brynsaas,Torger 84
Buchanan,James President 101
Buche,Helen 234,256,261
Buche,John 234
Buckeye,George J 86
Buckeye,Jon 85
Buckeye,Jon Halvorson 85
Bue,Hagbart 236
Bukkøy,Abraham 86
Bukkøy,Aleth 85
Bukkøy,Anne 85
Bukkøy,Cornelia 85
Bukkøy,Else 85,86
Bukkøy,Gunhild 85
Bukkøy,Jorgen 86
Bukkøy,Jørgen Jonsson 85
Bukkøy,Sigrid 85
Bukkøy,Susanne 86
Bukoi,J J 85
Bunnell,L H,Dr 139
Burket,Tom 234
Burtness,Halvor 169
Buxengard family 119
Byholt,Sveinung 12
Carlson family 187
Carlson,Jean M 234

Carlson,Lorraine 236
Carlson,Pehr 188
Carstensen,Peder 84,148
Caspersen,H C 236
Christ,Ruth 256
Christensen,Christan 236
Christiansen,F Melius 226
Christiansen,Paul G 237
Christianson,Andrew,Mrs 108
Christianson,Karen 256
Christianson,Peter 256
Christophersdtr,Helge 99
Christophersen,Carrie 84
Christopherson,Anna Olsen 179
Christopherson,Mary 157
Christopherson,Michael 179
Christopherson,Rachel 179
Christopherson,Rachel Hanson 180
Christopherson,Ragnhild Hansdtr 179
Christopherson,Ragnhild Hanson 180
Ciulen,Liviu 237
Clausen,C ,Pastor 7-9,32,33,51,
 151,156,167
Cleveland,Delores 234,241
Connolly,A P 190
Crooks,Mary 190
Custer,George Armstrong General 191
Dahl,Borghild 236
Dahl,Christian Johannessen 200
Dahl,Even Ellertson 27
Dahl,Ingeborg 50
Dahl,Liv 237
Dahl,Ole 50
Dahl,Syver 69
Dahle,Anna 101
Dahle,Engebor Nelson 101
Dahle,Hans 101
Dahle,John,Pastor 112
Dahlen,Anna Christina 176
Dalager,Elaine 234
Dale,Anders 102
Dale,Aslak 102
Dale,Dordi Gunnarsdtr 102,103
Dale,Gunnar 102
Dalen,Erhard Bruflat family 34
Dalen,Gullik A 33
Dalland,Sverre 236
Daly,William J 191
Daniels,Asa,Dr 187
Daniels,Helen 256
Daniels,John K 236
Danielson,Anne Helena 142
Danielson,Anton 142
Danielson,Daniel 142
Danielson,Hans 142
Danielson,Henry 142
Danielson,Lena 142
Danielson,Maren 142
Danielson,Nels 142
Danielson,Ragnild 142
Delano,Ann 234

Demeron,James 29
Dietrichson,J W C,Pastor 199
Dittmann,Reidar 237
Dodge,A man by the name of 139
Doely,Thorvald,Mrs 184
Dole,Tone 96
Dølehus,Ole Evensen 118
Dompendal,Birgith Kittelsdtr 149
Dompendal,Birgith Olsdtr 149
Dompendal,Kittel Kittelson 149
Donne,John 67
Dunham,Christian Mrs 98
Dunham,Jens Christian 77
Dutton,Mr 45
Duvick,Einar 237
Dybsand,Anton 180
Dyreson,Christen 176
Earl,Henry,Mrs 100
Eberhard,Governor 113
Ecklund,Johannes 188
Edstrom,Christine Ohnstad 138
Een,Andrea 237
Eggan,Benjamin Ross 236
Eggen,J Muller Mrs 151
Eggen,Kristen 149
Eich,Karen Kjerstine 49,94
Eidal,Jon Gundersen 72
Eide,Roy 237
Eielson,Elling 95
Eikhom,Aleth J Bukkøy 177
Eikhom,Halvor H 177
Eikhom,Halvor Halvorsson 85
Einong,Anne 167
Einong,Aslaug Jacobsdtr 167,168
Einong,John 168
Eischens,Paula 234
Eischens,Richard 234
Elandson,Christ 179
Elandson,Karen Enden 179
Elemoen,Jens 28
Elemoen,Thore Jensen 28
Ellefson,Ingeborg 86
Ellefson,John 86
Ellertson,Even 27
Ellestad,Sven 29
Ellingboe family 90
Ellingsen,Elling 28
Ellingsen,Hans 28
Ellingsen,Peder 84
Ellingson,Jåråm 94
Ellingson,Jon 76
Ellingson, Ole 48
Ellis,Anna 86
Ellis,Edwin 86
Ellis,Eldraine 86
Ellis,Guri 86
Ellis,Ingeborg Torgrimsdtr 86
Ellis,Johanna 86
Ellis,John 86
Ellis,Julia 86
Ellis,Ole 86

Ellis,Taurine 86
Ellis,Tone 86
Ellis,Yank 86
Ellson,Ellef 179
Ellson,Rena Hansdtr 179
Elstad,Anna Hogstad 177
Elstad,John H 178
Emmons,George 87
Emmons,Helge Gunderson 71
Emmons,Henry Gundersen 86
Emmons,Lewis 87
Enderud,Bjorn 99
Enderud,Embrick Benson 28
Enderud,Engebret Bensen 122
Enderud,Engebret Gundersen Benson 71
Endru,Bjorn 99
Endru,Helge 99
Engar,Elling Pedersen 71
Engebriktsen,Knud 119
Engell,Christian 29
Engelsgaard,Duane 248
Engelsgaard,Lorraine 248
Engen,Hans 70
Engen,Kristoffer Hansen 70
Engen,Margit 105
Engen,Ole 105
Engen,Ole Nilson 87,88
Engen,Sigri 16,105
Enger,Aase Ellingsdtr 176
Enger,Aase Sofie 88
Enger,Anne Ellingsdtr 176
Enger,Edward 88
Enger,Edward Ellingson 181
Enger,Elling 176
Enger,Elling Jr 88
Enger,Elling Pedersen 88
Enger,Elling Peterson Sr 88
Enger,Hannah Larson 181
Enger,Hjalmer 88
Enger,Ingrid Østensdtr 176
Enger,Lina 88
Enger,Peder Ellingsen 88,176
Enger,Peter 88
Enger,William Delander 181
Englestad,Karen 108
Engwalls,The 261
Erickson,Anna Johnson 181
Erickson,Bella 89
Erickson,Bent 196
Erickson,Carl 89
Erickson,Carl Edvardsen 180
Erickson,Charles Edvardsen 180
Erickson,Erick 176
Erickson,Erik 89
Erickson,Halvor 9,10,88,89,147
Erickson,Hans 89
Erickson,Inga 176
Erickson,John 148
Erickson,John 89,148
Erickson,John Olaf Ibsen 123,180
Erickson,Kari Overland 88

Erickson,Lena 89
Erickson,Michael 181
Erickson,Ole 89
Erickson,Steinar 89,148
Erickson,Tilla 89
Erik XIV,King 256
Eriksen,Eli Pedersdtr 177
Eriksen,Erik 201
Eriksen,Gustava 201
Eriksen,Martin 177
Erikson,Hans 55
Erikson,Kristi Iversdtr 55
Erlien,Ellef 241
Ernst,Luetta Earl 100
Erstad,Andreas Nilsen 69
Erstad,Nils 69
Eskar,Martin 101
Espeland,Aslaug Boen 179
Espeland,Osten 179
Estensen,Austin 82
Estensen,John 81
Estensen,Ole 81,200
Esterby,Andy 68
Esterby,Edith 68
Esterby,Gary 149
Esternsen,John 81
Evans,Arne 169,17
Evans,Eyvind 237
Evans,Gunhild Tostensdtr 82
Evensen,Aad 176
Evensen,Adeline 177
Evenson,Anders 71
Evenson,Borre 196
Evenson,Teman 89
Evenson,Thore 201
Faar,Barbro Torgersdtr 91
Faar,Torger Erikson 91
Farseth,Pauline 236
Felland,Esther 77,78
Felland,Ingeborg 78
Felland,Torger Tollefsen 78
Fendalsveit Halvor 204,212
Fetten,Anne G 77
Findreng,Andrew 101
Findreng,Anton 101
Findreng,Dorothy 101
Findreng,Emma 101
Findreng,Helma 101
Findreng,Olice 101
Findreng,Targe Gunnarson 100
Findreng,Theodore 101
Findreng,Tilde 101
Findreng,Tollef 101
Finhart,Kari 33
Finhart,Kari Hovda 33
Finhart,Kari,Mrs Ole 34
Finhart,Ole 31,32,33,34,38
Finney,Nat 236
Finseth,Anders 56
Finseth,Anne 56
Finseth,Herbrand 56

Finseth,Knut 56
Finseth,Knut Knudson 56
Finseth,Margit 56
Finseth,Margit Olsdtr 56
Finseth,Ole 56
Fjågesund,Gunnar Hanson 126
Fjågesund,Ingebjørg 126
Fjågesund,Olav 126
Fjeldhaug,Andrew Anderson 197
Flåberg,Ragnhild Johnsdtr 171
Fladager,Maurice 29
Fladager,Mons 29
Flandrau,Charles F 137
Flata,Ola Hellekson 50
Flateland,Talleff 206
Flaten,Aslesen 71
Flaten,Fingal Aslesen 28
Flaten,Ove 89
Flatland,Targe 100
Flatten,Targe Olson 176
Flattum,Martha 147
Fleming,William 28
Flesvig,Jorgen 193-196
Flom,Andrew Larsen 134
Florand,Martha 38,39
Florand,Ole 38
Florand,Ole,Mrs 39
Florand,Ragnhild 38
Forlie,Ambjor Olsdtr 77
Forlie,Gunhild Johnsdtr 77
Fosli,Even Olson 201
Fosli,Fingar 201
Fosli,Ole 201
Foss,Albert 184
Foss,Andrew Brynildsen 176,182-184
Foss,Anna Sophia 184
Foss,Barbara 184
Foss,Brady 184
Foss,Edward 184
Foss,Germa 184
Foss,Harriet 241
Foss,Johana 184
Foss,Julia 184
Foss,Leander 184
Foss,Martha 184
Foss,Mons K 182-184
Foss,Peter 184
Foss,Syver K 60
Fougner,Gustaf Pedersen 200
Fraagot,Anne Olsdtr 72
Fraagot,Beret Olsdtr 72
Fraagot,Guttorm Olson 72
Franson,Hans 10
Fredrickson,Andreas 46,48
Fredrickson,Andrew 46
Fredrik II,King 256
Fredriksen,Rev 34
Fried,Karen 234
Friestad,Lars Johannesen 124
Fritioff,Peter M 188
Froland,Martha 38

Froland,Ole 38
Froland,Ragnhild 38
Frygne,Aase Olsdtr 135
Frygne,Esther Olsdtr 135
Fuhr,Anna Theodora 235
Gaarder,Kari 131
Gaarder,Ole Knudsen 131
Gaarder,Oline Karine O Jørondlien 69
Gaardersæteren,Kari Nilsdtr 70
Gaare,John O 179
Gaaseberg,Marit Christophersdtr 161
Gaasedelen,Boye 89
Gaasedelen,Endre 89
Gaasedelen,Ingebjorg 89
Gaasedelen,Jon 89
Gaasedelen,Knut 89,90
Gaasedelen,Lars 89
Gaasedelen,Nils 89,90
Gaasedelen,Ole 89,90
Gaasedelen,Ole Knudsen 89
Gaasedelen,Ove 89
Gaasedelen,Peder Edward 90
Gaasedelen,Pete 90
Gaasedelen,Rangdi 90
Gaasedelen,Sara 90
Gaasedelen,Sissel 90
Gaasedelen,Torkel 89
Gamlemoen,Hans 33
Gamlemoen,Hans Andersen 38
Gamlemoen,Ragnhild 33
Gamme,Helga 220,231,234
Gamme,Ole 220,231,234,241
Garland,Samuel 116
Garnaas,Bjorn 91
Garnaas,Bjorn Olesen Sata 90
Garnaas,Engebret 90
Garnaas,Guri 90
Garnaas,Hans 90
Garnaas,Kari 90
Garnaas,Kittel O 178
Garnaas,Mari 90
Garnaas,Nils 90
Garnaas,Ole 90
Garnaas,Ole B 91
Garnaas,Sidsel Nilsdtr 91
Garvig,Erik Knudson 91
Garvik,Barbro Torgersdtr 92
Garvik,Erick 91
Garvik,Erik Knudson 91,92
Garvik,Gjertine 91
Garvik,Ingebret 91
Garvik,Knut 91
Garvik,Marit 91
Garvik,Nils 91
Garvik,Torger 91
Gautefall,Gunhild Halvo 172
Gilbertson,Andreas 95
Gilbertson,Berit Ellingsdtr 93
Gilbertson,Betsey 103
Gilbertson,Birgit Reiersdtr 103
Gilbertson,Elmer 103

Gilbertson,G E 93
Gilbertson,Geline 95
Gilbertson,Gilbert 92,103,118
Gilbertson,Gilbert Elias G 92,93
Gilbertson,Gulbrand 95
Gilbertson,Guri Peterson 176
Gilbertson,Harold 103
Gilbertson,Inga Augusta G 92,93
Gilbertson,Julia Peterson 176
Gilbertson,Knud 28
Gilbertson,Laura Emilie G 93
Gilbertson,Laura Galine G 93
Gilbertson,Lena G 92,93
Gilbertson,Martin G 92,93
Gilbertson,Norma 234,241
Gilbertson,Ole 176
Gilbertson,Ole Gulbrandsen 103
Gilbertson,Teman 28,29
Gillespie,Douglas 234
Gimmestad,Lars 246
Gire,Joran Christiansdtr 154
Gjeitsta,Aanon 207,210
Gjeitsta,Aanon Gunderson 203
Gjeitsta,Andreas 203
Gjeitsta,Gunder 203
Gjeitsta,Gustav 203
Gjeitsta,John 203
Gjeitsta,Thone 203
Gjermstad,Anne Louise 105
Gjermstad,Eline Mathea 105
Gjermstad,Ingebret 105
Gjermstad,Maren 105
Gjermstad,Rikka 105
Gjermstad,Soren Larsen 105,171
Gjermstad,Syverin 105
Gjermundsdtr,Joren Gjermundsdtr 128
Gjermundsdtr,Jorend 125,130
Gjermundson,Ingeborg 178
Gjermundson,Ole 178
Gjervert,Adam 220
Gjesme,Thora 112
Golberg,Tollef 51
Golden,Andrina Swanson 180
Golden,H I 180
Golden,Harold N 180
Goodrich,Halvor 10
Goodwin,Ashley 219,220,234
Gourley,Deb Nelson 221,230,234
Gøystdal,Aase Halvorsdtr 190
Graff,Caroline 180
Granskov,Clemens 235
Grant,General 92
Grant,President 53
Grant,Gunhild Grangard 104
Grasdalen,Ingeborg 94
Grasdalen,Julia 120
Grasdalen,Lars Olson 93,94
Grasdalen,Ole 94
Grasdalen,Ole Olson 93
Grefseng,Edward Pedersen 200
Griffin,Berthe Bjerke 177

Griffin,Ole Gullickson 177
Griffin,Oliver Gullickson 177
Grønsten,Anne Marie 49,52,94
Grønsten,Hans Johnsen 49.53.94
Grønsten,Henry 53
Grønsten,Ingeborg 94
Grønsten,James 94
Grønsten,Jens 53
Grønsten,John 49,51,94
Grønsten,Johnny 94
Grønsten,Nels 94
Grønsten,Nils 53
Grønsten,Norman 53
Grønvoll,Sissel Eivindsdtr 110
Groshong,Mary 147
Grover,Aase 95
Grover,Alexander 95,96,180
Grover,Christian 95,96,176
Grover,Clarence 180
Grover,Edward 95,96,176
Grover,Elise 95,96
Grover,Elmer T J 180
Grover,Geline Kassenborg
    94,95,96,178,219
Grover,Gustav 95,96
Grover,Kristi 103
Grover,Mary 95,96
Grover,Ole 94,95,103
Grover,Otto 96,179
Grover,Pauline Kroshus 180
Grover,Tarje,103
Grover,Tarje Aslaksen 94-96,178,219
Grover,Terry 95
Grover,Tilde 96
Grover,Tone 95,103
Groves,Inga Kinstad 53
Groves,Inga Kinstad Grønsten 94
Grovum,Aaste Nilsdtr 74
Grovum,Nils Olavson 74
Gubberud,Anders 20,21,25,96
Gubberud,Anders Øestensen 18
Gubberud,Anna 25,96
Gubberud,Anna Josephine 96
Gubberud,Christine 23,96
Gubberud,Edwin 96
Gubberud,Elias 96
Gubberud family 19
Gubberud,Gulbrand 18,21-25,96-97
Gubberud,Gulbrand Anderson 20
Gubberud,Gunhild 18,20,96
Gubberud,Gustav 96
Gubberud,Inger 96
Gubberud,Inger Olava 23
Gubberud,Johan 96
Gubberud,Julia 96
Gubberud,Kjersti 20.21.25
Gubberud,Kjersti Gudbrandsdtr 18
Gubberud,Malene 25,97
Gubberud,Martin 18,20
Gubberud,Øesten 18,20,22,25,96
Gubberud,Ole 96

Gubberud,Olia 18,20,21
Gubberud,Sigrid 96
Gubberud,Sophia 96
Gubberud,Sorine 96
Gubberud,Thina 25,96
Gubrud,Gust 171
Gudbrandsdtr,Kjersti 96
Gudbrandsdtr,Mari 84
Gulbrandsen,Elmer 97
Gulbrandsen,Gilbert 97
Gulbrandsen,Gulbrand 92,95,118
Gulbrandsen,Harold 97
Gulbrandsen,Ole 97
Gulbrandsgutten,Ole Olsen 71
Gulbrandson,Anders 77
Gulbrandson,Esther 236
Gulbrandson,Fredericka 77
Gulbranson,Eileen 256
Gullickson,Albert,Mrs 100
Gullickson,Anna 98
Gullickson,Gilbert 98
Gullickson,Hans 131
Gullickson,John 98
Gullickson,Knud 98
Gullickson,Margaret 98
Gullickson,Marit Knudsdtr 98
Gullickson,Martha O 131
Gulliksdtr,Anne 198
Gulmon,Aaste Tovsdtr 98
Gulmon,Alice 98
Gulmon,Anne Lawrence 99
Gulmon,Egel E 98
Gulmon,Egil G 98
Gulmon,Even 98
Gulmon,Gunnild 98
Gulmon,Ragnild 98
Gulmon,Sarah 98
Gulmon,Thomas 98
Gundersen,Anna 200
Gundersen,Asmund 99
Gundersen,Helge Gundersen 86
Gundersen,Olaus 176
Gunderson,Alma 100
Gunderson,Amanda Theodora 100
Gunderson,Andrew 101
Gunderson,Anna Maria 99
Gunderson,Anna Pauline Berg 100
Gunderson,Anne 101
Gunderson,Asborg Olsen Våsjo 181
Gunderson,Benhard 101
Gunderson,Bernt 99
Gunderson,Bjorgov 99
Gunderson,Bjørn 71,99,219
Gunderson,Charles 150
Gunderson,Christopher 99
Gunderson,Dagne 101
Gunderson,David 234,241,261
Gunderson,Emma Melvina 100
Gunderson,Engebrit 99
Gunderson,George 99
Gunderson,George Oscar 100

Gunderson,Gjert 99
Gunderson,Gunder 99,100
Gunderson,Gunhild 99
Gunderson,Gunil 176
Gunderson,Hannah 93
Gunderson,Harriet 99
Gunderson,Helen 99
Gunderson,Helene 99
Gunderson,Helge 219
Gunderson,Helge Christophersdtr 99
Gunderson,Henry Edwin 100
Gunderson,Hilda 100
Gunderson,Isabel 150
Gunderson,Joann 234
Gunderson,John Arnt 100
Gunderson,Kari 99
Gunderson,Knudt 179
Gunderson,Knut 99
Gunderson,Martin Theodore O 99,100
Gunderson,Ole 99,101
Gunderson,Osmund 99,100
Gunderson,Sigrid 99
Gunderson,Sophie 99
Gunderson,Targe 100,101
Gunderson,Tollef 101
Gunderson,Viola Rosalind 100
Gunderson,William Leonard 100
Gunhus,Lillian 123
Gunvalson,Ingeborg Tostensdtr 82
Guttormsdtr,Gunhild 82
Guttormsen,Jens 82
Guttormson,Guttorm 101,102
Guttormson,John 102
Guttormson,Liv 102
Guttormson,Ole 102
Haakaanes,Thurine 121
Haakenes,Ole Gjermundson 121
Haakenstad,Halvor Pedersen 179
Haakenstad,Sophia A Olson 179
Haarfarge,Harald 255
Haegtvedt,Mari Larsdtr 75
Haga,Truls 28,71
Hagen,Andrew 127
Hagen,Bersvend 178
Hagen,Dick 234
Hagen,Hans J 180
Hagen,Johanna Engen 181
Hagen,Karen 178,234
Hagen,Mary Annette Uggen 169
Hagen,Ole Jacobson,Rev 181
Hagen,Torsten Eriksen 71
Haglund,Chris 234
Halbert,Mary 234
Halbert,Ralph 234
Hallum,Nickolene Gustine 120
Hallvard,Saint 251
Halstenrud,Lars Reiersen 28,71
Halvorsdtr,Asborg 75
Halvorsdtr,Aslaug 75
Halvorsen,Alfred B 129
Halvorseth,Ole Ingebretson 155

Halvorseth,Sønnøv Olsdtr 155
Halvorson,Anna 103
Halvorson,Anne Knutsdtr 85
Halvorson,Asle 29
Halvorson,Belle 177
Halvorson,Bergine 103
Halvorson,Ellen 102
Halvorson,Ellev 102,103
Halvorson,Halvor 85
Halvorson,Helene 103
Halvorson,Ingeborg Halvorsdtr 177
Halvorson,Jon 85
Halvorson,Tilla 103
Halvorson,Helge 102,103
Hammel,Clyde Mrs 100
Hammer,Ellen 236
Hansdtr,Anne 140
Hansen,Andrew 200
Hansen,Anne Elise 200
Hansen,Carl G O 222,223,227
Hansen,Lars 70
Hansen,Lena 159
Hansen,Louis 200
Hansen,Wilhelm Marius 201
Hansen,William 201
Hansing,Ross 234
Hansing,Virginia 234
Hanson, Anton 48
Hanson,Christian 46,48
Hanson,Clara 181
Hanson, Hans 48
Hanson,Helen 177
Hanson,Hilda Myhre 236
Hanson,Johan 180,181
Hanson, Karen 48
Hanson,Karn Alitta 180,181
Hanson,Mari Sanden 177
Hanson,Michael 150
Hanson,Mikkel 150
Hanson,Ole 40,44,48,177
Hanson,Paul Hjelm 207
Harald,King 255
Haraldsen,Olav 255
Haraldson,Aase Aslaksdtr 103,104
Haraldson,Alex 104
Haraldson,Anne 104
Haraldson,Aslak 104
Haraldson,Edvin 104
Haraldson,Edwin 104
Haraldson,Harald 104
Haraldson,Kristian 104
Haraldson,Olav 255
Haraldson,Torjus 103,104
Hardråde,Harald 251
Hardy,Ole 93
Hårsaker,Johan Nilsen 76
Harstad,Aanond 83
Harstad,Margit 177
Harstad,Samuel 83
Harstad,Tollef A 177
Hasleberg,Aase Torgrimsdtr 98

Hasledalen,Ole 29
Hasleiet,Charles 177
Hasleiet,Gunhild Nielsdtr 177
Hasleiet,Kittel 177
Hasleiet,Thor Kittilson 177
Hatlestad,Anne Katrine 131
Hatling,Jakob Peter Olsen 200
Haug,Liv Knudsdtr 118
Hauge,Hans Nielsen 228
Hauge,Lawrence Olav 237
Haugen,Anders Peterson 20
Haugen,Christian 48
Haugen,Goro 71
Haugen,Ingeborg 69
Haugen,Inger 116
Haugen,Kittel Kittelson 150
Haugen, Kolbjorn 48
Hauger,Gustaf B 180
Haugerstuen,Anne 38
Haugerstuen,Jorand 39
Haugerstuen,Knut Nilsen 38
Haugerstuen,Nils Nelsen 38
Haugo,Hazel Syverson 181
Haugo,John 234
Haugo,Sharon 221,234
Haugrud,Edward 83
Haugsrudie,Anders Øestensen 18
Haugsrudie,Kjersti Gudbrandsdtr 18
Hauke,Eric Bjarne 235
Haukebo,G K 242
Hayes,Rutherford B 57
Hedberg,Blaine 260
Hefte,Bergit 15,104
Hefte,Guri 16,105
Hefte,Ingeborg 104,105
Hefte,Inger 15,16,105
Hefte,Ingri 104
Hefte,Ingrid 104,105
Hefte,Knut Nilsen 104
Hefte,Margit 105
Hefte,Nels 105
Hefte,Nils 15,104
Hefte,Olaus 105
Hefte,Ole Gofa 15-17,104,105
Hefte,Ole Lame 15,104
Hefte,Ole N 105
Hefte,Ole Oleson Storre 15-17,104,105
Hefte,Sarah 105
Hefte,Theoline 105
Hegedahl,Ole 236
Hegg,Colonel 196
Hegg,Even 167
Hegg,Gustav O 200
Heggtveit,Knud Olsen 190
Hegland,Alfred 181
Hegland,Allette 181
Hegland,Anton 181
Hegland,George Carlton 181
Hegland,Kristi 165
Hegland,Lina Berge 181
Hegland,Lorentz 181

Hegland,Mikkel 165
Hegland,Mikkel Tarjeisen 176
Hegland,Preston Martin 236
Hegland,Sissel Amundsdtr 176
Hegland,Sophie 181
Hegland,Thor Mikkelsen 165,181
Hegland,Torger 165
Hegvik,Ellevine 134
Hehaka Sapa,Black Elk 191
He-i-ya-win,Mah-kah-ta 190
Helgedalen,Anne Hanson 179
Helgedalen,Nels 179
Helgerudsveom,Engebret Johannesen 158
Helgesdtr,Kristi 86
Helle,Anna Hellicksdtr 196
Hendrickson,Nels 29
Hendrickson,Sandra 221,233,234
Hermansdtr,Borgil 122
Hertsgaard,Oscar 235
Hestenes,M J 245
Heusinkveld,Jan 234,241,261
Hilde,Ragnhild Gulbrandsdtr 97,103
Hillman,Robert 29
Hinkley,William 28
Hjamdal,Aaste Anundsdtr 126
Hjamdal,Anund Erikson 114,126
Hjamdal,Liv Olavsdtr 114,126
Hjamdal,Taran Anundsdtr 114
Hjermstad,Albert Louis 106
Hjermstad,Anne Marie 105
Hjermstad,Bergithe Gundersdtr Homme 105,106
Hjermstad, Bernt 105,106
Hjermstad,Betsey 105
Hjermstad,Edward 105
Hjermstad,Emma Bertine 106
Hjermstad,Gunder 105
Hjermstad,Lars Sorenson 105,106
Hjermstad,Olaus 106
Hjermstad,Ragnhild Caroline 106
Hjermstad,Soren 105
Hobe,Engereth 235
Hobe,Johanne A 235
Hoegh,Charles 29
Hoejesen,Ole 77
Hoelstad,Kjell 219,220,234
Hoelstad,Orpha 234
Hoen,Mette 124
Høgset,Helge Olsdtr 122
Hogstad,Anna Martha Melhus 177
Hogstad,Clara 181
Hogstad,Johanna Marie Olsen 179
Hogstad,John O 177
Hogstad,John Peder 177
Hogstad,Josephine 181
Hogstad,Lena 177
Hogstad,Ole Pedersen 177
Hogstad,Oline 177
Hogstad,Peder O 178
Hoime,Even 28

Høiset,Ole Torkelsen 122
Holand,Hjalmer Rued 150,155,172,224
Hole,Johan C 180
Holm,Christan 235
Holman,Kirsten 108
Holmquist,Inger Johnson 187,188
Holtan,Aline Svenungsdtr 106
Holtan,Andrew 106
Holtan,Anna Maria Pedersdtr Rygh 106,107
Holtan,Anne Maria 106
Holtan,Aslaug Svenungsdtr 106
Holtan,Charley 106
Holtan,Christina 106
Holtan,Gunhild Veum 106
Holtan,Gunnil 106
Holtan,Hans Hanson 106,107
Holtan,Hans Jr 106
Holtan,Henry 106
Holtan,Hulda 106
Holtan,John 106
Holtan,Louise 106
Holtan,Mary 106
Holtan,Peder 106
Holtan,Samuel 106
Holtan,Sophia J Moslet 106.107
Holte,Kari Mikkelsdtr 121
Holum,Amund Erickson 79
Holum,Anna Torsdtr 79
Homme,Bergithe 171
Homme,Bergithe Gundersdtr 105
Hopkins,W H 139
Horn,Barbara 234
Horsager,Johan Nilsen 76
Housker,Bartha 109
Hovda,Arne 38
Hovda,Engebret 38
Hovda,Guri 38
Hovda,Hermand 38
Hovda,Kari 32,34,38
Hovda,Ole 38
Hovda,Ole Olsen 38
Hovda,Syver 31
Hovda,Syver 38
Hoverstad,T A 225
Hovland,Anna Knudsdtr 142,143
Hovland,Peter August 236
Humble,Anne Cathrine Jensdtr 107
Humble,Ingeborg Marie 107
Humble,John 108
Humble,Karen 107
Humble,Lars Jr 107,108
Humble,Lars Larsen Sr 107,108
Humble,Marthea 107
Humphrey,E W 235
Huset,Anna 108
Huset,Anne Kirstine 108
Huset,Carl 108
Huset,Caroline 108
Huset,Christen 108
Huset,Halvor Olsen 108

Huset,Karen 108
Huset,Kirsten Christensdtr 108
Huset,Lauritz 108
Huset,Lettie 108
Huset,Lisbeth Olsdtr 108
Huset,Maren 108
Huset,Maria 108
Huset,Ole O 108
Huset,Peder 39
Hustvedt,Lloyd,Dr 67
Hutchinson,E R 207,209
Hvattum,Harold 241
Hvitbein,Harald 255
Ike,Knud 173,174
Ike,Martha 173,174
Ile,Mari Mikkelsdtr 171
Ingebrethsdtr,Kari 99
Ingemunsdtr,Bergit 201
Ingulfsland,Aagot 109,133
Ingulfsland,Aase 109
Ingulfsland,Aase Herbjornsdtr 133
Ingulfsland,Ausne 109
Ingulfsland,Bergit 109
Ingulfsland,Herbjorn 133
Ingulfsland,Herbjorn Nilssen 109
Ingulfsland,Nils 109
Ingulfsland,Oystein 109
Innvik,Erling 236
Isaksdtr,Marthe 84
Iverson,Andreas C 110
Iverson,Anna Axelsdtr 116
Iverson,Axel 48,115
Iverson,Bartha Housker 110
Iverson,Ben 110
Iverson,Børre 110
Iverson,Christian 109,110
Iverson,Christopher 110
Iverson,Daniel C 110
Iverson,Edward 110
Iverson,Ellen Marie 110
Iverson,Ingeborg 40
Iverson,Ingeborg 48,115,116
Iverson,Karoline 116
Iverson,Martha 41
Iverson,Martha Axelsdtr 115,116
Iverson,Ole 29
Iverson,Synneva 48
Iverson,Synneva Axelsdtr 116
Iverson,Syvert C 110
Jackson,Gunhild 176
Jackson,Gunhild Sigurdsdtr 160
Jackson,Jacob 160,176
Jackson,Oakey 235
Jacobsen,Hans M 236
Jacobsen,Nettie 57
Jacobsen,John 133,176
Jacobson,Kent A 103
Jacobson,Olaf 103
Jacobson,Ole 178
Jacobson,Olena Peterson 178
Jacobson,Walter E 237

Jahn,Nicolai 89
Jahr,Carl Mrs 149
Jakobsen,Abraham,Pastor 200
James,Jesse 169
Janda,Anne 234,241,261
Janda,Mark 234
Jellum,Berit 110
Jellum,Cecilia Eivindsdtr 110,111
Jellum,Even 110,111
Jellum,Ingebor 110
Jellum,Ingeborg Johnsdtr 110
Jellum,Jacob Johnson 110,111
Jellum,John 110
Jellum,Jon Jacobsen 110
Jellum,Kari 110
Jellum,Kristina 110
Jellum,Sissel 110
Jellum,Steingrim N 71
Jensen,Aaste 74
Jensen,Fred 198
Jensen,Lars 89
Jensen,Pastor 34,51
Jensen,Thore,Dr 29
Jenson,Bertha 101
Jenson,Michael 176
Jenswold,John R 227
Jergenson,Berger 180
Jergenson,Ingri 180
Jobraaten,Ole Simonson 33
Joerg,Frank,Mrs 184
Johannsen,Mallin 180
Johannssen,Mikkel 180
Johansen,Hans 70
Johnsdtr,Anne Marie 124
Johnsen,Amos 201
Johnsen,Aslak 200
Johnsen,Kari 201
Johnsen,Knudt 200
Johnsen,Marta Oline 200
Johnsen,Norman,Pastor 200
Johnsen,Thomas,Pastor 200
Johnson,Amund 38
Johnson,Andrew 69,181
Johnson,Anna 112
Johnson,Anne 38
Johnson,Anne Jakobsdtr 178
Johnson,Audrey H 234
Johnson,Barbra 39
Johnson,Christiane 124
Johnson,Christiane Martine 122
Johnson,Darlene 234
Johnson,Deborah M 234
Johnson,Elen Anna 178
Johnson,Ella 93
Johnson,Embrick 112
Johnson,Erik 187,188
Johnson,Fritz 181
Johnson,George 85,86
Johnson,Gertrude 112,113
Johnson,Gotthard 112
Johnson,Hans Grønsten 51

Johnson,Helge 39
Johnson,Inga 112
Johnson,Ingeborg 112
Johnson,Ingeborg Wahl 179,180
Johnson,Jacob 110
Johnson,James J 237
Johnson,Jane 112,113
Johnson,Jenny Alvilde 236
Johnson,John 52,53,112,133,188
Johnson,John R 70
Johnson,Johnny 53
Johnson,Jon 111
Johnson,Joran 188
Johnson,Julia 39
Johnson,Ludvig 179
Johnson,Mabel Isabel 181
Johnson,Maren Sohlgaard 112
Johnson,Maria 112
Johnson,Mark 234
Johnson,Mary 133,181,237
Johnson,Nils 53,178
Johnson,Olaus 178
Johnson,Ole 112
Johnson,Peder 111,179,180
Johnson,Pehr 187,188
Johnson,Peter 112
Johnson,Thomas 112,130
Johnson,Thomas Lommen,Pastor
  111,112
Johnson,Thora 112
Johnson,Tosten 112,130
Johnson,Tosten Lommen 112,113
Johnsrud,Harlan 114,234
Johnsrud,Harold 114
Johnsrud,Hovel Peterson 113,114
Johnsrud,Lars 114
Johnsrud,Maren 113
Johnsrud,Martha 114
Johnsrud,Mary Larsdtr 113,114
Johnsrud,Olaus 114
Johnsrud,Peter 114
Johnsrud,Sandy 234
Johnsrud,Theoline 114
Jones family 43
Jonsdtr,Berit 110
Jonsdtr Randi, 174
Jonsen,Sigurd 159
Jøntvet,Anne Halvorsdtr 108
Jørandlien,Karen Knudsdtr 131,132
Jorbraaten,Ole Simonson 33,38
Jordahl,Clara Bertina 181
Jordalen-Giljarhus,Anna Strksdtr 136
Jordgrav,Amelia Helene 115
Jordgrav,Andreas 115
Jordgrav,Carl 115
Jordgrav,Christian 115
Jordgrav,Clara 115
Jordgrav,Ellen Marie Kittelsdtr 114
Jordgrav,Gustav Julius 115
Jordgrav,Kari Kittelsdtr 114
Jordgrav,Karina Margret 115

Jordgrav,Kittel 115
Jordgrav,Kittel Olavson 114
Jordgrav,Lena 115
Jordgrav,Marget Karine 115
Jordgrav,Mary 115
Jordgrav,Michael 114
Jordgrav,Mikkel Kittelson 114,115,219
Jordgrav,Ole 115
Jordgrav,Taran Anundsdtr 115,219
Jorgens,Ole 33,38
Jorgensen,Herman 236
Jorssjoen,Oline 179
Jorstad,Lois A 234
Josiassen,Carl Anders 201
Josiassen,Johan Theodor 201
Julsen,Ole 38
Juve,Anne Kassenborg 117
Juve,Gjermund Jonsson 85
Juve,Gunhild 121
Juvrud,Anna 48
Juvrud,Inger 48
Juvrud,Martha 48,168
Juvrud,Martha Axelsdtr 116
Juvrud,Ole 42-45,48,168
Juvrud,Ole Mrs 44
Juvrud,Ole O 40
Juvrud,Ole Olsen 41,115,116
Juvrud,Oline 44,48,116,168,169
Juvrud,Serena 48
Juvrud,Thomas 48
Kaarstad,Gietru Nilsdtr 91
Kanten,Anne Gulbrandsdtr 177
Kanten,Iver Halvorsen 177
Kapperud,Erik Gudbrandsen 70
Kartvedt,Mikal 237
Kassenborg,A G 116
Kassenborg,Andreas G 178
Kassenborg,Andreas Gulbrandsen
  116-118
Kassenborg,Anne Karine 117
Kassenborg,Anne Marie 117
Kassenborg,Astri Andersdtr
  92,116,118,219
Kassenborg,Edward Ludwig 117
Kassenborg,Eliza A 117
Kassenborg,Geline Andrine 118
Kassenborg,Gilbert Olaus 117
Kassenborg,Gulbrand 219
Kassenborg,Gulbrand G 116
Kassenborg,Gulbrand Gulbrandsen 118
Kassenborg,Ingeborg Maline 117
Kassenborg,Julia Ogena 117
Kassenborg,Mina August 117
Kassenborg,Tone 121
Kassenborg,Tone Kragnes 178
Kassenborg,Gilbert 118
Kieland,Elling 28
Kieland,Elling Knutsen 71
Kieland,Haakon 29
Kieland,Knud Knudsen 71
Kieland,Knud Knudson 28

Kiil,Anders Nielsen 86
Kilane,Mary Thorvildsdtr 92
Kildahl,J N,Pastor 67
Kilen,Tone Olsdtr 146
Kinneberg,Glenn 119,234
Kinneberg,Ingeborg Oldsdtr 104
Kinneberg,Ingrid 15
Kinneberg,Ivar Pederson 119
Kinneberg,Iver 87
Kinneberg,Nels 119
Kinneberg,Nelvin 119
Kinneberg,Ola Iversen 104
Kittelsdtr,Ingebor 161
Kittelsdtr,Torgen 161
Kittelson,Bertha Bustul 178
Kittelson,Christopher 161
Kittelson,Hans 178
Kittelson,Ole 71
Kittelson,Tosten 161
Kittilsland,Ole Tollefsrud 26
Kittleson,Mamie 167
Kjos,Anne Karine Tostensdtr 99
Kjøsven,Anders Eriksen 200
Klastolen,Amund Johnson 38
Klastolen,Anne 38
Klastolen,Halvor Olsen 38
Klastolen,Johanne 38
Klastolen,Kjersti 38
Kleiv,Kari Steinarsdtr 110
Kleivstaul,Ingeborg Johannesdtr 74,76
Klemetsrud,Maren Gjertsdtr 99
Kleppo,Aasne Olsdtr 150
Kleppo,Mrs 151
Kleppo,Ole Drengson 150
Kleppo,Thrond 150
Kleven,Anna 257
Kleven,Irvin 257
Klovstadeie,Kirstie Olsdtr 140
Klovstadeie,Stephen 140
Knatvold,Anne 100
Knudsdtr,Helga 190
Knudsen,Carl Emil 200
Knudsen,Estelle H 237
Knudsen,Knud 82,201
Knudsen,Maria 201
Knudsen,Ole 190
Knudsen,Saave 75
Knudsen,Tolv 124
Knudson,Barbro 92
Knudson,Erik 92
Knudson,K A 48
Knudson,Mikkel 136
Knutsen,Lars 75
Knutson,Andreas 181
Knutson,Anna 181
Knutson,Arne 180
Knutson,Gjertrud 180
Knutson,Ole 119,120
Kodalen,Gunhild Larsdtr 99
Koll,Leo 235
Kolsrud,Ole Knudssen 179

272

Kopperud,Dorthe Larsdtr 200
Kopseng,Kristoffer Olsen 99
Kopsengeie,Eivind 110
Koren V,Pastor 14,129,152,166
Korsdalen,Ole Hanson 40,41,116
Korssjoen,Bernt P 179
Korssjoen,Marit O 179
Kragnes,A O 121,219
Kragnes,Aanund 120,121,178
Kragnes,Alvin 120
Kragnes,Anna 220
Kragnes,Anne 121
Kragnes,Bernhard 120
Kragnes,Caroline 120
Kragnes,Clarence 120
Kragnes,Gilbert 120
Kragnes,Gunhild 121
Kragnes,Isabelle 120
Kragnes,Kari 116,120
Kragnes,Luther 120
Kragnes,Ole 120,220
Kragnes,Ole Aanundson 121
Kragnes,Ole Anundson 116
Kragnes,Ole Emanuel 120
Kragnes,Oliver 120
Kragnes,Tone 116,117,121
Kragness,Anna 101
Kragness,Levi 101
Kragness,Sarah 101
Kragness,Thone 101
Kråkenes,Aanund Olesen 120
Kråkenes,Thone 101
Kringstad,Orlyn A 237
Krintolen,Gro Jørundsdtr 85
Kristensen, Botolv 174
Kristofersdtr,Synneva 201
Krogstrum,Carolina 159
Krohn,Fredrik 235
Kroshus,Albert 180
Kroshus,Anders 28
Kroshus,Anders Pederson 121,220
Kroshus,Fred 122
Kroshus,Halvor Anderson 179
Kroshus,John Anderson 122
Kroshus,Kjersti 179
Kroshus,Pauline 96
Kroshus,T A,Mrs 184
Krosshaug,Gunhild 122
Krosshaug,Gunhild Syversdtr 91
Krosshaug,Herman 122
Krosshaug,Sjur Hermansen 122
Krosshaug,Syver Hermannsen 122
Krueger,Allen 234
Krueger,Darwin 261
Krueger,Joyce 234
Krueger,Vangie 230,261
Krydshoug,Herman Nielsen 122
Kuecker,Evelith 221,234
Kuecker,Evy 248
Kulberg,Malene 179
Kulberg,Ole P 179

Kuross,Frances 236
Kvaale,Anders Ellingson 75
Kvaale,Torkel 89
Kvam,Karen Olsdtr 90
Kvanbekk,Ragnild Knudsdtr 98
Kvernodden,Anna T 124
Kvernodden,Annie 123
Kvernodden,Inga Amelia Nelson 179
Kvernodden,Inger T 124
Kvernodden,Jenny 123
Kvernodden,John T 124
Kvernodden,Mabel 123
Kvernodden,Martina 123
Kvernodden,Nels N T 124
Kvernodden,Nels Nelson 122
Kvernodden,Nels Tolvsen 122,124
Kvernodden,Ole T 124
Kvernodden,Tina 123
Kvernodden,Tolef T 124
Kvernodden,Tolif T 124
Lade,Johannes 103
Langejoen,Getrude Jordet 180
Langejoen,Peder 180
Langeland,Knut 9
Langeman,Amund 224
Langeman,Ingeborg Levorsdtr 224
Langemo,Jørgen,Mrs 149
Langhei,Ole O 179
Larsdtr,Berit 119
Larsen,Amund B 200
Larsen,Anders 177
Larsen,Anna Marie Wahl 179
Larsen,Anne Louise 171,172
Larsen,Bergithe Homme 172
Larsen,Christina 171,172
Larsen,Eline Mathea 171
Larsen,Ellen 172
Larsen,Gulbrand 107
Larsen,Gunder 171
Larsen,Hans 179
Larsen,Ingebret 171
Larsen,Kjersti I Vethammer 172
Larsen,Kristoffer 107
Larsen,Lars 171,172
Larsen,Lewis Olai 200
Larsen,Maren 171
Larsen,Ole 107
Larsen,Olavus 107
Larsen,Rebecca 172
Larsen,Rikka 171,172
Larsen,Soren 171
Larsen,Syverin 171
Larson,Brita Ohnstad 137
Larson,Christi 86
Larson,Christopher 171
Larson,Enoch 124,125,248
Larson,Erik 178
Larson family 187
Larson,J 188
Larson,Jo 261
Larson,Josephine 178,257

Larson,Karen Hanson 177
Larson,Karen Mathea H Melbyeie 125
Larson,Kjersti 86
Larson,LeRoy 221,233
Larson,Martin 181
Larson,Mathea Ellson 181
Larson,Orvin 257
Larson,Pastor 47
Larson,Tolline Johnson 178
Laumann,Theodora 160
Lavrantson,Aslak 98
Lawrence,Anne 98
Lee,Anna Johannesdtr 127
Lee,Anne 125
Lee,Aslak 95,103
Lee,Belle A 102
Lee,Berge 178
Lee,Berit Jonsdtr Lommen 125,126
Lee,Botolv 127
Lee,General 92
Lee,Hans Gunnarson 126
Lee,Ingeborg 102,120
Lee,Johannes Botolvsen Ytre 127
Lee,John 125
Lee, John J 174 Lee,Jorend 125
Lee,Knud 125
Lee,Mary 127
Lee,Ole 125
Lee,Olina Anderson 178
Lee,Raymond 235
Leimbach,Marian 234
Leirol,Knud Knudsen 89
Lennon,Joseph 182
Lewison,Ole 80,81
Lewiston family 201
Lia,Aaste Anundsdtr 219
Lia,Albert 126
Lia,Dorthia 127
Lia,Gunder Andreas 127
Lia,Gunder Andrias 126
Lia,Gunnil Annette 127
Lia,Hans Gunnarson 126,127,219
Lia,Hans Magnus 127
Lia,Ingebjørg 126
Lia,Karen Kristine 126
Lia,Lena 126
Lia,Ole 126
Libæk,Anders 71
Lie,Aaste Anundsdtr Hjamdal 127
Lie,Anna 127
Lie,Anna Johannesdtr 127
Lie,Botolv 127
Lie,Christina 127
Lie,Ellen 128
Lie,Johannes 127
Lie,Johannes Botolvson 127
Lie,Karine 127
Lie,Knud 125
Lie,Peroline 127
Lie,Randi 127
Liebe,Clare 234

Liebe,Larry 234
Lien,Kristi Olavsdtr 94,95
Lillejord,Signe Fossum 236
Lincoln,Abraham,President 52,190
Lindelien,Amund 33,39
Lindelien,Beret 38
Lindelien,Beret Knudsdtr 39
Lindelien,Engebret 33
Lindelien,Gulik 39
Lindelien,Gunhild 39
Lindelien,John Amundsen 39
Lindelien,Marit 38
Lindelien,Marit Johnson 33
Lindelien,Ole 39
Lindelien,Thora 39
Linder,Breanna 234
Linder,Jessica 234
Linder,Kim 234
Linder,Sammy Jo 234
Loe,Jerdine Eikeland 180
Loe,John O 180
Lofthus,Grandma 137
Lofthus,Ole 59
Lofthus,Svend 59
Loftness,Oline 146
Lommen,Aagot L Olson 129
Lommen,Andrew 130
Lommen,Anton 129
Lommen,Belle 130
Lommen,Christan 130
Lommen,Edward 129
Lommen,Elizabeth 130
Lommen,George 130
Lommen,Gjermund 129
Lommen,Gjermund Johnson 128
Lommen,Gjermund L Johnson 129
Lommen,Ingeborg 128,130
Lommen,Johanna 129
Lommen,John 28,129,130
Lommen,Jon Anfinson 111,125,128,130
Lommen,Jon Johnson 129
Lommen,Jorend 111,129,130
Lommen,Jorgen 130
Lommen,Kristofer,Big 128,129
Lommen,Marit 128-130
Lommen,Martin 129
Lommen,Ole 129,130
Lommen,Peder 129
Lommen,Peder Johnson 130
Lommen,Peter 129
Lommen,Peter Johnson 28
Lommen,Sigrid 128,130
Lommen,Thomas 129
Lommen,Tosten 129,130
Lone,Margaret 150
Lone,Margit 150
Lønnegrav,Knut 220
Lønnegrav,Sigrid 220
Lostegaard,Barbo 119
Lovoll,Odd,Dr 220,222,231
Lund,Joel A 234

Lund,Peter 123
Lund,Peter Foss 124
Lundby,Anders Larsen 130,131
Lundby,Anne 130
Lundby,Birthe 130
Lundby,Hans 130,131
Lundby,Inge 130,131
Lundby,Ingeborg 131
Lundby,J Andreas 131
Lundby,Johan Andreas 131
Lundby,Lars 130
Lundby,Laura 130
Lundby,Marte 130,131
Lundby,Ole 130
Lundby,Ole Anderson 131
Lunde,Amund 20-22
Lunde,Andreas 69
Lunde,Anne Andersdtr 124
Lunde,Carl A 132
Lunde,Caroline 132
Lunde,Christian P 69
Lunde,Christian Peterson 131,132
Lunde,Edwin 132
Lunde family 19
Lunde,Johannes Stenersen 131
Lunde,Josephine 132
Lunde,Matilda 132
Lunde,Nils 39
Lunde,Ole 39
Lunde,Sigrid 20,21
Lunde,William 132
Luther,Martin 53
Lybeck,Anders A 38
Lybeck,Hans Johansen 70
Lybeck,Johan Hansen 70
Lybeck,Kari 38
Lybeck,Signe 38
Maarem,Ole 133
Magelson,Christian 12
Magelson,Nils 12
Magnuson,Richard C 237
Magnusson,Haakon,King 255
Mah-za-koo-te-manne,Little Paul 190
Manheim,Egel Eivindson 98
Marthaler,Jean 234
Martin,Janet 220,232
Martin,Ole 177
Martinson,Johannes 178
Martinson,Karine Bjerke 178
Mathison,Karen 256
McCallum,Donis 256
McCormick,Robert 28
McCusick,Nils 224
Meland,Halvor 48
Melbostad,Anders Pederson 132
Melbostad,Carrie 132
Melbostad,Edward 132
Melbostad,Emma 132
Melbostad,Lars 132
Melbostad,Martha 132
Melbostad,Peter 132

Melbostad,Sigrid E 133
Melbostad,Sigrid Lynne 133
Melbostad,Siri 132
Melbostad,Siri Ellingsdtr 133
Melby,Elsie M 237
Melbyeie,Karen Mathea Hansdtr 124
Melgaard,Andrew 236
Melhus,Anne Marie 138
Melhus,Ingeborg Torsteinsdtr 78
Merten,Sharon 234
Metzger,Michelle 85
Meyer,David 234
Meyer,Sandra 234
Meyers,Ernest Mrs 149
Mickelsen,Marie 179
Mickelsen,Mathias 179
Midgarden,Ole 204,206,210-212
Midje,Martha Sjursdtr 174
Mikkelsdtr,Kari 120
Mikkelsdtr,Kjersti 87
Mikkelson,Ole 149
Milevandet,Marit Halvorsdtr 38
Miller,Elsie 234
Miller,Margaret 237
Miller,Marlene 234
Miller,Ole 196
Mills,Mr 45
Minne,Nels 236
Mo,Ole 201
Mo,Ole Olsen 201
Moe,Anne Marie 117
Moe,John 180
Moe,Mary Olesdtr 180
Moen,Elen 32,38
Moen,Gisle 94
Moen,Ingeborg Torgrimsdtr 86
Moen,Nils 33
Moen,Nils Syversen 32,38
Moen,Ragnhild Gisledtr 93,94
Moen,Thone 86
Moen,Torgrim 86
Mohn,Anders 50
Mokastad,Maria 81
Molee,John 167
Molsather,Lawrence 236
Molstad,Ole Gudmundsen 201
Monker,Claus C 216
Moore,Henry Mrs 32,34
Morben,Pamela 234
Morck,Conrad Deitlef 180,237,238
Morem,Aase Herbjørnsdtr 133
Morem,Austin 133
Morem,Gustie 133
Morem,Henry 133
Morem,Ingeborg 133
Morem,John 133
Morem,Ole 133
Mork,Einar Torgerson 179
Mork,Marte P Vollum 179
Mork,Torger Erickson 179
Morken,Mina Kassenborg 117

Morken,Thone 101
Morken,Torgrim 120
Mortensen,B E 237
Moslet,Sophia J 106
Muhle,Tarjei 204-207,210,212
Muller,Ingvald 29
Munch,P A 225
Munkhaugen,Ellen Lovise 146
Mutta,Anne 177
Mutta,Halvor 177
Muus,Pastor 48,51
Myhre,Kjell 241
Myrah,Gulbrand Nielsen 28
Myrah,Hans Nielsen 28
Myran,Gitta Eline 123
Myre,Nils 87
Myrhagen,Beta 147
Myrstuen,Geir Arne 241
N Tveiten,Anne Knutsdtr 165
Næse,Dorthea 134
Næse,Gjertrud Iversdtr 134
Næse,Iver 134
Næse,Ole Pedersen 134
Naeseth,Gerhard B 199,259
Naeseth,Hagan O 123
Næss,Hans 241
Narumshagen,Johannes Martinson 178
Narvesen,Haakon 71
Narveson,Haaken 28
Narvestad,Carl 237
Nedre Rindal,Cari 152
Nedre Rindal,Peder 152
Neggen,Even Gulliksen 72
Nelson,Alex 135
Nelson,Alfred Dewey 123
Nelson,Anders Kiil family 86
Nelson,Anna 135
Nelson,Annie 123
Nelson,Bertine 135
Nelson,C C 186
Nelson,Carl 180,188
Nelson,Caroline 135
Nelson,Char 234
Nelson,Edwin Nels 123
Nelson,Emma 123,135
Nelson,Evar 135
Nelson,Gottfried 84
Nelson,Guro 3
Nelson,Henry 135
Nelson,Herbjorn Ingulfsland 109
Nelson,Inga Amelia 123
Nelson,Ivar 135
Nelson,Iver Jr 135
Nelson,Jens 197,198
Nelson,Jon 76
Nelson,Joseph 68
Nelson,Jul 135
Nelson,Julia 135
Nelson,Julius 135
Nelson,Karlen 84
Nelson,Knud 135

Nelson,Knut 207
Nelson,Knute 227
Nelson,Mabel 123
Nelson,Martha 135
Nelson,Mary Laurense 123
Nelson,May 123
Nelson,N H,Mrs 184
Nelson,Nellie 198
Nelson,Nels Ekabot 135
Nelson,Nicholas 135
Nelson,Nils 135
Nelson,Nils Andreas 123
Nelson,Nora Louise 123
Nelson,O N 112
Nelson,Olava 135
Nelson,Petra Finsand 180
Nelson,Randi Otterness 68
Nelson,Sarah 135
Nelson,Sarah Neutsen 135
Nelson,Suzann 220,232
Nelson,Sylvan 156
Nelson,Thomas 135
Nelson,Thorild K 84,85
Nereson,Gunder 186
Nerhaugen,Andreas 69
Nerhaugen,Erik Johansen 69
Nerhaugen,Mari Syversdtr 69
Nerisdtr,Torbjor 159
Nerol,Kari 60
Nerol,Paul 60
Ness,Annette 89
Ness,Arnold 234
Nielsdtr,Inger 124
Nielson,Ingeborg 26
Niklasen,Hulda 96
Nilsen,Daniel 141
Nilsen,Gulbrand 149
Nilsen,Ingeborg 69
Nilsen,Jens 146
Nilsen,John 201
Nilsen,Knudt 201
Nilsen,Knut 38
Nilsen,Lars 200
Nilsen,Mathias Schmidt 29
Nilsen,Nils 201,224
Nilsen,Paul 201
Nilsen,Sina 201
Nilsen,Siri 201
Nilsen-Smebyhagen,Jens 197
Nissen,Voke 123
Nøbben,Tosten Larsen Ursdalen 82
Noem,Anne Pedersdtr 176
Noem,Petter Johnson 176
Nord Strand,Knud Bendixsen 135,136
Nord Strand,Ragnild Olsdtr 136
Nordlie,Elaine 219-221,232,234
Nordlie,Kjell 221,234
Nordskoug,Kari Olsdtr 163
Norland,Ralph 234
Norman,Albertina 136
Norman,Anna 136

Norman,Brynild 136
Norman,Christina 136
Norman,Christine Lofthus 136
Norman,David 234
Norman,Dick 234
Norman,Gloria 234
Norman,Kaye 234
Norman,Nels O 136
Norman,Ole 136
Norman,Ole N 136,137
Norskog,Evelyn 101
Nubgaard,Sidsel Nilsdtr 90
Nusvig,Aase Aslaksdtr 103
Nybro,Sigri 124
Nycklemoe,Henry 235
Ober,Joseph 23
Oddsen,Lars 66
Oddsen,Marta 66
Oddsen,Marte Knudsdtr 174
Odegaard,Halvor 56,57
Ødegaard,Liv P Valtvedt 176
Ødegaard,Sven Aslakson 176
Oellien,Bernice 257
Oellien,Lowell 257
Oestensen,Anders 96
Oftelie,Torkel 12,13,253,254
Ohnstad,Adolph 138
Ohnstad,Botolv 137
Ohnstad,Clarence 138
Ohnstad,Ingeborg 137
Ohnstad,Johanna 138
Ohnstad,Johannes Olsen 137
Ohnstad,Jon 137
Ohnstad,Joseph 138
Ohnstad,Kristine Olsdtr 137
Ohnstad,Marta 137
Ohnstad,Martha Ottum 138
Ohnstad,Ole 137
Ohnstad,Ole Andreas 137
Ohnstad,Peter Andreas 138
Ohnstad,Raymond 138
Ohnstad,Rensa 138
Ohnstad,Robert 138
Ohnstad,Rognald Johnson 137,138
Ohnstad,Tosten 138
Øino,Guttorm Guttormsen 118
Øistein, King of Oplands 255
Oium,Kasperinde Erickson 129
Okasås,O 220
Okland,Engel 181
Olav,Saint 257
Olav II,King 251
Oleson,Albert 138
Oleson,Amelia 139
Oleson,Andrew 138,139
Oleson,Anna 139
Oleson,Anne 140
Oleson,Anund 138
Oleson,Bear 91
Oleson,Bertha 138
Oleson,Caroline 139

Oleson,Christine 140
Oleson,Edna Madelia 139
Oleson,Eliza 139
Oleson,Hans 140
Oleson,Hattie 139
Oleson,Johanna 138
Oleson,Karl 140
Oleson,Margarette Stephensdtr 140
Oleson,Martha 138,139
Oleson,Mary Edna 139
Oleson,Ole 136,138,140
Oleson,Stephen 140
Oleson,Thore 140
Olness,Eliza Kassenborg 117
Olsdtr,Berte Marie 148
Olsdtr,Margit 201
Olsen,Aasulf 179
Olsen,Amund 178
Olsen,Astri 235
Olsen,Bertha Jennison 178
Olsen,Finbo 181
Olsen,Gulbrand 97,103
Olsen,Halvor 141
Olsen,Johannes 201
Olsen,Martha 176
Olsen,Martin 201
Olsen,Mathias 176
Olsen,Ole 115,181
Olsen,Ole Gunnerius 201
Olsen,Ole Kornelius 201
Olsen,Oline Christophersen 177
Olsen,Osalf 179
Olsen,Peter 177
Olsen,Susanna Jambakkmyra 179
Olsen,Torjus 159
Olson,Aagot L 128
Olson,Amelia 75
Olson,Andrew 138
Olson,Anna 83,140
Olson,Caroline 75,140
Olson,Christine 140
Olson,DeLos 220,234,241,261
Olson,Don 230,261
Olson,Dorothea Fuglehaug 176
Olson,Elise Andrea Grover 178
Olson,Emil B 112
Olson,Gary 219,231,247
Olson,George 140,256
Olson,Gilbert 76
Olson,Gilbert Monserud 176
Olson,Gulbrand 76
Olson,Gulleck 116
Olson,Gunlek 48
Olson,Isabella 140
Olson,John 181
Olson,Karen 234
Olson,Kate 178
Olson,Larry 68
Olson,Lewis 140
Olson,Louis 96
Olson,Lovise 140

Olson,Martha 76
Olson,Martin 101
Olson,Morgan 240
Olson,Ole P 196
Olson,Olia 177
Olson,Olina 75
Olson,Oline 83
Olson,Oline Olsdtr 181
Olson,Oliver 140
Olson,Peter 176,178
Olson,Peter,Mrs 177
Olson,preacher 47
Olson,Sigvald 178
Olson,Thor 177
Olson,Viggo 101
Olson,Wayne 101
Olson,William 140
Olson,William Jr 140
Omland,Jøran Aanesdtr 74
Ommelsæteren,Haldor Olsen 70
Ommelstadsæteren,Christian 69,157
Ommelstadsæteren,Halvor 157
Ommelstadsæteren,Ingeborg 152,157
Ommelstadsæteren,Ingeborg Olsdtr 69
Ommelstadsæteren,Isabel 152
Ommelstadsæteren,Johannes Olsen 69,157
Ommelstadsæteren,Lars 157
Ommelstadsæteren,Ole 157
Ommelstadsæteren,Ole Larsen Skogstad 157
Ommelstadsæteren,Tosten 157
Omsrud,Kari 141
Omsrud,Thord 141
Onsgard,Nels 29
Opheim,Embrick Knudsen 28
Oppegaard,Engebret 48
Opsahl,L 256
Opsal,Nels Danielson 141
Opsal,Ragnhild Halvorsdtr Røste 141
Opsal,Rasmus Rasmusson 177
Orton,Albert George 181
Orton,Anna 143
Orton,August Ludvig 176,181
Orton,C K 143
Orton,Carl Edward 143
Orton,Clara Alice Janette 142
Orton,Clark Walter 142
Orton,Cornelia 143
Orton,Cornelius K 143
Orton,Cornelius Knute 142
Orton,Dwight Wesley 143
Orton,Knute Ole 142,143
Orton,Mary Adella 142
Orton,Nell 142,143
Orton,Ole 143
Osmundsdtr,Metta 124
Ostensdtr,Ingrid 88
Østensdtr,Ingeri 92
Osterud,Lars 131
Other Day,John 190

Otternes,Guttorm 173
Otternes,Ingeborg Guttormsdtr 173
Otternes,Jens 173
Otternes,Jens Olsen 173
Otternes,Mari 173
Otternes,Martha 173
Otternes,Ole Olsen Skjerdal 173
Otterness,Anders 145
Otterness,Anders Oddsen 145,174
Otterness,Anna 144,174
Otterness,Anna Jensine 145
Otterness,Anne 67
Otterness,Ben 66
Otterness,Benjamin 67
Otterness,Benjamin Sivert 145
Otterness,Carl Edward 146
Otterness,E L 66,68
Otterness,Eddie 66,67
Otterness,Eddie E 145
Otterness,Edward 144,178
Otterness,Edward G 144
Otterness,Ellen 66,67
Otterness,Ellen Martini 145
Otterness,Erik 144
Otterness,Gurina E 146
Otterness,Guttorm Pederson 145
Otterness,Guttorm Pederson 144,145
Otterness,Ingeborg 66-68,144,174
Otterness,Ingeborg Pedersdtr 127
Otterness,Ingeborg Rebekke 145
Otterness,Irvina Petrina 146
Otterness,Jensine 66,145
Otterness,Johanne 144
Otterness,Knut 145
Otterness,Knute 174
Otterness,Lars 66,67,144,174
Otterness,Lars Larsen 145
Otterness,Lars Oddsen 145
Otterness,Lars Olaus 145
Otterness,Lawrence 66,67
Otterness,Lawrence Oliver 145
Otterness,Marta 145
Otterness,Marta Knutsdtr 145
Otterness,Marta Larsdtr 144,145
Otterness,Nels 144
Otterness,Odd 66-68,144-146
Otterness,Peder 144
Otterness,Petrine Olsdtr 138
Otterness,Randi 66,145,146
Otterness,William 67
Ottum,Martha 138
Ottun,Anna 146
Ottun,Berent 146
Ottun,Berta 146
Ottun,Caroline 146
Ottun,Elgerine 146
Ottun,Ellen 146
Ottun,Guro 146
Ottun,Inger 146
Ottun,Jacob 146
Ottun,Jens 146

Ottun,Julius 146
Ottun,Marianna 146
Ottun,Nels Jensen 146
Ottun,Peder 146
Ottun,Petrine 146
Ottun,Susan 146
Ottun,Susanna 146
Ouren,Jens 196,197
Ouren,John 196,198
Overbo,Anne Olsdtr 106
Overbo,Einar 106
Overland,Anne 146
Overland,Britt 146
Overland,Elias 147
Overland,Erick 88
Overland,Frans 147
Overland,Gunil 146
Overland,Gunil Franson Rue 148
Overland,Guro 146
Overland,Ingeborg Ulsness 88
Overland,Johannes 9,10,147
Overland,Johannes Olson 146,147
Overland,John 147
Overland,Kari 9,88,89,146
Overland,Knud 146
Overland,Knut 10
Overland,Olav 12
Overland,Olav Knutsen 146
Overland,Ole 9,10,88,146,147,148
Overland,Steinar 10,146
Overland,Thea 89,148
Overland,Tone 9,147
Overland,Tone Olsdtr Kilen 147
Øvestad,Christen Anderson 155
Oxnaberg,Anna 39
Oxnaberg,Torgeir 39
Øy,Anne Jørundsdtr 85
Oygarden,Aase Ellevsdtr Enger 88
Øygarden,Margit Mikkelsdtr 114
Padilla,Donald 237
Painter,William,Pastor 89
Paulsen,Marthe Andersen 177
Paulsen,Nils 201
Paulsen,Ole 177
Paulsen,Tilde Petrine Vaage 181
Paulsen,Truls 28,29
Paulson,Arthur 234
Paulson,Benhart Martin 180
Paulson,Helen Hansdtr 70
Paulson,Jerry 260
Paulson,Ole 70
Pedersdtr,Ragnhild 201
Pedersen,Anna Bertine 134
Pedersen,Anna Dortia 134
Pedersen,Anne 148
Pedersen,Anne Larsdtr 148
Pedersen,Berta Serine 176
Pedersen,Birthe 148
Pedersen,Christian 148
Pedersen,Iver 134
Pedersen,Johan Andrias 134

Pedersen,Johanne 134,148
Pedersen,Josephine 134
Pedersen,Kristine Maline 134
Pedersen,L O 216
Pedersen,Mari Sørensdtr 148
Pedersen,Oliver 134
Pedersen,Peder 134
Pedersen,Søren 148
Pennes,Peder Svensen 200
Pennes,Samuel Andreas 200
Peterson,Alfred 84
Peterson,Alice 84
Peterson,Andrew P 133
Peterson,Anna 84
Peterson,Annie 84
Peterson,Bernt 178
Peterson,Clara 84
Peterson,Emma 84
Peterson,Enge 178
Peterson,Gilbert 84
Peterson,Guri Thorson 177
Peterson,John,Mrs 108
Peterson,Julia Reierson 84
Peterson,Julia Thorson 177
Peterson,Martin 178
Peterson,Mary 84
Peterson,Ole 177,178,200
Peterson,Oscar 84
Peterson,Otilde 178
Peterson,Peter 177
Peterson,Peter G 84
Peterson,Sarah Borstad 149
Peterson,Theodore 84
Peterson Thiglum,Inger 137
Pfeffer,David 234,241,261
Pillsbury,Governor 173
Prestegaardseie,Else Halvorsdtr
 Klemstads 154
Prestegaardseie,Inger Ellingsdtr 154
Prestholdt,Bernice 257
Prestholdt,Rudy 257
Preus,A C,Pastor 134,147
Preus,H A,Pastor 51
Probstfield,R M 207,209,210
Quammen,N N,Pastor 110
Quarve,George Temandsen 28
Quarve,Levor Temandsen 28
Quie,Albert 57
Quie,Halvor 57
Radke,Albert 123
Ramsey,Alexander 7,9,224
Ramsey,Bottolf Pederson 177
Ramsey,Gertrud Mikkelsdtr 177
Ramstad,Anders 149
Ramstad,Anna 149
Ramstad,Bertha 149
Ramstad,Elizabeth 149
Ramstad,Hans 149
Ramstad,Hansine 149
Ramstad,Joseph 149
Ramstad,Josephine 138

Ramstad,Maren 149
Ramstad,Ole Anderson 149
Ramstad,Oscar 149
Ramstad,Ragnhild 149
Ramstad,Randi 149
Ramstad,William 149
Rand,Lois 237
Rasmusson,Knud 177
Reese,Cheryl 234
Reese,Matt 234
Reiersdtr,Birgit 97
Reiersen,Reier 97
Reierson,Elling 29
Reierson,Emile 84
Reierson,Gunhild Knutsdtr 84
Reierson,Helen 84
Reierson,Henry 84
Reierson,Knute 84
Reierson,Reier 103
Reierson,Steiner 29
Rekanes,Anne 150
Rekanes,Betsy 150
Rekanes,Birgit 150
Rekanes,Birgith Kittelsdtr 219
Rekanes,Birgith Kittelsdtr Dompendal 150
Rekanes,Helene 150
Rekanes,Helga 150
Rekanes,Ingeborg 150
Rekanes,Kittel 150
Rekanes,Margaret 150
Rekanes,Mikkel 150
Rekanes,Ole Mikkelson 149,150,219
Rekanes,Sevine 150
Rekstad,Erik 180
Rekstad,Martia 180
Renna,Gulbrand 39
Reque,S S,Rev 79
Richardson,Gunvor Halvorsdtr Vindlaus
 151,152
Richardson,Ole 150
Richardson,Rachael 150
Richardson,Rannei 150
Richardson,Thrond 150-152
Richardson,Tron 150
Ridder,Walter 236
Rikardson,Thrond 150
Rikardson,Tron 150
Ringdahl,Caroline 152
Ringdahl,Gusta 152
Ringdahl,Gustav 152
Ringdahl,Ingeborg Olsdtr Ommelsæteren
 69
Ringdahl,Matthias Pedersen 69,152
Ringdahl,Melvin 152
Ringdahl,Ole 152
Ringdahl,Olive 152
Ringdahl,Peder M 69
Ringdahl,Peter 152
Ringerud,Elling Frederikssen 88,92
Ringerud,Ingrid Ostensdtr 88
Risbrot,Engebret 200

Riste,Jorend Olson 130
Ristey,Marit Oldsdtr 129
Røbele,Knud Einarson 91
Røbele,Marit Eriksdtr 91
Rockswold,Palmer 241
Rodning,Lars Svenson 186
Rodningen,Lars S 59
Rodningen,Svend 58
Roe,Herman 236
Roed,Carl 123
Rogne,Leslie 241
Rogness,Kari Engebretson 179
Rogness,Knute Nelson 179
Roholt,Leiv Jonsson 85
Rokke,Lee 237
Rolegheta,Mikkel Gunnulvson 149
Rolfson,Asben S 178
Rolfson,Asbjørn 178
Rood,Agnete 69
Rood,Johan 70
Rood,Kristen Johansen 69
Rood,Kristian 69
Rood,Mari 70
Rood,Olava Olsdtr 69
Rood,Ole 69
Rood,Oline 69
Roppe,Ole 29
Rorhelle,Gunloug 147
Rorhelle,Signe Overland 148
Rosendahl,Georgia 220,232,234
Rosendahl,Hans 28
Rosendahl,Paul 28
Rosendahl,Robert 241
Røste,Ragnild Halvorsdtr 141
Rotegard,Barbro 153
Rotegard,Bernard 153
Rotegard,Carl Olavus 153
Rotegard,Hannah 153
Rotegard,Kari 153
Rotegard,Knudt 153
Rotegard,Knute 153
Rotegard,Nels 153
Rotegard,Ole 153
Rotneim,Arne 87
Rotneim,Helge 87
Rotneim,Kjerste 87
Rotneim,Margit 87
Rotneim,Margit Pedersdtr 87,88
Rotneim,Nils 87
Rotneim,Ole 87
Rotneim,Ole Olsen 87
Rotneim,Peder 87
Rotneim,Peder 87
Rotneim,Sara Sarabyne 87
Rotneim,Sarah 87
Rotneim,Sigri 87
Roundal,Aslaug Thimrud 178
Roundal,Knute 178
Rud,Agnete 69
Rud,Anders J 72
Rud,Hans C Gullickson 131

Rud,Ingeborg 131
Rud,Johan 70
Rud,Kristen Johansen 69
Rud,Kristian 69
Rud,Mari 70
Rud,Olava Olsdtr 69
Rud,Ole 69
Rud,Oline 69
Rudd,Anne Maria Engebretsdtr 158
Rudningen,Lars Sveinsen 164
Rudningen,Svein Sveinsen 164
Rue Family 9
Rue,Gunil Franson 147
Rue,Hans Franson 10
Rue,Harold Olson 10
Rue,Kari 147
Ruggeseter,Synneva Ellingsdtr 75
Rukke,Christian 154
Rukke,Else 154
Rukke,Halvor 154
Rukke,Jorand 154
Rukke,Knud 154
Rukke,Knud Olson 153,154
Rukke,Ole 154
Rukke,Sever Knutson 154
Runestad,Anne Serine Opsal 178
Runestad,Rasmus Olson 178
Rustad,Anna 20,97
Ruud,Kari Madsdtr 69
Ruud,Marte Marie Olsdtr 130
Rygh,Anna Maria Pedersdtr 106
Rygh,Torbjor Andersdtr 154,155
Rygh,Torger O 154,155
Rygh,Torger Torgersen 154
Sæteren,Stenetta Larsdtr 69
Sæther,Ole 200
Sæthre,Christen 155
Sæthre,Christie 155
Sæthre,Kari 155
Sæthre,Maria 155
Sæthre,Marthe 155
Sæthre,Tron Christenson 72,155
Saettre,Sjur 50,51
Sævre,Carl 156
Saevre,Charlotte 156
Sævre,Gunhild 82
Saevre,Henry 156
Sævre,Knud 82
Sævre,Knud Knudsen 155
Sævre,Mikkel 82,156
Sagedalen,Knud 28
Sagedalen,Ole 28
Sagnes,Berthe 177
Sagnes,Hans Sønsteby 177
Sagnes,Marie Mutta 178
Sagnes Jr,Hans 178
Salveson,Halvor 211
Salveson,Halvor Fendalsveit 203,204
Sampson,Andrena 157
Sampson,Anna 157
Sampson,Christina 157

Sampson,Christopher 157
Sampson,Hans 157
Sampson,Jessie 157
Sampson,Julia 157
Sampson,Kirstin 157
Sampson,Mary Christopherson 157
Sampson,Molina 157
Sampson,Ole 156
Sampson,Sven 157
Sand,Lars 102
Sanden,Aamund 101
Sandvig,Christopher Kristophersen 134
Sandvig,Kristine Maline 134
Sandwick,Andrew 96,180
Sandwick,Tilde Grover 178
Sannes,Anne 121
Sargent family 43
Sata,Bjorn Olesen 90
Sateren,Adolph 158
Sateren,Anna Maria Engebretsdtr Rudd 158
Sateren,Benjamin Otto 158
Sateren,Bennie 158
Sateren,Caroline 158
Sateren,Edvard 158
Sateren,Gunhild 158
Sateren,Hanna Olava 158
Sateren,Inger Mathia 158
Sateren,Johannes Olsen 157
Sateren,Joseph Albert 158
Sateren,Julia 158
Sateren,Leland 237
Sateren,Lise 158
Sateren,Lizzie 158
Sateren,Maria 158
Sateren,Mathia 158
Sateren,Oluf 158
Sauerlie,Ellef Stenerson 86
Sauerlie,Johannes Ellefson 86
Schartum,Marthe 155
Schibsted,Salve E 85
Schill,Mildred 234,248
Schmidt,Paul G 236
Schmidt,Søren 200
Schmitt,Barb 234,241
Schustad,Helle Hansdtr 141
Selland,Anna 136,159
Selland,Anna Styrkvårsdtr Jordalen-Giljarhus 159
Selland,Brynhild 136,159
Selland,Niels 136,159
Selland,Ola Nielsen 136,159
Selland,Ole 136,159
Sether,Betsy Gurine Olsdtr 200
Sevareid,Adolph 159
Sevareid,Alfred 159
Sevareid,Elias 159
Sevareid,Ephrian 159
Sevareid,Erik Eriksen 159
Sevareid,Ingeborg 159
Sevareid,Ingeborg Tollevsdtr 159

Sevareid,Marie 159
Sevareid,Martin 159
Sevareid,Mathilda 159
Sevareid,Osmund 159
Sevareid,Pauline 159
Sevareid,Tabitha 159
Sevareid,Vier 159
Severud,Ole Olson 32
Sherman,General 115
Shipnes,Anders Johnson 49
Sigstadoe,Ole P 196
Sigurdsen,Albert 159
Sigurdsen,Bergit 159
Sigurdsen,Gunhild 159
Sigurdsen,John 159,160
Sigurdsen,Margit 201
Sigurdsen,Ole 159
Sigurdsen,Sigurd 159
Sigurdsen,Tårånd Torjusdtr 160
Sigurdsen,Thomas 159
Sigurdsen,Torbjorn 159
Sigurdsen,Torjus 159
Sigurdsen,Tosten 201
Simdbu,Anne M Homlie 176
Simonsdtr,Aslaug 97,103
Simonsen,Liv 33
Simonsen,Ole 32-34
Simonson,Beret 38
Simonson,John 234
Simonson,Liv 38
Simonson,Simon 38
Simonson,Syver 38
Sinnes,Mikkel 101
Sinnes,Targe 100
Siqveland,Marie 236
Sjurud,Anne 38
Sjurud,Magdalene 38
Sjurud,Ole Olsen 38
Sjurud,Trond 38
Skalshaugen,Erland 38
Skalshaugen,Syver Olsen 38,39
Skaro,Alvah 160,161
Skaro,Askrim 189
Skaro,Askrim Knudsen 160,161
Skaro,Clara 160,161
Skaro,Edwin 160,161
Skaro,Guri Eriksdtr 160
Skaro,Joseph 160,161
Skaro,Knud Ellingsen 160
Skavland,Eric 20
Skiftun,Anna 19,20
Skiftun,Anne 19,20
Skiftun family 19
Skiftun,Gudmund 19
Skiftun,Malene 19,20,22,23,96
Skiftun,Ole Gudmundsen 19,96
Skiftun,Sissel 19,20
Skiftun,Sissela 19
Skiftun,Sissela Johnsdtr 96
Skjærstein,Anders Julsen 118
Skjærstein,Astri Andersdtr 118

Skjærstreneie,Gulbrand Gulbrandsen 118
Skjei,Arlene 257
Skjei,Bervin 257
Skjenstad,Lena 180
Skjenstad,Martha Oline 180
Skjerdal,Ole Knutson 143
Skogstad,Christian Olsen 70
Skoleland,Barbro 119
Skoleland,Ivar 119
Skree,Helge 220
Skree,Jim 220,232,234
Skree,Ola 220
Skrei,Gunhild 203
Skrei,Signe 203
Skrei,Tarjei 203,211
Skuleslatta,Herbrand Olsen 83
Skurdahl,Mildred 257
Sladky,Anne 219,222,231,234,241,261
Slette,Halvor Peterson 71
Slette,Ole Peterson 71
Slettemoen,Gunnar Tollefsdtr 58
Slettemoen,Guri Sandersdtr 58,164
Smebyhagen,Christina Nielsdtr 197
Smebyhagen,Jens Nielson 196
Smebyhagen,Theolina 197
Smebyhagen,Theolina Nielsdtr 196,198
Smebyhagen,Theoline Nilsdtr 198
Smebyhagen,Tonette Nielsdtr 196
Smedbyhagen,Johanna Nielsdtr 196
Smedvig,Magne 236
Smith,James 26,28
Smith,Ron D 237
Smith,T C 29
Smogard,Ellsworth 257
Smogard,Sylvia 257
Snæfred,King 255
Snedkerpladsen,Elling Erlandsen 71
Snedkerpladsen,Hans Erlandsen 71
Sohlgaard,Maren 111
Soine,Gertrude Elton 178,179
Soine,Ole 178,179
Solberg,Aashild Haugen 179
Solberg,Andros 184
Solberg,Anna 184
Solberg,Charles,Mrs 85
Solberg,Gerhardt 184
Solberg,Knut Knutson 179
Solbjør,Anders Julsen 118
Solomenson,Herman 188
Solomenson,Lars 188
Solomonson,John 187
Solseth,Julia Erickson 83
Solum,Tosten 201
Somdahl,Marilyn 237
Somdahl,Narv 251
Soredahl,Ole Larsen 124
Sorensen,Gunder 86
Sorenson,Marilyn 234
Sørenson,Ole 69
Sorum,Carol 234,241
Sorum,Dean 234,241

Sorum,Ingeborg 27
Sorum,Soren Olsen 26,27
Sørum,Andreas Olsen 69
Sørum,Anne Isaksdtr 118
Sørum,Søren Olsen 69
Spande,Beverly 234
Spigedalen,Johannes Mikkelsen 177
Spigedalen,Mina Holte 177
Sprague,Mr 16
Srp,Delores Jackson 160,234
Srp,Roy 234
St John,Levi 182
St Munch,Pastor 51
Stabbestad,Gunder 172
Stabeck,Clemet 161
Stabeck,Ingebor Kittelsdtr 161,172
Stabeck,Kittel Tostenson 161
Stabeck,Live 161
Stabeck,Tosten 161
Stall,Helga Hanson 176
Stall,Oliver 176
Stalland,Hanna G 236
Stangeland,Charlotte 214
Stangeland,Edmund 215
Stangeland,Elias 176
Stangeland,Elmer 214
Stangeland,George 214,215
Stangeland,Gratia 214,215
Stangeland,Gunhild 214
Stangeland,Gunhild Kørnbo 181
Stangeland,Gurine Einong 176
Stangeland,Hilda 214,215
Stangeland,James 214
Stangeland,Sam 214,215
Stangeland,Simon 181,214
Stangeland,William 214
Steen,Lauritz,Rev 54
Stefferud,Jacob K 236
Steinsrud,Gunhild Endresdtr 104
Stenehjem,Kari 17
Steneroden,Christ 171
Steneroden,Ole 28
Stensgaard family 107
Stensrud,Anders Christiansen 71
Stensrud,John Anderson 122
Stensrud,Mari Kittelsdtr 121
Stensrud,Ole 28
Stensrud,Ole Christiansen 71
Stenstadvalen,Christen Andreas Jensen 108
Stenstadvalen,Kirsten Maria Christensdtr 108
Stevens,Allard 219,220,234
Stevens,Anne 234
Stevens,Dennis 234
Stevens,Judy 234,261
Stoen,Nels Hendrickson 29
Stondahl,Ostena 127
Stone,Erling 236
Stone,Hans Olsen 178
Storaasli,Margit Germundsdtr 165

Storaasli,Ommund Thorsen 165
Storbo,Berit J 179
Storbo,Theodor P 179
Strand,Elling O 40,41,48,116
Strand,Guro 70
Strand,Martha 47
Strand,Theodore 46
Strandheim,Gunvor Larsdatter 180
Strandvold,Ola 206,207,209
Stras,Ingeborg Kleven 179
Stras,Theador E 179
Strass,Carl Johan 179
Strauman,Ludvig 236
Strenge,Edward 162,163
Strenge,Emma 162
Strenge,Even Olson 162,163
Strenge,Georgina 162
Strenge,Henry 162
Strenge,John 162
Strenge,Joseph 162,163
Strenge,Karen 163
Strenge,Karen Maria Ellefsdtr 162
Strenge,Maren 162
Strenge,May 162
Strenge,Olaves 162,163
Strenge,Severt 162
Strom,Hildegard M M 237
Stubberud,Karen Marie Danielson 77
Studley,Deborah M 234
Studlien,Oline 120
Stutelien,Brothers 118
Stuve,Gubjor Martea Larsdtr 157
Suckstorff,Hans 177
Suckstorff,Lena Peterson 177
Sumstad,Anton O 181
Sundby,Theodor A 176
Sundquist,Louis O 139
Susag,David 234
Svarte,Halvdan 251,255
Sveinsdtr,Sissel 165
Svennungsen,Christen 163
Svensen,Guri Sandersdtr 60
Svensen,Svend 60
Svensrud,Evan 181
Svensrud,Randi 181
Swenson,Arvid 101
Swenson,Aslaug 163
Swenson,Charlie 163,164
Swenson,Christian 163,164
Swenson,Evie 234
Swenson,Guri 58
Swenson,Hilda L 132
Swenson,Ingri Andersen 176
Swenson,Kari 163,164
Swenson,Kari Olsdtr 163,164
Swenson,Kittil 163
Swenson,Kristi 58,164
Swenson,Lars 58,164
Swenson,Lloyd 101,234
Swenson,Marthe 163
Swenson,Ole 58,163,164

Swenson,Ole C 163,164
Swenson,Owen 234
Swenson,Paul 58,164
Swenson,Pete 176
Swenson,Ramona 234
Swenson,Sander 58,164
Swenson,Sveining 163,164
Swenson,Sveinung 163
Swenson,Swen Jr 58,164,165
Swenson,Swen Sr 164
Swenson,Swen Swenson,Mrs 58
Swenson,Thomas 163
Swenson,Tolleiv 58,164
Synsteby,Ole 197
Syr,Sigurd 251
Syversdtr,Gunild 122
Syversen,Nils 32,38
Syverson,Elen 33
Syverson,Gunhild 33
Syverson,Marit 33
Syverson,Nils 33
Syversrud,Gunhild Guttormsdtr 155
Taflin,Sally 169
Talle,Ollegaard Nilsdtr 146
Ta-o-ya-te-du-ta,Little Crow 187
Tarjeisen,Aslak 94
Tart,J C 29
Teigen,Hans 177
Teigen,Marie 177
Teigen,Sylvia 234
Temanson,Sever 32,33
Tendeland,Torger 27,28
Tendeland,Torger Johannesen 26
Thesen,Captain 20
Thomasen,Ane Johanne 200
Thomasen,Isak 200
Thomleie,Gulbrand 118
Thompson,Clara 154
Thompson,Edwin,Mrs 100
Thompson,Peder 41
Thompson,Petrina Pedersdtr 179
Thompson,Thosten 48
Thorerson,Ole 140
Thoresdtr,Emma 201
Thoreson,Eddie 181
Thoreson,Jared 219
Thorsdtr,Marthe 135
Thorsen,Amund 219
Thorsen,Nils Abraham 201
Thorson,Amund 165
Thorson,Andrew 186
Thorson,Anne 165
Thorson,Betsey Dokkebakken 177
Thorson,Erick 177
Thorson,Gjermund 165
Thorson,Ingeborg 165
Thorson,Isaac 177
Thorson,Jan Haldorson 177
Thorson,Jorund Haldorson 177
Thorson,Margit 165
Thorson,Margit Germundsdtr 165

Thorson,Maria 177
Thorson,Minnie 177
Thorson,Olav 165
Thorson,Ole 177
Thorson,Oley 177
Thorson,Oline Norderhus 177
Thorson,Peter 177
Thorson,Sissel 165
Thorson,Thor 165
Thorson,Tory 177
Thorstensen,Aaste 201
Thortvedt,Joraand 203
Thortvedt,Leif Levi 203
Thortvedt,Olav 178
Thortvedt,Signe 203
Thortvedt,Thone 178,203,205,212
Thortvedt,Thone Saangdal 203
Thorvedt,Ola Gunderson 203
Thykesen,Anna M 236
Timrud,Ragnhild Olsdotter 86
Tofte family 216
Tokerud,Elene Olsdatter 176
To-ki-cha,Am-pa-tu 190
Tollefsgaardeie,Ole Thorsen 153
Tollefson,Johan 186
Tollefsrud,Christine Lovise 69
Tollefsrud,Christoffer Hovelsen 69
Tollefsrud,Hans Hovelsen 69
Tollefsrud,Johannes 69
Tollefsrud,John Hoovel 70
Tollefsrud,Olava Sophie Pedersdtr 70
Tone,Ole B 29
Torbiornsdtr,Gunnil 159
Torgersdtr,Johanne 148
Torgerson,Bendik 62
Torgerson,Briedy 63-65
Torgerson,Hannah Ohnstad 138
Torgerson,Ingeborg Ohnstad 138
Torgerson,Ole 61
Torgerson,Siri 61
Torgerson,Swenke 186
Torgerson,Torger 61-65
Torgersrud,Hans Olson 179
Torhaug,Anders 34,39
Torine,Anne 124
Torine,John 124
Torjusdtr,Tårånd 159
Torkelson,Lars 71
Tormoen,Helen B 236
Torsen,Amund 165
Torsen,Ommund 165
Torsteinsdtr,Ingeborg 104
Torstenson,Selma 257
Tostensen,Lars 87
Tostensen,Olaf 201
Tovsdtr,Bergit 146
Tovsdtr,Kari 155
To-wan-e-tan,Lorenzo Lawrence 190
Traaen,Gunder 28
Trehus,Endre 119
Trelstad,Randy 230

Trettrudhaugen,Ragnhild Tomasdtr 83
Tronsson,Olav 126
Trostheim,Gunhild Pedersdtr 179
Tuf,Anne 33
Tuf,Chresten 33
Tuf,Joseph 33
Tuff,Anna 38
Tuff,Christen 38
Tuff,Gulbrand Oleson 165
Tuff,Ole 10
Tunselle,Inga Eriksdtr 145
Turli,Knut Larsen 174
Turner,Sandra 234
Tuve,Anthony 166
Tuve,Gulbrand Oleson 165,166
Tuve,Ole Oleson 165
Tuve,Rangdi 166
Tuve,Torbjør Anundsdtr 166
Tvedten,Julia Kassenborg 117
Tveito,Aase 168
Tveito,Annie 168
Tveito,Aslaug Jacobsdtr Einong 167
Tveito,Clara 168
Tveito,Hans 167
Tveito,Hans Torgrimson 167,168
Tveito,Isabelle 168
Tveito,Jacob 168
Tveito,John 168
Tveito,Oscar 168
Tveito,Thomas 168
Tveito,Torgrim Halvorsen 167,168
Tverberg,Gro Sondresdtr 54
Tverberg,John 50-52
Tverberg,John Peterson 54
Twaiten,Julius 101
Tweeten,Geneva 234
Tweite,Ola Nielsen family 159
Tweito,Nels 28
Tyrebakken,Gunnar 87
Ueland,Branda 236
Uggen,Anders 168,169
Uggen,Andrew 48
Uggen,Elsie 48
Uggen,Erik A 40,48
Uggen,Erik Anderson 116
Uggen,Fingar 48
Uggen,Kristi 40,48
Uggen,Oline Juvrud 168
Ukkestad,Tina 89
Ulen,Anna 169
Ulen,Gunhild 169,170
Ulen,Ole 28
Ulen,Ole Olson 170
Ulen,Olson 169
Ulen,Randi 169,170
Ulen,Torgun Olsen 169,170
Ulland,Andrew Oleson 176
Ulsnes,Helga Olavsdtr 149
Ulsness,Ingeborg 88
Ulvestad,Martin 118
Underdahl,Ellen 127

Underdahl,Johan 127
Underdahl,Soren Hanson 127
Underdahl,Stena 127
Vaala,Berdeen 257
Vaala,Mable 257
Vaaler,Bernard 171
Vaaler,Christopher Larson 170,171
Vaaler,Halvor Olsen 170
Vaaler,Helena 171
Vaaler,Johan 171
Vaaler,Kaarn 171
Vaaler,Karl 171
Vaaler,Ludwig 171
Vaaler,Marie Larsdtr 170
Vaaler,Martha 171
Vaaler,Olaus 171
Vaaler,Rosalia 171
Vaaler,Christopher 171
Vaaslia,Christopher Kittilsen 72
Vaeting,Ivar 14
Vale,John 28
Vale,Maria Olsdtr 122,124
Vale,Ole Jonsen 124
Valla,Axel 237
Valle,Ole Halvorson 26
Valsenger,Ragne Hansdtr 148
Vanberg,Bent Jarl 236
Vastvedt,Anne Høljesdtr 93,94
Vastvedt,Hølje Halvorsen 93
Vernon,Edward N 137
Vethammer,Ingebret Olsen 171
Vethammer,Kjersti Ingebretsdtr 105,171
Veum,Ingeborg Larsdtr 174
Vexelsdtr,Berte 148
Vickesland,Amund Erickson 79
Vig,Halvor Johannesen 39
Vig,Johannes 39
Vig,Jorand Haugerstuen 39
Vig,Kari 39
Vig,Ragnhild 39
Vig,Siri 39
Vigeland,Carol 261
Vigeland,Dean 234,261
Vik,Per Inge,Pastor 220,232
Viljugrein,Kari Nilsdtr 78
Vindlaus,Gunvor Halvorsdtr 150
Vinje,Maria 159
Vinjum,Nils Olsen 176
Vislander,Louisa 198
Volstad,Charles 161,173
Volstad,Charlie 173
Volstad,Gullik 173
Volstad,Gunder 173
Volstad,Gunhild 161,173
Volstad,Halvor Knudsen 161,172,173
Volstad,Henry Johan 173
Volstad,Henry Johan 161,173
Volstad,Ingebor Stabeck 162,173
Volstad,Julia 173
Volstad,Julie 161
Volstad,Kittel 161,173

Volstad,Knud 161
Volstad,Knut 173
Volstad,Knut Gunleikson 172
Volstad,Marie 161,173
Volstad,Mary 161,173
Volstad,Peter 173
Vonen,Leiv 220
Voxland,Marie Langemo 149
Vraa,Tone Olsdtr 85
Wahl,Anders 179
Wahl,Anne Marie Swenson 180
Wahl,Berthe Syversen 179
Wahl,Edward 181
Wahl,Syver 180
Waihus,Anton Mrs 184
Walby,Thomas 240
Walhus,Mikkel 122
Wangensteen,Ragndi Nilsdtr 89
Warms,C M,Mrs 184
Weaver,William 139
Week,Halvor Johannesen 39
Week,Johannes 39
Week,Kari 39
Week,Ragnhild 39
Week,Siri 39
Weeks,J H J 38
Wells,Martin 213
Wenberg,Myrtle 198
Wentzel,Ardith 84,85
Western,Kirsten Heier 241
Westling,Augusta 142
Weum,G G 210,211
White,Robert 123
Wilhelmstad,Halvor Nielsen 154
Winjum,Anna Olsdtr Otternes 173,174
Winjum,Botolf 174
Winjum,Elling 173
Winjum,Jens Ellingsen 173,174
Winjum,Kari Jensdtr 176
Winjum,Marie 174
Winjum,Ole 174
Wold,Knud Olsen 28
Wold,Theodore 236
Wolstad,Helen 93
Wralstad,George 83
Ytre Lie, Ingeborg Pedersdtr 174
Ytre Lie,Johannes Botolvsen 127,174
Ytre Lie,Anders 174
Ytre Lie,Lars Oddsen 174
Ytre Lie,Marta 174
Ytre Lie,Marta Knudsdtr 174
Ytre Lie,Odd 174
Ytre Lie,Odd Amundson 174
Ytrefjornen,Gurina Carlsdtr 138
Ytrelie,Lars 144
Ytrelie,Lars Oddsen 144
Ytrelie,Marta Knutsdtr 144
Ytrelie,Marta Larsdtr 144
Ytrelie,Odd 144
Ytterbøe,Kari Thorsdtr 108
Ziesemer,Gerald 234

FIRST NAME ORDER

A C Preus,Pastor 134,147
A G Kassenborg 116
A man by the name of Dodge 139
A O Kragnes 121,219
A P Connolly 190
Aad Evensen 176
Aagot Ingulfsland 109,133
Aagot L Olson 128
Aagot L Olson Lommen 129
Aagot Oysteinsdtr Boen 109
Aamund Berland 147
Aamund Sanden 101
Aane Aaby 74
Aanon Gjeitsta 207,210
Aanon Gunderson Gjeitsta 203
Aanond Harstad 83
Aanund Berge 178
Aanund Kragnes 120,121,178
Aanund Olesen Kråkenes 120
Aase Aslaksdtr Haraldson 103,104
Aase Aslaksdtr Nusvig 103
Aase Bøen 81
Aase Brokken 82,83
Aase Ellevsdtr Enger Oygarden 88
Aase Ellingsdtr Enger 176
Aase Grover 95
Aase Halvorsdtr Gøystdal 190
Aase Herbjornsdtr Ingulfsland 133
Aase Herbjørnsdtr Morem 133
Aase Ingulfsland 109
Aase Olsdtr Frygne 135
Aase Sofie Enger 88
Aase Torgrimsdtr Hasleberg 98
Aase Tveito 168
Aashild Haugen Solberg 179
Aasne Jonsdtr Ingulfsland Boen 109
Aasne Olsdtr Kleppo 150
Aaste Aaby 74
Aaste Anundsdtr Hjamdal 126
Aaste Anundsdtr Lia 219
Aaste Anundsdtr Hjamdal Lie 127
Aaste Jensen 74
Aaste Nilsdtr Grovum 74
Aaste Thorstensen 201
Aaste Tovsdtr Gulmon 98
Aasulf Olsen 179
Abraham Bukkøy 86
Abraham Jakobsen,Pastor 200
Abraham Lincoln,President 52,190
Adam Gjervert 220
Adeline Evensen 177
Adelle Anderson 89
Adolf Bredesen,Pastor 199
Adolph Ohnstad 138
Adolph Sateren 158
Adolph Sevareid 159
Agnes Boraas 257
Agnete Rood 69

Agnete Rud 69
Albert Anderson 76
Albert Applen 78
Albert Foss 184
Albert George Orton 181
Albert Gullickson,Mrs 100
Albert Kroshus 180
Albert Lia 126
Albert Louis Hjermstad 106
Albert Oleson 138
Albert Peterson Aaberg 176
Albert Quie 57
Albert Radke 123
Albert Sigurdsen 159
Albertina Norman 136
Aleth Bukkøy 85
Aleth J Bukkøy Eikhom 177
Alex Haraldson 104
Alex Nelson 135
Alexander Grover 95,96,180
Alexander Ramsey,Governor 7,9,224
Alfred B Halvorsen 129
Alfred Dewey Nelson 123
Alfred Hegland 181
Alfred Peterson 84
Alfred Sevareid 159
Alice Gulmon 98
Alice Peterson 84
Aline Svenungsdtr Holtan 106
Allard Stevens 219,220,234
Allen Krueger 234
Allette Hegland 181
Alma Gunderson 100
Aslaug Boen Espeland 179
Alvah Skaro 160,161
Alvin Kragnes 120
Amalie Bruns 201
Amanda Theodora Gunderson 100
Ambjor Applen 77
Ambjor Olsdtr Forlie 77
Amelia Oleson 75,139
Amelia Helene Jordgrav 115
Amos Johnsen 201
Am-pa-tu To-ki-cha 190
Amund B Larsen 200
Amund Barskor 165
Amund Berekvam 79
Amund Blikom 165
Amund Erickson Holum 79
Amund Erickson Vickesland 79
Amund Johnson 38
Amund Johnson Klastolen 38
Amund Langeman 224
Amund Lindelien 33.39
Amund Lunde 20-22
Amund Olsen 178
Amund Thorsen 219
Amund Thorson 165

Amund Torsen 165
Amy Brokken 83
Anders A Lybeck 38
Anders Aaby 52,74
Anders Amundson 148
Anders Anderson 76
Anders Christiansen Stensrud 71
Anders Dale 102
Anders Ellingson Kvaale 75
Anders Eriksen Kjøsven 200
Anders Evenson 71
Anders Finseth 56
Anders Gubberud 20,21,25,96
Anders Gulbrandson 77
Anders J Rud 72
Anders Johnson Shipnes 49
Anders Jonsen Aaby 74,76
Anders Julsen Skjærstein 118
Anders Julsen Solbjør 118
Anders Kiil Nelson family 86
Anders Kroshus 28
Anders Larsen 177
Anders Larsen Lundby 130,131
Anders Libæk 71
Anders Mohn 50
Anders Nielsen Kiil 86
Anders Oddsen Otterness 145,174
Anders Oestensen 96
Anders Otterness 145
Anders Øestensen Gubberud 18
Anders Øestensen Haugsrudie 18
Anders Pederson Kroshus 121,220
Anders Pederson Melbostad 132
Anders Peterson Haugen 20
Anders Ramstad 149
Anders Torhaug 34,39
Anders Uggen 168,169
Anders Wahl 179
Anders Ytre Lie 174
Andrea Een 237
Andreas C Iverson 110
Andreas Fredrickson 46,48
Andreas G Kassenborg 178
Andreas Gilbertson 95
Andreas Gjeitsta 203
Andreas Gulbrandsen Kassenborg 116-118
Andreas Jordgrav 115
Andreas Knutson 181
Andreas Lunde 69
Andreas Nerhaugen 69
Andreas Nilsen Erstad 69
Andreas Olsen Sørum 69
Andrena Sampson 157
Andrew Anderson 178,181
Andrew Anderson 75
Andrew Anderson Fjeldhaug 197
Andrew Botoh Berekvam 79

Andrew Brynildsen Foss 176,182-184
Andrew Christianson 108
Andrew Findreng 101
Andrew Fredrickson 46
Andrew Gunderson 101
Andrew Hagen 127
Andrew Hansen 200
Andrew Holtan 106
Andrew Johnson 69,181
Andrew Larsen Flom 134
Andrew Lommen 130
Andrew Melgaard 236
Andrew Oleson 138,139
Andrew Oleson Ulland 176
Andrew Olson 138
Andrew P Peterson 133
Andrew Sandwick 96,180
Andrew Thorson 186
Andrew Uggen 48
Andrina Swanson Golden 180
Andros Solberg 184
Andy Esterby 68
Ane Johanne Thomasen 200
Anfinn Anfinnson 220
Anna Christina Dahlen 176
Ann Delano 234
Anna Axelsdtr Iverson 116
Anna Berekvam 79
Anna Bertine Pedersen 134
Anna Blexerud 22
Anna Dahle 101
Anna Dortia Pedersen 134
Anna Ellis 86
Anna Gubberud 25,96
Anna Gullickson 98
Anna Gundersen 200
Anna Halvorson 103
Anna Hellicksdtr Helle 196
Anna Hogstad Elstad 177
Anna Huset 108
Anna Jensine Otterness 145
Anna Johannesdtr Lee 127
Anna Johannesdtr Lie 127
Anna Johnson 112
Anna Johnson Erickson 181
Anna Josephine Gubberud 96
Anna Juvrud 48
Anna Kleven 257
Anna Knudsdtr Hovland 142,143
Anna Knutson 181
Anna Kragnes 220
Anna Kragness 101
Anna Lee Ellingsdtr Bergsundeie 88
Anna Lie 127
Anna M Thykesen 236
Anna Maria Gunderson 99
Anna Maria E Rudd Sateren 158
Anna Maria Pedersdtr Rygh 106
Anna Maria P Rygh Holtan 106,107
Anna Marie Wahl Larsen 179
Anna Martha Melhus Hogstad 177

Anna Nelson 135
Anna Norman 136
Anna Olsdtr Otternes Winjum 173,174
Anna Oleson 139
Anna Olsen Christopherson 179
Anna Olson 83,140
Anna Orton 143
Anna Otterness 144,174
Anna Ottun 146
Anna Oxnaberg 39
Anna Pauline Berg 100
Anna Pauline Berg Gunderson 100
Anna Peterson 84
Anna Ramstad 149
Anna Rustad 20,97
Anna Sampson 157
Anna Selland 136,159
Anna Skiftun 19,20
Anna Solberg 184
Anna Sophia Foss 184
Anna Strksdtr Jordalen-Giljarhus 136
Anna Styrkvårsdtr Jordalen-Giljarhus Selland 159
Anna T Kvernodden 124
Anna Theodora Fuhr 235
Anna Torsdtr Holum 79
Anna Tuff 38
Anna Ulen 169
Anne Amundsdtr Bjerkhagen 201
Anne Andersdtr Lunde 124
Anne Andersen 33,75
Anne Aslesdtr 141
Anne Bukkøy 85
Anne Cathrine Jensdtr Humble 107
Anne Einong 167
Anne Elise Hansen 200
Anne Ellingsdtr Enger 176
Anne Finseth 56
Anne G Fetten 77
Anne Gulbrandsdtr Kanten 177
Anne Gulliksdtr 198
Anne Gunderson 101
Anne Halvorsdtr Jøntvet 108
Anne Hansdtr 140
Anne Hanson Helgedalen 179
Anne Haraldson 104
Anne Haugerstuen 38
Anne Helena Danielson 142
Anne Høljesdtr Vastvedt 93,94
Anne Isaksdtr Sørum 118
Anne Jakobsdtr Johnson 178
Anne Janda 234,241,261
Anne Johnson 38
Anne Jørundsdtr Øy 85
Anne Karine Kassenborg 117
Anne Karine Tostensdtr Kjos 99
Anne Kassenborg Bergland 117
Anne Kassenborg Juve 117
Anne Katrine Hatlestad 131
Anne Kirstine Huset 108
Anne Klastolen 38

Anne Knatvold 100
Anne Knutsdtr Halvorson 85
Anne Knutsdtr N Tveiten 165
Anne Kragnes 121
Anne Larsdtr Pedersen 148
Anne Lawrence 98
Anne Lawrence Gulmon 99
Anne Lee 125
Anne Louise Gjermstad 105
Anne Louise Larsen 171,172
Anne Lundby 130
Anne M Homlie Simdbu 176
Anne Maria Holtan 106
Anne Maria Engebretsdtr Rudd 158
Anne Maria Pedersdtr Brynsaas 84
Anne Marie Grønsten 49,52,94
Anne Marie Hjermstad 105
Anne Marie Johnsdtr 124
Anne Marie Kassenborg 117
Anne Marie Melhus 138
Anne Marie Moe 117
Anne Marie Swenson Wahl 180
Anne Mutta 177
Anne Oleson 140
Anne Olsdtr Fraagot 72
Anne Olsdtr Overbo 106
Anne Otterness 67
Anne Overland 146
Anne Pedersdtr Noem 176
Anne Pedersen 148
Anne Rekanes 150
Anne Sannes 121
Anne Serine Opsal Runestad 178
Anne Sjurud 38
Anne Skiftun 19,20
Anne Sladky 219,222,231,234,241,261
Anne Stevens 234
Anne Thorson 165
Anne Torine 124
Anne Tuf 33
Annette Ness 89
Annie Kvernodden 123
Annie Nelson 123
Annie Peterson 84
Annie Tveito 168
Anthony Tuve 166
Anton Danielson 142
Anton Dybsand 180
Anton Findreng 101
Anton Hanson 48
Anton Hegland 181
Anton Julius Anderson 176
Anton Lommen 129
Anton O Sumstad 181
Anton Walhus,Mrs 184
Antonette Andersen 201
Anund Erikson Hjamdal 114,126
Anund Oleson 138
Ardith Wentzel 84,85
Arlene Skjei 257
Arne Agrimson 234

Arne Bohn 33
Arne Evans 169,17
Arne Hovda 38
Arne Knutson 180
Arne Rotneim 87
Arnold Applen 78
Arnold Ness 234
Arthur Bow 27
Arthur Paulson 234
Arvid Swenson 101
Asa Daniels,Dr 187
Asben S Rolfson 178
Asbjørn Rolfson 178
Asborg Halvorsdtr 75
Asborg Olsen Våsjo Gunderson 181
Ase Hansdtr Berge 167
Ashley Goodwin 219,220,234
Askild T Bekkerus 179
Askrim Knudsen Skaro 160,161
Askrim Skaro 189
Aslak Aaby 51,74
Aslak Anderson Aaby 74-75
Aslak Breidall,Mrs 149
Aslak Dale 102
Aslak Haraldson 104
Aslak Johnsen 200
Aslak Knudsen Aamodt 39
Aslak Knudsen Aamot 38
Aslak Lavrantson 98
Aslak Lee 95,103
Aslak Tarjeisen 94
Aslaug Halvorsdtr 75
Aslaug Jacobsdtr Einong 167,168
Aslaug Jacobsdtr Einong Tveito 167
Aslaug Simonsdtr 97,103
Aslaug Svenungsdtr Holtan 106
Aslaug Swenson 163
Aslaug Thimrud Roundal 178
Asle Halvorson 29
Aslesen Flaten 71
Asmund Gundersen 99
Astri Andersdtr 95
Astri Olsen 235
Astri Andersdtr Kassenborg
   92,116,118,219
Astri Andersdtr Skjærstein 118
Astrid Bøen 82
Astri Herbrandsdtr Børtnes 82
Astrid Johnsdtr Bøen 188
Astrid Jonsdtr Bøen 81,82
Audrey H Johnson 234
August Ludvig Orton 176,181
Augusta Bøen 82
Augusta Westling 142
Ausne Ingulfsland 109
Austin Estensen 82
Austin Morem 133
Axel Iverson 48,115
Axel Valla 237
Axel Bergh,Pastor 112
B E Mortensen 237

Barb Schmitt 234,241
Barbara Foss 184
Barbara Horn 234
Barbo Lostegaard 119
Barbra Johnson 39
Barbro Bakkene 83
Barbro Knudson 92
Barbro Rotegard 153
Barbro Skoleland 119
Barbro Torgersdtr Faar 91
Barbro Torgersdtr Garvik 92
Bartha Housker 109
Bartha Housker Iverson 110
Bear Oleson 91
Bella Erickson 89
Belle Halvorson 177
Belle Lommen 130
Belle A Lee 102
Ben Benson 99
Ben Iverson 110
Ben Otterness 66
Bendik Torgerson 62
Benhard Gunderson 101
Benhart Martin Paulson 180
Benjamin Otterness 67
Benjamin Otto Sateren 158
Benjamin Ross Eggan 236
Benjamin Sivert Otterness 145
Bennie Sateren 158
Bent Erickson 196
Bent Jarl Vanberg 236
Berdeen Vaala 257
Berent Ottun 146
Beret Bergetongen 79,80
Beret Lindelien 38
Beret Simonson 38
Beret Knudsdtr Lindelien 39
Beret Olsdtr Fraagot 72
Berge Lee 178
Berger Jergenson 180
Bergine Halvorson 103
Bergit Hefte 15,104
Bergit Ingemunsdtr 201
Bergit Ingulfsland 109
Bergit Sigurdsen 159
Bergit Tovsdtr 146
Bergithe G Homme Hjermstad 105,106
Bergithe Gundersdtr Homme 105
Bergithe Homme 171
Bergithe Homme Larsen 172
Berit Ellingsdtr Bergsundeie 92
Berit Ellingsdtr Gilbertson 93
Berit Jellum 110
Berit J Storbo 179
Berit Jonsdtr 110
Berit Jonsdtr Lommen Lee 125,126
Berit Larsdtr 119
Bernard Rotegard 153
Bernard Vaaler 171
Bernhard Kragnes 120
Bernice Oellien 257

Bernice Prestholdt 257
Bernt Gunderson 99
Bernt Hjermstad 105,106
Bernt P Korssjoen 179
Bernt Peterson 178
Bersvend Hagen 178
Berta Ottun 146
Berta Serine Pedersen 176
Berte Vexelsdtr 148
Berte Marie Olsdtr 148
Bertha Berekvam 79
Bertha Bustul Kittelson 178
Bertha Jennison Olsen 178
Bertha Jenson 101
Bertha Oleson 138
Bertha Ramstad 149
Berthe Bjerke Griffin 177
Berthe Hansdtr Aasen 70
Berthe Sagnes 177
Berthe Syversen Wahl 179
Bertine Nelson 135
Bervin Skjei 257
Beta Myrhagen 147
Betsey Dokkebakken Thorson 177
Betsey Gilbertson 103
Betsey Hjermstad 105
Betsy Gurine Olsdtr Sether 200
Betsy Rekanes 150
Betty Bailey 234
Betty Bergland 234
Beverly Spande 234
Birgit Reiersdtr 97
Birgit Reiersdtr Gilbertson 103
Birgit Rekanes 150
Birgith Kittelsdtr Dompendal 149
Birgith Kittelsdtr Dompendal Rekanes 150
Birgith Kittelsdtr Rekanes 219
Birgith Olsdtr Dompendal 149
Birthe Lundby 130
Birthe Pedersen 148
Bjorgov Gunderson 99
Bjorn Enderud 99
Bjorn Endru 99
Bjorn Garnaas 91
Bjørn Gunderson 71,99,219
Bjorn Olesen Sata 90
Bjorn Olesen Sata Garnaas 90
Black Elk 191
Blaine Hedberg 260
Borghild Dahl 236
Borgil Hermansdtr 122
Borre Evenson 196
Børre Iverson 110
Botoh Andrew Berekvam 79
Botolf Winjum 174
Botolv Botolvsen Berekvam 78
Botolv Johannesen Berekvam 78
Botolv Kristensen 174
Botolv Lee 127
Botolv Lie 127
Botolv Ohnstad 137

Bottolf Pederson Ramsey 177
Boye Adzlew,Captain 74
Boye Gaasedelen 89
Brady Foss 184
Branda Ueland 236
Breanna Linder 234
Briedy Torgerson 63-65
Brita Amundsdtr Berekvam 79
Brita Berekvam 145
Brita Ohnstad Larson 137
Britt Overland 146
Brown Anderson 29
Bruun Anderson 29
Brynhild Selland 136,159
Brynild Norman 136
C C Nelson 186
C K Orton 143
C L Clausen,Pastor
 7-9,32,33,51,151,156,167
C M Warms,Mrs 184
Captain Thesen 20
Cari Nedre Rindal 152
Carl A Lunde 132
Carl Applen 78
Carl Anders Josiassen 201
Carl Bronson 83,84
Carl Bruns 201
Carl Edvardsen Erickson 180
Carl Edward Orton 143
Carl Edward Otterness 146
Carl Emil Knudsen 200
Carl Erickson 89
Carl G O Hansen 222,223,227
Carl Huset 108
Carl Jahr,Mrs 149
Carl Johan Bottolfson 200
Carl Johan Strass 179
Carl Jordgrav 115
Carl Narvestad 237
Carl Nelson 180,188
Carl Olavus Rotegard 153
Carl Roed 123
Carl Sævre 156
Carol Sorum 234,241
Carol Vigeland 261
Carolina Krogstrum 159
Caroline Bendickson 135
Caroline Graff 180
Caroline Huset 108
Caroline Kragnes 120
Caroline Lunde 132
Caroline Nelson 135
Caroline Oleson 139
Caroline Olson 75,140
Caroline Ottun 146
Caroline Ringdahl 152
Caroline Sateren 158
Carolyn Benson 234
Carrie Christophersen 84
Carrie Melbostad 132
Cecilia Eivindsdtr Jellum 110,111

Char Nelson 234
Charles Edvardsen Erickson 180
Charles F Flandrau 137
Charles Gunderson 150
Charles Hasleiet 177
Charles Hoegh 29
Charles Solberg,Mrs 85
Charles Volstad 161,173
Charley Holtan 106
Charlie Swenson 163,164
Charlie Volstad 173
Charlotte Saevre 156
Charlotte Stangeland 214
Cheryl Reese 234
Chresten Tuf 33
Chris Haglund 234
Christ Elandson 179
Christ Steneroden 171
Christan Christensen 236
Christan Holm 235
Christan Lommen 130
Christen Anderson Øvestad 155
Christen Andreas Jensen Stenstadvalen
 108
Christen Dyreson 176
Christen Huset 108
Christen Sæthre 155
Christen Svennungsen 163
Christen Tuff 38
Christi Larson 86
Christian Ahlness 193-198
Christian Applen 78
Christian C Bergan 72
Christian Dunham,Mrs 98
Christian Engell 29
Christian Grover 95,96,176
Christian Hanson 46,48
Christian Iverson 109,110
Christian Johannessen Dahl 200
Christian Jordgrav 115
Christian Magelson 12
Christian Olsen Skogstad 70
Christian P Lunde 69
Christian Peterson Lunde 131,132
Christian Ommelstadsæteren 69,157
Christian Pedersen 148
Christian Rukke 154
Christian Swenson 163,164
Christiane Johnson 124
Christiane Martine Johnson 122
Christie Sæthre 155
Christina Holtan 106
Christina Larsen 171,172
Christina Lie 127
Christina Nielsdtr Smebyhagen 197
Christina Norman 136
Christina Sampson 157
Christine Gubberud 23,96
Christine Lofthus Norman 136
Christine Lovise Tollefsrud 69
Christine Ohnstad Edstrom 138

Christine Oleson 140
Christine Olson 140
Christoffer Hovelsen Tollefsrud 69
Christopher Abbott 139
Christopher Blexrud 81
Christopher Gunderson 99
Christopher Iverson 110
Christopher Kittilsen Vaaslia 72
Christopher Kittelson 161
Christopher Kristophersen Sandvig 134
Christopher Larson 171
Christopher Larson Vaaler 170,171
Christopher Sampson 157
Christopher Vaaler 171
Clara Alice Janette Orton 142
Clara Bertina Jordahl 181
Clara Hanson 181
Clara Hogstad 181
Clara Jordgrav 115
Clara Peterson 84
Clara Skaro 160,161
Clara Tveito 168
Clara Thompson 154
Clare Liebe 234
Clarence Grover 180
Clarence Kragnes 120
Clarence Ohnstad 138
Clark Walter Orton 142
Claus C Monker 216
Clemens Granskov 235
Clemet Stabeck 161
Clyde Hammel,Mrs 100
Colonel Hegg 196
Conrad Deitlef Morck 180,237,238
Cora Angeline Aslakson Akre 181
Cornelia Bukkøy 85
Cornelia Orton 143
Cornelius Anderson 75
Cornelius K Orton 143
Cornelius Knute Orton 142
Cornelius L Aasnes 200
Dagne Gunderson 101
Daniel C Iverson 110
Daniel Danielson 142
Daniel Nilsen 141
Darleen Bjugan 234
Darlene Johnson 234
Darwin Krueger 261
David Bauman 256
David Gunderson 234,241,261
David Meyer 234
David Norman 234
David Pfeffer 234,241,261
David Susag 234
Dean Sorum 234,241
Dean Vigeland 234,261
Deb Nelson Gourley 221,230,234
Deborah M Johnson 234
Deborah M Studley 234
Delores Cleveland 234,241
Delores Jackson Srp 160

Delores Srp 234
DeLos Olson 220,234,241,261
Dennis Stevens 234
Dick Norman 234
Dick Hagen 234
Don Olson 230,261
Donald Padilla 237
Donis McCallum 256
Donovan Brink 196
Dordi Gunnarsdtr Dale 102,103
Dorothea Fuglehaug Olson 176
Dorothy Findreng 101
Dorthe Amundsdtr Bleikedammen 76
Dorthe Larsdtr Kopperud 200
Dorthea Næse 134
Dorthia Lia 127
Douglas Gillespie 234
Duane Engelsgaard 248
Dwight Wesley Orton 143
E L Otterness 66,68
E R Hutchinson 207,209
E W Humphrey 235
Eddie Otterness 66,67
Eddie E Otterness 145
Eddie Thoreson 181
Edith Esterby 68
Edmund Stangeland 215
Edna Madelia Oleson 139
Edvard Sateren 158
Edvin Haraldson 104
Edward Ellingson Enger 181
Edward Enger 88
Edward Foss 184
Edward G Otterness 144
Edward Grover 95,96,176
Edward Haugrud 83
Edward Hjermstad 105
Edward Iverson 110
Edward Lommen 129
Edward Ludwig Kassenborg 117
Edward Melbostad 132
Edward N Vernon 137
Edward Otterness 144,178
Edward Pedersen Grefseng 200
Edward Sateren 158
Edward Severin Aasnes 200
Edward Strenge 162,163
Edward Wahl 181
Edwin Anderson 76
Edwin Ellis 86
Edwin Gubberud 96
Edwin Haraldson 104
Edwin Lunde 132
Edwin Nels Nelson 123
Edwin Skaro 160,161
Edwin Thompson,Mrs 100
Egel E Gulmon 98
Egel Eivindson Manheim 98
Egil Almaas 237
Egil G Gulmon 98
Eileen Gulbranson 256

Einar Duvick 237
Einar Overbo 106
Einar Torgerson Mork 179
Eivind Kopsengeie 110
Elaine Dalager 234
Elaine Nordlie 219-221,232,234
Eldraine Ellis 86
Elen Moen 32,38
Elen Syverson 33
Elen Anna Johnson 178
Elene Olsdatter Tokerud 176
Elgerine Ottun 146
Eli Pedersdtr Eriksen 177
Elias Gubberud 96
Elias Overland 147
Elias Sevareid 159
Elias Stangeland 176
Eline Mathea Gjermstad 105
Eline Mathea Larsen 171
Elise Andrea Grover Olson 178
Elise Grover 95,96
Eliza Oleson 139
Eliza A Kassenborg 117
Eliza Kassenborg Olness 117
Elizabeth Lommen 130
Elizabeth Ramstad 149
Ella Johnson 93
Ellef Ellson 179
Ellef Erlien 241
Ellef Stenerson Sauerlie 86
Ellen Halvorson 102
Ellen Hammer 236
Ellen Larsen 172
Ellen Lie 128
Ellen Lovise Munkhaugen 146
Ellen Marie Iverson 110
Ellen Marie Kittelsdtr Jordgrav 114
Ellen Martini Otterness 145
Ellen Otterness 66,67
Ellen Ottun 146
Ellen Underdahl 127
Ellev Halvorson 102.103
Ellevine Hegvik 134
Elling Anderson 75
Elling Bjertnes 71
Elling Eielson 95
Elling Ellingsen 28
Elling Enger 176
Elling Enger,Jr 88
Elling Erlandsen Snedkerpladsen 71
Elling Fredrikssen Ringerud 88,92
Elling Kieland 28
Elling O Strand 40,41,48,116
Elling Pedersen Engar 71
Elling Pedersen Enger 88
Elling Peterson Enger,Sr 88
Elling Reierson 29
Elling Winjum 173
Ellsworth Smogard 257
Elmer Gilbertson 103
Elmer Gulbrandsen 97

Elmer Stangeland 214
Elmer T J Grover 180
Elsa Marie Bergetongen 80
Else Bukkøy 85,86
Else Rukke 154
Else Halvorsdtr Klemstads
    Prestegaardseie 154
Elsie Bergland 96
Elsie M Melby 237
Elsie Miller 234
Elsie Uggen 48
Embrick Johnson 112
Embrick Benson Enderud 28
Embrick Knudsen Opheim 28
Emelie Dorthea Anderson 77
Emil B Olson 112
Emile Reierson 84
Emma Applen 77
Emma Bertine Hjermstad 106
Emma Bruns 201
Emma Findreng 101
Emma Melbostad 132
Emma Melvina Gunderson 100
Emma Nelson 123,135
Emma Peterson 84
Emma Strenge 162
Emma Thoresdtr 201
Endre Gaasedelen 89
Endre Trehus 119
Enge Peterson 178
Engebor Nelson Dahle 101
Engebret Bearson 91
Engebret Bensen Enderud 122
Engebret Bjørnsen Garnaas Bearson 122
Engebret Garnaas 90
Engebret Gundersen Benson Enderud 71
Engebret Hovda 38
Engebret Johannesen Helgerudsveom
    158
Engebret Lindelien 33
Engebret Oppegaard 48
Engebret Risbrot 200
Engebreth Hobe 235
Engebrit Gunderson 99
Engel Okland 181
Enoch Larson 124,125,248
Ephrian Sevareid 159
Erhard Bruflat 34
Eric Bjarne Hauke 235
Eric Skavland 20
Erick Erickson 176
Erick Garvik 91
Erick Oleson Alm 180
Erick Overland 88
Erick Thorson 177
Erik A Uggen 40
Erik Anderson Uggen 116
Erik Berekvam 145
Erik Erickson 89
Erik Eriksen 201
Erik Erikson Braaten 71

Erik Eriksen Sevareid 159
Erik Gudbrandsen Kapperud 70
Erik Johansen Nerhaugen 69
Erik Johnson 187,188
Erik Knudson 92
Erik Knudson Garvig 91
Erik Knudson Garvik 91,92
Erik Larson 178
Erik Otterness 144
Erik Rekstad 180
Erik Uggen 48
Erland Skalshaugen 38
Erling Innvik 236
Erling Stone 236
Ernest Meyers,Mrs 149
Estelle H Knudsen 237
Esther Felland 77,78
Esther Gulbrandson 236
Esther Olsdtr Frygne 135
Evan Svensrud 181
Evar Nelson 135
Evelith Kuecker 221,234
Evelyn Norskog 101
Even Ellertson 27
Even Ellertson Dahl 27
Even Gulliksen Neggen 72
Even Gulmon 98
Even Hegg 167
Even Hoime 28
Even Jellum 110,111
Even Olson Fosli 201
Even Olson Strenge 162,163
Evie Swenson 234
Evonne Anderson 234
Evy Kuecker 248
Eyvind Evans 237
F Melius Christiansen 226
Finbo Olsen 181
Fingal Aslesen Flaten 28
Fingar Fosli 201
Fingar Uggen 48
Floyd Boraas 257
Frances Kuross 236
Frank Joerg,Mrs 184
Frans Overland 147
Fred Jensen 198
Fred Kroshus 122
Fredericka Gulbrandson 77
Fredrik Krohn 235
Fredrika Bremer 224
Fremont Applen 78
Fritz Johnson 181
G E Gilbertson 93
G G Weum 210,211
G K Haukebo 242
Gary Esterby 149
Gary Olson 219,231,247
Geir Arne Myrstuen 241
Geline Gilbertson 95
Geline Andrine Kassenborg 118
Geline Kassenborg Grover 94-96,178,219

General Grant 92
General Lee 92
General Sherman 115
Geneva Tweeten 234
George Armstrong Custer, General 191
George Abbott 139
George Bakko 57
George Carlton Hegland 181
George Emmons 87
George Gunderson 99
George J Buckeye 86
George Johnson 85,86
George Lommen 130
George Olson 140,256
George Oscar Gunderson 100
George Stangeland 214,215
George Temandsen Quarve 28
George Wralstad 83
Georgia Rosendahl 220,232,234
Georgina Strenge 162
Gerald Ziesemer 234
Gerhard B Naeseth 199,259
Gerhardt Solberg 184
Germa Foss 184
Gertrud Mikkelsdtr Ramsey 177
Gertrude Johnson 112,113
Gertrude Elton Soine 178,179
Getrude Jordet Langejoen 180
Gietru Nilsdtr Kaarstad 91
Gilbert Elias G Gilbertson 92,93
Gilbert Gilbertson 92,103,118
Gilbert Gulbrandsen 97
Gilbert Gullickson 98
Gilbert Kassenborg 118
Gilbert Kragnes 120
Gilbert Olaus Kassenborg 117
Gilbert Olson 76
Gilbert Peterson 84
Gilbert Monserud Olson 176
Gisle Moen 94
Gitta Eline Myran 123
Gjermund Johnson Lommen 128
Gjermund Jonsson Juve 85
Gjermund L Johnson Lommen 129
Gjermund Lommen 129
Gjermund Thorson 165
Gjert Gunderson 99
Gjertine Garvik 91
Gjertrud Knutson 180
Gjertrud Iversdtr Næse 134
Glenn Kinneberg 119,234
Gloria Norman 234
Goro Haugen 71
Gottfried Nelson 84
Gotthard Johnson 112
Gratia Stangeland 214,215
Greta Bakke 78
Gro Jørundsdtr Krintolen 85
Gro Sondresdtr Tverberg 54
Gubjor Martea Larsdtr Stuve 157
Gudbrand Pedersen Brynsaas 84

Gudmund Skiftun 19
Gulbrand Andersen 76
Gulbrand Anderson Gubberud 20
Gulbrand G Kassenborg 116
Gulbrand Gilbertson 95
Gulbrand Gubberud 18,21-25,96-97
Gulbrand Gulbrandsen 92,95,118
Gulbrand Gulbrandsen Braker 118
Gulbrand Gulbrandsen Kassenborg 118
Gulbrand Gulbrandsen Skjærstreneie 118
Gulbrand Kassenborg 219
Gulbrand Larsen 107
Gulbrand Nielsen Myrah 28
Gulbrand Nilsen 149
Gulbrand Oleson Tuff 165
Gulbrand Oleson Tuve 165,166
Gulbrand Olsen 97,103
Gulbrand Olson 76
Gulbrand Renna 39
Gulbrand Thomleie 118
Gulik Lindelien 39
Gulleck Olson 116
Gullick Erhardson Bruflat 34
Gullik A Dalen 33
Gullik Volstad 173
Gunarius Anderson 76
Gunder Andreas Lia 127
Gunder Andrias Lia 126
Gunder Bjørnsen 99
Gunder Gjeitsta 203
Gunder Gunderson 99,100
Gunder Hjermstad 105
Gunder Larsen 171
Gunder Nereson 186
Gunder Sorensen 86
Gunder Stabbestad 172
Gunder Traaen 28
Gunder Volstad 173
Gunhild Andersdtr Aaby 75
Gunhild Bakke 78
Gunhild Bukkøy 85
Gunhild Endresdtr Steinsrud 104
Gunhild Grangard Grant 104
Gunhild Gubberud 18,20,96
Gunhild Gunderson 99
Gunhild Guttormsdtr 82
Gunhild Guttormsdtr Syversrud 155
Gunhild Halvo Gautefall 172
Gunhild Jackson 176
Gunhild Johnsdtr Forlie 77
Gunhild Juve 121
Gunhild Knutsdtr Reierson 84
Gunhild Kørnbo Stangeland 181
Gunhild Kragnes 121
Gunhild Krosshaug 122
Gunhild Larsdtr Kodalen 99
Gunhild Lindelien 39
Gunhild Nielsdtr Hasleiet 177
Gunhild Pedersdtr Trostheim 179
Gunhild Sævre 82
Gunhild Sateren 158

Gunhild Sigurdsen 159
Gunhild Sigurdsdtr Jackson 160
Gunhild Skrei 203
Gunhild Stangeland 214
Gunhild Syverson 33
Gunhild Syversdtr Krosshaug 91
Gunhild Ulen 169,170
Gunhild Volstad 161,173
Gunhild Tostensdtr Evans 82
Gunhild Veum Holtan 106
Gunil Benson 176
Gunil Franson Rue 147
Gunil Franson Rue Overland 148
Gunil Gunderson 176
Gunil Overland 146
Gunild Syversdtr 122
Gunleik Jonsen Bøen 81
Gunlek Olson 48
Gunloug Rorhelle 147
Gunnar Dale 102
Gunnar Hanson Fjågesund 126
Gunnar Tollefsdtr Slettemoen 58
Gunnar Tyrebakken 87
Gunnil Annette Lia 127
Gunnil Holtan 106
Gunnild Gulmon 98
Gunnile Torbiornsdtr 159
Gunnlaug Hansdtr Aarbak 176
Gunvor H Vindlaus Richardson 151,152
Gunvor Halvorsdtr Vindlaus 150
Gunvor Larsdatter Strandheim 180
Guri Ellis 86
Guri Eriksdtr Skaro 160
Guri Garnaas 90
Guri Hefte 16,105
Guri Hovda 38
Guri Peterson Gilbertson 176
Guri Sandersdtr Slettemoen 58,164
Guri Sandersdtr Svensen 60
Guri Svenungsdtr Bamle 86
Guri Swenson 58
Guri Thorson Peterson 177
Gurina Carlsdtr Ytrefjornen 138
Gurina E Otterness 146
Gurine Einong Stangeland 176
Guro Bakken 83
Guro Nelson 3
Guro Ottun 146
Guro Overland 146
Guro Strand 70
Gust Anderson 177
Gust Gubrud 171
Gusta Ringdahl 152
Gustaf B Hauger 180
Gustaf Pedersen Fougner 200
Gustav Gjeitsta 203
Gustav Grover 95,96
Gustav Gubberud 96
Gustav Julius Jordgrav 115
Gustav O Hegg 200
Gustav Oscar Anderson 77

Gustav Ringdahl 152
Gustava Eriksen 201
Gustie Morem 133
Guttorm Guttormson 101,102
Guttorm Guttormsen Øino 118
Guttorm Olson Fraagot 72
Guttorm Otterness 173
Guttorm Pederson Otterness 144,145
H A Preus, Pastor 51
H C Caspersen 236
H I Golden 80
Haaken Narveson 28
Haakon Kieland 29
Haakon Narvesen 71
Hagan O Naeseth 123
Hagbart Bue 236
Haldor Olsen Ommelsæteren 70
Hallstein Torson Bakke 78
Halvard Magnesen Berge 200
Halvdan Svarte 251,255
Halvor Ahlness 196,197
Halvor Anderson Kroshus 179
Halvor Burtness 169
Halvor Erickson 9,10,88,89,147
Halvor Fendalsveit 204,212
Halvor Fendalsveit Salveson 203,204
Halvor Goodrich 10
Halvor H Eikhom 177
Halvor Halvorson 85
Halvor Halvorsson Eikhom 85
Halvor Johannesen Vig 39
Halvor Johannesen Week 39
Halvor Knudsen Volstad 161,172,173
Halvor Meland 48
Halvor Mutta 177
Halvor Nielsen Wilhelmstad 154
Halvor Odegaard 56,57
Halvor Olsen 141
Halvor Olsen Huset 108
Halvor Olsen Klastolen 38
Halvor Olsen Vaaler 170
Halvor Ommelstadsæteren 157
Halvor Pedersen Haakenstad 179
Halvor Peterson Slette 71
Halvor Quie 57
Halvor Rukke 154
Halvor Salveson 211
Halvor Tolvssen Bratsberg 176
Hanna Brynsaas 84
Hanna G Stalland 236
Hanna Olava Sateren 158
Hannah Gunderson 93
Hannah Larson Enger 181
Hannah Ohnstad Torgerson 138
Hannah Rotegard 153
Hans Andersen 38
Hans Anderson 33,148
Hans Andersen Gamlemoen 38
Hans Bakke 28
Hans C Gullickson Rud 131
Hans Dahle 101

Hans Danielson 142
Hans Ellingsen 28
Hans Engen 70
Hans Erickson 89
Hans Erikson 55
Hans Erlandsen Snedkerpladsen 71
Hans Franson 10
Hans Franson Rue 10
Hans Gamlemoen 33
Hans Garnaas 90
Hans Grønsten Johnson 51
Hans Gullickson 131
Hans Gunnarson Lee 126
Hans Gunnarson Lia 126,127,219
Hans Hanson 48
Hans Hanson Holtan 106,107
Hans Holtan Jr 106
Hans Hovelsen Tollefsrud 69
Hans J Hagen 180
Hans Johann Blixerud 81
Hans Johansen 70
Hans Johansen Lybeck 70
Hans Johnsen Botten 177
Hans Johnsen Grønsten 49.53.94
Hans Kittelson 178
Hans Larsen 179
Hans Lundby 130,131
Hans M Jacobsen 236
Hans Magnus Lia 127
Hans Næss 241
Hans Nielsen Hauge 228
Hans Nielsen Myrah 28
Hans Oleson 140
Hans Oleson Alm 180
Hans Olsen Stone 178
Hans Olson Torgersrud 179
Hans Ramstad 149
Hans Rosendahl 28
Hans Sagnes Jr 178
Hans Sampson 157
Hans Sønsteby Sagnes 177
Hans Suckstorff 177
Hans Teigen 177
Hans Torgrimson Tveito 167,168
Hans Tveito 167
Hansine Ramstad 149
Harald Boe 90
Harald Haarfarge 255
Harald Haraldson 104
Harald Hardråde 251
Harald Hvitbein 255
Harlan Johnsrud 114,234
Harold Gilbertson 103
Harold Gulbrandsen 97
Harold Hvattum 241
Harold Johnsrud 114
Harold N Golden 180
Harold Olson Rue 10
Harriet Foss 241
Harriet Gunderson 99
Hattie Oleson 139

Hazel Syverson Haugo 181
Hehaka Sapa 191
Helen B Tormoen 236
Helen Buche 234,256,261
Helen Daniels 256
Helen Gunderson 99
Helen Hanson 177
Helen Reierson 84
Helen Wolstad 93
Helen Hansdtr Paulson 70
Helena Vaaler 171
Helene Gunderson 99
Helene Halvorson 103
Helene Rekanes 150
Helga Gamme 220,231,234
Helga Hanson Stall 176
Helga Knudsdtr 190
Helga Olavsdtr Ulsnes 149
Helga Rekanes 150
Helge Christophersdtr 99
Helge Christophersdtr Gunderson 99
Helge Endru 99
Helge Gundersen Gundersen 86
Helge Gunderson 219
Helge Gunderson Emmons 71
Helge Halvorson 102,103
Helge Johnson 39
Helge Olsdtr Høgset 122
Helge Rotneim 87
Helge Skree 220
Helle Hansdtr Schustad 141
Hellek Aakre 91
Helma Findreng 101
Henry Alfred Anderson 77
Henry Applen 77
Henry Danielson 142
Henry Earl,Mrs 100
Henry Edwin Gunderson 100
Henry Grønsten 53
Henry Gundersen Emmons 86
Henry Holtan 106
Henry Johan Volstad 161,173
Henry Louis Berge 200
Henry Moore,Mrs 32,34
Henry Morem 133
Henry Nelson 135
Henry Nycklemoe 235
Henry Reierson 84
Henry S Blexrud 81
Henry Saevre 156
Henry Strenge 162
Herbjorn Ingulfsland 133
Herbjorn Ingulfsland Nelson 109
Herbjorn Nilssen Ingulfsland 109
Herbrand Bronson 83
Herbrand Finseth 56
Herbrand Olsen Skuleslatta 83
Herman Krosshaug 122
Herman Roe 236
Herman Nielsen Krydshoug 122
Herman Solomenson 188

Herman Jorgensen 236
Hermand Hovda 38
Hilda Gunderson 100
Hilda L Swenson 132
Hilda Myhre Hanson 236
Hilda Stangeland 214,215
Hildegard M M Strom 237
Hilmar Alexandersen 220
Hjalmar Bjørnson 236
Hjalmer Enger 88
Hjalmer Rued Holand 150,155,172,224
Hølje Halvorsen Vastvedt 93
Hovel Peterson Johnsrud 113,114
Hulda Aus 236
Hulda Holtan 106
Hulda Niklasen 96
Ida Marie Benson 201
Inga Erickson 176
Inga Johnson 112
Inga Amelia Nelson 123
Inga Amelia Nelson Kvernodden 179
Inga Augusta G Gilbertson 92
Inga Eriksdtr Tunselle 145
Inga Kinstad Groves 53
Inga Kinstad Grønsten Groves 94
Inge Lundby 130,131
Ingebjorg Gaasedelen 89
Ingebjørg Fjågesund 126
Ingebjørg Lia 126
Ingebor Bronson 83,84
Ingebor Jellum 110
Ingebor Kittelsdtr 161
Ingebor Jorgensdtr Bakkene 83
Ingebor Jorgensdtr Bronson 83,84
Ingebor Kittelsdtr Stabeck 161,172
Ingebor Stabeck Volstad 162,173
Ingebord Iverson 40
Ingeborg Aaby 74
Ingeborg Berekvam 79
Ingeborg Dahl 50
Ingeborg Ellefson 86
Ingeborg Felland 78
Ingeborg Georgine Grønsten Aaby 50
Ingeborg Gjermundson 178
Ingeborg Grasdalen 94
Ingeborg Grønsten 94
Ingeborg Guttormsdtr Otterness 173
Ingeborg Halvorsdtr Halvorson 177
Ingeborg Haugen 69
Ingeborg Hefte 104,105
Ingeborg Iverson 48,115,116
Ingeborg Johannesdtr Kleivstaul 74,76
Ingeborg Johnsdtr Jellum 110
Ingeborg Johnson 112
Ingeborg Kleven Stras 179
Ingeborg Larsdtr Veum 174
Ingeborg Lee 120
Ingeborg Levorsdtr Langeman 224
Ingeborg Lommen 128,130
Ingeborg Lundby 131
Ingeborg Maline Kassenborg 117

Ingeborg Marie Humble 107
Ingeborg Morem 133
Ingeborg Nielson 26
Ingeborg Nilsen 69
Ingeborg Ohnstad 137
Ingeborg Ohnstad Torgerson 138
Ingeborg Oldsdtr Kinneberg 104
Ingeborg Olsdtr Ommelstadsæteren 69
Ingeborg Or Ommelsæteren Ringdahl 69
Ingeborg Ommelstadsæteren 152,157
Ingeborg Otterness 66-68,144,174
Ingeborg Pedersdtr Otterness 127
Ingeborg Pedersdtr Ytre Lie 174
Ingeborg Rebekke Otterness 145
Ingeborg Rekanes 150
Ingeborg Rud 131
Ingeborg Sevareid 159
Ingeborg Sorum 27
Ingeborg Thorson 165
Ingeborg Tollevsdtr Sevareid 159
Ingeborg Torgrimsdtr Ellis 86
Ingeborg Torgrimsdtr Moen 86
Ingeborg Torsteinsdtr 104
Ingeborg Torsteinsdtr Melhus 78
Ingeborg Tostensdtr Gunvalson 82
Ingeborg Ulsness 88
Ingeborg Ulsness Overland 88
Ingeborg Wahl Johnson 179,180
Ingebret Garvik 91
Ingebret Gjermstad 105
Ingebret Larsen 171
Ingebret Olsen Vethammer 171
Inger Applen 77
Inger Augusta G Gilbertson 93
Inger Ellingsdtr Prestegaardseie 154
Inger Gubberud 96
Inger Haugen 116
Inger Hefte 15,16,105
Inger Johnson Holmquist 187,188
Inger Juvrud 48
Inger Mathia Sateren 158
Inger Nielsdtr 124
Inger Olava Gubberud 23
Inger Olsdtr Appelen 77
Inger Ottun 146
Inger Peterson Thiglum 137
Inger T Kvernodden 124
Ingeri Østensdtr 92
Ingman Applen 78
Ingri Anderson 176
Ingri Andersen Swenson 176
Ingri Blekstad 105
Ingri Hefte 104
Ingri Jergenson 180
Ingrid Hefte 104,105
Ingrid Kinneberg 15
Ingrid Ostensdtr 88
Ingrid Østensdtr Enger 176
Ingrid Ostensdtr Ringerud 88
Ingvald Muller 29
Irvin Kleven 257

Irvina Petrina Otterness 146
Isaac Thorson 177
Isabel Gunderson 150
Isabel Ommelstadsæteren 152
Isabella Olson 140
Isabelle Anderson 76
Isabelle Brokken 83
Isabelle Kragnes 120
Isabelle Tveito 168
Isak Anderson 179
Isak Thomasen 200
Ivan Brattelid 234
Ivar Aasen 242
Ivar Aus 236
Ivar Nelson 135
Ivar Pederson Kinneberg 119
Ivar Skoleland 119
Ivar Vaeting 14
Iver Berekvam 79
Iver Branno 180
Iver Halvorsen Kanten 177
Iver Herman Alm 180
Iver Jensson Berge 138
Iver Kinneberg 87
Iver Næse 134
Iver Pedersen 134
Iver Nelson Jr 135
J Larson 188
J A Asgaard 235
J Andreas Lundby 131
J C Tart 29
J H J Weeks 38
J J Bukoi 85
J Muller Eggen,Mrs 151
J N Kildahl,Pastor 67
J W C Dietrichson,Pastor 199
Jacob Jackson 160,176
Jacob Johnson 110
Jacob Johnson Jellum 110,111
Jacob K Stefferud 236
Jacob Ottun 146
Jacob Tveito 168
Jakob Peter Olsen Hatling 200
James Demeron 29
James Grønsten 94
James Smith 26,28
James Stangeland 214
James J Johnson 237
James Buchanan,President 101
Jan Haldorson Thorson 177
Jan Heusinkveld 234,241,261
Jane Johnson 112,113
Janet Martin 220,232
Jåråm Ellingson 94
Jared Thoreson 219
Jean Marthaler 234
Jean M Carlson 234
Jenny Kvernodden 123
Jenny Alvilde Johnson 236
Jens Berekvam 78,145
Jens Christian Dunham 77

Jens Elemoen 28
Jens Ellingsen Winjum 173,174
Jens Grønsten 53
Jens Guttormsen 82
Jens Nelson 197,198
Jens Nielson Smebyhagen 196
Jens Nilsen 146
Jens Nilsen-Smebyhagen 197
Jens Olsen Otternes 173
Jens Otternes 173
Jens Ottun 146
Jens Ouren 196,197
Jensine Otterness 66,145
Jerdine Eikeland Loe 180
Jerry Paulson 260
Jesse James 169
Jessica Linder 234
Jessie Sampson 157
Jim Skree 220,232,234
Jo Larson 261
Joann Gunderson 234
Joel A Lund 234
Johan Andreas Lundby 131
Johan Andrias Pedersen 134
Johan Berekvam 79
Johan C Hole 180
Johan Gubberud 96
Johan Hansen Lybeck 70
Johan Hanson 180,181
Johan Nilsen Hårsaker 76
Johan Nilsen Horsager 76
Johan Rood 70
Johan Rud 70
Johan Theodor Josiassen 201
Johan Tollefson 186
Johan Underdahl 127
Johan Vaaler 171
Johana Foss 184
Johanna Brynsaas 84
Johanna Ellis 86
Johanna Engen Hagen 181
Johanne Klastolen 38
Johanna Lommen 129
Johanna Marie Olsen Hogstad 179
Johanna Nielsdtr Smedbyhagen 196
Johanna Ohnstad 138
Johanna Oleson 138
Johanne A Hobe 235
Johanne Hansdtr Alm 180
Johanne Otterness 144
Johanne Pedersen 134,148
Johanne Torgersdtr 148
Johannes Botolvsen Ytre Lie 127,174
Johannes Botolvson Lie 127
Johannes Ecklund 188
Johannes Ellefson Sauerlie 86
Johannes Lade 103
Johannes Lie 127
Johannes Martinson 178
Johannes Martinson Narumshagen 178
Johannes Mikkelsen Spigedalen 177

Johannes Olsen 201
Johannes Olsen Ohnstad 137
Johannes Olsen Ommelstadsæteren 69,157
Johannes Olsen Sateren 157
Johannes Olson Overland 146,147
Johannes Overland 9,10,147
Johannes Stenersen Lunde 131
Johannes the elder Berekvam 79
Johannes the younger Berekvam 79
Johannes Tollefsrud 69
Johannes Vig 39
Johannes Week 39
John Aaby 51,74
John Aanonsen 205
John Amundsen Lindelien 39
John Anderson 75,76
John Anderson Kroshus 122
John Anderson Stensrud 122
John Arnt Gunderson 100
John Berquist 220,231
John H Blexrud 81
John Blixerud 81
John Bredeson 178
John Brokken 83
John Buche 234
John Dahle,Pastor 112
John Donne 67
John Einong 168
John Ellefson 86
John Ellis 86
John Erickson 148
John Erickson 89,148
John Estensen 81
John Gjeitsta 203
John Grønsten 49,51,94
John Gullickson 98
John Guttormson 102
John H Elstad 178
John Haugo 234
John Holtan 106
John Hoovel Tollefsrud 70
John Humble 108
John J Lee 174
John Jacobson 133,176
John Jellum 110
John Johnson 52,53,112,133,188
John K Daniels 236
John Lee 125
John Lommen 28,129,130
John Moe 180
John Molee 167
John Morem 133
John Nilsen 201
John O Bakken 21
John O Gaare 179
John O Hogstad 177
John O Loe 180
John Olaf Ibsen Erickson 123,180
John Olson 181
John Østenson Bøen 81

John Other Day 190
John Ouren 196,198
John Overland 147
John Peder Hogstad 177
John Peterson,Mrs 108
John Peterson Tverberg 54
John R Jenswold 227
John R Johnson 70
John Sigurdsen 159,160
John Simonson 234
John Solomonson 187
John Steingrimsen Bergrud 71
John Strenge 162
John T Kvernodden 124
John Torine 124
John Tveito 168
John Tverberg 50-52
John Vale 28
Johnny Applen 77
Johnny Grønsten 94
Johnny Johnson 53
Jon Anfinson Lommen 111,125,128,130
Jon Buckeye 85
Jon Ellingson 76
Jon Gaasedelen 89
Jon Gundersen Eidal 72
Jon Gunleikson Bøen 81
Jon Halvorson Buckeye 85
Jon Jacobsen Jellum 110
Jon Halvorson 85
Jon Johnson 111
Jon Johnson Lommen 129
Jon Nelson 76
Jon Ohnstad 137
Jon Olsen Bøen 81
Jonas Nelsen Berg 38
Joraand Thortvedt 203
Jøran Aaby 74
Jøran Aanesdtr Omland 74
Joran Christiansdtr Gire 154
Joran Johnson 188
Jorand Haugerstuen 39
Jorand Haugerstuen Vig 39
Jorand Rukke 154
Joren Gjermundsdtr 128
Jorend Gjermundsdtr 125,130
Jorend Lee 125
Jorend Lommen 111,129,130
Jorend Olson Riste 130
Jorgen Bronson 83,84
Jorgen Bukkøy 86
Jorgen Flesvig 193-196
Jørgen Jonsson Bukkøy 85
Jørgen Langemo,Mrs 149
Jorgen Lommen 130
Jorund Haldorson Thorson 177
Joseph Albert Sateren 158
Joseph Anderson 176
Joseph Edvin Aslakson 128
Joseph Lennon 182
Joseph Nelson 68

Joseph Ober 23
Joseph Ohnstad 138
Joseph Ramstad 149
Joseph Skaro 160,161
Joseph Strenge 162,163
Joseph Tuf 33
Josephine Brack 236
Josephine Hogstad 181
Josephine Larson 178,257
Josephine Lunde 132
Josephine Pedersen 134
Josephine Ramstad 138
Joyce Krueger 234
Judy Stevens 234,261
Jul Aaby 74
Jul Nelson 135
Julia Bollie 178
Julia Botten 179
Julia Brokken 83
Julia Ellis 86
Julia Erickson Solseth 83
Julia Foss 184
Julia Grasdalen 120
Julia Gubberud 96
Julia Hansdtr Aarbak 176
Julia Johnson 39
Julia Kassenborg Tvedten 117
Julia Nelson 135
Julia OgenaKassenborg 117
Julia Peterson Gilbertson 176
Julia Reierson Peterson 84
Julia Sampson 157
Julia Thorson Peterson 177
Julia Volstad 173
Julianes Sateren 158
Julie Volstad 161
Julius Nelson 135
Julius Ottun 146
Julius Twaiten 101
K A Knudson 48
Kaarn Vaaler 171
Karen Berekvam 79
Karen Christianson 256
Karen Christopherson Anderson 181
Karen Enden Elandson 179
Karen Englestad 108
Karen Fried 234
Karen Hagen 178,234
Karen Hanson 48
Karen Hanson Larson 177
Karen Humble 107
Karen Huset 108
Karen Kjerstine Eich 49,94
Karen Knudsdtr Jørandlien 131,132
Karen Kristine Lia 126
Karen Maria Ellefsdtr Strenge 162
Karen Marie Danielson Stubberud 77
Karen Mathea Hr Melbyeie Larson 125
Karen Mathea Hansdtr Melbyeie 124
Karen Olson 234

Karen Olsdtr Kvam 90
Karen Strenge 163
Karen Wahl Bakken 181
Kari Berekvam 145
Kari Engebretson Rogness 179
Kari Finhart 33,34
Kari Gaarder 131
Kari Garnaas 90
Kari Gunderson 99
Kari Hovda 32,34,38
Kari Hovda Finhart 33
Kari Ingebrethsdtr 99
Kari Jellum 110
Kari Jensdtr Winjum 176
Kari Johnsen 201
Kari Kittelsdtr Jordgrav 114
Kari Kragnes 116,120
Kari Lybeck 38
Kari Madsdtr Ruud 69
Kari Mikkelsdtr 120
Kari Mikkelsdtr Holte 121
Kari Nilsdtr Gaardersæteren 70
Kari Nilsdtr Viljugrein 78
Kari Nerol 60
Kari Olsdtr Nordskoug 163
Kari Olsdtr Swenson 163,164
Kari Overland Erickson 88
Kari Omsrud 141
Kari Overland 9,88,89,146
Kari Rotegard 153
Kari Rue 147
Kari Sæthre 155
Kari Steinarsdtr Kleiv 110
Kari Stenehjem 17
Kari Swenson 163,164
Kari Thorsdtr Ytterbøe 108
Kari Tovsdtr 155
Kari Vig 39
Kari Week 39
Karina Margret Jordgrav 115
Karine Bjerke Martinson 178
Karine Christensdtr Bjerke 178
Karine Bronson 84
Karine Lie 127
Karl G Andersen 235
Karl Oleson 140
Karl Vaaler 171
Karlen Nelson 84
Karn Alitta Hanson 180,181
Karoline Henrikke Andersen 76
Karoline Iverson 116
Kasperinde Erickson Oium 129
Kate Olson 178
Kaye Norman 234
Kendrick Charles Babcock 226
Kent A Jacobson 103
Kierstine Andersen 76
Kim Linder 234
King Alf 255
King Erik XIV 256
King Fredrik II 256

King Haakon Magnusson 255
King Harald 255
King Olav II 251
King Snæfred 255
Kirsten Berg 38
Kirsten Christensdtr Huset 108
Kirsten Heier Western 241
Kirsten Holman 108
Kirsten Maria Christensdtr Stenstadvalen 108
Kirstie Olsdtr Klovstadeie 140
Kirstin Sampson 157
Kittel Hasleiet 177
Kittel Jordgrav 115
Kittel Rekanes 150
Kittel Kittelson Dompendal 149
Kittel Kittelson Haugen 150
Kittel O Garnaas 178
Kittel Olavson Jordgrav 114
Kittel Tostenson Stabeck 161
Kittel Volstad 161,173
Kittil Swenson 163
Kjell Bergh 237
Kjell Hoelstad 219,220,234
Kjell Myhre 241
Kjell Nordlie 221,234
Kjerste Rotneim 87
Kjersti Gubberud 20,21,25
Kjersti Gudbrandsdtr 96
Kjersti Gudbrandsdtr Gubberud 18
Kjersti Gudbrandsdtr Haugsrudie 18
Kjersti I Vethammer Larsen 172
Kjersti Ingebretsdtr Vethammer 105,171
Kjersti Klastolen 38
Kjersti Kroshus 179
Kjersti Larson 86
Kjersti Mikkelsdtr 87
Knud Bendixsen Nord Strand 135,136
Knud Bergo 28
Knud Einarson Røbele 91
Knud Ellingsen Skaro 160
Knud Engebriktsen 119
Knud Gilbertson 28
Knud Gullickson 98
Knud Ike 173,174
Knud Knudsen 82,201
Knud Knudsen Kieland 71
Knud Knudsen Leirol 89
Knud Knudsen Sævre 155
Knud Knudson Kieland 28
Knud Lee 125
Knud Lie 125
Knud Nelson 135
Knud Olsen Heggtveit 190
Knud Olsen Wold 28
Knud Olson Rukke 153,154
Knud Overland 146
Knud Rasmusson 177
Knud Rukke 154
Knud Saavesen Aaker 75
Knud Sævre 82

Knud Sagedalen 28
Knud Volstad 161
Knudt Gunderson 179
Knudt Johnsen 200
Knudt Nilsen 201
Knudt Rotegard 153
Knut Applen 77
Knut Finseth 56
Knut Gaasedelen 89,90
Knut Garvik 91
Knut Gunderson 99
Knut Gunleikson Volstad 172
Knut Knudson Finseth 56
Knut Knutson Solberg 179
Knut Langeland 9
Knut Larsen Turli 174
Knut Lønnegrav 220
Knut Nelson 207
Knut Nilsen 38
Knut Nilsen Haugerstuen 38
Knut Nilsen Hefte 104
Knut O Blixerud 80
Knut Otterness 145
Knut Overland 10
Knut Volstad 161,173
Knute Bergetongen 79,80
Knute Bronson 83,84
Knute Nelson 227
Knute Nelson Rogness 179
Knute Ole Orton 142,143
Knute Olsson Aaretun 143
Knute Otterness 174
Knute Reierson 84
Knute Rotegard 153
Knute Roundal 178
Kolbjorn Haugen 48
Kristen Eggen 149
Kristen Johansen Rood 69
Kristen Johansen Rud 69
Kristi Aslackson 95
Kristi Grover 103
Kristi Hegland 165
Kristi Helgesdtr 86
Kristi Iversdtr Erikson 55
Kristi Olavsdtr Lien 94,95
Kristi Swenson 58,164
Kristi Uggen 40,48
Kristian Haraldson 104
Kristian Rood 69
Kristian Rud 69
Kristin Brynsaas 84
Kristina Jellum 110
Kristine Maline Pedersen 134
Kristine Maline Sandvig 134
Kristine Olsdtr Ohnstad 137
Kristofer,Big Lommen 128,129
Kristoffer Larsen 107
Kristoffer Olsen Kopseng 99
Krostoffer Hansen Engen 70
L Opsahl 256
L H Bunnell,Dr139

L K Aaker 200
L O Pedersen 216
Larry Liebe 234
Larry Olson 68
Lars Andersen 201
Lars Gaasedelen 89
Lars Gimmestad 246
Lars Hansen 70
Lars Humble,Jr 107,108
Lars Jensen 89
Lars Johannesen Friestad 124
Lars Johnsrud 114
Lars Knudson Aaker 75
Lars Knutsen 75
Lars Larsen 171,172
Lars Larsen Otterness 145
Lars Larsen Humble,Sr 107,108
Lars Lundby 130
Lars Melbostad 132
Lars Nilsen 200
Lars Oddsen 66
Lars Oddsen Otterness 145
Lars Oddsen Ytre Lie 174
Lars Oddsen Ytrelie 144
Lars Olaus Otterness 145
Lars Olson Grasdalen 93,94
Lars Ommelstadsæteren 157
Lars Osterud 131
Lars Otterness 66,67,144,174
Lars Reiersen Halstenrud 28,71
Lars S Rodningen 59
Lars Sand 102
Lars Solomenson 188
Lars Sorenson Hjermstad 105,106
Lars Sveinsen Rudningen 164
Lars Svenson Rodning 186
Lars Swenson 58,164
Lars Torkelson 71
Lars Tostensen 87
Lars Ytrelie 144
Laura Lundby 130
Laura Emilie G Gilbertson 93
Laura Galine G Gilbertson 93
Lauritz Huset 108
Lauritz Steen,Rev 54
Lawrence Molsather 236
Lawrence Olav Hauge 237
Lawrence Oliver Otterness 145
Lawrence Otterness 66,67
Leander Foss 184
Lee Rokke 237
Leif Levi Thortvedt 203
Leiv Jonsson Roholt 85
Leiv Vonen 220
Leland Sateren 237
Lena Anderson 177
Lena Bakke 78
Lena Danielson 142
Lena Erickson 89
Lena G Gilbertson 92,93
Lena Hansen 159

Lena Hogstad 177
Lena Jordgrav 115
Lena Lia 126
Lena Skjenstad 180
Lena Peterson Suckstorff 177
Leo Koll 235
LeRoy Larson 221,233
Leslie Rogne 241
Lettie Huset 108
Levi Kragness 101
Levi St John 182
Levor Temandsen Quarve 28
Lewis Anderson 75
Lewis Emmons 87
Lewis Olai Larsen 200
Lewis Olson 140
Lillian Gunhus 123
Lina Berge Hegland 181
Lina Enger 88
Lisa Martinsdtr Alm 180
Lisbeth Olsdtr Huset 108
Lise Sateren 158
Little Crow 187
Little Paul 190
Liv Aslakson 128
Liv Dahl 237
Liv Guttormson 102
Liv Knudsdtr Haug 118
Liv Olavsdtr Hjamdal 114,126
Liv P Valtvedt Ødegaard 176
Liv Simonsen 33,38
Live Stabeck 161
Liviu Ciulen 237
Lizzie Sateren 158
Lloyd Swenson 101,234
Lloyd Hustvedt,Dr 67
Lois A Jorstad 234
Lois Rand 237
Lorentz Hegland 181
Lorenzo Lawrence 190
Lorraine Carlson 236
Lorraine Engelsgaard 248
Louis Bøen 82
Louis Hansen 200
Louis O Sundquist 139
Louis Olson 96
Louisa Vislander 198
Louise Bøen 82
Louise Holtan 106
Lovise Olson 140
Lowell Oellien 257
Ludvig Johnson 179
Ludvig Strauman 236
Ludwig Vaaler 171
Luetta Earl Ernst 100
Luther Kragnes 120
M J Heste 245
Mabel Applen 78
Mabel Isabel Johnson 181
Mabel Kvernodden 123
Mabel Nelson 123

Mable Vaala 257
Magdalene Sjurud 38
Maggie Applen 77
Magne Smedvig 236
Mah-kah-ta He-i-ya-win 190
Malene Gubberud 25,97
Malene Kulberg 179
Malene Skiftun 19,20,22,23,96
Mallin Johannsen 108
Mah-za-koo-te-manne 190
Mamie Kittleson 167
Maren Danielson 142
Maren Gjermstad 105
Maren Gjertsdtr Klemetsrud 99
Maren Huset 108
Maren Johnsrud 113
Maren Larsen 171
Maren Ramstad 149
Maren Sohlgaard 111
Maren Sohlgaard Johnson 112
Maren Strenge 162
Margaret Gullickson 98
Margaret Lone 150
Margaret Miller 237
Margaret Rekanes 150
Margarette Stephensdtr Oleson 140
Marget Karine Jordgrav 115
Margit Bakko 56,57
Margit Engen 105
Margit Finseth 56
Margit Germundsdtr Storaasli 165
Margit Germundsdtr Thorson 165
Margit Harstad 177
Margit Hefte 105
Margit Mikkelsdtr Øygarden 114
Margit Olsdtr 201
Margit Olsdtr Finseth 56
Margit Pedersdtr Rotneim 87,88
Margit Rotneim 87
Margit Sigurdsen 201
Margit Thorson 165
Mari Aaker Bordsen 176
Mari Garnaas 90
Mari Gudbrandsdtr 84
Mari Kittelsdtr Stensrud 121
Mari Larsdtr Haegtvedt 75
Mari Mikkelsdtr Ile 171
Mari Otternes 173
Mari Rood 70
Mari Rud 70
Mari Sanden Hanson 177
Mari Sørensdtr Pedersen 148
Mari Syversdtr Nerhaugen 69
Maria Arntson 130
Maria Huset 108
Maria Johnson 112
Maria Knudsen 201
Maria Mokastad 81
Maria Olsdtr Vale 122,124
Maria Sæthre 155
Maria Thorson 177

Maria Vinje 159
Marian Leimbach 234
Marian Sateren 158
Marianna Ottun 146
Marie Brown 256
Marie Langemo Voxland 149
Marie Larsdtr Vaaler 170
Marie Mickelsen 179
Marie Mutta Sagnes 178
Marie Sevareid 159
Marie Siqveland 236
Marie Teigen 177
Marie Volstad 161,173
Marie Winjum 174
Marilyn Somdahl 237
Marilyn Sorenson 234
Marit Christophersdtr Gaaseberg 161
Marit Eriksdtr Røbele 91
Marit Garvik 91
Marit Halvorsdtr Milevandet 38
Marit Johnson Lindelien 33
Marit Knudsdtr Gullickson 98
Marit Lindelien 38
Marit Lommen 128-130
Marit O Korssjoen 179
Marit Oldsdtr Ristey 129
Marit Syverson 33
Mark Janda 234
Mark Johnson 234
Marlene Miller 234
Marta Knutsdtr Otterness 145
Marta Knudsdtr Ytre Lie 174
Marta Knutsdtr Ytrelie 144
Marta Larsdtr Otterness 144,145
Marta Larsdtr Ytrelie 144
Marte Lundby 130,131
Marta Oddsen 66
Marta Ohnstad 137
Marta Oline Johnsen 200
Marta Otterness 145
Marta Ytre Lie 174
Marte Hansdtr Bjørkeie 158
Marte Knudsdtr Oddsen 174
Marte Marie Olsdtr Ruud 130
Marte P Vollum Mork 179
Martha Anderson 76
Martha Anfinnson 220
Martha Axelsdtr Iverson 115,116
Martha Axelsdtr Juvrud 116
Martha Berekvam 79
Martha Brynsaas 84
Martha Christopherson Anderson 178
Martha Flattum 147
Martha Florand 38,39
Martha Foss 184
Martha Froland 38
Martha Ike 173,174
Martha Iverson 41
Martha Johnsrud 114
Martha Juvrud 48,168
Martha Melbostad 132

Martha Nelson 135
Martha O Gullickson 131
Martha Oleson 138,139
Martha Oline Skjenstad 180
Martha Olsen 176
Martha Olson 76
Martha Otternes 173
Martha Ottum 138
Martha Ottum Ohnstad 138
Martha Sjursdtr Midje 174
Martha Strand 47
Martha Vaaler 171
Marthe Andersen Paulsen 177
Marthe Isaksdtr 84
Marthe Sæthre 155
Marthe Schartum 155
Marthe Swenson 163
Marthe Thorsdtr 135
Marthea Humble 107
Martia Rekstad 180
Martin Anderson 196-198
Martin Brynsaas 84
Martin Eriksen 177
Martin Eskar 101
Martin G Gilbertson 92,93
Martin Gubberud 18,20
Martin Larson 181
Martin Lommen 129
Martin Luther 53
Martin Olsen 201
Martin Olson 101
Martin Peterson 178
Martin Sevareid 159
Martin Theodore O Gunderson 99,100
Martin Ulvestad 118
Martin Wells 213
Martina Kvernodden 123
Mary Adella Orton 142
Mary Annette Uggen Hagen 169
Mary Bakke 78
Mary Christopherson 157
Mary Christopherson Sampson 157
Mary Crooks 190
Mary Edna Oleson 139
Mary Groshong 147
Mary Grover 95,96
Mary Halbert 234
Mary Holtan 106
Mary Johnson 133,181,237
Mary Jordgrav 115
Mary Larsdtr Johnsrud 113,114
Mary Laurense Nelson 123
Mary Lee 127
Mary Olesdtr Moe 180
Mary Peterson 84
Mary Thorvildsdtr Kilane 92
Mary Volstad 161,173
Mathea Ellson Larson 181
Mathia Sateren 158
Mathias Olsen 176
Mathias Mickelsen 179

Mathias Schmidt Nilsen 29
Mathilda Sevareid 159
Matilda Lunde 132
Matt Reese 234
Matthias Pedersen Ringdahl 69,152
Maurice Fladager 29
May Nelson 123
May Strenge 162
Melvin Ringdahl 152
Metta Osmundsdtr 124
Mette Hoen 124
Michael Christopherson 179
Michael Erickson 181
Michael Hanson 150
Michael Jenson 176
Michael Jordgrav 114
Michelle Metzger 85
Mikal Kartvedt 237
Mikkel Gunnulvson Rolegheta 149
Mikkel Hanson 150
Mikkel Hegland 165
Mikkel Johannssen 180
Mikkel Kittelson Jordgrav 114,115,219
Mikkel Knudson 136
Mikkel Rekanes 150
Mikkel Sævre 82,156
Mikkel Sinnes 101
Mikkel Tarjeisen Hegland 176
Mikkel Walhus 122
Mildred Schill 234,248
Mildred Skurdahl 257
Millie Ardorfer 256
Mina August Kassenborg 117
Mina Holte Spigedalen 177
Mina Kassenborg Morken 117
Minnie Thorson 177
Molina Sampson 157
Mons Bottolfson 200
Mons Fladager 29
Mons K Foss 182-184
Morgan Olson 240
Myrtle Wenberg 198
N H Nelson,Mrs 184
N N Quammen,Pastor 110
Narv Somdahl 251
Nat Finney 236
Nell Orton 142,143
Nellie Applen 77
Nellie Nelson 198
Nels Anderson 75
Nels Danielson 142
Nels Danielson Opsal 141
Nels Ekabot Nelson 135
Nels Grønsten 94
Nels Hefte 105
Nels Helgedalen 179
Nels Hendrickson 29
Nels Hendrickson Stoen 29
Nels Jensen Ottun 146
Nels Kinneberg 119
Nels Minne 236

Nels N T Kvernodden 124
Nels Nelson Kvernodden 122
Nels O Norman 136
Nels Olsen Blexerud 20
Nels Onsgard 29
Nels Otterness 144
Nels Rotegard 153
Nels Tolvsen Kvernodden 122,124
Nels Tweito 28
Nelvin Kinneberg 119
Nettie Brown 150
Nettie Jacobsen 57
Nicholas Nelson 135
Nickolene Gustine Hallum 120
Nicolai Jahn 89
Niels Selland 136,159
Nils Aaby 74
Nils Anderson 135
Nils Bakke 78
Nils Bøen 82,188
Nils Erstad 69
Nils Gaasedelen 89,90
Nils Garnaas 90
Nils Garvik 91
Nils Grønsten 53
Nils Hefte 15,104
Nils Ingulfsland 109
Nils Johnson 53,178
Nils Lunde 39
Nils Magelson 12
Nils McCusick 224
Nils Moen 33
Nils Myre 87
Nils Nelson 135
Nils Nilsen 201,224
Nils Paulsen 201
Nils Rotneim 87
Nils Syversen 32,38
Nils Syverson 33
Nils Abraham Thorsen 201
Nils Andreas Nelson 123
Nils Nelsen Haugerstuen 38
Nils O Brandt,Pastor
   51,111,152,158,199-202
Nils Olavson Grovum 74
Nils Olsen Vinjum 176
Nils Syversen Moen 32,38
Nora Louise Nelson 123
Norma Gilbertson 234,241
Norma Gilbertson 234
Norman Grønsten 53
Norman Johnsen,Pastor 200
O Okasås 220
O N Nelson 112
O W Anderson,Dr 39
Oakey Jackson 235
Odd Otterness 66-68,144-146
Odd Ytre Lie 174
Odd Ytrelie 144
Odd Amundson Ytre Lie 174
Odd Lovoll,Dr 220,222,231

Odell Bjerkness 237
Øesten Gubberud 18,20,22,25,96
Øistein, King of Oplands 255
Ola Anderson 204,210,212
Ola Bakke 78
Ola FroysakBrekke 104
Ola Gunderson Thorvedt 203
Ola Hellekson Flata 50
Ola Iversen Kinneberg 104
Ola Nielsen Selland 136,159
Ola Nilson Brekke 15
Ola Skree 220
Ola Strandvold 206,207,209
Ola Tostensen Appelen 77
Ola Tostensen Applen 77
Olaf Jacobson 103
Olaf Tostensen 201
Olaus Gundersen 176
Olaus Hefte 105
Olaus Hjermstad 106
Olaus Johnson 178
Olaus Johnsrud 114
Olaus Vaaler 171
Olav Fjågesund 126
Olav Haralds0n 255
Olav Knutsen Overland 146
Olav Overland 12
Olav Thorson 165
Olav Tronsson 126
Olav Thortvedt 178
Olava Branno 180
Olava Nelson 135
Olava Olsdtr Rood 69
Olava Olsdtr Rud 69
Olava Sophie Pedersdtr Tollefsrud 70
Olaves Strenge 162,163
Olavus Larsen 107
Ole Aanundson 120
Ole Asleson 169-170
Ole Aanundson Kragnes 121
Ole Amundson Berg 28
Ole Andersen 76
Ole Anderson 75,178
Ole Anderson Lundby 131
Ole Anderson Ramstad 149
Ole Andreas Ohnstad 137
Ole Anundson Kragnes 116
Ole Appelen 77
Ole Applen 77,78
Ole Aslakson Grover 94,95
Ole B Garnaas 91
Ole B Tone 29
Ole Bakke 78
Ole Bakko 56,57
Ole Benson 89
Ole Berekvam 79,145
Ole Bergetongen 79
Ole Borjum 112
Ole Botten 179
Ole Brokken 83
Ole Bronson 83,84

Ole C Swenson 163,164
Ole Christiansen Stensrud 71
Ole Dahl 50
Ole Drengson Kleppo 150
Ole Emanuel Kragnes 120
Ole Ellingson 48
Ole Ellis 86
Ole Engen 105
Ole Erickson 89
Ole Erickson Alm 180
Ole Evensen Dølehus 118
Ole Estensen 81,200
Ole Finhart 31,32,33,34,38
Ole Finseth 56
Ole Florand 38
Ole Florand,Mrs 39
Ole Fosli 201
Ole Froland 38
Ole Gaasedelen 89,90
Ole Gamme 220.231.234,241
Ole Garnaas 90
Ole Gilbertson 176
Ole Gjermundson 178
Ole Gjermundson Haakenes 121
Ole Grasdalen 94
Ole Grover 103
Ole Gubberud 96
Ole Gudmundsen Molstad 201
Ole Gudmundsen Skiftun 19,96
Ole Gulbrandsen 97
Ole Gulbrandsen Gilbertson 103
Ole Gullickson Griffin 177
Ole Gunderson 99,101
Ole Gunnerius Olsen 201
Ole Guttormson 102
Ole Halvorson Valle 26
Ole Hanson 40,44,48,177
Ole Hanson Korsdalen 40,41,116
Ole Hardy 93
Ole Hasledalen 29
Ole Hefte,Gofa 15-17,104,105
Ole Hefte,Lame 15,104
Ole Hegedahl 236
Ole Herbrandson Bronson 83,84
Ole Hoejesen 77
Ole Hovda 38
Ole Ingebretson Halvorseth 155
Ole Iverson 29
Ole Jacobson 178
Ole Jacobson Hagen,Rev 181
Ole Johnson 112
Ole Jordgrav 115
Ole Jorgen Bakko 56
Ole Jorgens 33,38
Ole Julsen 38
Ole Juvrud 42-45,48,168
Ole Jonsen Vale 124
Ole Juvrud,Mrs 44
Ole Kittelson 71
Ole Knudsen 190
Ole Knudsen Gaarder 131

Ole Knudsen Gaasedelen 89
Ole Knudssen Kolsrud 179
Ole Knutson 119,120
Ole Knutson Skjerdal 143
Ole Kornelius Olsen 201
Ole Kragnes 120,220
Ole L Blexrud 81
Ole Larsen 107
Ole Larsen Soredahl 124
Ole L Skogstad Ommelstadsæteren 157
Ole Lee 125
Ole Lewison 80,81
Ole Lewison Blexrud 80
Ole Lewison Blixerud 80
Ole Lia 126
Ole Lindelien 39
Ole Lofthus 59
Ole Lommen 129,130
Ole Lundby 130
Ole Lunde 39
Ole Maarem 133
Ole Martin 177
Ole Midgarden 204,206,210-212
Ole Mikkelson 149
Ole Mikkelson Rekanes 149,150,219
Ole Miller 196
Ole Mo 201
Ole Morem 133
Ole N Hefte 105
Ole N Norman 136,137
Ole Nilson Engen 87,88
Ole Norman 136
Ole O Huset 108
Ole O Juvrud 40
Ole O Langhei 179
Ole Ohnstad 137
Ole Oleson 136,138,140
Ole Oleson Tuve 165
Ole Oleson Hefte,Storre 15-17,104,105
Ole Olsen 115,181
Ole Olsen Berekvam 145
Ole Olsen Gulbrandsgutten 71
Ole Olsen Hovda 38
Ole Olsen Juvrud 41,115,116
Ole Olsen Mo 201
Ole Olsen Rotneim 87
Ole Olsen Sjurud 38
Ole Olsen Skjerdal Otternes 173
Ole Olson Grasdalen 93
Ole Olson Severud 32
Ole Olson Ulen 170
Ole Ommelstadsæteren 157
Ole Orton 143
Ole Østensen Bøen 186,188
Ole Østenson Bøen 81,82
Ole Overland 9,10,88,146,147,148
Ole P Anderson 70
Ole P Olson 196
Ole P Sigstadoe 196
Ole P Kulberg 179
Ole Paulsen 177

Ole Paulson 70
Ole Pedersen Hogstad 177
Ole Pedersen Næse 134
Ole Peterson Slette 71
Ole Peterson 177,178,200
Ole Richardson 150
Ole Ringdahl 152
Ole Rood 69
Ole Roppe 29
Ole Rotegard 153
Ole Rotneim 87
Ole Rud 69
Ole Rukke 154
Ole Sæther 200
Ole Sagedalen 28
Ole Sampson 156
Ole Selland 136
Ole Selland 159
Ole Sigurdsen 159
Ole Simonsen 32-34
Ole Simonson Jorbraaten 33,38
Ole Soine 178,179
Ole Sørenson 69
Ole Steneroden 28
Ole Stensrud 28
Ole Swenson 58,163,164
Ole Synsteby 197
Ole T Aanderud 201
Ole T Kvernodden 124
Ole Thorerson 140
Ole Thorsen Tollefsgaardeie 153
Ole Thorson 177
Ole Torgerson 61
Ole Tollefsrud Kittilsland 26
Ole Torkelsen Høiset 122
Ole Tuff 10
Ole Ulen 28
Ole Winjum 174
Olena Peterson Jacobson 178
Oley Thorson 177
Olia Gubberud 18,20,21
Olia Olson 177
Olice Findreng 101
Olina Anderson Lee 178
Olina Olson 75
Oline Applen 78
Oline Christophersen Olsen 177
Oline Hogstad 177
Oline Jorssjoen 179
Oline Juvrud 44,48,116,168,169
Oline Juvrud Uggen 168
Oline Karine Olsdtr Jørondlien Gaarder 69
Oline Loftness 146
Oline Norderhus Thorson 177
Oline Olsdtr Olson 181
Oline Olson 83
Oline Rood 69
Oline Rud 69
Oline Studlien 120
Olive Ringdahl 152

Oliver Gullickson Griffin 177
Oliver Kragnes 120
Oliver Olson 140
Oliver Pedersen 134
Oliver Stall 176
Ollegaard Nilsdtr Talle 146
Oluf Sateren 158
Ommund Torsen 165
Ommund Thorsen Storaasli 165
Oraine Bjugan 234
Orlyn A Kringstad 237
Orpha Hoelstad 234
Orvin Larson 257
Osalf Olsen 179
Oscar Alm 180
Oscar Hertsgaard 235
Oscar Peterson 84
Oscar Ramstad 149
Oscar Tveito 168
Osmund Gunderson 99,100
Osmund Sevareid 159
Østen Bøen 188
Osten Espeland 179
Østen Olsen Bøen 82
Ostena Stondahl 127
Otilde Peterson 178
Otto Applen 77
Otto Grover 96,179
Ove Flaten 89
Ove Gaasedelen 89
Owen Swenson 234
Oystein Ingulfsland 109
P A Munch 225
Palmer Rockswold 241
Pamela Morben 234
Pastor Jensen 34,51
Pastor Koren 152
Pastor Larson 47
Pastor Muus 48,51
Pastor St Munch 51
Paul Anderson 234
Paul G Christiansen 237
Paul G Schmidt 236
Paul Nerol 60
Paul Nilsen 201
Paul Rosendahl 28
Paul Swenson 58,164
Paul Hjelm Hanson 207
Paula Eischens 234
Pauline Farseth 236
Pauline Kroshus 96
Pauline Sevareid 159
Pauline Kroshus Grover 180
Peder Carstensen 84,148
Peder Edward Gaasedelen 90
Peder Ellingsen 84
Peder Ellingsen Enger 88,176
Peder Holtan 106
Peder Huset 39
Peder Jensen Bratlien 131
Peder Johnson 111,179,180

Peder Johnson Lommen 130
Peder Langejoen 180
Peder Lommen 129
Peder M Ringdahl 69
Peder Nedre Rindal 152
Peder O Hogstad 178
Peder Otterness 144
Peder Ottun 146
Peder Pedersen 134
Peder Rotneim 87
Peder Svensen Pennes 200
Peder Thompson 41
Pehr Benson 188
Pehr Carlson 188
Pehr Johnson 187,188
Per Inge Vik,Pastor 220,232
Peroline Lie 127
Pete Gaasedelen 90
Pete Swenson 176
Peter Aadnes 70
Peter Andreas Ohnstad 138
Peter Aslagson Boe 178
Peter August Hovland 236
Peter Bakke 78
Peter Borgesen,Mrs 100
Peter Brynsaas 84
Peter Christianson 256
Peter Enger 88
Peter Foss 184
Peter Foss Lund 124
Peter G Peterson 84
Peter Johnson 112
Peter Johnson Lommen 28
Peter Johnsrud 114
Peter Lommen 129
Peter Lund 123
Peter M Fritioff 188
Peter Melbostad 132
Peter Olsen 177
Peter Olson 176,178
Peter Olson,Mrs 177
Peter Peterson 177
Peter Ringdahl 152
Peter S Aslakson 78
Peter Thorson 177
Peter Volstad 173
Petra Finsand Nelson 180
Petrina Pedersdtr Thompson 179
Petrine Ottun 146
Petrine Olsdtr Otterness 138
Petter Johnson Noem 176
Preacher Olson 47
President Grant 53
Preston Martin Hegland 236
R M Probstfield 207,209,210
Rachael Richardson 150
Rachel Christopherson 179
Rachel Hanson Christopherson 180
Ragna Adilsdtr 255
Ragna Bergetongen 80
Ragndi Nilsdtr Wangensteen 89

Ragne Hansdtr Valsenger 148
Ragnhild Andersen 33,38
Ragnhild Berg 38
Ragnhild Caroline Hjermstad 106
Ragnhild Florand 38
Ragnhild Froland 38
Ragnhild Gamlemoen 33
Ragnhild Gisledtr Moen 93,94
Ragnhild Gulbrandsdtr Hilde 97,103
Ragnhild Halvorsdtr Røste Opsal 141
Ragnhild Hansdtr Christopherson 179
Ragnhild Hanson Christopherson 180
Ragnhild Johnsdtr Flåberg 171
Ragnhild Olsdotter Timrud 86
Ragnhild Pedersdtr 201
Ragnhild Ramstad 149
Ragnhild Tomasdtr Trettrudhaugen 83
Ragnhild Vig 39
Ragnhild Week 39
Ragnild Bronson 83
Ragnild Danielson 142
Ragnild Gulmon 98
Ragnild Halvorsdtr Røste 141
Ragnild Knudsdtr Kvanbekk 98
Ragnild Olsdtr Nord Strand 136
Ralph Halbert 234
Ralph Norland 234
Ramona Swenson 234
Randi Jonsdtr 174
Randi Lie 127
Randi Olsdtr Berekvam 66,145
Randi Otterness 66,145,146
Randi Otterness Nelson 68
Randi Ramstad 149
Randi Svensrud 181
Randi Ulen 169,170
Randy Trelstad 230
Rangdi Gaasedelen 90
Rangdi Tuve 166
Rannei Richardson 150
Rasmus Olson Runestad 178
Rasmus Rasmusson Opsal 177
Raymond Lee 235
Raymond Ohnstad 138
Rebecca Larsen 172
Reidar Dittmann 237
Reier Reiersen 97
Reier Reierson 103
Rena Hansdtr Ellson 179
Rensa Ohnstad 138
Rev Fredriksen 34
Richard Eischens 234
Richard C Magnuson 237
Rikka Gjermstad 105
Rikka Larsen 171,172
Roald Benson 201
Robert Brodin 234
Robert Hillman 29
Robert McCormick 28
Robert Ohnstad 138
Robert Rosendahl 241

Robert White 123
Rognald Johnson Ohnstad 137,138
Ron D Smith 237
Rosalia Vaaler 171
Rosalie Brodin 234
Ross Hansing 234
Roy Eide 237
Roy Srp 234
Rozalyn Boyer 234
Rudy Prestholdt 257
Ruth Christ 256
Rutherford B Hayes 57
S S Reque,Rev 79
Saave Knudsen 75
Saint Hallvard 251
Saint Olav 257
Sally Taflin 169
Salve E Schibsted 85
Sam Stangeland 214,215
Sammy Jo Linder 234
Samuel Andreas Pennes 200
Samuel Garland 116
Samuel Harstad 83
Samuel Holtan 106
Samuel Olaus Aslakson 128
Sander Swenson 58,164
Sandra Hendrickson 221,233,234
Sandra Meyer 234
Sandra Turner 234
Sandy Johnsrud 234
Sara Gaasedelen 90
Sara Sarabyne Rotneim 87
Sarah Borstad Peterson 149
Sarah Gulmon 98
Sarah Hefte 105
Sarah Kragness 101
Sarah Nelson 135
Sarah Rotneim 87
Sarah Neutsen Nelson 135
Selma Boraas 257
Selma Torstenson 257
Serena Juvrud 48
Sever Knutson Rukke 154
Sever Temanson 32,33
Severin Aaby 74
Severt Strenge 162
Sevine Rekanes 150
Sharon Haugo 221,234
Sharon Merten 234
Sidsel Nilsdtr Garnaas 91
Sidsel Nilsdtr Nubgaard 90
Signe Fossum Lillejord 236
Signe Lybeck 38
Signe Overland Rorhelle 148
Signe Skrei 203
Signe Thortvedt 203
Sigri Brenna 87
Sigri Engen 16,105
Sigri Nybro 124
Sigri Rotneim 87
Sigrid Bukkøy 85

Sigrid E Melbostad 133
Sigrid Gubberud 96
Sigrid Gunderson 99
Sigrid Lommen 128,130
Sigrid Lønnegrav 220
Sigrid Lunde 20,21
Sigrid Lynne Melbostad 133
Sigurd Jonsen 159
Sigurd Sigurdsen 159
Sigurd Syr 251
Sigvald Olson 178
Simon A-nah-wag-manne 190
Simon Bakken 181
Simon Simonson 38
Simon Stangeland 181,214
Sina Nilsen 201
Siri Ellingsdtr Melbostad 133
Sissel Gaasedelen 90
Sissel Jellum 110
Siri Melbostad 132
Siri Nilsen 201
Siri Torgerson 61
Siri Vig 39
Siri Week 39
Sissel Amundsdtr Hegland 176
Sissel Eivindsdtr Grønvoll 110
Sissel Skiftun 19,20
Sissel Sveinsdtr 165
Sissel Thorson 165
Sissela Johnsdtr Skiftun 96
Sjur Hermansen Krosshaug 122
Sjur Saettre 50,51
Snæfred 255
Sønnøv Olsdtr Halvorseth 155
Sophia Gubberud 96
Sophia A Olson Haakenstad 179
Sophia J Moslet 106
Sophia J Moslet Holtan 106.107
Sophie Gunderson 99
Sophie Hegland 181
Soren Hanson Underdahl 127
Soren Hjermstad 105
Soren Larsen 171
Søren Pedersen 148
Søren Schmidt 200
Soren Larsen Gjermstad 105,171
Soren Olsen Sorum 26,27,69
Sorine Gubberud 96
Steinar Erickson 89,148
Steinar Overland 10,146
Steingrim N Jellum 71
Steiner Reierson 29
Stella Brunsvold 237
Stena Underdahl 127
Stenetta Larsdtr Sæteren 69
Stephen Klovstadeie 140
Stephen Oleson 140
Susan Anderson 75,76
Susan Applen 77
Susan Ottun 146
Susanna Ottun 146

Susanna Jambakkmyra Olsen 179
Susanne Bukkøy 86
Suzann Nelson 220,232
Svein Sveinsen Rudningen 164
Sveining Swenson 163,164
Sveinung Byholt 12
Sveinung Swenson 163
Sven Aslakson 128
Sven Ellestad 29
Sven Sampson 157
Sven Aslakson Ødegaard 176
Svend Lofthus 59
Svend Rodningen 58
Svend Svensen 60
Sverre Dalland 236
Swen Benson 188
Swen Swenson Jr 58,164,165
Swen Swenson,Mrs 58
Swen Swenson Sr 164
Swenke Torgerson 186
Sylvan Nelson 156
Sylvia Smogard 257
Sylvia Teigen 234
Synneva Axelsdtr Iverson 116
Synneva Ellingsdtr Ruggeseter 75
Synneva Iverson 48
Synneva Kristofersdtr 201
Syver Dahl 69
Syver Hermannsen Krosshaug 122
Syver Hovda 31,38
Syver K Foss 60
Syver Olsen Skalshaugen 38,39
Syver Simonson 38
Syver Wahl 180
Syverin Gjermstad 105
Syverin Larsen 171
Syvert C Iverson 110
T A Hoverstad 225
T A Kroshus,Mrs 184
T C Smith 29
Tabitha Sevareid 159
Tallack W Brokken 82,83
Talleff Flateland 206
Ta-o-ya-te-du-ta 187
Taran Anundsdtr Hjamdal 114
Taran Anundsdtr Jordgrav 115,219
Tårånd Torjusdtr 159
Tårånd Torjusdtr Sigurdsen 160
Targe Flatland 100
Targe Gunderson 100,101
Targe Gunnarson Findreng 100
Targe Olson Flatten 176
Targe Sinnes 100
Tarje Grover 103
Tarje Aslakson Grover 94-96,178,219
Tarjei Muhle 204-207,210,212
Tarjei Skrei 203,211
Taurine Ellis 86
Teman Evenson 89
Teman Gilbertson 28,29
Terry Grover 95

Thaddeus Brokken 83
Thea Overland 89,148
Theodor A Sundby 176
Theodor Baardsen 200
Theador E Stras 179
Theodor P Storbo 179
Theodora Laumann 160
Theodore Applen 78
Theodore Bekkerus 180
Theodore Findreng 101
Theodore Peterson 84
Theodore Strand 46
Theodore Wold 236
Theolina Nielsdtr Smebyhagen 196,198
Theolina Smebyhagen 197
Theoline Hefte 105
Theoline Johnsrud 114
Theoline Nilsdtr Smebyhagen 198
Thina Gubberud 25,96
Thomas Gulmon 98
Thomas Johnsen,Pastor 200
Thomas Johnson 112,130
Thomas Juvrud 48
Thomas Lommen 129
Thomas Lommen Johnson,Pastor
  111,112
Thomas Nelson 135
Thomas Sigurdsen 159
Thomas Swenson 163
Thomas Tveito 168
Thomas Walby 240
Thone Gjeitsta 203
Thone Kragness 101
Thone Kråkenes 101
Thone Moen 86
Thone Morken 101
Thone Olsen Berge 178
Thone Saangdal Thortvedt 203
Thone Thortvedt 178,203,205,212
Thor Anderson 71
Thor Bakke 78
Thor Hegland 165
Thor Kittilson Hasleiet 177
Thor Mikkelsen Hegland 181
Thor Olson 177
Thor Thorson 165
Thora Gjesme 112
Thora Johnson 112
Thora Lindelien 39
Thord Omsrud 141
Thore Evenson 201
Thore Jensen Elemoen 28
Thore Jensen,Dr 29
Thore Oleson 140
Thorild K Nelson 84,85
Thorstein Olsen Appelen 77
Thosten Thompson 48
Thorvald Doely,Mrs 184
Thrond Kleppo 150
Thrond Richardson 150-152
Thrond Rikardson 150

Thurine Haakaanes 121
Tilda Brokken 83
Tilde Findreng 101
Tilde Grover 96
Tilde Grover Sandwick 178
Tilde Petrine Vaage Paulsen 181
Tilla Erickson 89
Tilla Halvorson 103
Tina Kvernodden 123
Tina Ukkestad 89
Tine Hanna Bergitta Aanderud 201
Tolef T Kvernodden 124
Tolif T Kvernodden 124
Tollef A Harstad 177
Tollef Amundson Berg 28
Tollef Findreng 101
Tollef Golberg 51
Tollef Gunderson 101
Tolleiv Swenson 58,164
Tolline Johnson Larson 178
Tolv Knudsen 124
Tom Burket 234
Tone Aslaksdtr Grover 95
Tone Dole 96
Tone Ellis 86
Tone Grover 103
Tone Kassenborg 121
Tone Kleven Bekkerus 179
Tone Kragnes 116,117,121
Tone Kragnes Kassenborg 178
Tone Olsdtr Kilen 146
Tone Olsdtr Kilen Overland 147
Tone Olsdtr Vraa 85
Tone Overland 9,147
Tonette N Smebyhagen Ahlness 197
Tonette Nielsdtr Smebyhagen 196
Tor Aanundsen 165
Torbjor Andersdtr Rygh 154,155
Torbjør Anundsdtr Tuve 166
Torbjor Nerisdtr 159
Torbjorn Sigurdsen 159
Torgeir Oxnaberg 39
Torgen Kittelsdtr 161
Torger Brynsaas 84
Torger Erickson Mork 179
Torger Erikson Faar 91
Torger Garvik 91
Torger Hegland 165
Torger Johannesen Tendeland 26
Torger O Rygh 154,155
Torger Tendeland 27,28
Torger Torgerson 61-65
Torger Tollefsen Felland 78
Torger Torgersen Rygh 154
Torgrim Halvorsen Tveito 167
Torgrim Moen 86
Torgrim Morken 120
Torgrim Tveito 167,168
Torgun Olsen Ulen 169,170
Torjus Haraldson 103,104
Torjus Olsen 159

Torjus Sigurdsen 159
Torkel Gaasedelen 89
Torkel Kvaale 89
Torkel Oftelie 12,13,253,254
Torstein Berekvam 78
Torstein Bøen 82
Torstein Østensen Bøen 81,185,186
Torsten A Aabye 72
Torsten Eriksen Hagen 71
Tory Thorson 177
Tosten Applen 77
Tosten Johnson 112,130
Tosten Kittelson 161
Tosten Larsen Ursdalen Nøbben 82
Tosten Lommen 129,130
Tosten Lommen Johnson 112,113
Tosten Ohnstad 138
Tosten Ommelstadsæteren 157
Tosten Sigurdsen 201
Tosten Solum 201
Tosten Stabeck 161
To-wan-e-tan 190
Tron Richardson 150

Tron Rikardson 150
Tron Christenson Sæthre 72,155
Trond Sjurud 38
Truls Haga 28,71
Truls Paulsen 28.29
Tudor Applen 78
V Koren,Pastor 14,129,166
Vangien Krueger 230,261
Verla Anderson 234
Verlyn Anderson 234,237,241
Vier Sevareid 159
Viggo Olson 101
Viola Rosalind Gunderson 100
Virginia Hansing 234
Voke Nissen 123
W H Hopkins 139
Wallace Beaver 49
Walter Ridder 236
Walter E Jacobson 237
Walther S Booth 33
Wayne Olson 101
Wilhelm Marius Hansen 201
William Delander Enger 181

William Fleming 28
William Hansen 201
William Hinkley 28
William J Daly 191
William Leonard Gunderson 100
William Lunde 132
William Olson 140
William Olson Jr 140
William Otterness 67
William Painter,Pastor 89
William Ramstad 149
William Stangeland 214
William Weaver 139
Yank Ellis 86